Ordnance Survey

STRE ⬛⬛⬛ S

C000065015

Oxforashire

Contents

PHILIP'S

First edition published 1994
First colour edition published 1998
Reprinted in 1999 by

Ordnance Survey®   and   George Philip Ltd, a division of
Romsey Road   Octopus Publishing Group Ltd
Maybush   2-4 Heron Quays
Southampton   London
SO16 4GU   E14 4JP

ISBN 0-540-07514-0 (pocket)

To the best of the Publishers' knowledge, the information in this
atlas was correct at the time of going to press. No responsibility
can be accepted for any errors or their consequences.

The representation in this atlas of a road, track or path is no
evidence of the existence of a right of way.

**The mapping between pages 1 and 260 (inclusive) in this
atlas is derived from Ordnance Survey® OSCAR® and
Land-Line® data and Landranger® mapping.**

Ordnance Survey, OSCAR, Land-line and Landranger are
registered trade marks of Ordnance Survey, the national
mapping agency of Great Britain.

Printed and bound in Spain by Cayfosa

Digital Data

The exceptionally high-quality
mapping found in this book is
available as digital data in TIFF
format, which is easily convertible
to other bit-mapped (raster) image
formats.

The index is also available in digital
form as a standard database table.
It contains all the details found in
the printed index together with the
National Grid reference for the map
square in which each entry is
named and feature codes for places
of interest in eight categories such
as education and health.

For further information and to
discuss your requirements, please
contact the Ordnance Survey
Solutions Centre on 01703 792929.

Key to map symbols

III

	Motorway (with junction number)
	Primary route (dual carriageway and single)
	A road (dual carriageway and single)
	B road (dual carriageway and single)
	Minor road (dual carriageway and single)
	Other minor road
	Road under construction
	Pedestrianised area
	Railway
	Tramway, miniature railway
	Rural track, private road or narrow road in urban area
	Gate or obstruction to traffic (restrictions may not apply at all times or to all vehicles)
	Path, bridleway, byway open to all traffic, road used as a public path
	The representation in this atlas of a road, track or path is no evidence of the existence of a right of way
179 / **106**	**Adjoining page indicators**

Acad	**Academy**	Mon	**Monument**
Cemy	**Cemetery**	Mus	**Museum**
C Ctr	**Civic Centre**	Obsy	**Observatory**
CH	**Club House**	Pal	**Royal Palace**
Coll	**College**	PH	**Public House**
Ent	**Enterprise**	Recn Gd	**Recreation Ground**
Ex H	**Exhibition Hall**	Resr	**Reservoir**
Ind Est	**Industrial Estate**	Ret Pk	**Retail Park**
Inst	**Institute**	Sch	**School**
Ct	**Law Court**	Sh Ctr	**Shopping Centre**
L Ctr	**Leisure Centre**	Sta	**Station**
LC	**Level Crossing**	TH	**Town Hall/House**
Liby	**Library**	Trad Est	**Trading Estate**
Mkt	**Market**	Univ	**University**
Meml	**Memorial**	YH	**Youth Hostel**

■ The dark grey border on the inside edge of some pages indicates that the mapping does not continue onto the adjacent page

■ The small numbers around the edges of the maps identify the 1 kilometre National Grid lines

	British Rail station
	Underground station
D	**Docklands Light Railway station**
	Private railway station
	Bus, coach station
	Ambulance station
	Coastguard station
	Fire station
	Police station
	Accident and Emergency entrance to hospital
H	**Hospital**
+	**Church, place of worship**
i	**Information centre** (open all year)
P	**Parking**
PO	**Post Office**
Sch	**Important buildings, schools, colleges, universities and hospitals**
	County and unitary authority boundaries
River Medway	**Water name**
	Stream
	River or canal (minor and major)
	Water
	Tidal water
	Woods
	Houses
House	**Non-Roman antiquity**
VILLA	**Roman antiquity**

The scale of the maps is 3.92 cm to 1 km (2¹/₂ inches to 1 mile)

0	¹/₄	¹/₂	³/₄	1 mile
0	250m 500m	750m 1 kilometre		

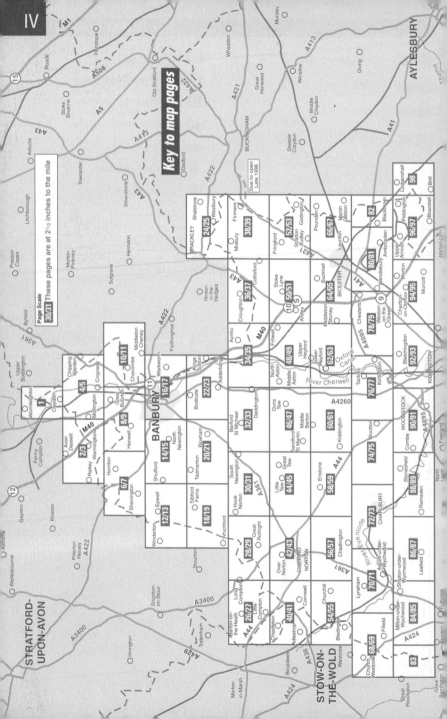

IV

Key to map pages

Page Scale
30/31 These pages are at 2½ inches to the mile

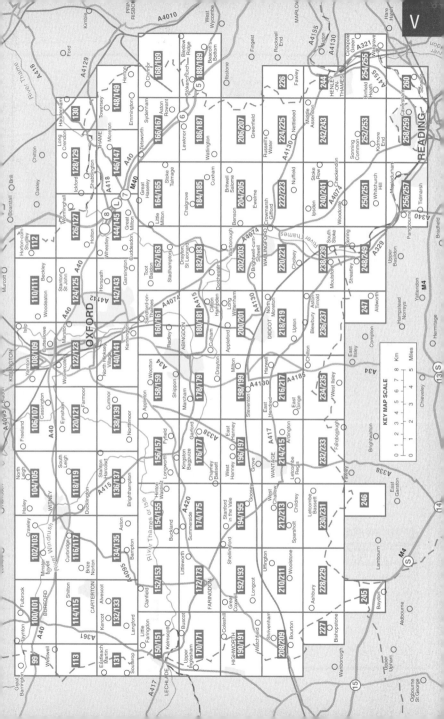

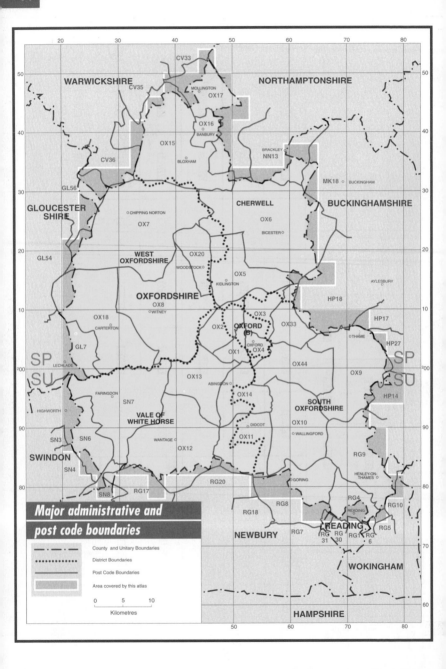

VI

Major administrative and post code boundaries

	County and Unitary Boundaries
	District Boundaries
	Post Code Boundaries
	Area covered by this atlas

0   5   10
Kilometres

A B C

Oxford Canal

Manor House

Wormleighton

Wormleighton Hall

Berryhill Plantation

Fox Covert

4

Saville's Pool

The Hall Farm

Three Shires

53

3

Claydon Hay Farm

52

Wormleighton Reservoir

Granmore Hill Farm

Wormleighton Crossing

Hay Bridge

2

Canal Feeder

Oxford Canal

Glebe Farm

51

Farnborough Fields Farm

FENNY COMPTON RD

BODDINGTON RD

Claydon Top Lock

Claydon Locks

1

Leys Farm

Claydon

Poultry Farm

Butlin Farm

50

44 A 45 B 46 C

D E F

AVON CARROW

Stonewold

Dassett Fields

Windmill Lodge
Farm

Sch

NEWDONS TERR

Sourland Pool

Butchers Arms
(PH)

Park
Lodge

Farnborough

A423

4

Farnborough
Hall

The Rookery

Farnborough Park

Oak Hill

49

Obelisk

Tile Barn

SOUTHAM RD

3

Markhamhole
Spinney

College
Farm

Mollington
Wood

Keepers
Cottage

48

CHAPEL
ST

SCHOOL LA

WELLFORD RD

MOLLINGTON LA

Warmington

PH

CHURCH ST SCOUT LA

Warmington
Wood

Deddington Hill

1 ROUNDHILL RD
2 TINKERS LA
3 SCHOOL HILL

WEST WAY

MAIN ST

2

THE
PADDOCKS

THE HOLT

MARCH RD

LOWER FARM
LA

Sch

BANBURY RD

47

Warmington
Fox Covert

The
Wobbly Wheel
(PH)

Angel
Piece

1

Valley Farm

M40

46

D 42 E 43 F

B4100

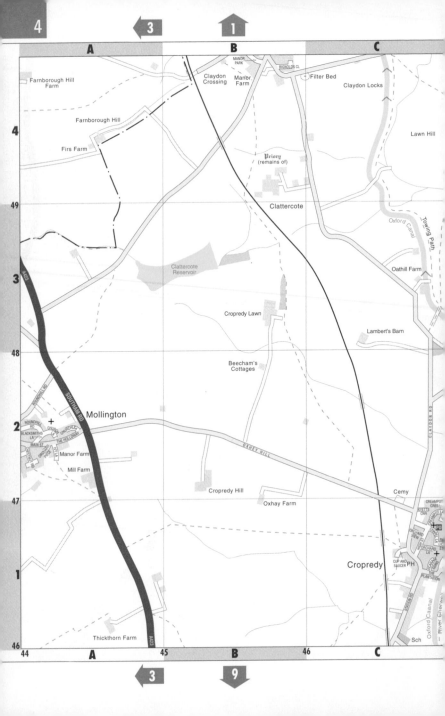

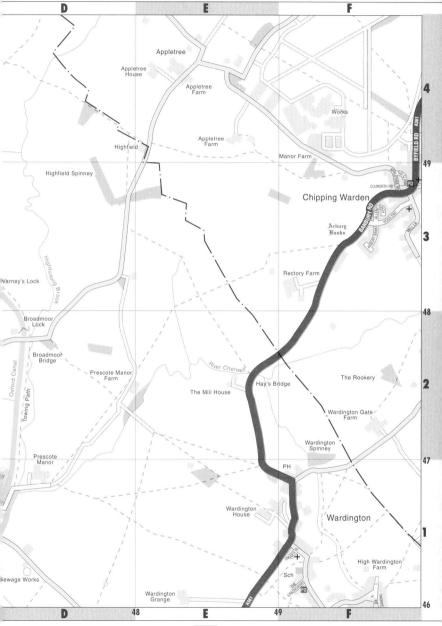

A   **B**   **C**

Sun Rising

A422

Home Farm

Sun Rising
Covert

Sugarswell
Cottages

Blackwell
Wood

Upton
House

4

Spring Hill

Black Hut

45

Old Lodge Farm

Foxbury
Barn

Temple Pool

Heath
Wood

Sugarswell
Farm

SUGARSWELL LA

3

Shenington Hirons
Covert

STRATFORD RD

New
Covert

Dairy

Sugarswell Farm

44

The Bungalow

2

Lodge
Farm

Christmas
Corner

Vehicle Proving
Ground

Hill Barn

43

Hill Farm

Rectory
Farm

Manor
Farm

Alkerto

STOCKING LA

BUSHILL RD

PH

Sch

+

Shenlow Hill

Quarry Farm

PO

+

Mill
Farm

MARSHALLS CL

1

Shenlow
Farm

RATTLECOMBE RD

Shenington

Gliding
Club

Mill Lane

Oxfordshire Circular Walks

42

35   **A**   **36**   **B**   **37**   **C**

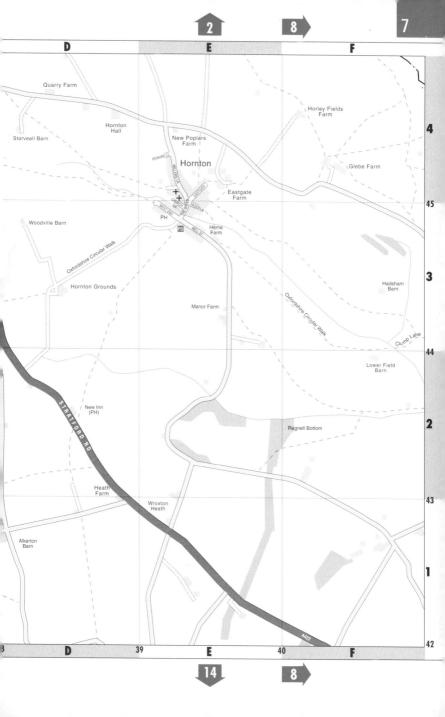

D
E
F

Quarry Farm

Horley Fields
Farm

4

Hornton
Hall

Starveall Barn

New Poplars
Farm

PERKINS LD

Hornton

Glebe Farm

Eastgate
Farm

45

Woodville Barn

PH

Home
Farm

Oxfordshire Circular Walk

3

Hornton Grounds

Manor Farm

Hadsham
Barn

Oxfordshire Circular Walk

Clump Lane

44

Lower Field
Barn

New Inn
(PH)

2

Ragnell Bottom

STRATFORD RD

Heath
Farm

43

Wroxton
Heath

Alkerton
Barn

1

A422

42

D
39
E
40
F

7
3

A   B   C

4

Slated Barn

Slade Barn

Laurel Farm

Bury Court Farm

Shotteswell

45

Sor Brook

Hadsham House
Manor Farm

3

Water Tower

Horley House

Clump Lane

44

Hanwell

LANE CL

MANOR ORCH

PH

Bramhill Park Farm

Horley

Hanwell Castle

Park Farm

2

WARWICK RD

43

Oxfordshire Circular Walk

1

Cemy

Lord's Spinney

Drayton Lodge

Golf Course

42

41   A   42   B   43   C

A422

7
15

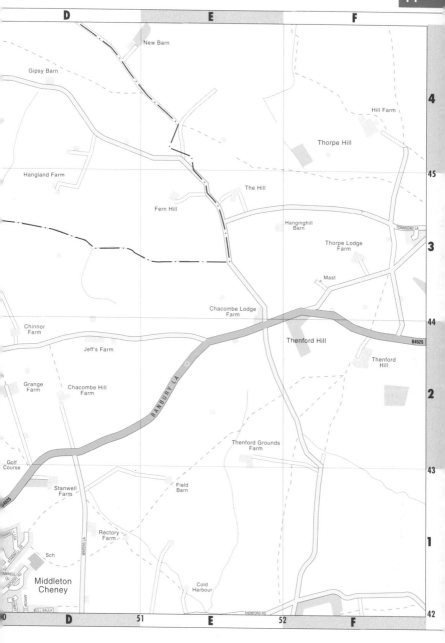

New Barn

Gipsy Barn

Hill Farm

Thorpe Hill

4

Hangland Farm

45

The Hill

Fern Hill

Hanginghill
Barn

Thorpe Lodge
Farm

TOWNSEND LA

3

Mast

Chacombe Lodge
Farm

44

Chinnor
Farm

Thenford Hill

B4525

Jeff's Farm

Thenford
Hill

Grange
Farm

Chacombe Hill
Farm

BANBURY LA

2

Thenford Grounds
Farm

43

Golf
Course

Stanwell
Farm

Field
Barn

4525

WHITEHILL LA

Rectory
Farm

1

Sch

ANWELL CL

STERHILL DR

ANWELL RD

ARDENS RD

Middleton
Cheney

Cold
Harbour

THENFORD RD

BULL BAULK

TO MOWN

42

A   **B**   **C**

Compton Wynyates

Lady Elizabeth's Hill

Windertonroad Spinney

New Meadow Spinney

Compton Wynyates

4

Comptn Pike

Orchard Hill

Broomhill Farm

Quarry Farm

Broom Hill

41

Birch Wood

White House

Winderton Farm

Winderton

The Warren

3

+

Alice Hyde's Cottage

Hill Barn

Mast

40

The Brake

Sibford Heath Farm

Hall Meadow Farm

Beggars' Lane

Sutton Brook

Sibford Heath

2

B4035

Gallow Hill Farm

39

Gallow Hill

Hill Barn

B4035

HOLLOWAY HILL

Ryehill Barn

Ditchedge Lane

1

Eddeneshill Barn

Hasty Leys Farm

Elmridge

Coombe Slade Farm

38

32   **A**   **33**   **B**   **34**   **C**

6
14

D   E   F

Rough Hill

Rough Hill Farm

OC Walks

Epwell Hill

Yarn Hill Farm

Field Barn

4

Lower Barn

Rectory Farm

Yarn Hill

Epwell Grounds Farm

41

Shutford Grounds Farm

Epwell

BIRDS LA

Long Hill

EPWELL RD

3

THE CLOSE

THATCHERS

Epwell Mill

Cranes Farm

Gage Farm

PH

Slatters Barn

Cemy

Bottle Barn

Woodington Spinney

40

Heath Plantation

Woodington Barn

Barton Hill

Chillaway Barn

Farmington Farm

2

Lake Spinney

Heathnell Spinney

SHAMS RD

Blenheim Farm

Redland Barn

39

Handywater Farm

POUND LA

Brakelands Farm

1

Tyne Hill

BACKHILL LA

Tyne Hill Farm

SHARPS

38

5   D   36   E   37   F

19
14

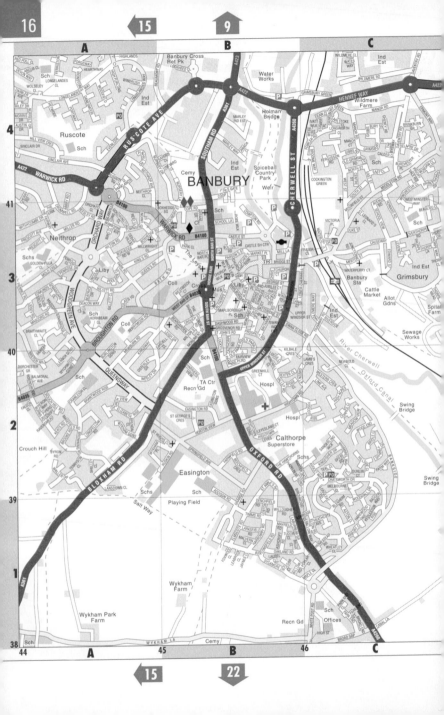

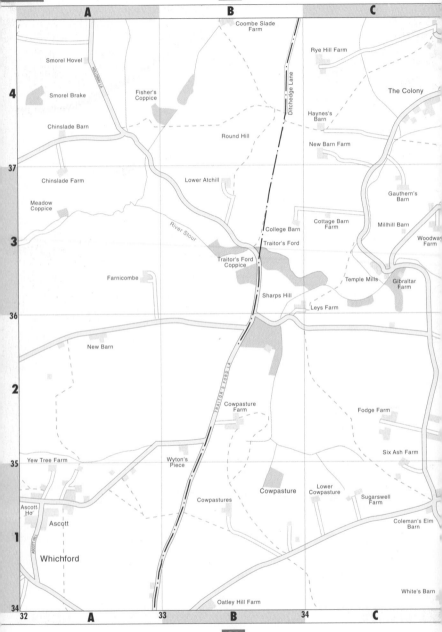

Coombe Slade Farm

Rye Hill Farm

Smorel Hovel

The Colony

Smorel Brake

Fisher's Coppice

Haynes's Barn

Chinslade Barn

Round Hill

New Barn Farm

4

37

Chinslade Farm

Lower Atchill

Gauthern's Barn

Meadow Coppice

Millhill Barn

River Stour

Cottage Barn Farm

College Barn

Woodway Farm

Traitor's Ford

3

Traitor's Ford Coppice

Farnicombe

Temple Mills

Gibraltar Farm

Sharps Hill

Leys Farm

36

New Barn

Fodge Farm

2

Cowpasture Farm

Six Ash Farm

35

Yew Tree Farm

Wyton's Piece

Cowpasture

Lower Cowpasture

Sugarswell Farm

Ascott Ho.

Ascott

Cowpastures

Coleman's Elm Barn

1

Whichford

White's Barn

34

Oatley Hill Farm

Broughton Grange

Castle Farm

Wykham Mill Farm

Wykham Mill

BLOXHAM RD   A361

Sor Brook

4

Ell's Farm

Chaddle Barn Farm

ELL'S LA

37

Tadmarton Lodge

Nayland Farm

BANBURY RD

Bloxham Grove Rd

Sch

Playing Field

Tadmarton House Farm (Industrial Estate)

Firs Hill Farm

Hobb Hill

Firs Hill

Woollen Hale

Sch

3

TADMARTON RD

Playing Fields

THE POUND

GAUNTLET CL

STRAW BERRY HILL CL

GREENS GARTH

Park Farm

Bloxham

Sch

The Goggs

COURTINGTON LA

HD HORNTON HOLLOW

HIGH ST

PO

Sch

BARLEY CL

HOGG END

36

Sch

WIND MILL ST

STONE WALL

CHAPEL ST

Yew Tree Piggeries

QUARRY CL

THE GASCONS

WALKS

GOOSE WALK

CHURCH ST

PH

MERRIVALE'S LA

Sewage Works

Coates's Spinney

2

HYDE GR

BRIDGES WAY

COLESBOURNE

WEST BUNGS

LUDFORD GDNS

MILTON RD

35

Milcombe Hall

BLOXHAM RD

Happy Valley Farm

BANFORD CL

MAULE CL

BARFORD RD

Factory

Brompton Farm

HORN

Milcombe

SOUTH NEWINGTON RD

Hollie's Barn

Mast

Wireless Station

Mast

1

Mast

A361

34

A   **B**   **C**

Cemy

PADDOCK FARM LA
PH
MALTHOUSE LANE
HOUSE LANE
RYDES CL
THE RYDE
CHAPEL LA
WEEPING CROSS
PH
EAST ST
Cottage Farm
WALTON CL
A 4260
OXFORD RD

Sch

Bodicote
DEERS CLOSE
CHAPEL CL
ROOKERY
ROSE CL
RISE CL
MELTREVA RD
BLACKWO
SEELEIGH RD
PD

BEARGARDEN
EVANS RD

DEER B
FARM
WARDS CL
AUSTIN RD
SEFTON PL

Cotefield
House

4

Bodicote Mill
House

Water Works

Upper Grove
Mill

37

Old Barn Farm

Lower Grove
Mill

BLOXHAM GROVE RD

Bloxham
Grove

Sor Brook

Windmill

3

Wayhouse Farm

36

2

MANOR RD
CROSS HILL RD
NEW RD

Brickhouse
Farm

AUSTEN
FARM
ROUND CL

West Adderbury
PH
Recn G

Manor Farm

Milton
CHAPEL LA
PH

HIGH ST
TWELVE ACRE DRIVE

Works

35

Church Farm

MILTON RD

NORRIS CL
KATE'S CL

AYNHO RD B 4100

1

Mast

Wyatt's Barn

Airfield
(disused)

Wireless Station

Mast

A 4260
OXFORD RD

34

44   **A**   **45**   **B**   **46**   **C**

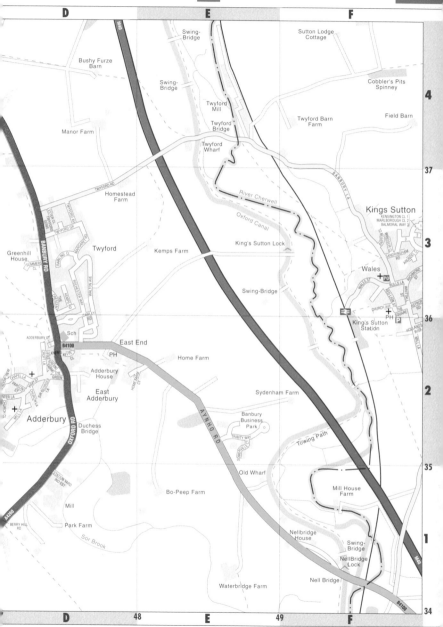

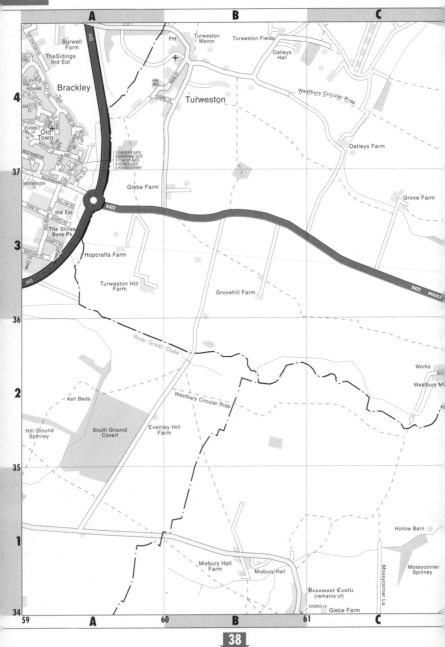

A · B · C

Burwell Farm

The Sidings Ind Est

VALLEY CRES

PH

Turweston Manor

Turweston Fields

Oatleys Hall

Brackley

VALLEY AVE

YEOMANS

EGERTON CL

4

PO

CHAPEL LA

Turweston

Westbury Circular Ride

CHURCH

Old Town

WESTMINSTER CRES

37

WESTMINSTER CL

BUCKINGHAM LA

Oatleys Farm

Glebe Farm

1 CAESERS GATE
2 HADRIANS GATE
3 FLAVIUS GATE
4 REMUS GATE
5 ROMULUS WAY

FARM RD

A422

Grove Farm

WILLOW RD

Ind Est

SHIRES RD

The Shires Bsns Pk

COUNTY RD

3

BOROUGH RD

Hopcrafts Farm

A43

Turweston Hill Farm

Grovehill Farm

A422 BRACKLE

36

River Great Ouse

Works

2

Westbury M

Ash Beds

Westbury Circular Ride

Hill Ground Spinney

South Ground Covert

Evenley Hill Farm

35

Hollow Barn

1

Mixbury Hall Farm

Mixbury Hall

Mossycorner La

Mossycorner Spinney

Beaumont Castle
(remains of)

34

CHURCH LA

Glebe Farm

59 · A · 60 · B · 61 · C

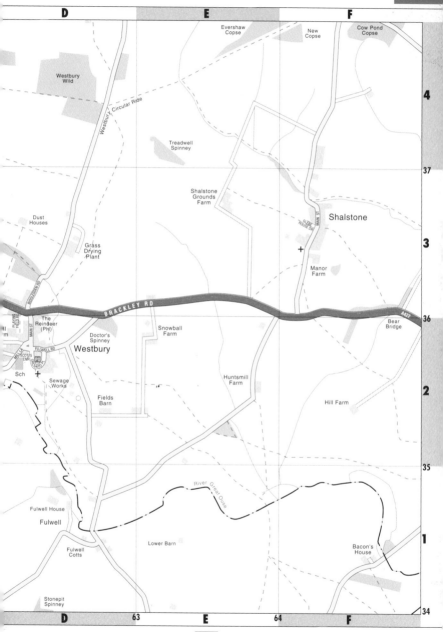

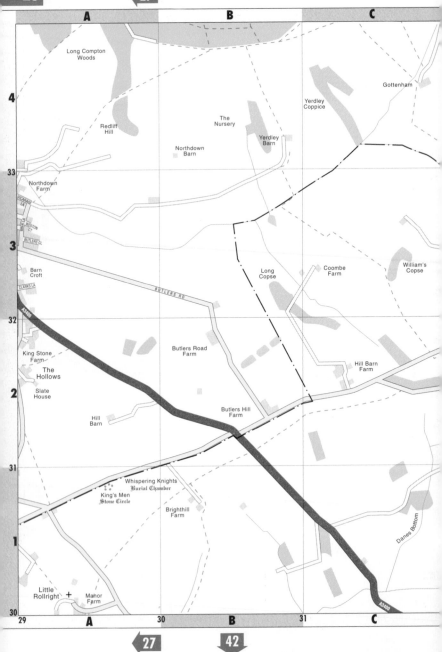

4

Long Compton
Woods

Gottenham

Yerdley
Coppice

Redliff
Hill

The
Nursery

Yerdley
Barn

33

Northdown
Barn

Northdown
Farm

3

William's
Copse

Long
Copse

Coombe
Farm

BUTLERS RD

Barn
Croft

CLARKS LA

32

Butlers Road
Farm

Hill Barn
Farm

King Stone
Farm

The
Hollows

2

Slate
House

Hill
Barn

Butlers Hill
Farm

31

Whispering Knights
Burial Chamber

King's Men
Stone Circle

Brighthill
Farm

Danes Bottom

1

Little
Rollright

Mahor
Farm

A3400

30

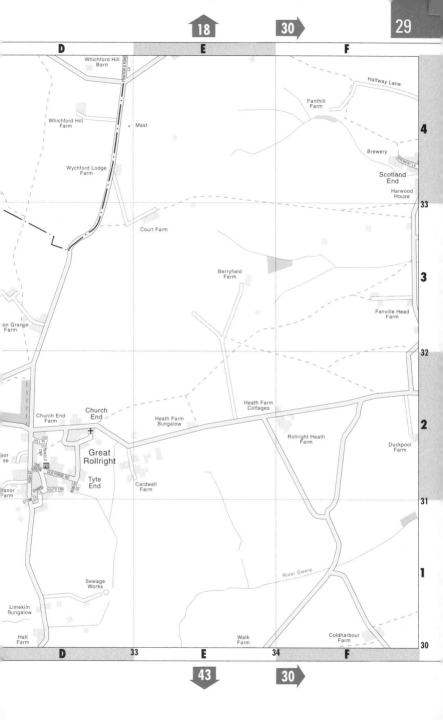

Whichford Hill Barn

TRAITOR'S FORD LA

Halfway Lane

Fanthill Farm

Whichford Hill Farm

Mast

Brewery

BREWERY LA

Scotland End

Wychford Lodge Farm

Harwood House

33

4

Court Farm

Berryfield Farm

3

Fanville Head Farm

on Grange Farm

32

Church End Farm

Church End

Heath Farm Cottages

2

Heath Farm Bungalow

HILL RD

THE COTSWOLD CLUP

OLD FORGE RD

Great Rollright

Rollright Heath Farm

Duckpool Farm

HIGH ST

THE GREEN

Tyte End

Cardwell Farm

CHAPEL LA

SOUTH END

RISING LA

STONE

anor arm

31

or se

Sewage Works

River Swere

1

Limekiln Bungalow

Halt Farm

Walk Farm

Coldharbour Farm

30

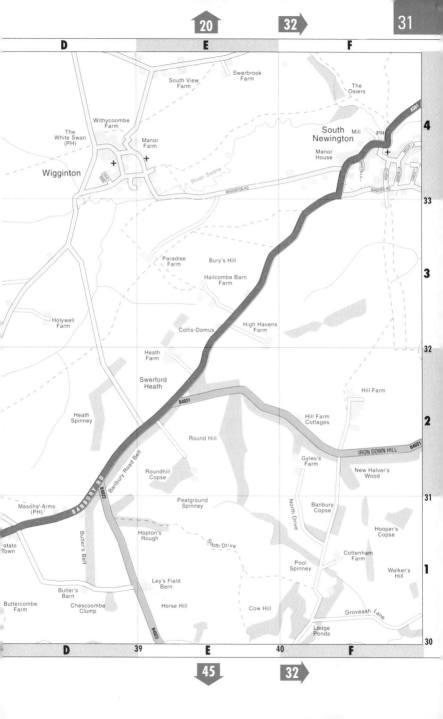

33
23

A   **B**   **C**

4

River Swere

Adderbury Grounds
Farm

Paper Mill
Cottages

Sor Brook

Weir
Lock

Nellbridge
Farm

Aynho
Junction

Hazelhedge
Farm

Wilson's
Gorse

Aynho
Wharf

33

3

Field
Barn

Hazel
Hedge

Oxford Canal

Great Western
Arms
(PH)

B4031 STATION RD

Towing Path

32

Duke of Cumberlands
Head
(PH)

County
Bridge

EARL'S

CASTLE ST **B4031**

CLIFTON RD

COUNTY FARM

THE CRESCENTS

PEPPER ALLEY

ST WALNUT CL

2

The
Poplars

Castle Earthworks

Appletree
Farm

Manor
Farm

Clifton

Wharf
Farm

31

STONEBRIDGE LA

The
Fishers

Sewage
Works

1

Leadenporch
Farm

Danehill
Covert

Bowman's
Bridge

Chisnell
Farm

30

47   **48**   **49**

A   **B**   **C**

33
48

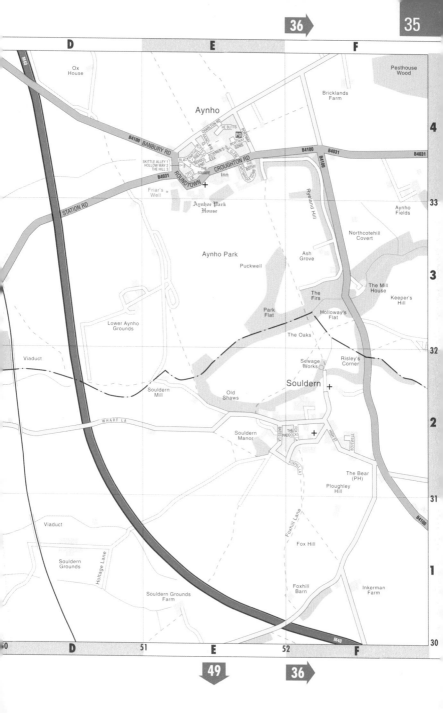

35

A B C

Cemy

Home Farm

Sch

The Moors

Warren Farm

Blackbird (PH)

WHEELER'S RISE

HIGH ST

BRACKLEY RD

NEW TERR

PARK END

B4031

4

BLENHEIM

The Green

CHURCH LA

Croughton

PORTWAY
PORTWAY DR

SOUTHFIELD

PORTWAY CLOSE

B4031

MILL LA

Old Down Covert

Ford

Sewage Works

SIXTH ST

FIFTH AVE

33

Old Down Pond

Park Farm

FIFTH ST E. Schs

FOURTH AVE

FOURTH ST

FIRST ST

THIRD

SECOND

Padbury's Bottom

Smanhill Covert

New Buildings

Masts

3

Middle Covert

32

Upper Aynho Grounds

Pimlico Farm

2

Crook's Firs

Ockley Brook

Thriftwood House

A43

31

Tower Farm

Roundhill Farm

Lower Rookery

1

B4100

Horwell Corner

Round Hill

Wr Twr

Hermitage Belt

Horwell Farm

Oxford Lodge

Park Farm

A43

30

Sharmans Pit

53 A 54 B 55 C

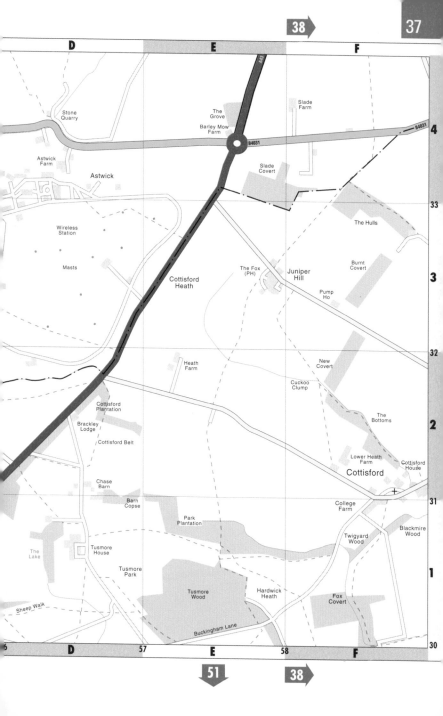

D   E   F

4

Stonepit
Spinney

Tile House
Farm

Finmere
Grounds

Sandpit Hill
Farm

Warren
Farm

Hill Leys

Finmere

Glebe Farm

33

Widmore
Plantation

SANDPIT HILL A421

Widmore
Farm

Finmere
Plantation

Gravel
Farm

Little
Tingewick

3

Grassy
Plantation

Road under construction

Airstrip

32

West
Wood

2

Barleyfields Barn
Farm

Barley
Fields

Shelswell Inn
(PH)

The Rectory

Home
Farm

Kings End
Farm

31

Ismere
Wood

Elms
Farm

Barton Hartshorn

Manor
Farm

Manor
House

Newton
Purcell

Barn
Copse

1

A421

School
End

Church
Copse

Courtfield
Farm

30

26

A B C

Newtown

Grove
End

Hogg's
Barn

Cowley's
Copse

4

Chastleton

THE LANE

Chastleton House

Hill
Farm

29

Harcomb
House

HORN LA

Horn
Farm

Harcomb
Wood

Chastleton
Hill

Peasewell
Wood

Barrow
House

3

Larch
Plantation

Adlestrop
Hill

Chastleton Bar
Fort

Hill
Barn

28

Peak
Coppice

Fern
Farm

Quarry
(dis)

Pit
(dis)

Hillside
Farm

Coomb
Wood

The
Naite

Wayside

Outlands

Evenlode
Grounds
Farm

2

Fern Drive

The
Pheasantry

The Long Drive

Lower
Farm

BACK ROW

ODDLE LA

MAIN ST

Manor Farm

27

PO

Adlestrop
House

Adlestrop

Green
Plantation

Sch

Adlestrop
Park

Adlestrop
Park Lodge

Daylesford
House

Daylesford
Hill Farm

1

River Evenlode

Baywell
Wood

Oddington
Lodge

A436

SANDITS LA

The
Dell

26

23 A **24** B **25** C

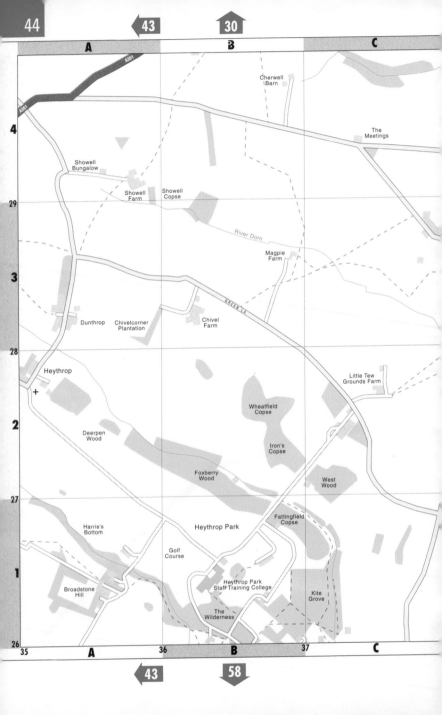

D
E
F

Cowhill
Hanging

Mill Lane

The Avenue

Hollow
Lake

Leys
Farm

4

Clay
Bank

THE AVENUE

ROOKERY RD

THE LANE

PO

Great Tew

COUNCIL HOUSES

Sch

PH

Home
Farm

OLD RD

BUTCHER'S HILL

Court
Farm

NEW RD

Great Tew Park

29

Mast

The Warren

Cross Roads
Clump

The Grove

WATER LA

Little Tew

CHAPEL LA

ENSTONE RD

Ledwell Lane Spinney

3

Park Farm
Barn

Sandford
Belt

The Lodge

28

Hookerswell Farm

Beggars
Lodge

Tracey Barn
Farm

The
Wallet

2

Beaconsfield
Farm

Mill
Covert

River Dorn

Lady Grove

27

Tracey
Farm

Poor Bridge

Hungryhill
Barn

Green Lane

Apple Pie
Wood

1

B4022

B4022

Airstrip

26

D
39
E
40
F

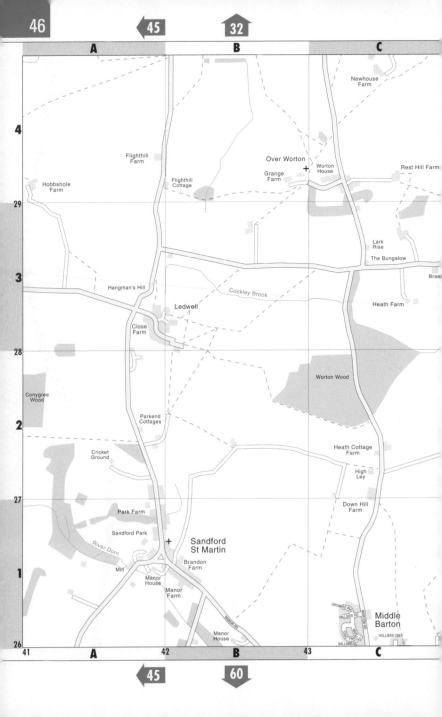

A **B** **C**

4

Coldharbour
Farm

Dane Hill
Farm

Ram
Spinney

Somerton
Lock

Manor House
Farm

Mill
Cottage

Millhouse

Rectory
Farm

29

The
Green

North Aston
Hall

North Aston
Farm

North
Aston

Somerton

Towing Path

3

The
Folly

Manor
Farm

28

Hendon
Farm

River Cherwell

Oxford Canal

Warren
Copse

Warren
Lodge

Grange
Farm

Somerton
Crossing

2

Pig
Unit

Middle
Aston

27

Middle Aston
House

Heyford Common
Lock

Lakeside
Farm

1

Poultry
Unit

Schs

The
Brambles

Barley Mow
(PH)

Allen's
Lock

Cow Lane

26

D E F

M40

Holtage
Barn

Hill
House

Tower

Manor
Farm

4

Tunnel

Portway
Farm

NORTH ST
THE LABURNUMS

Sch
George &
Dragon
(PH)

EAST ST

KIRTLINGTON RD

Park
Farm

Heath
Farm

Fritwell

PO

SOUTHFIELD
LA

29

FORGE PL

The
Rectory

ST VIEW

King's Head
(PH)

Lodge
Farm

Sewage
Works

Aqueduct

RAGHOUSE LA

3

Village
Farm

Troy
Cottages

28

Troy Farm

Village
Farm

Cross Roads
Farm

Mudginwell
Farm

2

Kennel
Copse

27

Upper Heyford Airfield

1

Letchmere
Farm

PHIPPS ROAD

TRENCHARD DRIVE

26

0 D 51 E 52 F

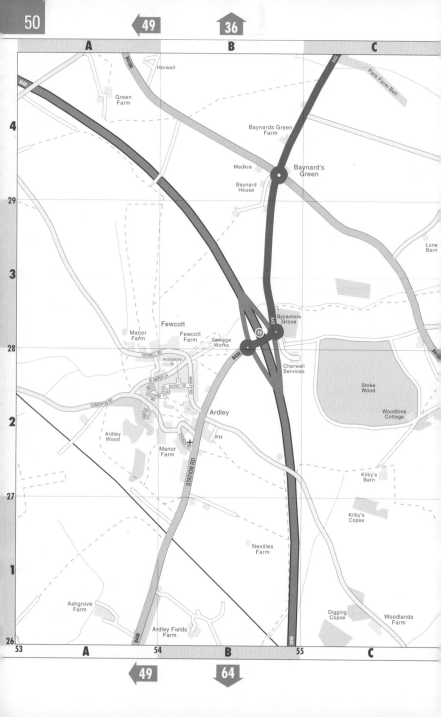

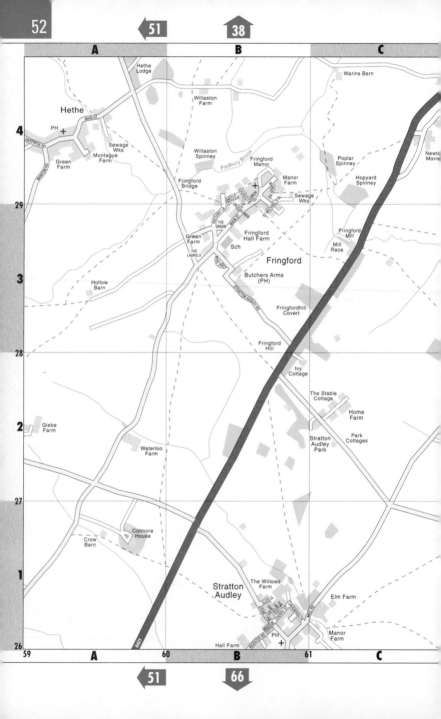

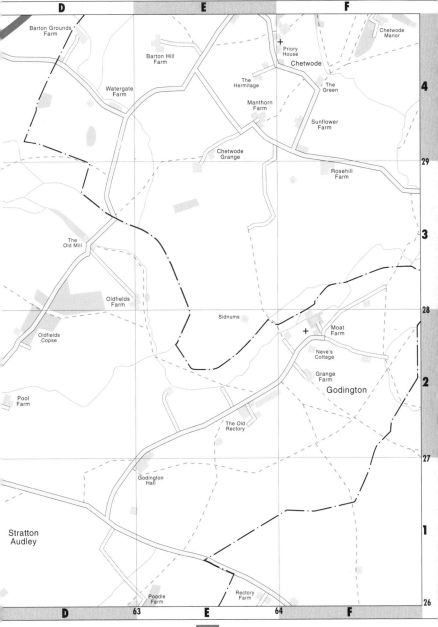

D   E   F

Barton Grounds
Farm

Chetwode
Manor

Barton Hill
Farm

Priory
House

Chetwode

Watergate
Farm

The
Hermitage

The
Green

4

Manthorn
Farm

Sunflower
Farm

Chetwode
Grange

29

Rosehill
Farm

The
Old Mill

3

Oldfields
Farm

Sidnums

28

Oldfields
Copse

Moat
Farm

Neve's
Cottage

Grange
Farm

Godington

2

Pool
Farm

The Old
Rectory

27

Godington
Hall

Stratton
Audley

1

Poodle
Farm

Rectory
Farm

26

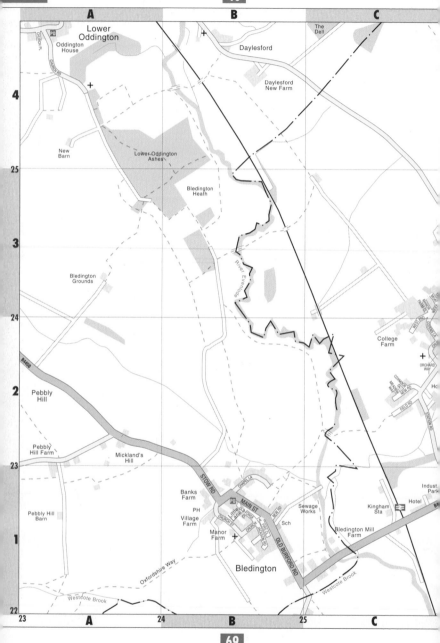

40

A · B · C

Lower
Oddington

Oddington
House

PO CHURCH PL

CHURCH RD

New
Barn

+

Lower Oddington
Ashes

Bledington
Heath

Bledington
Grounds

Daylesford

The
Dell

+

Daylesford
New Farm

River Evenlode

College
Farm

ORCHARD
WAY

+

WEST END

COMMON
MEADOW
WAY

FIELD RD

STATION RD

4

25

3

24

2

Pebbly
Hill

Pebbly
Hill Farm

Mickland's
Hill

Pebbly Hill
Barn

B4450

STOW RD

Banks
Farm

PH
Village
Farm

Manor
Farm

+

Bledington

Oxfordshire Way

Westcote Brook

CHAPEL LA

MAIN ST

CHURCH ST

HIGH ST

CROFT LA

MILL LA

Sch

Sewage
Works

OLD BURFORD RD

Kingham
Sta

Indust
Park

Hotel

Bledington Mill
Farm

Westcote Brook

23

1

22

23 · A · 24 · B · 25 · C

69

D
E
F

4

Warden's
House

Churchill Grounds
Farm

Churchill Grounds
Cottages

ade
arm

Lower
Kingham Hill
Cottages

25

Churchill
Mill

Sarsden
Halt

3

Mount
Farm

Sch

Churchill
Crossing

+

Grange
Farm

BEBURY LA

CHURCHILL RD

The
Caravan

Meadow
Place

SANDYS RD

HASTINGS HILL

KINGHAM RD

+

Churchill
Farm

PH

LANGSTON CL.

Hill
View

Churchill

PO

+

24

Kingham

HARPERS LA

WILLIAM SMITH LA

JUNCTION RD

Mount
Farm

The Mount *

The
Lodge

2

York
Cottage

Home
Farm

Sarsden

+

23

Sarsden
House

Rynehill
Farm

Sars Brook

1

Churchill Heath
Farm

Churchill Heath
Bungalow

Lower
Buildings

22

D
27
E
28
F

A
B
C

East Churchill Grounds Farm

B4450

Greystones (Council Offic

Bellpiece

Boulter's Barn

Chadlington Downs Farm

Boulter's Barn House

Sarsbank

4

B4450

25

BERBURY LA

Conduit Farm

Sarsgrove Farm

Downs Hollow

Sarsgrove Wood

Dower House

The Barns Plantation

3

Sars Brook

Lowland Barn

24

Sarsden Glebe

Parsonage Farm

CHIPPING NORTON RD

Iron Buildings

Sarsden Glebe Farm

Nursery Plantation

2

Squire's Clump Tumulus

The Belt

Home Farm

Kennels Belt

Knollbury

23

Skew Plantation

1

Fairgreen Farm

Castle Barn

Jubilee Plantation

CROSS'S LA

Blaythorne Cottages

22

29
A
30
B
A381
31
C

Furlong
Farm

my

Airfield

Enstone Airfield Complex
(Industrial Estate)

Cuckold's Holt
Farm

4

Gagingwell

The
Farm

Abbey
Farm

Quarrypiece
Farm

25

he
uare

Drystone Hill
House

Woodford
Bridge

3

Upper Farm

Cleveley
Bank

Radford

24

Cleveley

The
Millhouse

River Glyme

Radford
Farm

Manor Farm

Green Eye Way
Plantation

Radfordbridge

Radford
Bridge

2

Jollys Ricks

Bagnall

Skew Barn

23

Roche's
Plantation

Kiddington
Park

Deadman's
Riding
Wood

Pp Ho &
Wr Twr

Park
Farm

1

Ellen's Lodge

Asterleigh
Farm

Laurel Wood

Asterleigh
Wood

Dudgely
Pool

PO

22

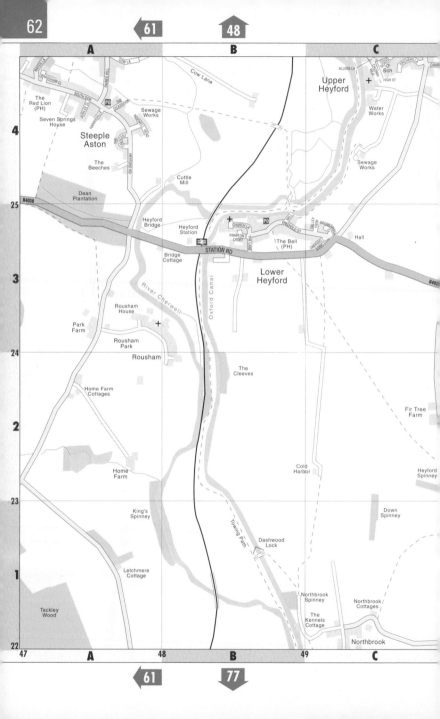

49
64

D E F

Upper Heyford Airfield

CAMP RD

Leys Farm

Cheesman's Barn

Field Barn

Sewage Works

The Heath

4

25

The Gorse

Timberyard Clump

Lime Hollow

Hill View Farm

LOWER HEYFORD RD

3

Caulcott

Horse and Groom (PH)

Ryman's Stable

Park Farm

Daisy Head Farm

Caulcott Farm

Manor Farm

Lyndhurst

GREENWAY

24

B4030

Old Nursery

Home Wood

Sainfoinhill Clump

Cricket Ground

2

Gallos Brook

Gold Barn

Breaklands Clump

Middleton Park

Middleton Park

23

Wheats Covert

Goldwell Spinney

Mangthorn Wood

Cowground Covert

Cowground Clump

1

Brakeslode Spinney

The Downs

Mushroom Cottages

Slade Farm

Roomer's Spinney

Swiss Cottage

22

D 51 E 52 F

78
64

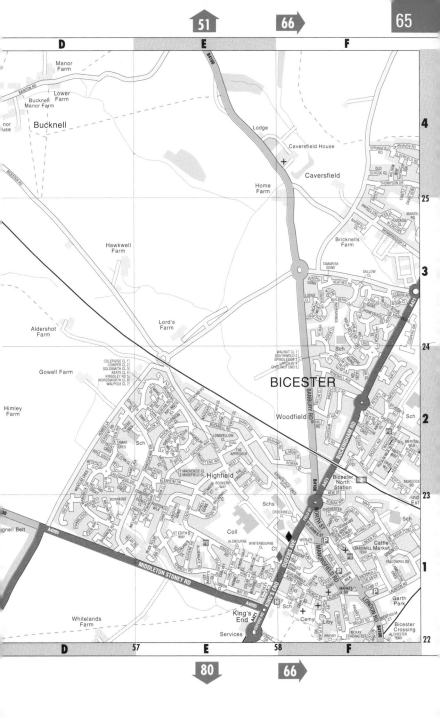

D   **E**   **F**

Poodle
Gorse

Rectory
Farm

Hill View Farm

Sow & Pigs
(PH)

Lower Farm

Home
Farm

4

Wireless Station

Poundon

Manor
Farm

Cross Bucks Way

Masts

Poundon
House

Sewage
Works

Poundon
Hill

25

Beacon Hill

Hare Leys
Farm

Cross Bucks Way

Field
Farm

3

Rhonhill
Barn

Rhon
Hill

Kensington
Villas

24

Westbury
Court Farm

2

The
College

STATION RD

MILLFIELD AVE

Marsh
Gibbon

RECTORY CT

Sch

Manor Ho

CASTLE ST

Folly Farm

WEST CT CL

CHURCH ST

SUFFOLK CT

Box

The
Plough
(PH)

Farm

23

Pear Tree
Farm

ST STYLES

BULL'S LA

Cemy

Town's End

WEST EDGE

BICESTER RD

TOWNSEND

WADES LA

LAMBS LA

SPIERS LA

Towns
End
Farm

Priory
Farm

SPIERS LA

1

Sewage
Works

The Leverets

22

D   63   **E**   64   **F**

A624

Booth's Barn

Westcote Brook

Oxfordshire Way

Gawcombe

Wyck Beacon Farm

Gawcombe Woods

Hawkwell

Wyck Beacon

Court Hayes Farm

Church Westcote

New Inn (PH)

Nether Westcote

Far Hill Coppice

Far Hill Barn

DE HAVILLAND RD

Bunting's Hill Copse

Little Glebe Farm

Brookfield

SNIPE RD

Peak's Coppice

Westcote Hill

SANDY LA

SMITH BARN RD

Ansell's Hill Copse

Imjin Barracks (dis)

Collier's Hill Barn

SANDY LANE

SOUTH GATE

F. ELLIS RD

KANDAL RD

Idbu

Workham Farm

Workha Bottom

Little Rissington Airfield (disused)

Ram Plantation

Limekiln Plantation

Warren Farm

A
B
C

Churchill Heath Wood

Sarsden Lodge Cottages

The Norrells.

Merriscot Farm

Sarsden Lodge

4

Lyneham Heath Farm

Sarsden Gorse

21

LC

3

Cocksmoor Copse

Lyneham Farm

HIGH ST

Lyneham

Bruern Abbey

PRIORY LA

Priory Farm

PRIORY RD

Mill

20

Conduit Copse

Bruern Wood

Meadow Copse

The Crossings

Round Pound

2

Pool Copse

Outside Copse

Mast

SPRING RD

River Evenlode

Pyrton Farm

Heath Farm

Oxfordshire Way

Glebe Farm

Littlecott

LYNEHAM RD

19

Cemy

Shipton Station

The Heath

Cottage Farm

Heath Farm

Sewage Works

Mill

CHURCH RD

STATION RD

1

PH

SHIPTON RD

LITTLEMORE MEADOW

REYNOLDS CL

MEADOW LA

1ST MICHAELS CL
2 COOMBES CL

CHURCH MEADOW

PEAR TREE

PUSSELL WAY

WOOD LA

ROSE LA

MILTON RD

A361

JUBILEE LA

Liby

Sch

18

26

A

27

B

28

C

D   **E**   **F**

CROSS'S LA

Blaythorne

Blaythorne House

The Roundabout

Barter's Hill Farm

4

Lyneham Barrow

Newclose Copse

21

Hill Barn

Five Shilling Corner

Pudlicote Farm

Springhill Cottages

PUDLICOTE LA

3

Pudlicote House

20

Oxfordshire Way

River Evenlode

Chilson Farm

Ascott Mill

Chilson

2

SCHOOL LA

+

B4437

19

LC

Yew Tree Farm

Oxfordshire Way

Wychwood Farm

Ascott-under-Wychwood Station

Churchill Arms (PH)

HIGH ST

Mill Lane

Ascott d' Oyley

Ascott-under-Wychwood

Sch

LONDON LA

Ascott Earl

Smallstones Farm

1

ngley Mill

B4437

18

D   30   **E**   31   **F**

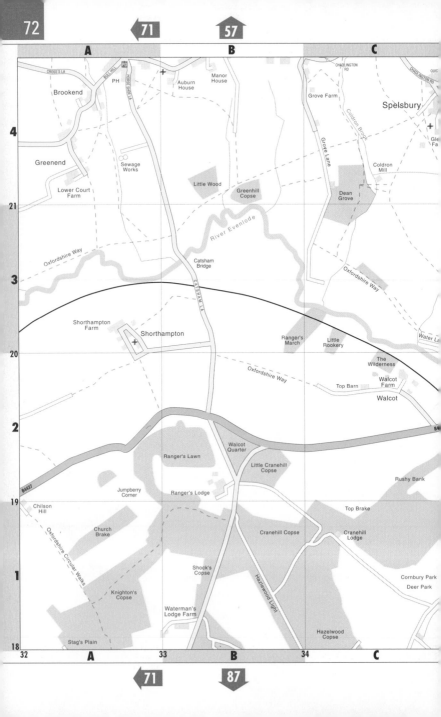

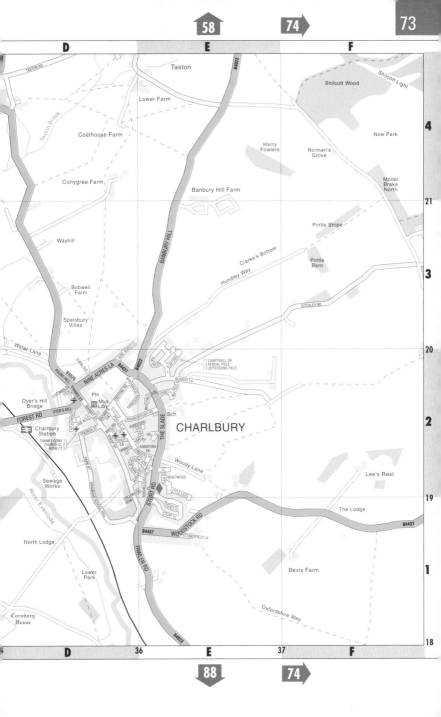

A B C

4

21

3

20

2

19

1

18

44 45 46

A B C

Woottondown Farm

Upper Dornford Farm

Upper Dornford Cottages

Woottondown Cottages

Tackley Hea

Old Man Leys Cottage

Old Man Leys

Holly Bank

River Dorn

Lower Dornford Farm

Dornford Lane

B4027

Dornford Grove

A4260

BANBURY RD

Home Farm

OXFORD PL

LODGE VIEW

Milford Bridge

Snakestail Clump

Hordley Farm

Oxfordshire Way

Sturdy's Castle (PH)

Sansoms Cottage

River Glyme

STRATFORD LA

Sansom's Farm

Upper Weaveley Farm

Stratford Bridge

Sansom's Platt

Sansoms Lane

BAGLEY RD

Old Weaveley Farm

Field Barn

Weaveley Farm

Weaveley Furze

A4260

Ban

D
E
F

4

SANDPIPER CL
FALCON MEAD

OSPREY
MERGANSER CT

NG CL
PEREGRINE WAY

Sch

KESTREL RD
KINGFISHER WAY

SWANFIELD RD
RAVENCROFT

PEREGRINE WAY

ROCKET WAY

WRETCHWICK WAY

Middle
Wretchwick
Farm

Little
Wretchwick
Farm

RAVENHILL
RD N

A41

21

Blackthorn Hill

LC

PIONEER RD

LC

LINCOLN RD

Wretchwick
Farm

Mill House
Farm

Stone Pits
Farm

3

Hill Farm

B4011

A41

20

Willow
End

BIRCH RD

ALDER DR

SYCAMORE RD

WILLOW RD

ELM CT

ELM PL

BEECH HAWTHORN RD

PEAR TREE

EAST HAWTHORN RD

LIMETON RD

GLEBE CLOSE

CHESTNUT WK

AKEMAN AVE

ENDCOTT CL

Sch

THAME RD

LOWER
RD

LABURNUM
CL

MERTON RD

PH

Ambrosden

Pound
Farm

2

HOME FARM
CL

OLD ARNCOTT RD

LC

PH

B4011

19

Home Farm

PLOUGHLEY RD

Arncott
Bridge

River Ray

1

Jasper's
Copse

LC

Manor
Farm

Astley Bridge
Farm

Brook
Farm

The
Tally-Ho
(PH)

Lower
Arncott

18

D
60
E
61
F

D
E
F

Great Rissington Farm

North Lodge

Great Rissington Hill

Resr

The Follies

Airfield (disused)

4

Littlehill Bank

Choake's Brake

Choake's Barn

Ell Brake

17

Washpool Copse

Barrington Bushes

Downs Cottages

Hazelford Brook

3

Taynton Bushes

Mill Hill

Hill Barn

16

Bromham Plantation

Miletree Clump

2

15

1

Comb Hill Plantation

Grosvenor Plantation

Barrington Park

Mortar Pits

14

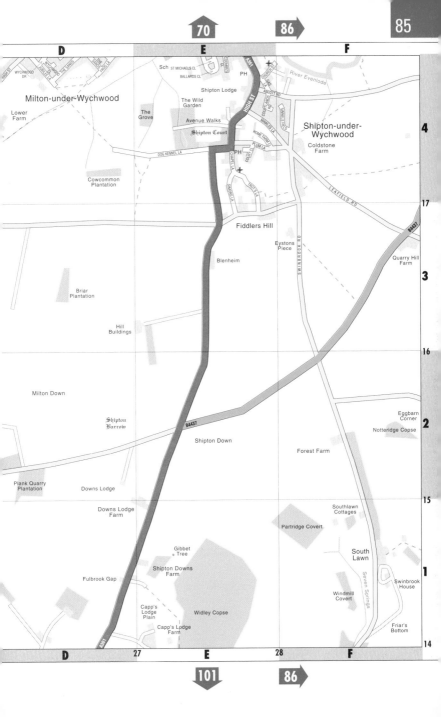

87
73

A | B | C

Cornbury Park
(Deer Park)

Park Farm

Oxfordshire Way

4

Little Park

Fawler Mill
House

Merryfall

Variety

Finstock
Station

Fawler

David's Hill

Stockfield
Brake

Manor House

Coldshore
Cottage

17

Patch Riding

Illcott
Copse

Manor
House

Manor
Farm

Oxfordshire Circular Walks

Wallborough
Grove

Sewage Works

River Evenlode

The Crown
(PH)

3

Finstock
House

Ward's Lane

Dark Lane

Topples Lane

Sch

Finstock

Topples Wood

Finstock
Heath

WITNEY RD

Blackberry
Lane

Strange's
Farm

HIGH ST

The Plough
(PH)

WILCOTE RIDING

Lady Grove

16

The Ridings

Wilcotefield
Longcut

Wilcote
House

Mount Skippett

Keeper
House

Home Farm

Sumteth's
Coppice

2

Ramsden Hill
Longcut

Wilcote Manor

HIGH ST

The Grange

WILCOTE LA

Wilcote

Ramsden

PH

The Hays

Wilcote Grange

Sch

15

Lower Farm

Holly Grove

Bridewell Farm
Cottages

Bridewell
Farm

Coneygar Copse

1

Hell Brake

Saint John's Lane

Shakenoak Farm

TURLEY LA

14

35 | A | 36 | B | 37 | C

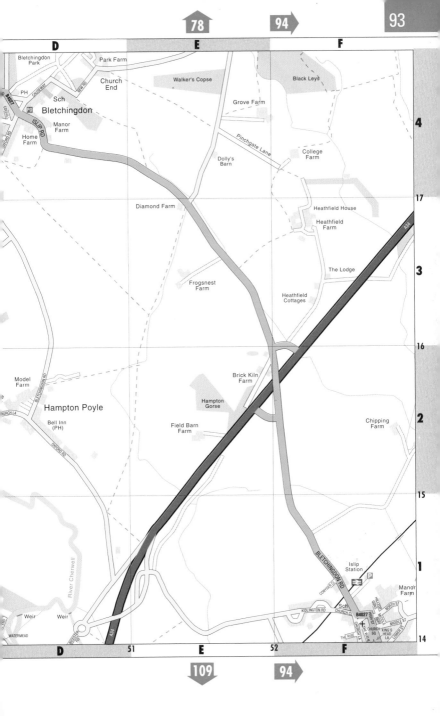

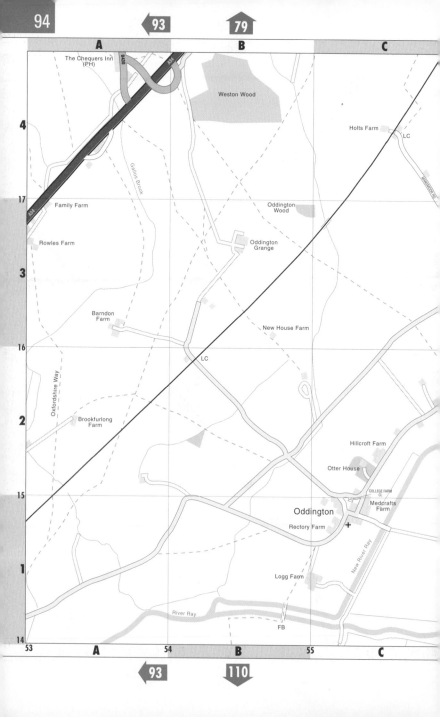

D
E
F

Sewage Works

West End
Farm

PH

Merton

River Ray

4

17

Street Hill

3

The
Homestead

Fencott Bridge

Bridge House
Farm

Mill Lane

Wks

Bull's
Lane

Fencott

Pound Lane

Murcott

Sch

Manor Farm

16

PH

Charlton-on-Otmoor

Moor Lands

New River Ray

PH

Pigeonhouse
Farm

2

15

1

Ot Moor

Danger Area

14

Astley Bridge Farm

River Ray

Murcott

Marlake House

Latchmeads

Whitecross Green

Manor Farm

Panshill Farms

Whitecross Green Wood
Nature Reserve

Upper Wood

Oriel Wood

Boarstall Lane

New Park Farm

Four Winds Farm

Upper Panshill Farm

Depot

LCs

LC

LC

LC

LC

Upper Arncott

The Plough (PH)

Bridge Farm

PALMER AVE

PATRICK HAUGH RD

Arncott Hill

Arncott Wood

Arncott Hill Farm

Depot

CH

Red House Farm

Oldhouse Spinney

Pans Hill

M40

LC

LC

LC

LC

LC

LC

LC

97

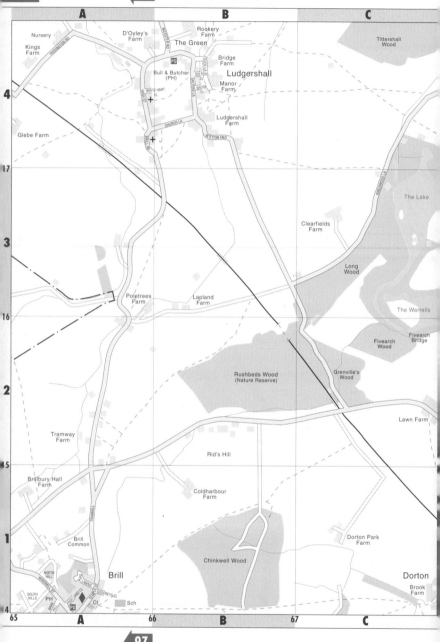

D

E

F

Barrington Park

Park Farm

Barrington Farm

Sch

Great
Barrington

4

Barrington Park

+

erloo
pse

The
Fox Inn
(PH)

Barrington
Mill

River Windrush

13

Green Drive
Farm

PO

Church
Farm

MINNOW LA

MIDDLE RD

+

Barrington
Grove

Paper Mill
Cottages

Sanctuary
Wood

Guggle
Wood

Little
Barrington

Home Farm

Drive
Covert

Boundary
Covert

3

B4

Allotment
Plantation

The Lodge

Brindles

12

The Inn for
all Seasons
(PH)

Ell
Plantation

Upton Downs
Farm

B4425

Hurst Barn
Farm

2

Upton Down

Cat's Abbey
Barn

Leys Farm

11

Poverty

Handpost
Covert

Freeland
Plantation

1

Hollowbarn
Farm

Westwell

+

Freelands
Farm

Pig Unit

10

D

21

E

22

F

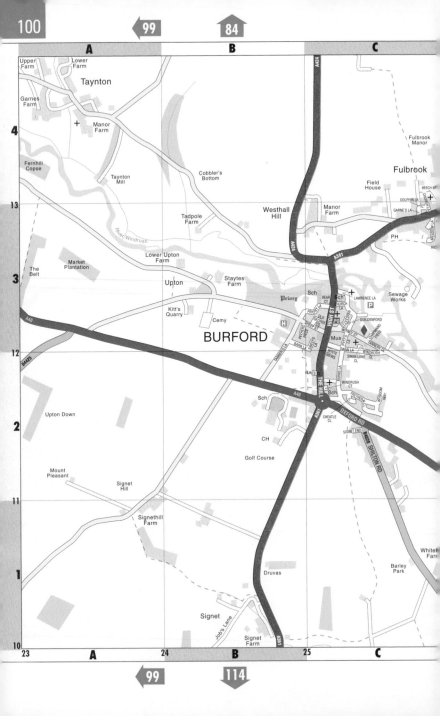

Waterloo Farm

Kingswood Lane

Pain's Farm Cottages

East Hill

Tudhill Bushes

4

Furzy Leaze

Salter's Corner

Furzyleaze Lodge

Faws Grove

Pain's Farm

Handley Plain

13

Beech Grove Farm

Beech Grove

Poulten's Walk Spinney

Dean Bottom

Swinbrook Manor Farm

Swinbrook

3

Widford Village

Oxford Circular Walks

PEBBLE CT

SWIN LA

The Old Farm

River Windrush

12

Manor Farm

Widford

Widford Mill Farm

PH

Chalk Hill Cover

2

THE COLLEGE

PH

Whitehill Farm

WHITE HILL

Flat Barn Farm

The Manor

Asthall

WALKER'S CL

11

Quarry

Sturt Farm

1

Home Close Farm

BURFORD RD

Barrow Plantation

Asthall Barrow

A40

A4047

10

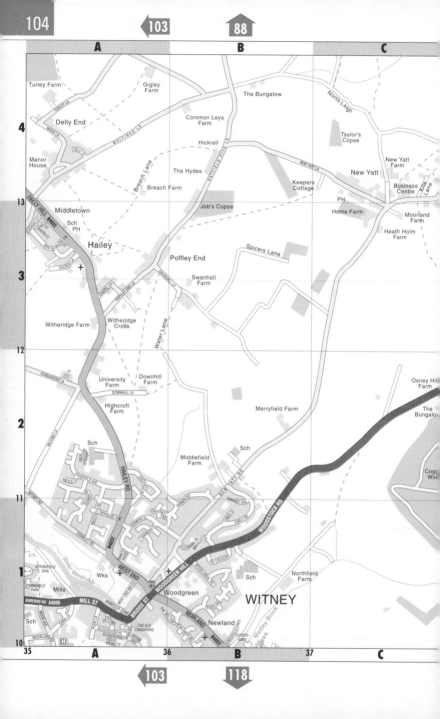

107
92

D
E
F

Gosford Bridge
Gosford Farm

Mill Farm
LC
LC
River Ray
Weir
Islip
LOWER ST
WHEATLEY RD
COLLEGE ST
BRIDGE ST
B4027
MILL ST

4

Hillside Farm

Northfield Farm

13

Water Eaton Crossing

River Cherwell

3

Middle Farm

Water Eaton
+

12

Sparsey Bridge

2

St Frideswide Farm

11

CH

Cutteslowe

Cemy
+

OXFORD RD
BANBURY RD
NORTH WAY

Sports Ground

Cutteslow Park

Sescut Farm

1

Bayswater Brook

SUNDERLAND AVE
ELSFIELD WAY
HAWKSMOOR RD
NORTHERN BY-PASS RD
A40
Sch

D
51
E
52
F

10

109 94

River Ray

Sewage Works

B4027

Oxfordshire Way

4

Manor Farm

Rectory Farm

13

Noke

Rectory Farm

Lower Farm

Prattle
Wood

3

Prattle Lane

Home
Farm

The
Bungalow

Lower Wood's
Farm

Sch

Old Upper Farm

12

Woodeaton

Woodmoor
Copse

Lower Farm

Parson's
Copse

Sewage Works

2

Drun's Hill

Upper Wood's
Farm

Noke
Wood

Woodeaton
Wood

Robert's
Copse

The Common

11

COMMON RD

Folly Farm

Long Wood

Lyme
Hill

Fox
Covert

1

Sewage
Works

Little Wood

Stow Wood

Manor House

Home Farm

Lodge
Farm

10

Elsfield

53   A   54   B   55   C

109 124

D
E
F

4

Danger Area

Ot Moor

Danger Area

13

Butts

Danger Area

Rifle Range

The Spinney

Lower Green Farm

West Hill Farm

Ventfield Farm

3

Lower Farm

Beckley Park

12

Oxfordshire Way

2

Sch

Grove Farm

Abingdon Arms (PH)

Middle Park Farm

Upper Park Farm

Stanton Little Wood

HIGH RD

Blackwater Wood

COMMON RD

Beckley

11

SANDY LA

WOODPERRY RD

BECKLEY RD

BROWN'S CLOSE

Masts
Television Station

Woodperry House Farm

1

Rifle Range

Royal Oak Farm

Woodperry

Woodperry Farm

Holly Wood

New Inn Farm

B4027

10

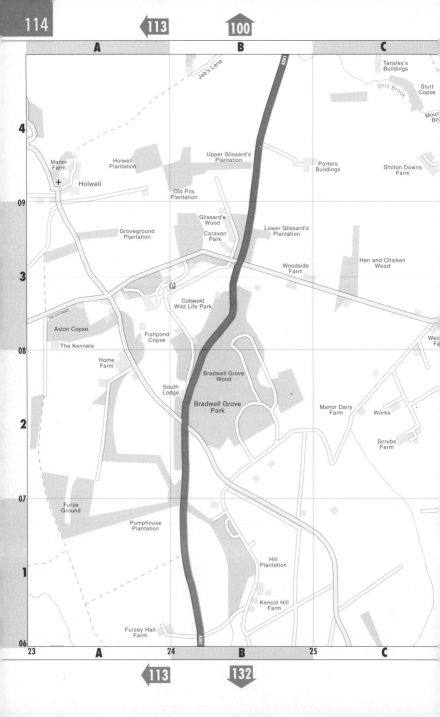

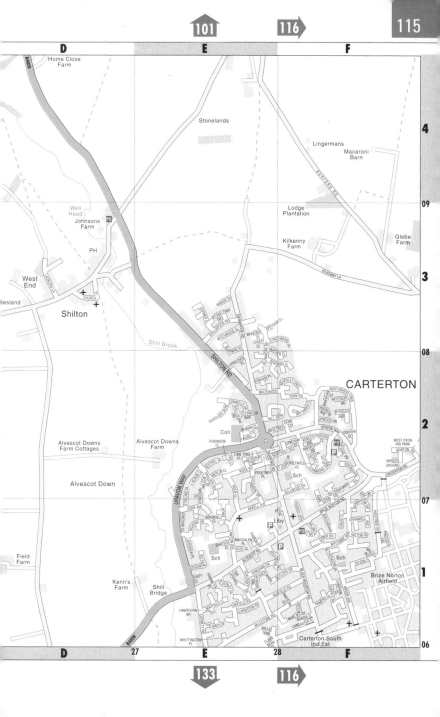

D
E
F

A40

Green House Farm
Ash Plantations

Green Farm

Chil Brook

4

Furzy Breach

Little Bartlett's
Kimber's Brake

SOUTH LEIGH RD

Glebe House

Oxfordshire Circular Walks
09

CHURCH RD

CHAPEL RD

Church End

Church End Farm

Margery Cross

The Masons Arms (PH)

South Leigh

Horman's Farm

Oxfordshire Circular Walks
3

PO

STATION RD

LIMBROOK CL

Station Farm

Limb Brook

Warners

Moor Lane

STATION/CHURCH RD

Blue Barn House
08

College Farm

Rushy Common

Tar Wood

2

Tar Farm

07

Tar Farm Cottages

Blue Barn

River Windrush

Friar's Farm

1

Hardwick Farm

Standlake Brook

B4449

06

D
39
E
40
F

119
106

A B C

4

Twelve Acre Farm

Paddock Close

Chil Brook

09

Oxfordshire Circular Walks

Chil Brook

3

The Nunnery

Southfield Cottages

Southfield Barn

Foxley Farm

08

Limb Brook

2

Bell Bridge

The Bungalow

Pinkhill Farm

07

University Cottages

Nicholls' Farm

Sutton Farm

Sutton Green

1

Beaumont House

Cox's Farm

Sutton

The Fox (PH)

Lower Farm

Sewage Works

06

41 A 42 B 43 C

A40

PH

MARLBOROUGH CL

HANBOROUGH CL

GREEN'S RD

OLD WITNEY RD

DUNCAN

STRATFORD

Sch

HAWTHORN RD

BARTHOLOMEW CL

WILLOW'S EDGE

THORNBURY RD

Sch

CLOVER PL

FALSTAFF CL

NEWLAND ST

Liby

ORCHARD CL

TANNERS LA

PO

CHILBROOKE RD

Litchfield Farm

ACRE END ST

HIGH ST

SWAN ST

Eynsham

Abbey Farm

THE TILER
THE SQUARE
CHURCH ST
ABBEY PL

Oxfordshire Circular Walks

PINKHILL LA

B4044

Sch

CASSINGTON

River Thames or Isis

Thames Path

D
E
F

4

CASSINGTON RD

Cassington Mill

River Evenlode

Old Canal

Towing Path

Ten Acre Copse

Oxfordshire Circular Walks

Hither Clay Hill

Thorney Croft

09

PH

Wharf Stream

Great Ash Hill

Further Clay Hill

Wytham Great Wood

Common Piece

River Thames or Isis

Weir

Great Plain

Keepers Cottage

winford Bridge (Toll)

Lock

Water Works

Little Ash Hill

3

Swinford

Swinford Farm

Hill Copse

Towing Path

OXFORD RD

The Five Sisters

Wytham Hill

08

Beacon Hill

My Lady's Seat

Woodcroft Copse

Radbrook Common

2

Stroud Copse

Rough Copse

The Plantation

Nealing's Copse

Pinkhill Lock

Farmoor

07

Woodend Farm

Cowleaze Copse

BEACON RD

BAYWELL RD

CHURCH CL

B4017

Oaken Holt

Bean Wood

Hill End Camp

CUMNOR RD

Valley Farm

EYNSHAM RD

Hill End Camp Farm House

1

Farmoor Reservoir

P

P

B4017

Red House Farm

B4044

06

D
45
E
46
F

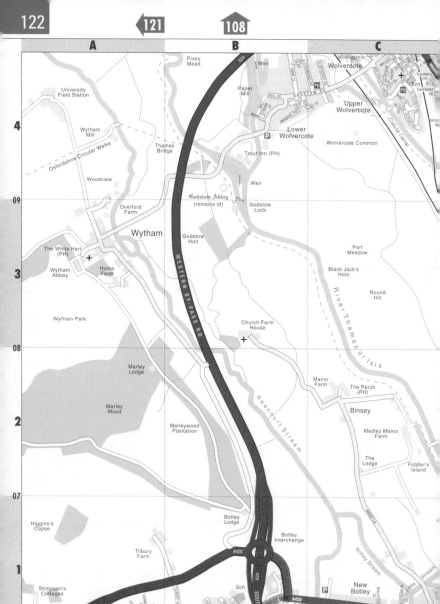

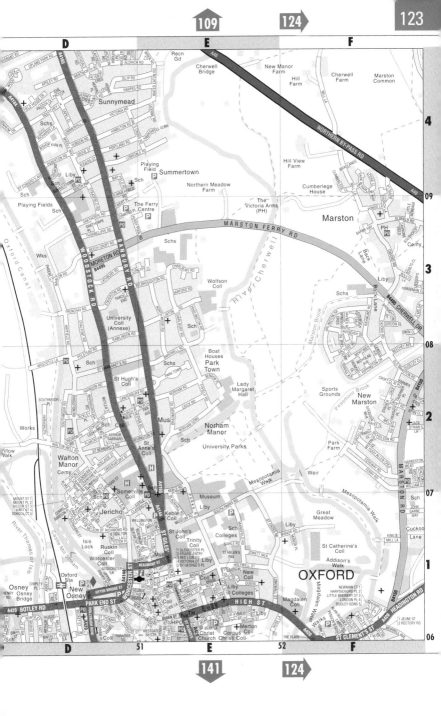

A   B   C

4

09

3

08

Woodway Farm

Westfield Farm

Lower
Peppershill Farm

Peppershill

Peppershill Farm

Crendon
House

Peacehaven Farm

Marsh
Farm

2

Ickford

07

SOLDER'S CL
ACORN CL
FIELD CL
TURNPIKE
SHELDON RD
Sch
BULLY'S

Little
Ickford

Sewage
Works

Rookery
Farm

THE BURNHAMS
LOWER
FARM
CL
MEADOW RD
LONG CRENDON RD

Upper
Farm

Thame Valley Wlk

MORTON KING
CL

Shabbington

Village
Farm

SCHOOL LA

ICKFORD RD
LOWE'S WAY

PO

QUEENS CL

NEW ST CL

River Thame

1

River Thame

Franklins
Farm

Old
Fisherman
(PH)

06

Manor Farm

Nor
Wes

65   A   66   B   67   C

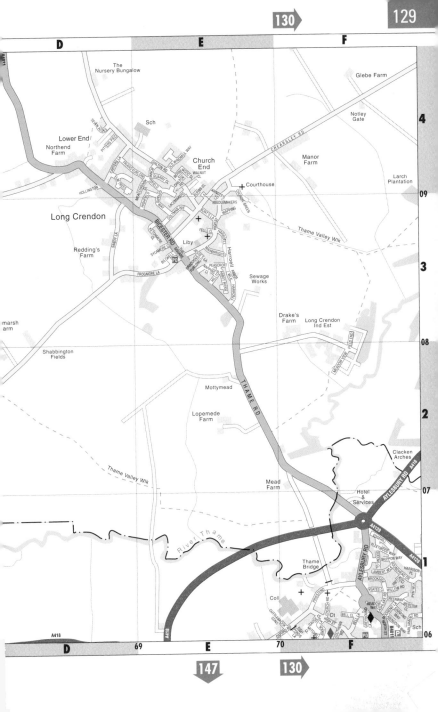

A **B** **C**

4

05

Hillview Farm

Peartree Farm

Filkins

Home Farm

3

Asthall Farm

Filkins Farm

CROSS TREES CT

Filkins Hall

Kencot

Mus

BULL CL

Manor Farm

Factory

PH

HONEY LA

PH

04

Scb

PH

Manor Farm

Broughton Hall

LEIGH LA

Broadwell

Broughton Poggs

2

Lower Farm

Filkins Mill Broadshire Bridge

Broadwell Brook

Holly Cottage

CALCROFT LA

03

Langford

PH

Ansells Farm

LECHLADE RD

BROADWELL RD

Broadwell Mill

1

THE LANE

Sch

Rectory Farm

Lower Farm

Little Faringdon Wood

HIGH ST

Hulse Grounds Farm

HOOKS CL

Leys View

02

23 **A** 24 **B** 25 **C**

D
E
F

B4020

CORBETT RD
MILESTONE RD
THE CRESCENT
GLEBE FARM

Shill Brook

Brize Norton
Airfield

4

The
Poplars

Elmwood
House

Springfield
House

05

Sewage
Works

Home
Farm

MILL LA

Mill
House

Butlers
Court
Farm

PH

Black
Bourton

Alvescot

Glebe
Farm

MILL LA

Piggery

3

Sch

PH

BOURTON RD

Bedwell
Pond

College

CHURCH RD

THE GREEN
THE VINEYARD
OLD ROAD

Park
Farm

Lower End

OAKEY CL

STATION RD

SCHOOL LA

SHILBROOK
MANOR

Glebe
Farm

04

Manor
Farm

Long
Copse

Black Bourton Brook

Draught Ditch

2

Clanfield Brook

03

Bazeland

CALCROFT LA

1

B4020

Edgerly
Farm

BLACK BOURTON RD

Chestlion
Farm

ROUND LA

PH

02

BAMPTON RD

A4095

D
27
E
28
F

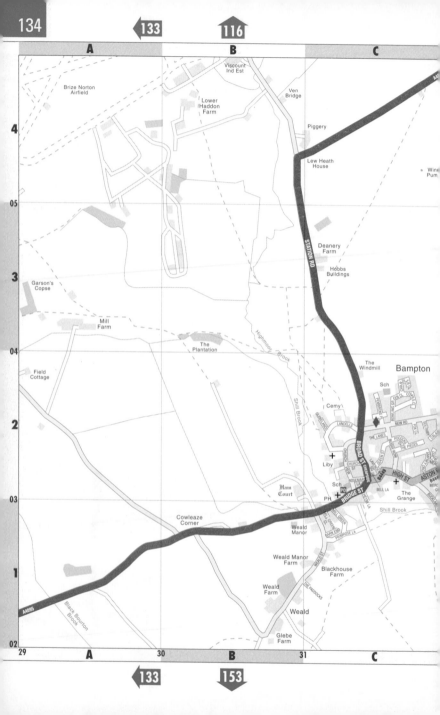

D
E
F

University
Farm

Rushy
Butts

Claywell
Hill

Ditcham
Wood

Newhouse
Farm

Elm Bank Ditch

4

Lew
Lodge

Newhouse
Farm Cottages

05

Mount Owen
Farm

Far
Horizons

3

Coalpit
Farm

04

White
Owl
Farm

CALAIS DENE

Cote Ditch

2

North Street
Farm

Aston

B4449

KILN

BOVINGTON'S
YD

MERCURY CL

Aston Ditch

OAKFIELD CL

HIGH STREET

LONGWOOD
CL

COTE RD

Home
Farm

Sch

Kingsway
Farm

THE
SQUARE

WOODBRIDGE
CL

MANOR
CL

03

Calais Oak
Farm

BAMPTON RD

HIGH ST

P

SIMMS
CL

PENNY FARTHING

MAIN CL

BELL LA

Sewage
Works

Bull Inn
(PH)

Lower
Farm

Nursery

Paradise
Farm

Westmoor Lane

Shill Brook

HART LA

1

ursery

Kennels

Rainbow
Farm

Hedgefields
Farm

02

D
33
E
34
F

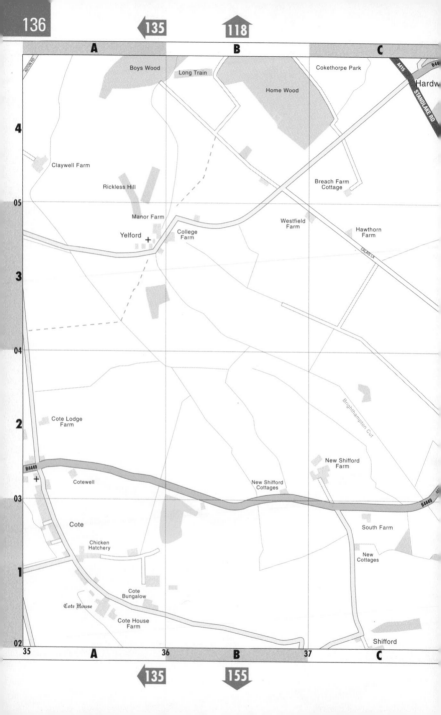

139
122

A   B   C

TUDOR CT
B4044
EYNSHAM RD   B4044

Nobles
Farm
Cottages

FERRY HINKSEY RD   New
Botley

Kin
Mea
Ind

Dean
Court

Botley

NORTH HINKSEY LA
SOUTHERN BY-PASS RD

Sch

4

Hid's
Copse

TOYNBEE CL
CHESTNUT
RD
BEECH RD

Raleigh
Park

The
Fold

Hine
Stre

PH

Chawley

Cumnor
Hill

ARNOLD'S WAY
Sch

LIME RD

North
Hinksey
Village

PH

05

Long
Copse

Dene
House
Coll

Water
Tower

VERNON AVE

Harcourt
Hill

3

NORELL RD

HURST LA

Playing
Field

Hinksey Heights
Golf Course

04

Hurst
Hill

Powder
Hill
Copse

2

Hen
Wood

Chiswell
Farm

Chiswell House
(Priory)

Circular   Walks

Whitebarn

Youlbury
Wood

Oxfordshire

CHISWELL LA

Birch
Copse

Chiswell
Farm
Cottages

03

Henwood
Farm

Youlbury
Pond

Mast
Pickett's
Heath
Farm

Upper
Youlbury
Heath

West
Gardens

Boars
Hill

Yatscombe
Copse

1

CANDY LA

RIDGEWAY

BERKELEY HEATH

Oxford
Preservation
Trust

HENWOOD HILL LA
CUMNOR RD   B4017

Wootton
Close

Jarn
Mound

Mayo's
Farm

JARN WAY

Foxcombe
Hall

BERKELEY RD

FOXCOMBE LA

White Hill
Farm

Old Boars
Hill

ORCHARD LA

02

47   A   48   B   49   C

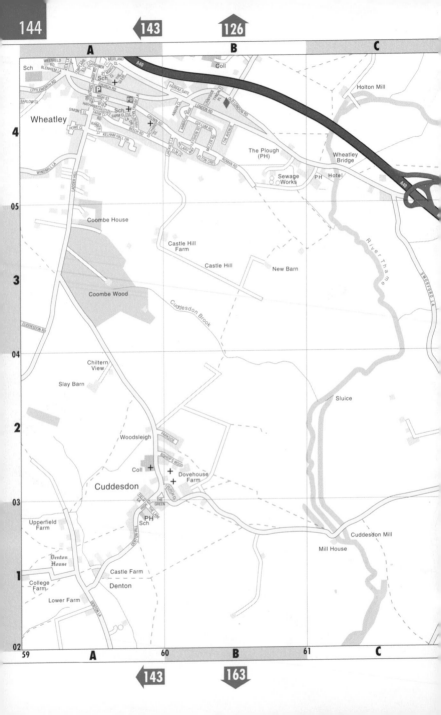

D **E** **F**

Bumpers

Grange Farm

Parkhill
Covert

Ilmer **4**

Manor Farm

Upper
Farm

MANOR RD **05**

North Mill
Farm

Penn Farm **3**

Grovehill Farm

NORTH MILL RD

Grovehill
Covert

Hinton Crossing
Cottage

New Close Farm **04**

Down
Covert

Whites Close

Forty Green **2**

New Close Farm Road

Fortygreen
Farm

Great
Covert

Cattle Brook

Sewage Works

FORTY GREEN

The
Peacock
(PH) **03**

Home Farm

Henton

College Farm

Village Farm

nor
rm

Manor Farm **1**

Emmington

Rectory

Allnut's Farm

Church Covert

Westbrook
Farm

Upper Farm

LOWER ICKNIELD WAY

B A609

B A609

D 75 **E** 76 **F** **02**

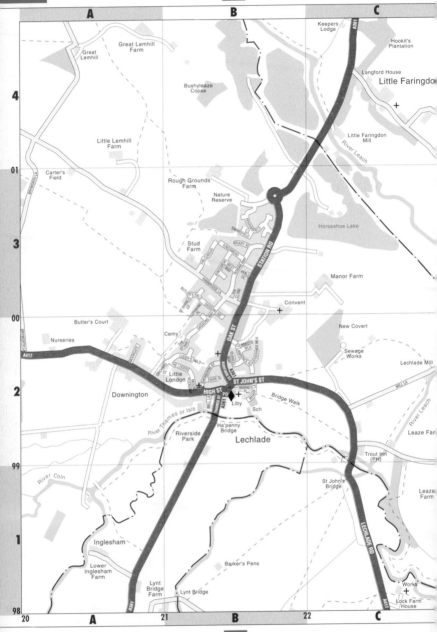

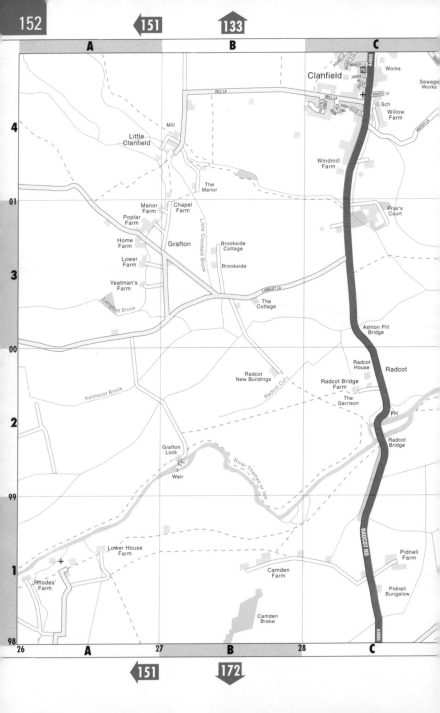

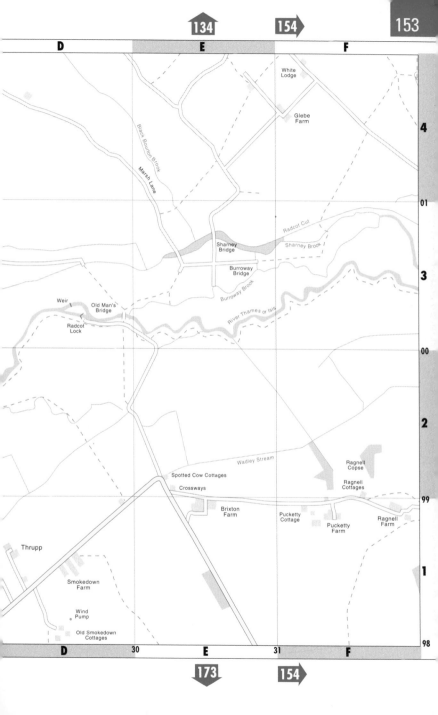

153
135

A B C

4

01

3

00

2

99

1

98

32 A 33 B 34 C

153
174

Shill Brook

Meadow Arch Bridge

Meadow Farm Cottages

Meadow Brook

BUCKLAND RD

Great Brook

Meadow Farm

Hoskins Barn

Isle Of Wight Bridge

Tadpole Bridge

Tadpole

The Trout Inn (PH)

Rushey Lock

Weir

River Thames or Isis

Buckland Marsh

Buckland Marsh Farm

Gore Farm

Carswell Marsh

Marriage Hill

The Lakes

Weir

Deer Park

Manor House

Sewage Works

Vicar's Copse

CASWELL LA

Middle Brake

Rivey Brake

Rivey Copse

Buckland House (College)

Arch Plantation

BUCKLAND RD

ST GEORGE'S RD

Buckland

ORCHARD RD

157
139

A B C

Lower England's
Copse

Home
Farm

Bessels Leigh

The Greyhound
(PH)

THE
ORCHARD

Radcliffe
House

The Cottage

Sch

Bessels Leigh
Common

Hull's Copse

New
Copse

4

PH

Dean's Farm

Appleton

Hall

Colliers
Copse

Sch

Holt
Copse

01

Tubney Manor
Farm

The Keepers
House

The Old
Rectory

Great Park Farm

New Plantation

Upwood
Cottages

Sch

THE FIELD

Triangle
Plantation

A338

Upwood Park

Rowleigh
House

Dry
Sandford

3

Tubney Wood

Upwood Park

Manor
Farm

White Hart
Wood

Brushwood Farm

Parsonage Moor

00

Factory

Hitch Copse

String Lane

Sch

COTHILL RD

Fleur-de-lys
(PH)

Cothill

Tubney Wood

2

Woodside

Hitchcopse
Farm

Blackgate Lane

Golf Course

The
Warren

Cothill
Farmhouse

Sewage Farm

99

The Dog House Hotel
(PH)

Oakley Park

Gozzard's Ford

Grey
Walls

Black Horse
(PH)

Black Horse
Farm

Golf Course

Hylston

Buildings
Farm

1

CH

Sheepstead
Park

Sheepstead Folly

98

44 45 46

A B C

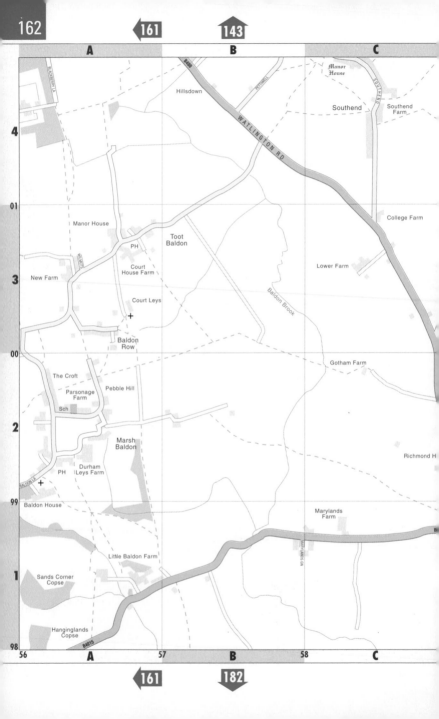

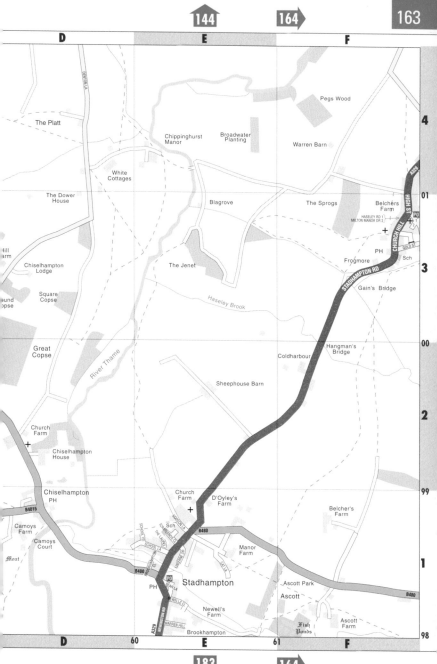

D E F

4

Pegs Wood

The Platt

Chippinghurst
Manor

Broadwater
Planting

Warren Barn

White
Cottages

01

The Dower
House

Blagrove

The Sprogs

Belchers
Farm

HASELEY RD 1
MILTON MANOR DR 2

Hill
arm

Chiselhampton
Lodge

The Jenet

PH

Frogmore

Sch

3

Square
Copse

ound
opse

Haseley Brook

Gain's Bridge

00

Great
Copse

River Thame

Hangman's
Bridge

Coldharbour

Sheephouse Barn

2

Church
Farm

Chiselhampton
House

99

Chiselhampton
PH

Church
Farm

D'Oyley's
Farm

Belcher's
Farm

B4015

Sch

Camoys
Farm

Camoys
Court

THE DRIVE

SCHOOL LA

GOODSON LA

B480

LUCERNE RD

Manor
Farm

Moat

B480

STADHAMPTON RD

HIGH ST

A329

CHURCH HILL

GOLD ST

PO

+

Newell's
Farm

PH

Stadhampton

BEAM LA

WELLS CL

A329

Ascott Park

Ascott

Fish
Ponds

B480

Ascott
Farm

WARREN HILL

Brookhampton

MILTON HILL RD

D 60 E 61 F

98

D
E
F

M40

Manor Farm

Goldpits Farm

Jointer's Farm

Oxhouse Farm

4

Latchford House

LATCHFORD LA

Latchford Farm

Latchford

Latchford Copse

Haseley Brook

01

Sheepbridge Copse

Peggs Farm

Cornwell Copse

3

Stoke Grange

The Island

00

Poppets Hill

Oxfordshire Way

Poppets Hill Farm

2

Stoney Lane

Stoke Talmage

Manor Farm

99

Clare

1

Clare Copse

Manor Farm

98

D
66
E
67
F

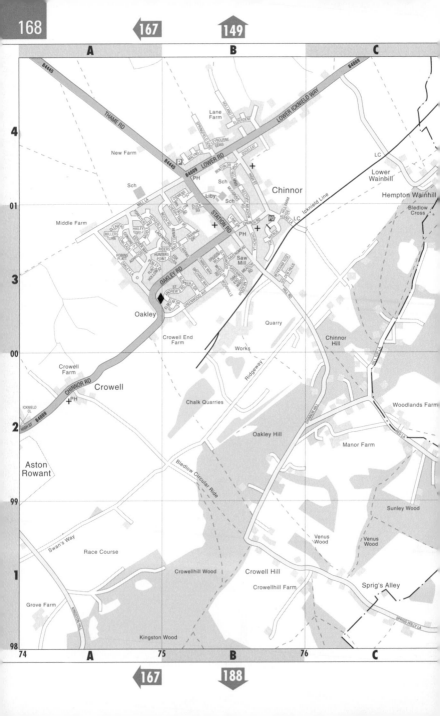

A   B   C

A419

Buscot Wick

Buscot Wick Farm

Weston Cottages

LECHLADE RD

The Rectory

4

Weir

River Thames or Isis

Weston Farm

97

Upper Inglesham

Manor Farm

Lynt Farm

3

LYNT RD

Snowswick Cottages

Broadlea Farm

River Cole

96

Snowswick Copse

Snowswick Farm

College Farm

2

Pennysw Farm

95

Worsall Farm

1

LECHLADE RD

A361

Roundhill Farm

94

20   21   22

A   B   C

D
E
F

Buscot Wharf

Buscot

P
PO

Kilmester Farm

Eaton Hastings

4

West Lodge

Taylor's Hill

LECHLADE RD

Stud Farm

Little Lake

A417

97

Buscot House

The Lake

Roadside Cottages

Resr

Buscot Park

Canada Wood

Bury Hill

Cannon Hill

3

Cannonhill Wood

Old Wood

Black Plantation

Longmead Plantation

Eaton Wood

Bushy Heath

Heath Barn

Resr

Woodacre Wood

96

Oldfield Farm

Rowleaze Wood

Gorse Hill

2

Brimstone Farm

95

Coxwell Wood

Middle Leaze Farm

Fern Copse

1

B4019

Cuckoopen Plantation

B4019

Colleymore Farm

94

D
24
E
25
F

D   E   F

Barcote Manor

Barcote
Farm

Barcote Hill

4

Park Farm

Leaze Hill

Waney Hill

Littleworth

Fox & Hounds
(PH)

A420

97

Church Walk

Haremoor Wood

Grove Wood

Haremoor
Farm

3

Church Walk   Grove
Lodge

Wadley
Cottages

Wadley Lodge

Wadley Manor

96

Church Path
Farm

LONDON ST

Cromwell's
Battery

Ewedown Copse

Oxpen Copse

Oxpen Farm

Chinham Copse

Hotel

The Folly

Faringdon Hill

CROMWELL CL

STANFORD RD

Folly Farm

Standford Place

2

GOODLAKE AVE
FLETCHER CL

Jespers Hill

A417 STANFORD RD

Kennels

Bowling Green
Farm

Chinham Farm

95

Chinham Farm

PARK RD

el Cottages

A417

Wichwood

Bowling Green
Cottages

Kitemoor
Copse

1

A417

Kitemoor Farm

Kitemoor
House

Wickleshamlodge Farm

94

D   30   E   31   F

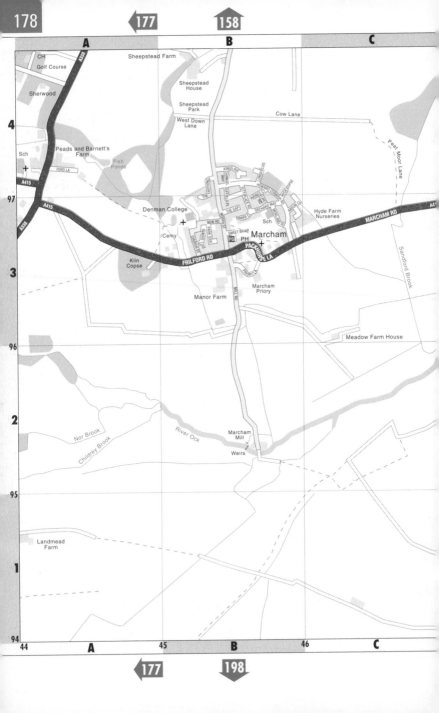

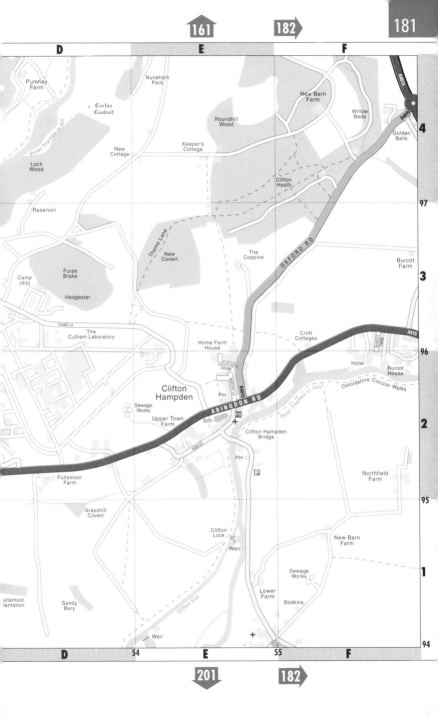

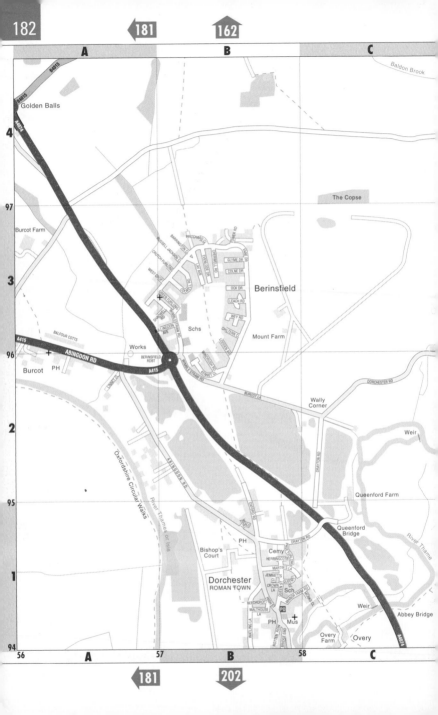

A
B
C

Baldon Brook

Golden Balls

4

97

The Copse

Burcot Farm

PATCHARD CL
RUSSELL JACKSON CL
BARRINGTON CL
TOWER RD
FANE RD
CHERWELL RD
GLYME DR
CRATCH FURLONG
LIT JOE RD
COLNE DR
WEST CROFT
CONEY
EVENLODE DR
DCK DR

Berinsfield

3

LEACH RD
SANDFIELD
BRIMPTON RD
FERRY FARM RD
LINGDON AVE

Schs

WEY RD
CHILTERN CL

Mount Farm

A415

BALFOUR COTTS

Works

ABINGDON RD

BERINSFIELD RDBT
A415

UDSEY LN
WAITES CL

Burcot
PH

96

TUNNEL CL

WATERMEADOW CL
CONNET CL
THAME RD

BURCOT LA

DORCHESTER RD

Wally
Corner

Weir

2

Oxfordshire Circular Walks

DRAYTON RD

Queenford Farm

River Thames

River Thames or Isis

WATLING LA

95

Queenford
Bridge

OXFORD RD

Bishop's
Court

PH

Cemy
HERRINGCOTE
MARTIN'S LA

DRAYTON RD

GLEBE

Dorchester
ROMAN TOWN

JEMMETTS
CL
CROWN
LA

BEANS CL

Sch

1

BEECHCROFT
CL
MALTHOUSE
LA
PH

WATLING LA
ROTTEN ROW
BRIDGE END

PO
Mus

Weir

Abbey Bridge

Overy
Farm

Overy

94

56
A
57
B
58
C

D   E   F

4

97

3

96

2

95

1

94

Newall's Pond

Newbury Hill

Sewage Wks

Lower Covert

Hayward Bridge

Hill Farm

HOLCOMBE LA

Great Holcombe

Newington

River Thame

Newington House

Drayton St Leonard

LONG LA
THE OSIERS
CHURCH
CHURCH LA
STADHAMPTON RD
PH
WATER LA
THE OSIERS
WATER LA

Manor Farm

Upper Grange

Drayton House Farm

Ford

DORCHESTER RD

A329

Primrose Hill

Lower Grange

Lane End Farm

Ewe Farm

Town Hill

Pain Way

FERRIS LA

Upper Farm

Priests' Moor Lane

Violets Farm

THAME RD   A329

Court Farm

Green Lane

Ladybrook Copse

D   60   E   61   F

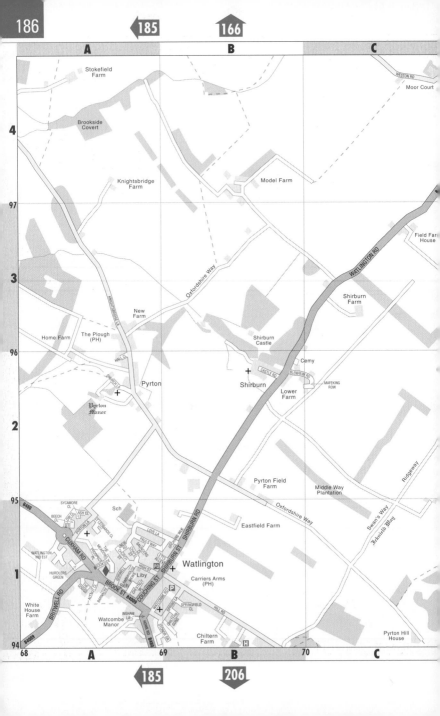

Stokefield Farm

Brookside Covert

WESTON RD

Moor Court

4

Knightsbridge Farm

Model Farm

Field Far House

97

Oxfordshire Way

WATLINGTON RD

Shirburn Farm

3

New Farm

Home Farm

The Plough (PH)

HALL CL

Shirburn Castle

Cemy

CASTLE RD

BLENHEIM RD

MAFEKING ROW

96

CHURCH LA

Pyrton

Shirburn

Lower Farm

Pyrton Manor

2

Pyrton Field Farm

Middle Way Plantation

Ridgeway

95

B480

SYCAMORE CL

ASH GR

BEECH

Sch

Oxfordshire Way

Eastfield Farm

Swan's Way

Icknield Way

WATLINGTON IND EST

HURDLERS GREEN

ST EDMUND'S

LOVE LA

PAUL'S WAY

HIGH ST

GORWELL

Watlington

Liby

Carriers Arms (PH)

1

CUXHAM RD

BROOK ST

COUCHING ST

P

SHIRBURN RD

HILL RD

White House Farm

BRITWELL RD

B4009

Watcombe Manor

INGHAM LA

Chiltern Farm

SPRINGFIELD CL

H

Pyrton Hill House

94

B4009

68

A

69

B

70

C

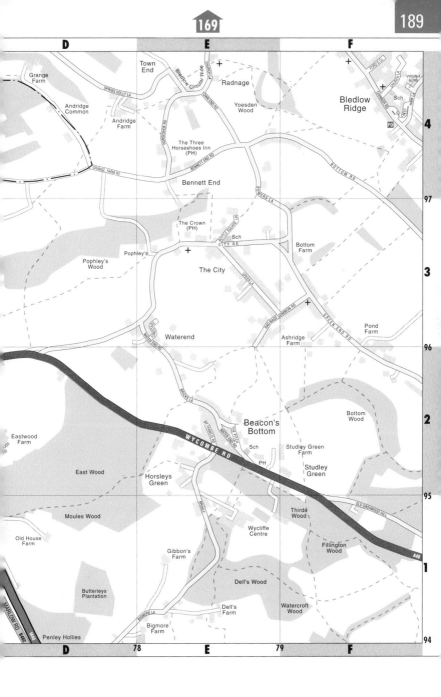

D **E** **F**

Grange
Farm

Town
End

Radnage

Andridge
Common

SPRIGS HOLLY LA

Andridge
Farm

Bledlow Circuit Ride

TOWN END RD

Yoesden
Wood

FORD'S C.CL

VIRGINIA
GDNS

Sch

CHURCH RD

Bledlow
Ridge

PO

4

HORSESHOE RD

The Three
Horseshoes Inn
(PH)

BENNETT END RD

GRANGE FARM RD

Bennett End

BOTTOM RD

97

BOYERS LA

The Crown
(PH)

Sch

BOTTLE SQUARE LA

CITY RD

Bottom
Farm

Pophley's

Pophley's
Wood

The City

GREEN LA

3

Waterend

WATER END RD

BECKS LA

ANDRIDGE COMMON RD

Ashridge
Farm

GREEN END RD

Pond
Farm

96

Eastwood
Farm

BOLTER END LA

East Wood

Horsleys
Green

ST FRANCIS RD

HORSE RD

THE DITTON

Beacon's
Bottom

WYCOMBE RD

Sch

PH

Studley Green
Farm

Bottom
Wood

2

Studley
Green

OLD DASHWOOD HILL

95

Moules Wood

Old House
Farm

BRAKE

Gibbon's
Farm

Wycliffe
Centre

Thirds
Wood

Fillington
Wood

A40

1

Butterleys
Plantation

Dell's Wood

Dell's
Farm

Watercroft
Wood

MARLOW RD B482

BIGMORE LA

Bigmore
Farm

Penley Hollies

D **78** **E** **79** **F** **94**

A B C

4

BLACKWORTH

93

HIGHWORTH

Lower
Barn

Common
Farm

Eastrop
Farm

Wickstead
Farm

Fresden
Wood

River Cole

Ragl
Wo

3

EASTROP

Eastrop
Grange

Starveall
Barn

Fresde
Far

92

Schs

91

The
Buildings

Wrag
Farm

CH

Golf Course

Highmoor
Copse

Friars Hill

Round
Robin
Farm

Folly
Plantation

Round
Robin
Wood

River Cole

B4508

Coombes
Copse

River Cole

2

SHRIVENHAM RD

1

Bellingham
Farm

The
Rookery

Sevenhampton

Sevenhampton
Farm

Thorny
Copse

New
Covert

Little
Coombes
Copse

Friars
Farm

Homegrown
Copse

HIGHWORTH RD

Swan's Nest
Copse

B4000

90

20 A 21 B 22 C

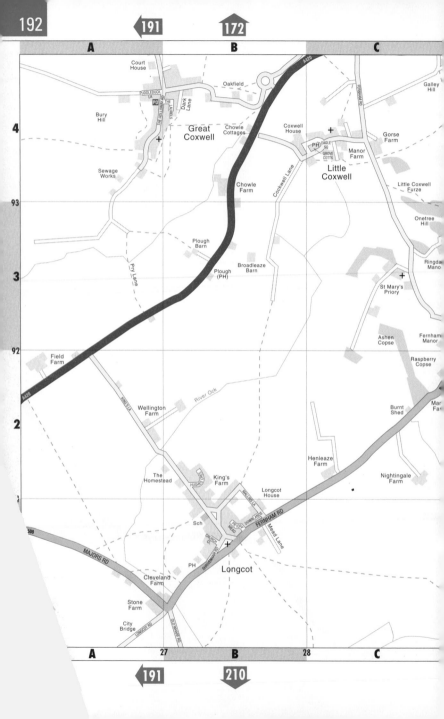

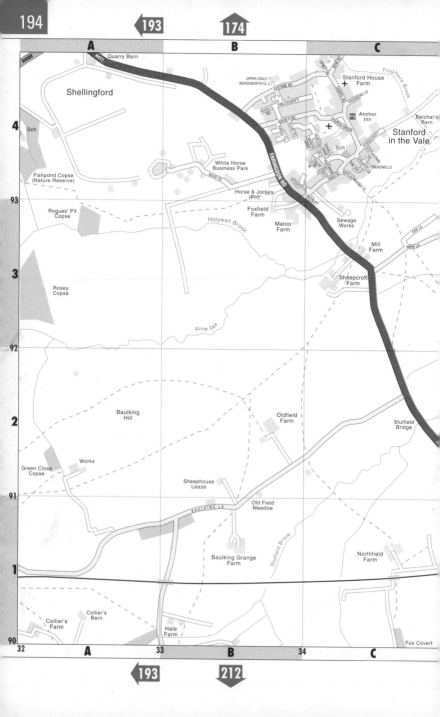

A B C

4

Shellingford

Quarry Barn

Sch

Fishpond Copse
(Nature Reserve)

UPPER CRALE 1
WORDSWORTH CL 2

COTTAGE RD

ST DIEMAN'S

PERRY'S RD

JOYCE'S RD

Upper Green Farm

Stanford House
Farm

CHURCH GREEN

Anchor
Inn

PO

Sch

Belcher's
Barn

Stanford
in the Vale

TREADWELLS

Frogmore Brook

White Horse
Business Park

WISE RD

FARINGDON RD

Horse & Jockey
(PH)

Foxfield
Farm

Manor
Farm

Sewage
Works

Mill
Farm

93

Rogues' Pit
Copse

Holywell Brook

OAK LA

PARK LA

3

Rosey
Copse

Sheepcroft
Farm

River Ock

92

2

Baulking
Hill

Oldfield
Farm

Stutfield
Bridge

Green Close
Copse

Works

Sheephouse
Leaze

BAULKING LA

Old Field
Meadow

91

Stutfield Brook

Northfield
Farm

1

Baulking Grange
Farm

Collier's
Farm

Collier's
Barn

Hale
Farm

Fox Covert

90

32 A 33 B 34 C

A B C

4

Drayton
Copse

93

Steventon Field

Cow Common

Honeybottom
Boarding
Kennels

Goose
Willow

El Sub Sta

3

Orchard Farm

HANNEY RD

Three
Elms

The
Views

92

Depot

Steventon

Sewage
Works

Causeway
Farm

Sch

Causeway
Crossing

LC

2

Little
Lane

VICARAGE RD

MILL ST

CASTLE ST

Steventon
Copse

91

CHURCH LA

Ginge Brook

Hill Farm

1

East Hendred Brook

Hill Barn

Wood's Farm

WOOD'S FARM RD

90

44 A 45 B 46 C

D
E
F

B4017

DRAYTON RD
B4016
B4016

CHIERS DR

Hulgrove
Farm

BROOK ST

Sutton
Courtenay

THE NURSERY

Hall

EAST WAY

Drayton East Way

STEVENTON RD

HAYWARDS RD

Sewage
Works

Brook Farm

Drayton Mill

MILL LA

TULLIS RD

Uptown
Farm

HIGH ST

4

Mill Brook

93

ABINGDON RD

Ginge Brook

Courtfield House

Frog Hole

MILTON RD

KATCHSIDE

BARRETT'S WAY

BRADSTOCK'S WAY

Sch

Milton Mill

MILL LA

SUTTON RD

CHURCH RD

Cemy

HARWELL RD

3

FIELD END

PH

Butcher's
Farm

THE GREEN

Milton Lane

Milton
Manor

PH

Milton

WILLOW LA

Sch

SCHOOL LA

SUTTON COURTENAY RD

92

MILTON LA

BREWER CL

THE PADDOCKS CL

Inn

PUGSDEN LA

Sch

OLD MNOR

PEMBROKE LA

Manor
Farm

Moor Ditch

MILTON PARK

MILTON PARK

MILTON PARK

Milton Park

2

HIGH ST

AUGER LA

VEY RD

STATION YD

Recn
Gd

Depot

Stockslane
Farm

Milton Bridge

Mast

MILTON RD

A4130

A4130

A4130

Bachill Lane

New Farm

A4130

91

Steventon Hill

B4017

SCHOOL RD

TRENCHARD AVE

LAMBELL RD

MAYERS AVE

DUKE OF YORK AVE

Sch

Milton Heights

Cow Lane

Midwinters
Farm

Steventon
House

1

Milton
Hill

FERNBRELL LA

The Grove
Farm

Research
Centre

The
Pack Horse
(Inn)

Hungerford Road

A4130

Milton Hill
House

Stert
Plantation

90

D
48
E
49
F

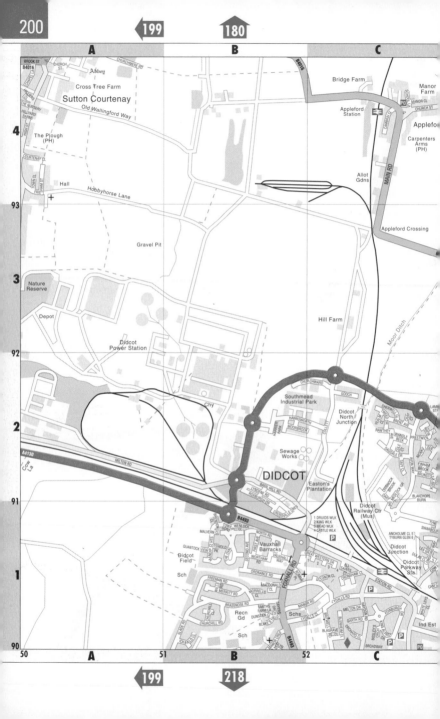

4

93

3

92

2

91

1

90

B4009

Turner's Green Lane

Lower Farm
The Old Rectory
The Priory
Cooper's Farm

Heath Plantation
Ashley's Wood
Turner's Green
Britwell Salome
PH

Grove Farm
Brightwell Grove

Home Farm

GROVE LA

Mon

Britwell Salome House
Mon

Brockholes Lane
Brockholes Covert

Icknield Way
Ridgeway

North Farm

Huntingland

Swan's Way

Icknieldbank Plantation

Lower Warren

Swyncombe Downs

Warren Bottom

Sliding Hill

Lower Farm

The Nuttery

Littleworth Hill

Lowerfarm Cottages

Down Farm

Grindon Lane

Ladies Walk

Colliers Hill

Potters Lane

Ewelme Downs

Colliers Bottom

D   E   F

Portways
Shotridge Wood
Buckingham Bottom
Hungryhill Wood
Barnfield Hanging Wood
-fordshire Way
Mast
4
Christmas Common
Ibstone
Fox & Hounds (PH)
Mast
Copper's Wood
Blackmoor Wood
93
Prior's Grove
Northend
Northend Farm
Launder's Farm
HOLLOW LA
3
Queen Wood
The White Hart (PH)
Fire Wood
Swain's Wood
92
HOLLANDRIDGE LA
Greenfield
Hollandridge Farm
Longhill Hanging Wood
Blundells
2
College Wood
Turville Park Farm
Greenfield Wood
Turville Park
91
Roll's Shaw
Shambridge Wood
Whitehill Shaw
1
Pishill Bottom
Whitelands House
Primrose Cottage
Pishill Bank
Oxfordshire Way
PH
B480
90

Sevenhampton Place
Hill Farm
Dogkennel Copse
Sandhill Farm
Hurststone Barn
Stallpits Farm
Roves Farm
Nightingale Farm
Lowerfield Wood
Lowerfield Farm
Prior's Farley Cottages
Rowborough Farm
River Cole
Acorn End
Acorn Bridge
Lower Bourton
Gran Farr
The Carpenter's Arms (PH)
Manor Farm
Longleaze Farm
Acorn Bridge Farm
A420
Acorn Wood
River Cole
Hibberd's Piece
Mill Road Cottages
Lower Earlscourt Farm
New Barn

ROSE LA
NIGHTINGALE LA

D
E
F

BARRINGTON RD

Sewage
Works

Golf
Course

Bower Brook

CH

Beckett
Stables

Northford
Bridge

FARINGDON RD

LAKE RD

THE MALL

BECKETT RD

Broadleaze
Farm

4

Royal Military College
of Science

Shrivenham

BECKETT AVE

LAND HILL

STALLPITS RD

Sch

Golf Course

Home Farm

89

FARLEIGH RD

FORREST CL
TREES

MARTENS CL

SPRINGFIELD
CL

CHAPEL HILL RD

COMMON

HIGH ST

MARTENS RD

HIGH ST

PH

LONGLEAT
CL

Rhyme's
Cottages

COLTON RD

CURTIS RD
THE GREEN

TOWNSEND RD

CLAYDON CL

CAMBRIA CL
VICARAGE LA

STOMEFIELD WAY

FAIRTHORNE WAY

Works

STATION RD

COWLEAZE CL

Cemy

STAINSWICK LA

Reservoir

Old Canal

3

Forty Acre
Plantation

Steppingstone Lane

Chapelwick Farm

88

Cowleaze
Farm

FB

Ashbury
Crossing

The Victoria
(PH)

STAINSWICK CL

2

Stainswick Copse

CLAYFIELDS

AVENUE RD

Stainswick
Farm

THE HILL

THE DROVE

Bourton

New Road

87

CURTISS PIECE

ch

Home Farm

Five Acres
Farm

Bourton End

Fern Farm

1

A420

Zulu Buildings

86

D
24
E
25
F

A   B   C

LONGCOT RD

River Ock

4

Talbot
Cottage

Lock's
Cottage

89

Cowleaze
Farm

CLAYPIT LA

Galleyherns
Farm

Knighton
Copse

Breaches
Copse

3

Ruffinswick
Farm

88

Odstone
Lands

Hardwell
Farm

Hardwell Lane

2

New Rd

Compton Marsh
Farm

Odstone
Marsh

Knighton

87

Snivelling
Corner

Compton
Beauchamp

Compton
House

Knighton
Farm

Hardwell
Wood

Memorial

KNIGHTON HILL

1

Knighton
Coombes

Odstone
Farm

Pit
(dis)

86

Bourton
Gate

B4507

26   A   27   B   28   C

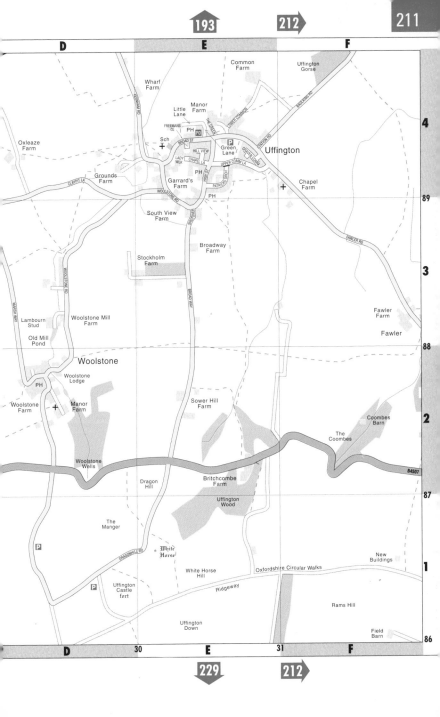

A   B   C

Fox Covert

Ladycroft Pond

Cross Bargain
Farm

Gabbits Copse

Church's
Copse

Featherbed Lane

Stutfield Brook

Sout
Farm

4

Long Spinney
Copse

Westcot Lane

Round Spinney
Copse

Broadleaze Farm

89

Kingston Common
Farm

3

WEST COT LA

Fawler Manor

Cemy

Fawler

Georgesgreen
Farm

88

Drove Way

Hall Place
Home Farm

Kingston Lisle

Star
(PH)

The Plough
(PH)

Sch

Sparsholt

Manor Farm

North
Park

WEST ST

Kingston Lisle
Farm

Westcot
Farm

CHURCH WAY

2

Kingston Lisle
House

Green
Park

Westcot

Sparsholt Park

Kingston Lisle Park

B4507

Blowing Stone

87

The Warren

Seven Acre Hill

Oakbank
Plantations

Oakbank Barn

1

The Rides

Sparsholt Field

Oxfordshire

Kingstonhill Barn

Ridgeway
Circular Walks

Field Barn

Sheephouse Bottom

Clements Cottages

Lodge Farm

86

32 A   **33**   B   **34**   C

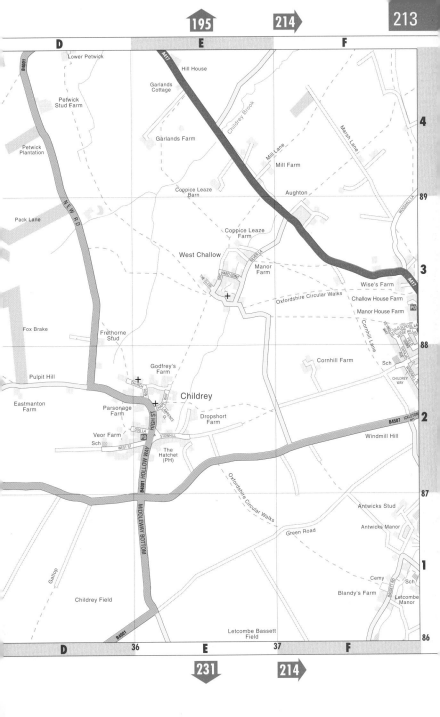

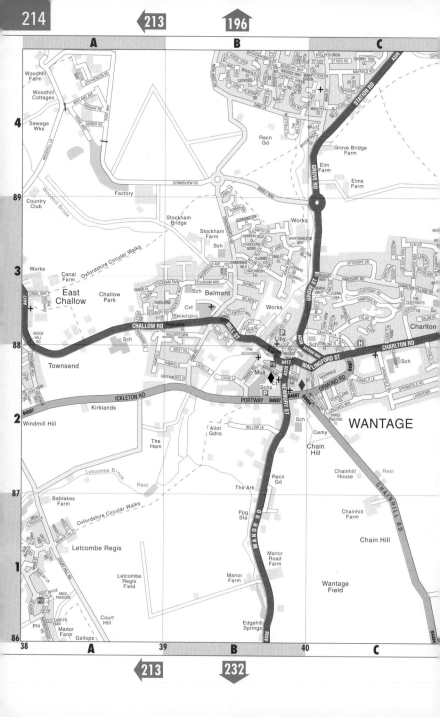

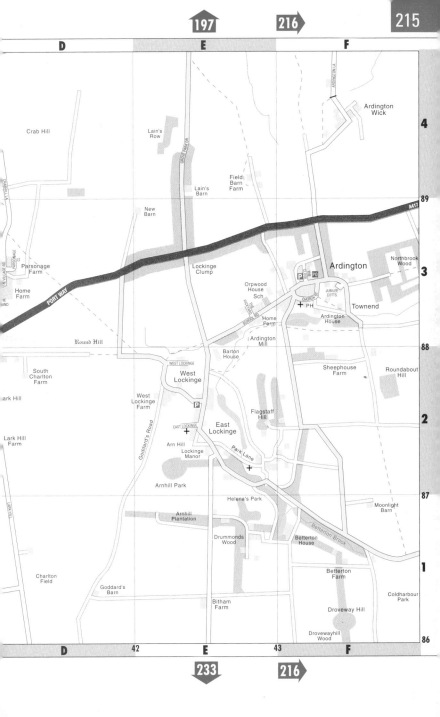

D

E

F

4

Ardington
Wick

Crab Hill

CHAPEL LA

Lain's
Row

GROVE PARK DR

Lain's
Barn

Field
Barn
Farm

89

New
Barn

A417

Parsonage
Farm

CLUBHOUSE RD

THE VILLAGE RD
MOUND

Lockinge
Clump

PORT WAY

Orpwood
House
Sch

Northbrook
Wood

Ardington

P
THE
GLEBE
P PO

CHURCH

Home
Farm

THE RICKYARD

SCHOOL RD

JUBILEE
COTTS

Ardington
House

Townend

Home
Farm

PH

Ardington
Mill

3

Round Hill

Ardington
Mill

88

South
Charlton
Farm

WEST LOCKINGE

Barton
House

West
Lockinge

Sheephouse
Farm

Roundabout
Hill

ark Hill

West
Lockinge
Farm

P

Flagstaff
Hill

2

Lark Hill
Farm

EAST LOCKINGE

East
Lockinge

Goddard's Road

Arn Hill

Lockinge
Manor

Park Lane

LARK HILL

Arnhill Park

Helena's Park

87

Moonlight
Barn

Arnhill
Plantation

Drummonds
Wood

Betterton
House

Betterton Brook

Charlton
Field

Goddard's
Barn

Bitham
Farm

Betterton
Farm

Droveway Hill

Coldharbour
Park

1

Droveway hill
Wood

86

D

42

E

43

F

219
202

A   **B**   **C**

Mackney

Sherwood Farm

MACKNEY LA

Kibble Ditch

4

ELM RD
LME WY ELM RD

The Bear (PH)

BEAR LA

89

Mill Brook

Glebe Cottage

Hithercroft Farm

3

HITHERCROFT

The Crown (PH)

CROWN LA
POST MILL LA

MILL LA

INGLE BE LA

Pumping Station

Cholsey Hill

88

Hillgreen Farm

BRIGHTON RD

2

Poultry Farm

The Manor

Sew Work

Manor Farm

87

GOLDFINC

The Lees

Red Lion (PH)

Schs

CHURCH RD
MANOR RD

CHEQUERS PL

THE FORTY

Lees Cottages

ELLIS LA

1

West End

POUND LA

STATION RD
DROVE SIDE
EAST ST
FORD CL
CRESCENT RD

BUCK THORN LA

COLLEG CL

Bancroft Farm

WEST ST

KENTWOOD CL

The Elms

WESTFIELD RD

PAPIST WAY

Cholsey Station

86

A   56   57   **B**   58   **C**

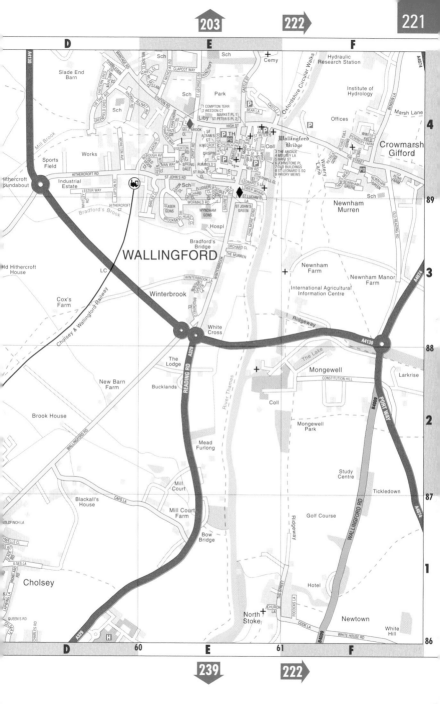

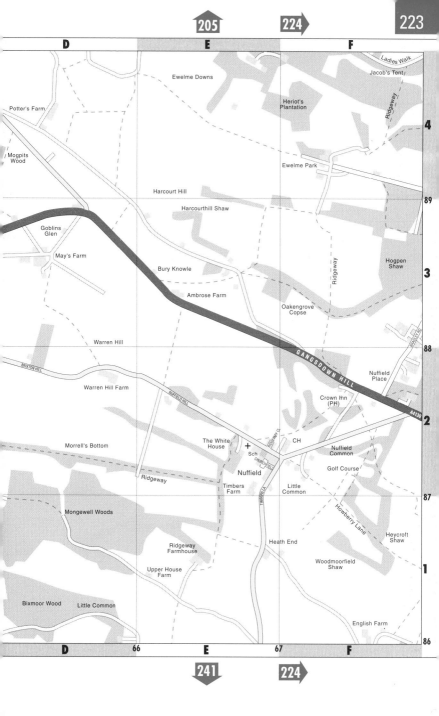

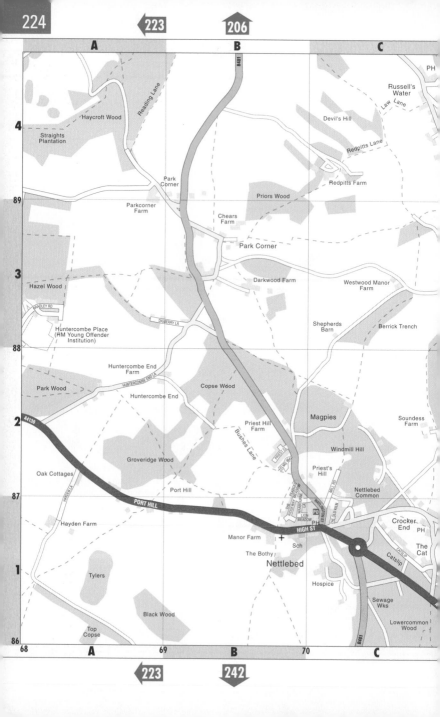

4

89

3

88

2

87

1

86

PH

Russell's
Water

Law Lane

Devil's Hill

Reading Lane

Haycroft Wood

Straights
Plantation

Redpitts Lane

Park
Corner

Priors Wood

Redpitts Farm

Parkcorner
Farm

Chears
Farm

Park Corner

Hazel Wood

Darkwood Farm

Westwood Manor
Farm

BRADLEY RD

DIGBERRY LA

Huntercombe Place
(HM Young Offender
Institution)

Shepherds
Barn

Berrick Trench

Huntercombe End
Farm

HUNTERCOMBE END LA

Park Wood

Copse Wood

Huntercombe End

A4130

Groveridge Wood

Priest Hill
Farm

Bushes Lane

Magpies

Soundess
Farm

Windmill Hill

Oak Cottages

Port Hill

PORT HILL

Priest's
Hill

Nettlebed
Common

Hayden Farm

HIGH ST

Crocker
End PH

The
Cat

Manor Farm

Sch

Catslip

The Bothy

Nettlebed

PUBLIC

Tylers

Hospice

Sewage
Wks

Black Wood

B481

Lowercommon
Wood

Top
Copse

A   B   C

4

85

3

84

2

83

1

82

32   A   33   B   34   C

Hillbarn Clump

Oxfordshire Circular Walks

Ridgeway

Rubblepit Plantation

Old Plantation

Hill Barn

Down Barn

Pigtrough Bottom

Gallops

Hackpen Hi

Mast

Radio Station

Sparsholt Firs

Scary Hill

Galliops

Sparsholt Down

Moss Hill

Faringdon Down Gallop

Green Down

Gallop

Eastmanton Down

84

Crog Hill

Westcot Down

Boundary Covert

Oxfordshire Circular Walks

Long Barrow

Pit Down

Old Warren

Sevenbarrows House

Seven Barrows

Post Down

Long Covert

Gallops

Faringdon Road Down

Gallops

Crow Down

Postdown Farm

Croker's Hole

Sheepdrove Farm

Wormhill Bottom

| D | E | F |

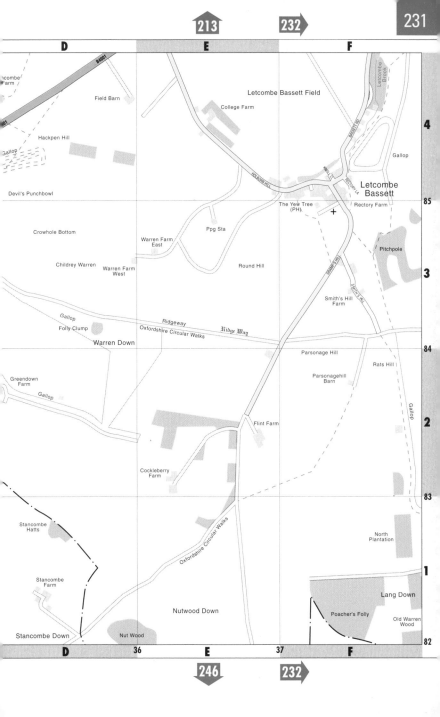

B4001

Field Barn

Letcombe Bassett Field

College Farm

Hackpen Hill

Gallop

Devil's Punchbowl

The Yew Tree
(PH)

Letcombe
Bassett

HOLBURN HILL

KING LA

RECTORY LA

BASSETT RD

Letcombe
Brook

Gallop

Rectory Farm

Crowhole Bottom

Ppg Sta

Warren Farm
East

Pitchpole

Childrey Warren

Warren Farm
West

Round Hill

Smith's Hill
Farm

BLOWING STONE HILL

FAWLEY HL

Gallop

Folly Clump

Ridgeway
Oxfordshire Circular Walks

Ridge Way

Warren Down

Parsonage Hill

Rats Hill

Greendown
Farm

Gallop

Parsonagehill
Barn

Flint Farm

Gallop

Cockleberry
Farm

Oxfordshire Circular Walks

North
Plantation

Stancombe
Hatts

Stancombe
Farm

Lang Down

Old Warren
Wood

Poacher's Folly

Stancombe Down

Nut Wood

Nutwood Down

| D | 36 | E | 37 | F |

4
85
3
84
2
83
1
82

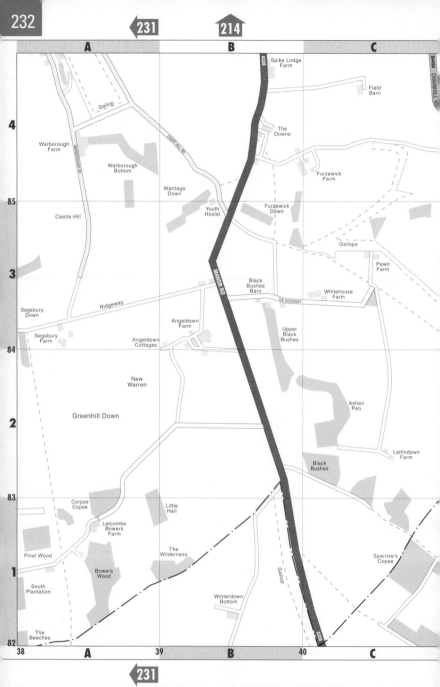

231
214

A   B   C

4

85

3

84

2

83

1

82

38   A   39   B   40   C

Gallop

Warborough Farm

WARBOROUGH RD

COURT HILL RD

Warborough Bottom

Wantage Down

Castle Hill

Youth Hostel

Segsbury Down

Ridgeway

MANOR RD

Angeldown Farm

Segsbury Farm

Angeldown Cottages

New Warren

Greenhill Down

Corpse Copse

Little Hall

Letcombe Bowers Farm

Pinal Wood

The Wilderness

Bowers Wood

South Plantation

Winterdown Bottom

The Beeches

Spike Lodge Farm

A338

Field Barn

The Downs

Furzewick Farm

Furzewick Down

Black Bushes Barn

Gallops

Pewit Farm

Whitehouse Farm

THE RIDGEWAY

Upper Black Bushes

Ashen Pen

Lattindown Farm

Black Bushes

Galop

Sparrow's Copse

A338

B4494 CHAIN HILL RD

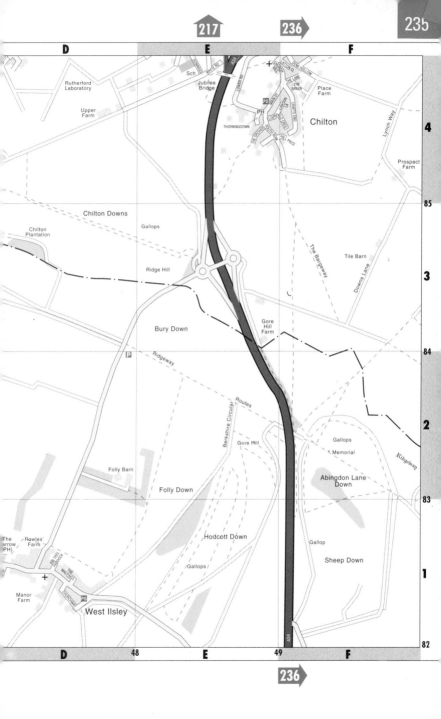

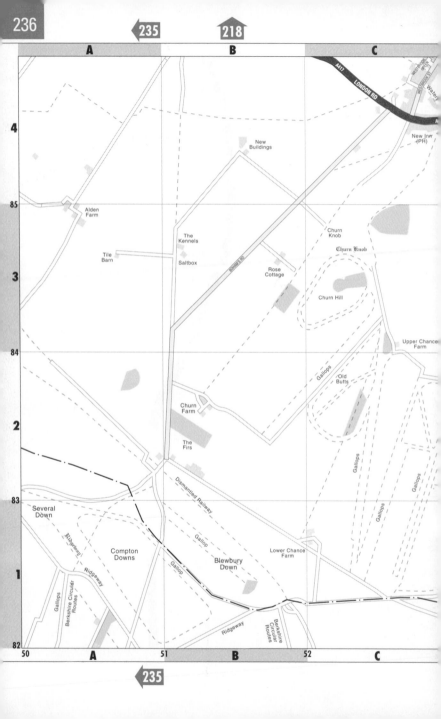

D E F

CHARLES RD
PAPIST WAY
A329
EA PL PH
holsey
Cholsey Marsh
(Nature Reserve)
WHITE HOUSE RD

Inn

Barracks
Farm

The
Gables

READING RD

Littlestoke
Manor
Farm

Ash
Cottage

HALFPENNY LA

4

85

Offlands
Farm

Middle
Barn
Swan's Way

Sch

The
Oak

Watch
Folly

River Thames

Ridgeway

Sch

WALLINGFORD RD

White Hill

3

84

Lower
Farm

Freedom
Cottages

Ivol
Barn

Hotel

FERRY LA

FERRY RD

WOODCOTE RD

**South
Stoke**

Sowberry
Court

FERRY LA

CHAPEL LA

PH

Lower
Cadley's

THE BEER
THE HOUSE

CROSS KEYS RD

The
Old
Vicarage

DEACONFIELD

THE CROSSES

Glebe
Cottages

South
Bank

2

83

Grove Farm
House

Runsford
Hole

Sewage
Works

Grove
House

WALLINGFORD RD

Grove
Farm

Ichnield Way

1

Streatley
Farm

A329

PH

Spring
Farm

B4009

BEECH LA

ICKNIELD RD

Spring Farm
Cottages

D 60 E 61 F

82

Starveall Farm

Swinley Down

Swinley Copse

Oxfordshire Circular Walks

Ashdown Farm

Upper Wood

Pumping Station

B4000

Harley Bushes

Whiteshere

Bishopstone Downs

Idstone Down

Botley Bottom

Dean Bottom

Botley Copse

Russley Park

Bailey Hill

Goor Lane Farm

GORE LA

Bailey Hill Copse

Peaks Down

Hazelbury Farm

Peaks Wood

Bailey Hill Farm

Gallop

Baydon

Bailey Hill Farm

East Leaze Farm

BAYDON RD

DOWNSMEAD

PO

Sch

FINCHES LA

Westfield Farm

Finche's Farm

M4

249
240

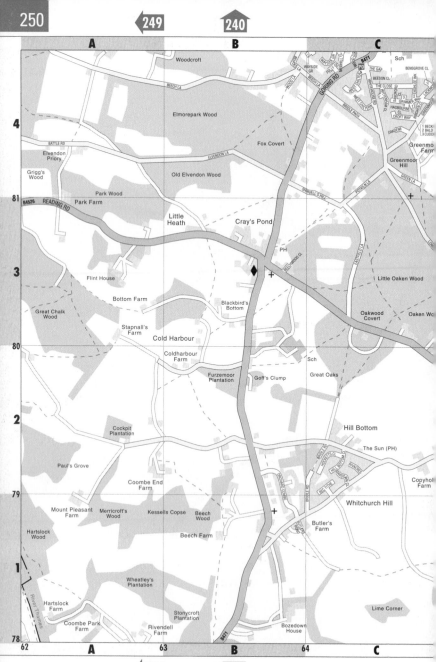

D
E
F

PH
Cocks Hill
Rumerhedge Farm

Ward's Farm
Sch
Lower Farm
Rumerhedge Wood

Ward Shaw
Poultry Farm
4

Ashlee Wood
Hook End Farm
Hook End

Lackmore Wood
Nippers Grove

The Oaks
81

College Wood or Abbot's Wood
Valentine Wood

Whitewood Heath
Parklane Shaw

Common Wood
3

Common Covert
Bensgrove Wood

Bensgrove Farm
The Hocket
Collegewood Farm
Kempwood Cottage
80

Newhouse Farm
Little College Wood

Poultry Farm
Abbotsfield
Hawhill Wood

Charity Farm
Highfield Shaw
Cane End House

Sch
H
Holme Copse
2

Ladygrove Farm
Haw Farm
Nuney Copse
Nuney Green
Walk Shaw

Goring Heath
PO
Thicket Copse
Nuney Wood

Withy Shaw
Querns
Gutteridge's Wood
79

Westholme Farm
Collins End
King Charles's Head (PH)
Nuney Wood

Bunce's Lane
Collinsend Common

Holmes's Farm
Coxsetter's Wood

Path Hill
Holly Copse

Pathhill Farm
Long Ground Plantation
Whittles Farm
Cross Lanes
1

Bottom Wood

The Baulk
Stirrups

78

D
66
E
67
F

Peppard
Farm
Sch
Church La
Arundel
Bottom
Barn
Stony Bottom
Shiplake
Hill
Butcher's Arms
(PH)
Blounts
Court
Blountscourt
Farm
Blounts Court Rd
Brinds Cl
Blackmore
Farm
Pond
Farm
Blackmore La
House Dr
Young
Wood
Sewage
Works
Bird
Wood
Bird in Hand
(PH)
Peppard Rd
Kennylands Rd
Cucumber
Plantation
Chalkhouse Green
Farm
Chalkhouse Green La
Chalkhouse
Green
Club
Rugby Football
Ground
B481

Silgrove
Wood
Crosslanes
The
Paddock
Round
Wood
Flowercroft
Wood
Kent's Hill
King's
Farm
Crosscroft
Wood
Scot's Hill
Kingshill
Wood
King's Hill
Crosscroft
Masts
Crowsley Park
Wireless
Station
Mast
Crowsley
Park
Frieze
Farm
Crowsley
Crowsley
Grange
Morgan's
Wood
Crowsley Park
Farm
Lady's
Shaw
Bishopsland
Farm

Cowfields
Farm
Upper House
Farm
Pond
Copse
King's Farm La
Mag's
Wood
Old
Place
Gillsmithers
Wood
Peppard Rd
Redhill
Wood
Crowsley Park
Woods
Barn
Grounds
Coppid
Hall
Wild
Orchard
The
Belt
The
Common
Thames Kipling Lane
Comp
Farm
Comp
Wood
The Coach & Horses
(PH)
Sandon
Lane
Tagg
Lane
Gravel Rd

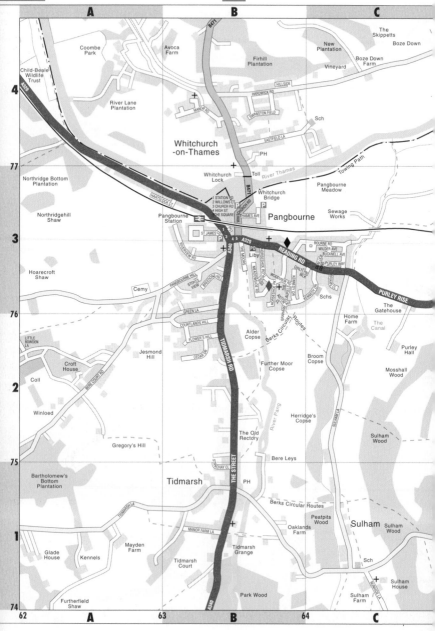

A   B   C

4

Coombe Park

Avoca Farm

The Skippetts

Boze Down

New Plantation

Firhill Plantation

Boze Down Farm

Vineyard

Child-Beale Wildlife Trust

HILLSIDE

HARDWICK RD

Sch

River Lane Plantation

SWANSTON FIELD

MANOR RD

Whitchurch -on-Thames

EASTFIELD LA

77

PH

Northridge Bottom Plantation

Whitchurch Lock

Toll

River Thames

Towing Path

Whitchurch Bridge

Pangbourne Meadow

HARTSLOCK CT

Northridgehill Shaw

Pangbourne Station

THAMES AVE

Pangbourne

Sewage Works

1 STATION RD
2 WILLOWS RD
3 CHURCH RD
4 HIGH ST
5 THE SQUARE

3

St JAMES CL

A340

A329

BOURNE RD

WILDER AVE

BUCKNELL AVE

PURLEY WAY

READING RD

Hoarecroft Shaw

PO

Liby

BELLEVUE RD

PANGBOURNE HILL

STOKES VIEW

BREEDONS HILL

Cemy

Schs

Home Farm

The Gatehouse

76

GREEN LA

COURTLANDS HILL

FLOWER'S HILL

Berks Circular Routes

PURLEY RISE

The Canal

Purley Hall

LITTLE BOWDEN LA

CEDAR LA

Alder Copse

Broom Copse

Mosshall Wood

Croft House

Jesmond Hill

BERE COURT RD

Coll

Further Moor Copse

2

Winloed

River Pang

TIDMARSH RD

Herridge's Copse

Sulham Wood

Gregory's Hill

The Old Rectory

75

Bere Leys

Bartholomew's Bottom Plantation

BUCHAY CL

Tidmarsh

THE STREET

PH

Berks Circular Routes

Peatpits Wood

Sulham

Sulham Wood

1

Glade House

Kennels

Mayden Farm

MANOR FARM LA

Oaklands Farm

TIDMARSH LA

Tidmarsh Grange

Sch

Tidmarsh Court

Sulham House

BERWICK LA

Furtherfield Shaw

Park Wood

Sulham Farm

A340

62   A   **63**   B   **64**   C

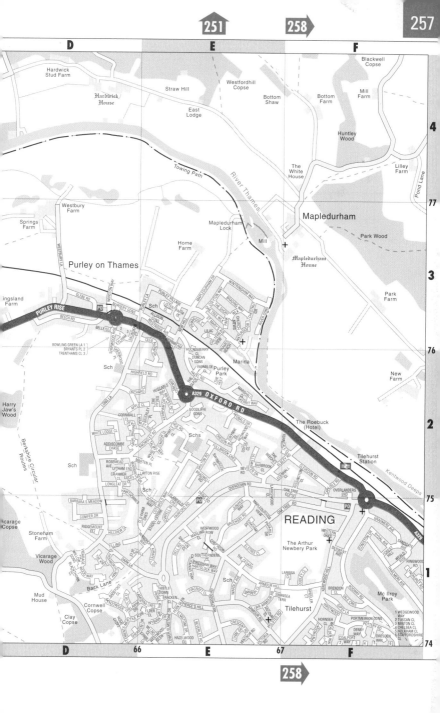

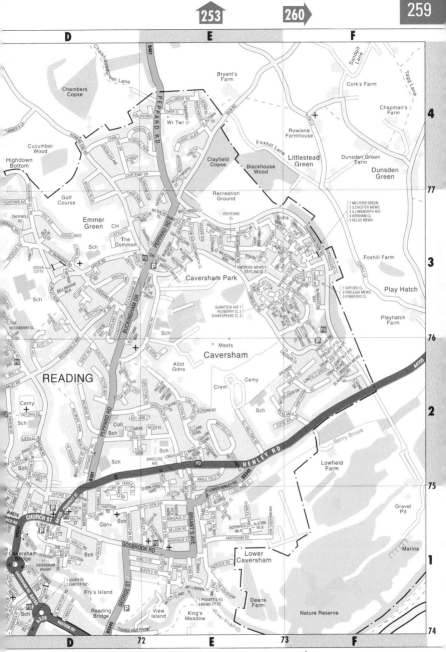

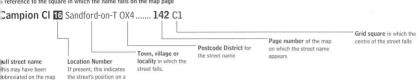

Street names are listed alphabetically and show the locality, the Postcode District, the page number and a reference to the square in which the name falls on the map page

Campion Cl 16 Sandford-on-T OX4 ...... 142 C1

Full street name
this may have been
abbreviated on the map

Location Number
If present, this indicates
the street's position on a
congested area of the
map instead of the name

Town, village or
locality in which the
street falls.

Postcode District for
the street name

Page number of the map
on which the street name
appears

Grid square in which the
centre of the street falls

Abbreviations used in the index

App Approach	Cl Close	Ent Enterprise	La Lane	Rdbt Roundabout
Arc Arcade	Comm Common	Espl Esplanade	N North	S South
Ave Avenue	Cnr Corner	Est Estate	Orch Orchard	Sq Square
Bvd Boulevard	Cotts Cottages	Gdns Gardens	Par Parade	Strs Stairs
Bldgs Buildings	Ct Court	Gn Green	Pk Park	Stps Steps
Bsns Pk Business Park	Ctyd Courtyard	Gr Grove	Pas Passage	St Street, Saint
Bsns Ctr Business Centre	Cres Crescent	Hts Heights	Pl Place	Terr Terrace
Bglws Bungalows	Dr Drive	Ho House	Prec Precinct	Trad Est Trading Estate
Cswy Causeway	Dro Drove	Ind Est Industrial Estate	Prom Promenade	Wlk Walk
Ctr Centre	E East	Intc Interchange	Ret Pk Retail Park	W West
Cir Circus	Emb Embankment	Junc Junction	Rd Road	Yd Yard

Town and village index

Abingdon 180 B4	Chilson 71 F2	Goring 249 E3	Marston 123 F3	Stanford in the Vale 194 C4
Adderbury 23 D2	Chilton 235 F4	Great Barrington 99 E4	Merton 95 E4	Stanton Harcourt 137 F4
Adlestrop 40 B1	Chinnor 168 B4	Great Bourton 9 E4	Middle Barton 46 C1	Stanton St John 125 F4
Aldworth 247 F2	Chipping Norton 42 C1	Great Coxwell 192 B4	Middleton Cheney 11 D1	Steeple Aston 62 A4
Alvescot 133 E3	Chipping Warden 5 F3	Great Haseley 164 C4	Middleton Stoney 64 A2	Steventon 198 C2
Ambrosden 81 E2	Cholsey 221 D1	Great Milton 145 E1	Milcombe 21 D1	Stoke Lyne 51 D3
Appleton 158 A4	Church Westcote 68 B3	Great Rollright 29 D2	Milton (Abingdon) 199 E3	Stoke Row 241 F2
Ardington 215 F3	Churchill 55 F3	Great Tew 45 E4	Milton (Banbury) 22 B2	Stoke Talmage 165 F2
Ardley 50 B2	Clanfield 152 C4	Grove 196 C1	Milton-under-Wychwood 85 D4	Stokenchurch 188 C3
Ascott-under-Wychwood 71 E1	Claydon 1 B1	Haddenham 130 C3	Minster Lovell 102 C1	Stonesfield 89 E4
Ashbury 228 A4	Clifton Hampden 181 E2	Hailey 104 A3	Mixbury 38 B4	Stonor 225 F3
Aston 135 F2	Cockpole Green 255 F4	Hampton Poyle 93 D2	Mollington 4 A2	Stratton Audley 52 B1
Aston Rowant 167 E1	Coleshill 191 D4	Hanwell 8 C2	Moulsford 238 C2	Streatley 249 D4
Aston Tirrold 237 F4	Combe 90 A3	Hardwick 51 E4	Murcott 95 F2	Sunningwell 159 F3
Avon Dassett 2 C4	Compton Wynates 12 B4	Harwell 217 F4	Nettlebed 224 B1	Sutton Courtenay 200 A4
Aynho 35 E4	Cottisford 37 F2	Henley-on-Thames 244 B1	North Aston 48 A3	Swalcliffe 19 F4
Bampton 134 C2	Crawley 103 F2	Hethe 52 A4	North Hinksey Village 140 C4	Swerford 30 C2
Banbury 16 B4	Cropredy 4 C1	Highworth 190 A3	North Leigh 105 D4	Swinbrook 101 F3
Barford St Michael 32 C3	Croughton 36 B4	Hinton Waldrist 155 F2	North Moreton 219 F4	Sydenham 167 E4
Barton-on-the-Heath 26 C3	Crowmarsh Gifford 221 F4	Holton 126 B1	North Newington 15 D2	Tackley 77 E3
Baydon 245 F1	Cuddesdon 144 A2	Hook Norton 30 A4	Northmoor 138 B1	Tadmarton 20 B4
Beckley 111 D2	Culham 180 A1	Horley 8 A2	Nuneham Courtenay 161 F2	Tetsworth 166 A4
Begbroke 108 A4	Cumnor 139 E3	Hornton 7 E4	Oddington 94 C1	Thame 147 F4
Benson 204 A2	Curbridge 117 E3	Horspath 143 E3	Over Norton 42 C3	Tiddington 145 F4
Berinsfield 182 B3	Cutteslowe 109 D1	Horton-cum-Studley 112 A3	Oxford 123 F1	Tidmarsh 256 B1
Berrick Salome 184 A1	Cuxham 185 E2	Ibstone 207 F4	Pangbourne 256 B3	Towersey 148 C4
Bicester 65 F2	Deddington 33 F2	Ickford 128 A2	Piddington 97 F4	Turweston 24 B4
Bishopstone 227 E2	Denchworth 196 A2	Idbury 69 D2	Poundon 67 F4	Uffington 211 E4
Bix 243 E4	Didcot 218 C4	Islip 109 F4	Purley on Thames 257 D3	Upper Arncott 96 C4
Black Bourton 133 F3	Dorchester 182 B1	Kencot 132 C3	Radley 160 C2	Upper Heyford 62 C4
Blackthorn 82 A3	Drayton 179 D1	Kennington 141 F1	Ramsden 88 A2	Upton 218 B1
Bladon 91 E1	Drayton (Banbury) 15 E4	Kidlington 92 C1	Ratley 2 A2	Wallingford 221 E3
Bledington 54 B1	Drayton St Leonard 183 D3	Kidmore End 252 B2	Reading 259 D2	Wantage 214 C2
Bledlow Ridge 189 F4	Ducklington 118 A2	Kingham 55 D2	Rotherfield Peppard 252 C4	Warborough 203 D4
Bloxham 21 E3	Duns Tew 47 E3	Kings Sutton 23 F3	Salford 41 F3	Wardington 5 F1
Bodicote 22 B4	East Challow 214 A3	Kingston Bagpuize 156 C1	Sandford-on-Thames 161 D4	Wargrave 255 E1
Bourton 209 D2	East Hagbourne 218 C3	Kingston Lisle 212 A1	Shabbington 128 B2	Warmington 3 D2
Brackley 24 A4	East Hanney 197 D3	Kirtlington 77 F2	Shalstone 25 F3	Watchfield 191 F1
Brightwell-cum-Sotwell 202 B1	East Hendred 216 C4	Langford 132 B1	Shellingford 194 A4	Watlington 186 B1
Brize 98 A1	Eastleach Martin 131 D4	Launton 66 B1	Shenington 6 C1	Wendlebury 80 A2
Brize Norton 116 B2	Enstone 58 C3	Leafield 86 C2	Shilton 115 D3	West Hagbourne 218 B2
Broughton 15 E1	Epwell 13 D3	Lechlade 150 B2	Shiplake 254 C1	West Hanney 196 C3
Buckland 154 C1	Ewelme 204 C2	Letcombe Bassett 231 F4	Shipton-on-Cherwell 92 A3	West Ilsley 235 D1
Bucknell 65 D4	Eynsham 120 C4	Lewknor 187 D4	Shipton-under-Wychwood 85 F4	Westbury 25 D2
Burford 100 B3	Faringdon 172 C2	Little Compton 26 C1	Shotteswell 8 B4	Weston-on-the-Green 79 D1
Buscot 171 D4	Farnborough (Berks) 233 F1	Little Coxwell 192 C4	Shrivenham 209 D4	Wheatley 144 A4
Carterton 115 F2	Farnborough (Warks) 3 F4	Little Milton 164 A3	Shutford 14 A3	Whichford 18 A1
Cassington 107 E1	Fawley 226 B1	Sibford Ferris 19 D4	Whitchurch-on-Thames 256 B4
Caversham 259 E2	Fernham 193 D2	Little Compton 27 F3	Sibford Gower 19 D4	Wigginton 31 D4
Chacombe 10 C2	Fifield 69 E1	Long Crendon 129 D3	Sonning 260 C2	Witney 104 B1
Chadlington 57 D1	Filkins 132 B3	Long Hanborough 90 B1	Sonning Common 252 C3	Woodcote 240 B1
Chalgrove 184 C3	Finmere 39 E4	Long Wittenham 201 E4	Souldern 35 F2	Woodstock 91 D3
Charlbury 73 D2	Finstock 88 B3	Longcot 192 B1	South Hinksey 141 E3	Woolstone 211 D2
Charlton-on-Otmoor 95 D2	Forest Hill 125 F2	Longworth 156 B2	South Leigh 119 E3	Wootton 75 F3
Charney Bassett 176 A1	Freeland 106 A4	Lower Basildon 249 F1	South Moreton 219 F3	Wootton (Oxford) 159 D4
Chastleton 40 B4	Fringford 52 B3	Lower Heyford 62 B3	South Newington 31 F4	Worminghall 127 F3
Checkendon 241 E4	Fritwell 49 F4	Lower Odington 54 A4	South Stoke 239 E2	Wroxton 15 D4
Chesterton 79 F4	Fulbrook 100 C4	Ludgershall 98 B4	Southend 226 B4	Wytham 122 A3
Childrey 213 E2	Fyfield 157 E1	Lyneham 70 C3	Sparsholt 212 C2	Yarnton 108 A3
	Garford 177 D3	Mapledurham 257 F3	Spelsbury 72 C4	
	Garsington 143 F1	Marcham 178 B3	Stadhampton 163 E1	
	Glympton 75 E4	Marsh Gibbon 67 F2	Standlake 137 E2	

A P Ellis Rd GL54 .... 68 A2
Abberbury Ave OX4 .... 142 A2
Abberbury Rd OX4 .... 141 F2
Abbey Centre OX14 .... 180 A4
Abbey Cl OX14 .... 179 F4
Abbey Pl Eynsham OX8 ...... 120 C4
Oxford OX4 .... 141 D4
Abbey Rd Banbury OX16 ...... 16 A4
Oxford OX2 .... 123 D1
Witney OX8 .... 117 F4
Abbey St OX8 .... 120 C4
Abbot Ridge HP18 .... 129 E3
Abbot Wlk HP18 .... 129 E3
Abbots Wlk GL7 .... 150 B2
Abbots Wood (E) OX3 .... 142 C4
Abbots Wood (W) OX3 ...... 142 C4
Abbott Cl OX11 .... 218 C4
Abbott Rd Abingdon OX14 .. 179 F4
Didcot OX11 .... 218 C4
Abelwood Rd OX8 .... 90 A1
Aberaman RG8 .... 258 C3
Abingdon Dr RG4 .... 259 E3
Abingdon Rd
Carterton OX18 .... 115 F2
Clifton Hampden OX14 ...... 181 E2
Culham OX14 .... 180 B2
Cumnor OX2 .... 139 F2
Didcot OX11 .... 201 D1
Dorchester OX10 .... 182 B2
Drayton OX14 .... 179 D2
Kennington OX1 .... 141 E2
Oxford OX1, OX2 .... 141 E3
Standlake OX8 .... 137 E2
Steventon OX13 .... 199 D3
Sutton Courtenay OX14 .... 180 A1
Abingdon Way OX14 .... 129 F1
Ablett Cl OX4 .... 142 A4
Abotts Mead OX10 .... 239 D4
Abrahams Rd RG9 .... 244 B2
Acacia RG9 .... 244 B1
Acacia Ave OX4 .... 142 C1
Acacia Cl OX18 .... 115 F1
Acacia Gdns OX13 .... 156 C1
Bicester OX6 .... 65 F3
Ackerman Rd OX7 .... 42 C2
Acland Cl OX3 .... 124 B1
Acorn Cl OX6 .... 65 F3
Acorn Way OX16 .... 9 F1
Acre Ditch OX15 .... 19 D4
Acre End St OX8 .... 120 C4
Acremead Rd OX33 .... 143 F4
Adderbury Ct OX17 .... 23 D2
Adderbury Park OX17 .... 22 C2
Addiscombe Chase RG31 .... 257 D2
Addison Cres OX4 .... 141 F3
Addison Dr OX4 .... 142 B2
Addison Rd Banbury OX16 .. 16 B2
Reading RG1 .... 259 D1
Adeane Rd OX44 .... 184 B4
Adelaide St OX2 .... 123 D2
Adkin Way OX12 .... 214 B3
Admiral Cl OX4 .... 142 C1
Adwell Sq RG9 .... 244 B1
Akeman Ave OX6 .... 81 E2
Akeman Cl OX5 .... 78 A3
Akeman St OX6 .... 90 A3
Akers La OX10 .... 202 C1
Alan Bullock Cl OX4 .... 123 F1
Albermarle Dr OX14 .... 214 B4
Albert Rd Caversham RG4 .. 258 C2
Henley-on-T RG9 .... 244 C1
Albert St Banbury OX16 ..... 16 B3
Oxford OX2 .... 123 D1
Albion Pl Chipping Norton OX7 42 C2
Oxford OX1 .... 141 E4
Albion St OX7 .... 42 C2
Albury Cl RG30 .... 258 B1
Albury View OX9 .... 146 A3
Alchester Rd OX6 .... 80 A4
Alchester Terr OX6 .... 65 F1
Aldbarton Dr OX3 .... 124 C2
Aldbourne Cl OX6 .... 65 E1
Aldeburgh Cl RG4 .... 259 E4
Alden Cres OX3 .... 124 C2
Aldenham Cl RG4 .... 259 E3
Alder Dr OX6 .... 81 E2
Alder Gate Rd OX16 .... 65 E1
Alderley Cl Carterton OX18 . 115 E1
Woodstock RG5 .... 260 C1
Aldrich Rd OX2 .... 123 D4
Aldridge Cl OX10 .... 204 A2
Aldsworth Ct OX18 .... 117 F4
Aldworth Ave OX12 .... 214 C3
Alesworth Gr OX3 .... 124 A3
Alexander Cl
Abingdon OX14 .... 160 A2
Upton OX11 .... 218 B1
Alexandra Rd OX2 .... 122 C1
Alexandra Sq OX7 .... 42 B1
Alfred St Oxford OX1 .... 123 E1
Wantage OX12 .... 214 B2
Alfred Terraces OX7 .... 42 C1
Alfredstone Pl OX12 .... 214 C2
Alfriston Pl OX16 .... 16 C1
Alice Smith Sq OX4 .... 142 B1
Alister Taylor Ave OX10 .... 204 B1
All Hallows Rd RG4 .... 259 E1
All Saints Cl OX13 .... 158 C3
All Saints Ct OX13 .... 200 C1
All Saints La OX14 .... 180 A1
All Saints Rd OX3 .... 124 B1
Allam St OX2 .... 123 D2
Allder Cl OX14 .... 159 F1
Allectus Ave OX6 .... 81 E2

Allens La OX6 .... 48 C1
Allens Orch OX17 .... 5 F3
Alley The OX7 .... 73 D2
Allin Cl OX4 .... 142 C2
Allin's La OX12 .... 216 B4
Allison Gdns RG8 .... 257 E3
Allnatt Ave OX10 .... 221 E4
Allnut Cl OX9 .... 186 A1
Alma Green RG9 .... 242 A2
Alma Pl OX4 .... 141 F4
Almond Ave OX5 .... 108 C3
Almond Dr RG4 .... 259 F2
Almond Rd OX6 .... 65 F2
Alpha Ave OX44 .... 143 E1
Alston Wlk RG4 .... 259 E1
Altus St OX6 .... 63 D4
Alvescot Rd OX18 .... 115 E1
Alvis Gate OX16 .... 15 E1
Amberley Ct OX6 .... 9 D1
Ambleside Dr OX3 .... 124 A2
Ambrose Rise OX33 .... 144 B4
Ambury Rd RG4 .... 247 F2
Amersham Rd RG4 .... 259 E1
Amey Cres OX13 .... 159 D3
Amos Ct OX4 .... 142 B2
Ampney Orch OX18 .... 134 C2
Amwell Pl OX10 .... 220 C1
Amyce Cl OX14 .... 160 A1
Ancastle Gr RG9 .... 244 B1
Ancholme Cl OX14 .... 200 C1
Anchor La OX11 .... 220 A2
Ancil Ave OX6 .... 66 B1
Andersey Way OX14 .... 179 F2
Anderson Cl HP14 .... 188 C2
Andersons Cl OX5 .... 108 B4
Andover Cl Bicester OX6 ... 66 A2
Reading RG31 .... 257 E1
Andover La OX18 .... 115 F1
Andover Rd OX14 .... 204 B2
Andrew Rd OX10 .... 203 D1
Andrews Ave NN13 .... 36 C3
Andromeda Cl OX44 .... 142 C1
Anemone Cl OX4 .... 161 F4
Angelica Cl OX4 .... 142 C1
Angle Field Rd RG4 .... 259 E2
Anglesey Pl HP14 .... 188 C3
Angus Cl OX16 .... 16 A4
Anne Greenwood Cl OX4 .. 142 A2
Annesley Cl OX5 .... 93 D4
Annesley Rd OX4 .... 142 A2
Ansell Way OX7 .... 70 A1
Anson Ave OX18 .... 115 E1
Anson Cl Marcham OX13 ... 178 B3
Wheatley OX33 .... 144 B4
Anson Rd OX10 .... 204 B2
Anson Way OX6 .... 66 A2
Anthony Hill Rd OX10 ...... 204 B1
Anvil Cl SN7 .... 194 C4
Anvil La OX12 .... 214 A1
Anvil Paddock OX12 .... 214 A1
Anxey Cl HP17 .... 130 C3
Apley Way OX18 .... 117 F4
Apple Cl RG31 .... 257 D2
Appleby Cl OX16 .... 15 F4
Appleford Dr OX14 .... 160 A1
Appleford Rd OX14 .... 180 A1
Appleton Rd Cumnor OX2 .. 139 E2
Kingston Bagpuize OX13 ... 156 B2
Longworth OX13 .... 156 B2
Appletree Cl
Sandford-on-T OX4 .... 161 F4
Sonning Common RG4 ..... 252 C3
Appletree Rd OX17 .... 5 F3
Appletree The OX6 .... 65 F3
Apsley Rd OX2 .... 123 D4
Arbury Banks OX17 .... 5 F3
Arbury Cl OX16 .... 16 C1
Arcade The Goring RG8 .... 249 E3
Wallingford OX10 .... 221 E4
Archery Rd OX17 .... 11 D1
Archway Rd RG4 .... 259 D1
Ardington La OX12 .... 197 F1
Ardler Rd RG4 .... 259 E1
Ardley Rd Ardley OX6 ...... 50 B2
Bucknell OX6 .... 64 B2
Upper Heyford OX6 .... 48 C3
Argentan Cl OX14 .... 179 E2
Argosy Cl OX44 .... 184 C3
Argosy Rd Benson OX10 .... 204 B2
Carterton OX18 .... 115 F1
Argyle St OX4 .... 141 F3
Aristotle La OX2 .... 123 D2
Arkell Ave OX18 .... 115 E1
Arkwright Rd OX6 .... 66 A2
Arlington Cl OX18 .... 115 E1
Arlington Dr OX3 .... 123 F3
Armour Hill RG31 .... 257 E1
Armour Rd RG31 .... 257 E1
Armour Wlk RG31 .... 257 E1
Arncott Rd OX6 .... 97 E4
Arncott Wood Rd OX6 ..... 96 C1
Arndale Beck OX11 .... 201 D1
Arnold Rd OX4 .... 141 F3
Arnold Way OX9 .... 147 F4
Arnold's Way OX2 .... 140 B4
Arnott's Yd HP18 .... 129 E3
Arran Gr OX16 .... 16 C1
Arrow Cl OX16 .... 11 D1
Arthray Rd OX2 .... 140 B4
Arthur Evans Cl OX13 ..... 159 D2
Arthur Garrard Cl OX2 .... 123 D2
Arthur St OX2 .... 123 D1
Arun Mews OX11 .... 201 D1
Arundel Cl Carterton OX18 . 115 E1
Kings Sutton OX17 .... 23 F3
Arundel Pl OX16 .... 15 F3
Ascott Hill OX16 .... 18 A1

Ascott Rd OX7 .... 85 E4
Ash Cl Faringdon SN7 ...... 172 C2
Kidlington OX5 .... 108 C4
Watlington OX9 .... 186 A1
Ash Gr Chesterton OX6 ..... 79 F4
Deddington OX15 .... 34 A2
Ash La OX6 .... 81 E2
Ashburton La OX15 .... 30 A3
Ashbury Hill SN6 .... 228 A3
Ashby Ct OX16 .... 16 B3
Ashcombe Cl OX8 .... 118 A4
Ashcroft Cl
Caversham RG4 .... 258 C3
N Hinksey Vill OX2 .... 122 A1
Ashcroft Rd OX16 .... 16 B4
Ashdene Rd OX6 .... 65 E1
Ashdown Way OX14 .... 214 B4
Ashenden Cl OX11 .... 159 F1
Ashfield Rd OX18 .... 115 F1
Ashfields Cl OX12 .... 197 E4
Ashfields La OX12 .... 197 E4
Ashford Ave RG4 .... 252 C3
Ashgate OX14 .... 179 F2
Ashhurst Way OX4 .... 142 A2
Ashlee Wk RG8 .... 250 C4
Ashley Hill Pl RG10 .... 255 F4
Ashlong Rd OX3 .... 124 A3
Ashmole Pl OX4 .... 142 C2
Ashmole Rd OX14 .... 179 F2
Ashridge OX9 .... 168 A3
Ashville Way OX4 .... 142 C2
Aspen Cl OX6 .... 65 F3
Aspen Sq OX4 .... 142 C1
Asquith Rd OX4 .... 142 A2
Astley Ave OX5 .... 108 B3
Astley Rd OX9 .... 130 A1
Aston Ave RG31 .... 257 D3
Aston Cl Abingdon OX14 ... 179 F4
Banbury OX16 .... 16 C1
Pangbourne RG8 .... 256 B3
Wallingford OX10 .... 221 E4
Aston Gdns OX9 .... 167 E2
Aston Hill OX9 .... 187 F4
Aston Park OX9 .... 167 E1
Aston Rd Ducklington OX8 . 118 A1
Standlake OX8 .... 137 D2
Aston St Aston Tirrold OX12 237 F4
Oxford OX4 .... 141 F4
Astrop Rd Kings Sutton OX17 23 F3
Middleton Cheney OX17 ... 17 F3
Atkinson Cl OX3 .... 124 C2
Atkyns Rd OX3 .... 142 C4
Atno Rd OX17 .... 23 E2
Atwell Cl OX16 .... 221 E4
Atwell Pl OX3 .... 124 B1
Aubrey Ct OX4 .... 142 A2
Audlett Dr OX4 .... 180 A4
Austen Wlk OX6 .... 65 E1
Austin Dr OX16 .... 15 F4
Austin Pl OX14 .... 159 F1
Austin Rd OX15 .... 21 E3
Austin's Way OX15 .... 30 B4
Austin Pl OX9 .... 254 B4
Autumn Cl RG4 .... 259 E4
Autumn Wlk RG10 .... 255 E1
Avens Way OX4 .... 142 C1
Avenue Four OX18 .... 116 A4
Avenue La OX4 .... 141 F4
Avenue One OX18 .... 118 A4
Avenue Rd Banbury OX16 .. 16 C3
Bourton SN6 .... 209 D2
Avenue The Bloxham OX15 21 E2
Chinnor OX9 .... 168 B3
Great Tew OX7 .... 45 E4
Kennington OX1 .... 160 C4
Wheatley OX33 .... 144 B4
Worminghall HP18 .... 127 F3
Avenue Three OX18 .... 118 A3
Avenue Two OX18 .... 118 A3
Avington Cl RG31 .... 257 D3
Avocet Way Banbury OX16 . 16 C2
Bicester OX6 .... 81 D4
Avon Carrow OX17 .... 3 D4
Avon Cres OX6 .... 65 D2
Avon Rd Abingdon OX13 ... 159 E1
Harwell OX11 .... 217 E1
Avon Way OX11 .... 200 C2
Avonbury Ct NN13 .... 24 A3
Avro Rd GL54 .... 68 A3
Axis Rd SN6 .... 191 F1
Axtell Cl OX5 .... 92 B1
Aylesbury Rd
Haddenham HP17,HP18 .... 130 B3
Thame OX9 .... 129 E3
Ayrshire Cl OX16 .... 9 D1
Aysgarth Rd OX5 .... 108 A3
Azalea Ave OX5 .... 108 C3
Azalea Wlk OX16 .... 9 D1
Azor's Ct OX4 .... 142 A2

Badblock Hythe Rd OX13 .. 139 D2
Back La Aston OX18 .... 135 E2
Ducklington OX8 .... 118 A2
Eynsham OX8 .... 120 C4
Long Compton CV36 ...... 28 A3
Silford Ferris OX15 .... 19 D4
Back Row OX12 .... 40 B2
Back St Stokenchurch HP14 . 188 B3
Tetsworth OX9 .... 166 A4
Backside La OX15 .... 19 D4
Backsideans RG10 .... 255 E1
Bader Dr OX6 .... 63 E4
Badgemoor La RG9 .... 244 B2
Badger Cl OX33 .... 125 F2
Badger La OX1 .... 141 D1
Badger Way OX16 .... 16 C1
Badgers Copse OX14 ...... 160 C1
Badgers Rise RG4 .... 259 D3
Badgers Wlk RG9 .... 255 D2
Badswell La OX13 .... 158 A4
Bagley Cl OX1 .... 141 E1
Bagley Wood Rd OX1 ...... 160 B4
Bailey Cl OX12 .... 214 B3
Bailey Rd OX4 .... 142 B2
Bailie Cl OX14 .... 179 F3
Bainton Rd Bucknell OX6 .. 64 B2
Hethe OX6 .... 52 A4
Oxford OX2 .... 123 D3
Bakehouse La OX17 .... 8 B4
Baker Ave OX10 .... 204 B1
Baker Cl Benson OX10 .... 204 B2
Bicester OX6 .... 65 F4
Oxford OX3 .... 124 C1
Baker St OX14 .... 179 F3
Baker's Piece OX9 .... 167 F2
Bakers La
East Hagbourne OX11 ...... 218 C3
Oxford OX4 .... 141 F2
South Newington OX15 .... 31 F4
Swalcliffe OX15 .... 19 F4
Tadmarton OX15 .... 20 B4
Bakers Piece OX8 .... 104 A1
Bakers Sq SN7 .... 193 D2
Bakery La Clanfield OX18 .. 152 C4
Letcombe Bassett OX12 ... 214 A1
Baldon La OX44 .... 161 F2
Baldons Cl RG8 .... 250 C4
Balfour Cotts OX14 .... 182 A3
Balfour Rd OX4 .... 142 C2
Balfour's Field RG8 .... 241 E2
Balham's La Ibstone RG9 .. 225 F4
Stonor RG9 .... 225 F3
Ball La OX5 .... 77 D3
Ballard Chase OX14 .... 160 A2
Ballard Cl OX7 .... 46 C1
Ballards Cl OX7 .... 85 E4
Balliol Cl OX5 .... 77 F3
Balliol Dr OX11 .... 219 D4
Balliol Rd Bicester OX6 ... 65 F2
Caversham RG4 .... 258 B2
Balmoral Ave Bewbury OX16 15 F3
Banbury, Crouch Hill OX16 . 15 F2
Oxford OX1 .... 219 D4
Balmoral Way OX17 .... 23 F3
Balmore Dr RG4 .... 259 D2
Bampton Cl OX4 .... 142 B2
Bampton Rd Aston OX18 .. 135 E1
Carterton OX18 .... 115 E2
Curbridge OX8 .... 117 D2
Banbury Gdns RG4 .... 259 E2
Banbury Hill OX7 .... 73 E3
Banbury La
Kings Sutton OX17 .... 23 F3
Middleton Cheney OX17 ... 10 C1
Banbury Rd Adderbury OX17 23 D3
Aynho OX17 .... 35 E4
Bicester OX6 .... 65 F2
Bloxham OX15 .... 21 F3
Chacombe OX2 .... 10 B2
Chipping Norton OX7 ...... 42 C2
Chipping Warden OX17 .... 5 F3
Cuttleslowe OX2 .... 109 D1
Deddington OX15 .... 33 F3
Kidlington OX5 .... 92 B1
North Newington OX16 .... 15 E2
Over Norton OX7 .... 43 E3
Oxford OX2 .... 123 D3
Shipton-on-C OX5 .... 92 A3
Shutford OX15 .... 14 A3
Swerford OX7 .... 30 B3
Tackley OX5 .... 77 D4
Warmington OX17 .... 3 D1
Woodstock OX20 .... 91 E4
Banbury Rd Crossing OX7 . 42 C2
Bandet Way OX9 .... 148 A3
Banesberie Cl OX16 ...... 15 F3
Banjo Rd OX4 .... 142 B3
Banks Furlong OX6 .... 79 F4
Bankside Banbury OX16 .. 16 C2
East Hendred OX12 .... 216 A3
Kidlington OX5 .... 92 B1
Long Hanborough OX8 .... 90 C1
Oxford OX3 .... 124 C2
Bannister Cl OX4 .... 141 F3
Bannister Rd OX9 .... 148 B4
Barbaras Meadow RG31 .. 257 E2
Barbrook Cl RG31 .... 257 E2
Barbury Dr OX12 .... 214 B4
Barclose Ave RG4 .... 259 E2
Barcombe Cl OX16 .... 6 C1
Barcote La SN7 .... 174 A3
Bardolphs Cl RG4 .... 258 B4
Bardwell Rd OX2 .... 123 E2
Bardwell Terr OX6 .... 65 F1
Barefoot Cl RG31 .... 257 D2
Barfleur Cl OX14 .... 214 A1
Barford Rd Bloxham OX15 . 21 F1
South Newington OX15 ... 32 A3
Barksdale Ave NN13 ...... 36 C3
Barkus Way HP14 .... 188 C3
Barley Cl Lewknor OX9 .... 187 E4
Silford Gower OX15 ...... 19 D4
Wallingford OX10 .... 221 E3
Barleycott La OX1 .... 141 E2
Barleyfields OX11 .... 218 B4
Barlow Cl Milcombe OX15 . 21 D1
Wheatley OX33 .... 143 F4
Barn Cl Denchworth OX12 . 196 A4
Kidlington OX5 .... 108 B4
Barn End OX18 .... 134 C1
Barn La Burford OX18 .... 100 B3
Henley-on-T RG9 .... 244 B2
Barn's Rd OX4 .... 142 B2

Barnacre OX9 .... 186 A1
Barnard Cl RG4 .... 259 E3
Barnards Way OX12 .... 214 C3
Barncroft OX10 .... 221 E4
Barnes Cl OX11 .... 218 C4
Barnes Rd OX11 .... 218 C3
Barnet St OX4 .... 142 A4
Barnett Rd
Middleton Cheney OX17 ... 17 F4
Steventon OX13 .... 198 C3
Barnett Way OX10 .... 204 B1
Barnfield OX12 .... 175 F1
Barnfield Cl OX5 .... 65 F3
Barns Cl OX3 .... 140 A3
Barns Hay OX3 .... 124 A3
Barns La OX18 .... 100 C2
Baroma Way RG9 .... 244 C1
Baronhurst Dr OX44 ...... 184 B3
Barons Mead RG9 .... 244 B1
Barracks La Oxford OX4 ... 142 A4
Oxford OX4 .... 142 B3
Barrett St OX2 .... 123 D1
Barrett's Way OX14 .... 199 F3
Barretts Ct OX18 .... 89 E4
Barrington Ave SN6 .... 191 F1
Barrington Cl
Bernisfield OX10 .... 182 B3
Oxford OX3 .... 124 B1
Witney OX8 .... 117 F4
Barrington Rd SN6 .... 209 E4
Barrow Hill Ct OX14 ...... 160 B1
Barrow La OX11 .... 217 F4
Barrow Rd Abingdon OX13 . 179 D4
Harwell OX11 .... 217 F4
Barry Ave OX6 .... 65 E2
Barry Pl RG4 .... 259 D1
Bartholomew Ave OX5 .... 108 A3
Bartholomew Cl
Ducklington OX8 .... 118 A2
Eynsham OX8 .... 120 B4
Bartholomew Rd OX4 ..... 142 A2
Bartholomew Tipping Way
HP14 .... 188 C3
Bartlemas Cl OX4 .... 142 A4
Bartlemas Rd OX4 .... 142 A4
Bartlett Cl OX8 .... 118 A4
Barton Ct OX17 .... 23 F3
Barton La Abingdon OX14 .. 180 A4
Oxford OX3 .... 124 B2
Barton Rd
Long Compton CV36 ...... 27 D1
Oxford OX3 .... 124 B2
Barton Village Rd OX3 .... 124 B3
Barwell OX12 .... 214 B3
Basil Hill Rd OX11 .... 200 B2
Baskerville La RG9 .... 255 D2
Baskerville Rd RG4 .... 259 D3
Basmore La RG9 .... 255 D2
Basset Way OX5 .... 108 C4
Bassett Ave OX6 .... 65 F2
Bassett Rd
Letcombe Bassett OX12 ... 231 F4
Oxford OX3 .... 124 C2
Batchelors Row OX15 .... 33 D2
Bateman St OX3 .... 124 B1
Bates La OX6 .... 35 E2
Bath Pl OX1 .... 123 E1
Bath Rd Banbury OX16 ... 16 B3
Sonning RG4 .... 260 C1
Bath St Abingdon OX14 ... 179 F4
Oxford OX4 .... 123 F1
Battle Cl OX6 .... 66 A2
Battle Rd Benson OX10 ... 204 B1
Goring RG8 .... 249 F4
Baulking La OX12 .... 194 B1
Baulking Rd SN7 .... 211 F4
Bay Rd OX6 .... 65 E1
Bay Tree Cl OX4 .... 142 A2
Baydon Rd RG17 .... 245 E1
Bayliss Rd RG10 .... 255 E1
Bayliss Yd OX7 .... 73 D2
Bayswater Farm Rd OX3 .. 125 D2
Bayswater Rd Oxford OX3 . 124 C2
Stanton St John OX3 ..... 125 D3
Bayworth La OX1 .... 159 F4
Beaconsfield Rd OX16 .... 16 B1
Beagle Cl OX14 .... 160 B1
Beagles Cl OX5 .... 109 D4
Beanacre Rd OX15 .... 30 C3
Beanfurlong OX17 .... 22 C2
Beanhill Cl OX18 .... 118 A2
Beanhill Rd OX18 .... 118 A3
Bear Cl OX20 .... 91 D3
Bear Ct OX18 .... 100 C3
Bear La
North Moreton OX11 ...... 220 A4
Oxford OX1, OX44 .... 123 E1
Stadhampton OX44 .... 163 E1
Wallingford OX10 .... 221 E4
Bearsden Rd OX16 .... 16 A3
Bears Hedge OX4 .... 142 A2
Beatrice Dr OX16 .... 16 A3
Beauchamp La OX4 ...... 142 B2
Beauchamp Pl OX4 ...... 142 A2
Beaufort Cl Bicester OX6 .. 66 A2
Didcot OX11 .... 219 D4
Beaulieu Cl OX16 .... 16 C3
Beaulieu Ct OX13 .... 159 F3
Beaulieu Mews OX11 .... 201 D2
Beaumaris Cl OX16 ...... 15 E3
Beaumont Bldgs OX1 .... 123 D1
Beaumont Dr OX14 ...... 160 A2
Beaumont Pl OX1 .... 123 E1
Beaumont Rd OX11 ...... 219 D4
Beaumont Rd Banbury OX16 16 B1
Oxford OX3 .... 124 C2
Beaumont St OX1 .... 123 E1
Bec Cl OX12 .... 214 A3

Bec Tithe RG8 .... 250 C2
Beckdale Cl OX6 .... 65 D2
Becket St OX1 .... 123 D1
Becket Ave SN6 .... 209 E4
Becket Dr SN6 .... 209 E4
Becketts Cl OX3 .... 90 A1
Beckley Cl RG8 .... 250 C4
Beckley Ct OX3 .... 111 D1
Becquerel Ave OX11 .... 217 D1
Bedford Cl OX16 .... 15 F4
Bedford St OX4 .... 141 F3
Bedwells Heath OX1 .... 140 B1
Beech RG9 .... 244 B1
Beech Cl Farringdon SN7 .... 172 C2
  Stokenchurch HP14 .... 188 C2
  Watlington OX9 .... 186 A1
Beech Cres OX5 .... 108 C3
Beech Croft Rd OX2 .... 123 D3
Beech Gr OX18 .... 100 C3
Beech La RG8 .... 250 B4
Beech Rd Chinnor OX9 .... 168 B3
  Eynsham OX8 .... 120 C4
  Mapledurham RG4 .... 258 B4
  N Hinksey Vill OX2 .... 140 B4
  Oxford OX3 .... 124 B2
  Purley on T RG8 .... 257 D3
  Thame OX9 .... 147 E4
  Wheatley OX33 .... 144 A4
  Witney OX8 .... 117 F4
Beech Rise RG4 .... 252 C3
Beechcroft OX10 .... 182 B1
Beeches The
  Deddington OX15 .... 33 F2
  Goring RG8 .... 249 D3
  Oxford OX3 .... 124 C2
  Reading RG31 .... 257 E2
Beechey Ave OX3 .... 123 F2
Beechfield Cres OX16 .... 16 B2
Beechgate OX8 .... 118 A3
Beeching Cl OX1 .... 218 B1
Beechwood Cl RG8 .... 250 B3
Beesley Rd OX16 .... 16 A3
Beeson Cl RG8 .... 250 C4
Begbroke Cres OX5 .... 92 A1
Begbroke La OX5 .... 92 A1
Beggar's La OX11 .... 156 B1
Beggarsbush Hill OX10 .... 204 B1
Behoes La RG8 .... 240 B1
Beir Path The RG8 .... 239 D2
Belbroughton Rd OX2 .... 123 E3
Belfast Rd OX10 .... 204 C2
Belgrove Cl OX5 .... 108 B4
Bell Cl Cassington OX8 .... 107 D1
  Grove OX12 .... 196 C1
  Thame OX9 .... 129 F1
Bell Hill OX15 .... 30 A4
Bell La Adderbury HP28 .... 247 F2
  Bampton OX18 .... 134 C2
  Bicester OX6 .... 65 F1
  Brightwell-cum-S OX10 .... 202 C1
  Cassington RG8 .... 107 E1
  Henley-on-T RG9 .... 244 C2
  Lechlade GL7 .... 150 B2
  Thame OX9 .... 129 F1
  Wheatley OX33 .... 144 A4
Bell St Henley-on-T RG9 .... 244 C1
  Hornton OX15 .... 7 E3
Bell's La OX15 .... 30 A4
Bellamy Cl OX13 .... 156 C1
Belle Terr OX18 .... 115 E1
Belle Vue Rd RG9 .... 254 B4
Belleisle RG8 .... 257 D3
Bellenger Way OX5 .... 108 B4
Bellingham La SN6 .... 190 A1
Bellingham Wlk RG4 .... 259 D3
Belmont OX12 .... 214 B3
Belmont Mews OX9 .... 147 F4
Belvedere Rd OX4 .... 142 A4
Ben Cl OX5 .... 92 C1
Benares Gr RG9 .... 242 A2
Benhams La RG9 .... 226 B1
Bennett Cl OX17 .... 10 C2
Bennett End Rd HP14 .... 189 E4
Bennett Rd SN7 .... 172 C2
Bensgrove Cl RG8 .... 250 C4
Benson Cl OX6 .... 66 A2
Benson La Benson OX10 .... 204 A1
  Crownmarsh G OX10 .... 221 F4
Benson Pl OX2 .... 123 E2
Benson Rd Abingdon OX14 .... 159 F1
  Oxford OX3 .... 142 B4
Bentley Cl OX16 .... 15 F4
Benton Dr OX9 .... 168 B4
Benwells OX9 .... 168 B3
Bere Court Rd RG8 .... 256 A2
Berens Rd SN6 .... 209 D3
Bergamont Pl [20] OX4 .... 142 C1
Bergen Ave OX14 .... 179 E2
Berins Hill OX10 .... 241 D3
Berinsfield Rdbt OX10 .... 182 A2
Berkeley Cl OX16 .... 15 F4
Berkeley Rd
  Sunningwell OX1 .... 140 C1
  Thame OX9 .... 130 A1
Berkshire Rd RG9 .... 254 B4
Bernard Cl OX5 .... 108 B3
Berner's Way SN7 .... 173 D2
Bernewood Cl HP18 .... 129 E4
Bernwood Rd Bicester OX6 .... 65 F1
  Oxford OX3 .... 124 C2
Berrick Rd OX4 .... 184 B3
Berry Cl OX4 .... 142 C2
Berry Croft OX13 .... 159 F1
Berry Hill Rd OX17 .... 22 C1
Berry La Blewbury OX11 .... 219 D1
  East Hanney OX12 .... 197 D3
Berrylands Rd RG4 .... 259 D2

Berrymere Rd OX13 .... 159 D4
Berrymoor Rd OX16 .... 16 A3
Bertie Pl OX1 .... 141 E3
Bertie Rd OX2 .... 139 F3
Besbury La OX7 .... 55 F3
Bessels Lea OX11 .... 219 D1
Bessels Way OX11 .... 237 D4
Besselsleigh Rd
  Appleton OX13 .... 158 C4
  Wootton (Oxford) OX13 .... 159 D4
Bessemer Cl OX6 .... 66 A1
Bettina Cres OX16 .... 9 D1
Betty La OX1 .... 141 E2
Between Towns Rd OX4 .... 142 B3
Beverley Cl
  Abingdon OX14 .... 159 F1
  Benson OX10 .... 204 B2
  Chalgrove OX44 .... 184 C3
Beverley Cres OX18 .... 115 F2
Beverley Gdns
  Bicester OX6 .... 66 A2
  Wargrave RG10 .... 255 F1
Beverley Rd RG31 .... 257 E1
Bevington Rd OX2 .... 123 E2
Bibury Cl OX8 .... 117 E4
Bicester Rd Bucknell OX6 .... 64 C4
  Enstone OX7 .... 58 C3
  Kidlington OX5 .... 109 D4
  Launton OX6 .... 66 B1
  Long Crendon HP18 .... 129 E3
  Ludgershall HP18 .... 98 B4
  Marsh Gibbon OX6 .... 67 F2
  Middleton Stoney OX6 .... 64 A2
  Stratton Audley OX6 .... 66 B4
Bickerton Rd OX3 .... 124 B1
Biddel Springs SN6 .... 190 A3
Biddlesden Rd NN13 .... 25 D3
Bigmore La HP14 .... 189 E1
Bignell View OX6 .... 79 F4
Bignolds Cl OX17 .... 4 B4
Billings Cl HP14 .... 188 C3
Billwell HP18 .... 129 E3
Bingley Gr RG5 .... 260 C1
Binsey La OX2 .... 122 C1
Binswood Ave OX3 .... 124 C1
Birch Cl OX3 .... 124 C2
Birch Rd Ambrosden OX6 .... 81 E2
  Garsington OX44 .... 143 E1
Birchen Cl RG8 .... 250 C4
Birches The RG8 .... 249 D3
Birchfield Cl OX4 .... 142 C1
Birchwood Banbury OX16 .... 16 B2
  Carterton OX18 .... 115 F1
Birchwood Cl RG4 .... 259 E3
Birchwood Dr OX2 .... 92 B3
Birchwood The RG31 .... 257 D3
Bird Cl OX16 .... 16 B2
Bird Wood Ct RG4 .... 253 D2
Birdlip Cl OX8 .... 103 E1
Birds La OX15 .... 13 D3
Bishop Kirk Pl OX2 .... 123 D1
Bishop's Wood OX44 .... 144 B2
Bishops Cl OX13 .... 138 C3
Bishops Orch OX11 .... 218 C4
Bisley Cl OX4 .... 142 C2
Bitham Rd OX12 .... 233 E4
Bitterell OX8 .... 120 C4
Bix Hill Bix RG9 .... 243 F4
  Henley-on-T RG9 .... 243 A4
Black Bourton Rd
  Carterton OX18 .... 115 F1
  Clanfield OX18 .... 133 E1
Black Croft OX12 .... 214 B3
Black's La OX8 .... 86 C1
Blackberry La OX4 .... 162 A4
Blackbird Assarts La OX7 .... 88 A1
Blackbird Leys Rd OX4 .... 142 B1
Blackburn Wlk OX6 .... 66 A2
Blackditch OX8 .... 138 A4
Blackfriars Rd OX1 .... 141 D4
Blackhall Rd OX1 .... 123 E1
Blackhorse La OX13 .... 158 C2
Blacklands Rd OX10 .... 224 A1
Blacklands Way OX14 .... 179 E4
Blacklocks Hill OX17 .... 17 D4
Blackman Cl OX1 .... 141 F1
Blackmore La RG4 .... 253 D3
Blacknall Rd OX14 .... 179 F3
Blacksmith La OX5 .... 95 D2
Blacksmiths Hill OX17 .... 3 E4
Blacksmiths La OX17 .... 4 A4
Blacksmiths Meadow [9]
OX4 .... 142 C1
Blackstock Cl OX3 .... 142 C4
Blackstone Rd OX10 .... 203 E1
Blackthorn Cl
  Blackthorn OX6 .... 82 A2
  Oxford OX3 .... 124 C2
  Reading RG31 .... 257 D2
Blackthorn Rd OX6 .... 66 C1
Blackwater Cl RG4 .... 259 F2
Blackwater Way OX11 .... 201 D2
Blackwood Pl OX15 .... 22 C4
Blackworth SN6 .... 190 A4
Bladon Cl OX2 .... 122 C4
Bladon Rd OX20 .... 91 E2
Blaenant RG4 .... 258 C3
Blaenavon RG4 .... 258 C3
Blagrave Cl OX14 .... 160 A2
Blagrave La RG4 .... 258 B2
Blake Rd OX6 .... 66 A1
Blake Way OX9 .... 130 A1
Blake's Field OX11 .... 200 B1
Blakehope Burn OX11 .... 200 C2
Blakes Ave OX8 .... 118 B4
Blakes Rd RG10 .... 255 F2
Blandford Alley SN6 .... 190 A3
Blandford Ave OX2 .... 109 D1

Blandford Rd OX5 .... 92 B1
Blandy Ave OX13 .... 156 C1
Blandy Rd RG9 .... 254 B4
Blankstone Cl OX8 .... 120 B4
Blay Cl OX4 .... 142 B3
Bleache Pl OX4 .... 142 B3
Bledlow Rd HP27 .... 169 E4
Bledlow Ridge Rd HP27 .... 169 E4
Blencowe Cl OX6 .... 65 F3
Blenheim NN13 .... 36 A4
Blenheim Cl OX11 .... 200 C1
Blenheim Dr Bicester OX6 .... 65 E2
  Cutteslowe OX2 .... 123 D4
  Launton OX6 .... 66 C1
  Witney OX8 .... 117 F4
Blenheim Gdns OX12 .... 196 B1
Blenheim Hill OX11 .... 217 F4
Blenheim La OX18 .... 106 A3
Blenheim Orch OX12 .... 197 D3
Blenheim Pl OX11 .... 204 B1
Blenheim Rd
  Banbury OX16 .... 16 C1
  Caversham RG4 .... 259 D2
  Kidlington OX5 .... 108 C4
  Lewknor OX9 .... 186 B2
  Little Milton OX44 .... 164 A3
Blenheim Rise OX17 .... 23 F3
Blenheim Way OX33 .... 143 E4
Blenheim La OX33 .... 144 A4
Bleriot Rd GL54 .... 68 A2
Bletchingdon Rd
  Bletchingdon OX5 .... 78 A2
  Hampton Poyle OX5 .... 93 D2
  Islip OX5 .... 93 F1
Blewbury Hill OX11 .... 237 E4
Blewbury Rd OX11 .... 219 D2
Blomfield Pl OX2 .... 123 D2
Blossoms Glade OX14 .... 160 C3
Blounts Court Rd RG4 .... 253 D3
Blowings The OX6 .... 106 A4
Bloxhamgrove Hill OX12 .... 212 A1
Bloxham Grove Rd OX15 .... 22 A3
Bloxham Rd
  Banbury OX15, OX16 .... 16 A2
  Barford St M OX15 .... 32 C4
  Broughton OX15 .... 21 D1
  Milcombe OX15 .... 21 D1
Blue Boar St OX1 .... 123 E1
Bluebell Cl ☑ OX4 .... 142 C1
Bluebell Ride OX14 .... 160 C4
Blythe Pl OX6 .... 65 D2
Boathouse Reach RG9 .... 244 C1
Bobby Fryer Cl OX4 .... 142 C2
Boddington La OX8 .... 105 E4
Bodley Pl OX2 .... 123 D4
Bodley Rd OX4 .... 142 B2
Bohams Rd OX11 .... 236 B3
Bolney La RG9 .... 255 D3
Bolney Rd RG9 .... 255 D3
Bolsover Cl OX8 .... 90 A1
Bolton Rd OX16 .... 16 B3
Bolton's La OX8 .... 90 A2
Bonar Rd OX3 .... 124 C1
Bones La RG9 .... 254 A2
Bonham Pl OX18 .... 115 E2
Bonnersfield HP18 .... 129 E4
Boot St OX8 .... 89 E4
Boreford Rd OX14 .... 160 A2
Borough Ave OX10 .... 221 E4
Borough Rd NN13 .... 24 A3
Borough Wlk OX4 .... 159 F1
Borrowmead Rd OX3 .... 124 A3
Bosley Cres OX10 .... 221 E4
Bostock Rd OX14 .... 179 F4
Boston Rd Bicester OX6 .... 66 A2
  Henley-on-T RG9 .... 254 C4
Boswell Rd OX4 .... 142 B2
Bothy The Aynho RG10 .... 35 E4
  Wargrave RG10 .... 255 E1
Botley Cl OX2 .... 122 C4
Bottle Square La HP14 .... 189 E3
Bottom La RG8 .... 241 D2
Bottom Rd HP14 .... 189 E4
Boucher Cl OX12 .... 214 B4
Boulevard The OX5 .... 92 B3
Boulter Dr OX14 .... 160 A2
Boulter St OX4 .... 123 F1
Boults Cl OX3 .... 123 F3
Boults La OX3 .... 123 F3
Boundary Brook Rd OX4 .... 142 A3
Boundary Cl OX6 .... 66 B2
Boundary La RG4 .... 258 C2
Boundary Rd NN13 .... 24 A3
Bourlon Wood OX14 .... 159 E1
Bourne Cl Bicester OX6 .... 65 E1
  Cutteslowe OX2 .... 109 D1
Bourne La OX15 .... 30 A4
Bourne Rd RG8 .... 256 C3
Bourne St OX11 .... 218 C4
Bourne The
  Eastleach Martin GL7 .... 131 D4
  Hook Norton OX15 .... 30 A4
Bourton Cl Clanfield OX18 .... 133 F1
  Witney OX8 .... 117 F4
Bovewell OX6 .... 79 F4
Bovingdon Rd OX18 .... 115 F2
Bovington's Yd OX18 .... 133 E2
Bow Rd SN7 .... 174 C1
Bowbank OX3 .... 124 A3
Bowbank Cl OX13 .... 156 B2
Bower Green SN6 .... 191 F1
Bowerman Cl OX5 .... 108 B4
Bowers La HP14 .... 189 E4
Bowfell Cl RG31 .... 257 E1
Bowgrave Copse OX14 .... 160 B1

Bowling Ct RG9 .... 244 B2
Bowling Gr HP14 .... 188 B3
Bowling Green Cl OX18 .... 134 C2
Bowling Green La RG8 .... 257 D3
Bowmont La OX17 .... 35 E4
Bowmont Sq OX6 .... 65 D1
Bowness Ave Didcot OX11 .... 218 B4
  Oxford OX3 .... 124 A2
Bowyer Rd OX14 .... 179 F4
Box Tree La OX9 .... 166 C2
Boxhedge Rd OX16 .... 16 A3
Boxhedge Rd W OX16 .... 16 A3
Boxhedge Sq OX16 .... 16 A3
Boxhill Rd OX14 .... 179 F4
Boxhill Wlk OX14 .... 179 F4
Boxwell Cl OX14 .... 160 A1
Bracegirdle Rd OX3 .... 124 C1
Bracken Cl
  Carterton OX18 .... 115 E2
  Reading RG31 .... 257 E1
Brackley Rd
  Croughton NN13 .... 36 B4
  Westbury NN13 .... 25 D3
Bradburys The OX6 .... 66 A1
Braddons Furlong HP18 .... 129 E3
Brading Way RG8 .... 257 E3
Bradlands OX3 .... 123 F4
Bradley Rd RG9 .... 224 A3
Bradley's St RG8 .... 241 D2
Bradmore Rd OX2 .... 123 E2
Bradshaw Cl OX6 .... 66 A1
Bradstock's Way OX14 .... 199 F3
Bradwell Rd RG31 .... 257 E2
Brae Hill HP18 .... 98 A1
Braemar Cl OX18 .... 115 E3
Braithwaite Cl OX16 .... 16 B3
Brake Hill OX4 .... 143 D1
Bramber Cl OX16 .... 15 F4
Bramber Mews RG4 .... 259 F2
Brambling Way OX4 .... 142 B1
Bramblings OX4 .... 258 C3
Bramblings The OX6 .... 66 A1
Bramley Cres RG4 .... 252 C3
Bramley Hts OX8 .... 117 F4
Brampton Chase RG9 .... 255 D2
Brampton Cl OX14 .... 159 F1
Brampton Dr OX14 .... 115 F1
Brampton Rd OX3 .... 124 C2
Bramshaw Rd RG30 .... 258 A1
Bramwell Pl OX4 .... 141 F4
Brandon Cl OX5 .... 108 B4
Brantwood Rise OX16 .... 16 A2
Brasenose Dr OX5 .... 92 C1
Brasenose Driftway
OX4 .... 142 C3
Brasenose La OX1 .... 123 E1
Brasenose Rd OX11 .... 200 B1
Brashfield Rd OX6 .... 65 F2
Braybrooke Cl OX7 .... 42 C3
Braybrooke Gdns RG10 .... 255 E1
Braybrooke Rd RG10 .... 255 E1
Braze La OX10 .... 204 A3
Braziers La OX10 .... 205 D4
Breedons Hill RG8 .... 256 B3
Brenda Cl OX16 .... 16 A2
Brendon Cl Didcot OX11 .... 200 B1
  Reading RG31 .... 257 F1
Brentford Cl OX10 .... 221 E3
Brereton Dr OX12 .... 196 B1
Bretch Hill OX16 .... 15 F3
Brett Cl OX9 .... 148 A4
Brewer Cl OX13 .... 199 D2
Brewer Rd OX8 .... 90 A1
Brewers Ct OX14 .... 179 F3
Brewery La OX15 .... 29 F4
Brewery Row GL56 .... 26 C1
Brewery St SN6 .... 190 A3
Briants Ave RG4 .... 259 E1
Briar Cl Banbury OX16 .... 16 B1
  Caversham RG4 .... 259 D3
  Kidlington OX5 .... 92 B1
Briar End OX5 .... 92 B1
Briar Thicket OX20 .... 91 E3
Briar Way OX4 .... 142 C2
Briars Cl RG8 .... 256 C3
Briarswood HP14 .... 188 C3
Briary Rd GL7 .... 150 B3
Brice Rd OX6 .... 63 E4
Brick Hill OX15 .... 30 A3
Brickle La OX15 .... 21 F3
Bricks La HP14 .... 189 E2
Briden's Way HP17 .... 130 C3
Bridewell Cl OX8 .... 105 D4
Bridge Cl OX11 .... 219 D1
Bridge End OX10 .... 202 B4
Bridge Farm Cl OX12 .... 214 C4
Bridge Rd HP18 .... 127 F1
Bridge St Abingdon OX14 .... 179 F4
  Bampton OX18 .... 134 C2
  Banbury OX16 .... 16 C2
  Caversham RG4 .... 259 D1
  Islip OX5 .... 109 F4
  Witney OX8 .... 104 A1
Bridges Cl OX11 .... 200 C1
Bridgewater Cl RG30 .... 258 B1
Bridle Cl OX16 .... 16 C2
Bridle Path RG8 .... 250 C4
Bridle Way RG8 .... 250 C4
Bridstow Rd OX1 .... 141 D1
Bridus Mead OX11 .... 219 D1
Bridus Way OX11 .... 219 D1
Brierley Pl RG31 .... 257 E1
Briggs Cl OX15 .... 15 F2
Brightwell Cl OX10 .... 202 C1
Brightwell St OX10 .... 202 C1
Brill Cl RG4 .... 259 D2
Brill Rd HP18 .... 98 A4

Brinds Cl OX11 .... 253 C3
Brinkburn Gr OX16 .... 16 C4
Brinkinfield Rd OX44 .... 184 B4
Bristol Rd Bicester OX6 .... 64 C4
  Church Westcote GL54 .... 68 A3
Britannia Cl OX18 .... 115 F2
Britannia Rd OX16 .... 16 B3
Britnell Cl HP14 .... 188 C3
Britwell Rd Didcot OX11 .... 200 C1
  Ewelme OX10 .... 204 C2
  Watlington OX9 .... 186 A1
Brixton Hill OX10 .... 223 D2
Brize Norton Rd
  Carterton OX18 .... 115 F1
  Minster Lovell OX8 .... 102 C1
Brizewood OX18 .... 115 F1
Broad Cl Barford St M OX15 .... 32 C3
  Kidlington OX5 .... 108 B4
  N Hinksey Vill OX2 .... 122 A1
Broad End OX15 .... 16 C1
Broad Gap OX15 .... 16 C1
Broad Marsh La OX8 .... 106 A3
Broad Oak OX3 .... 142 C4
Broad St Abingdon OX14 .... 179 F4
  Bampton OX18 .... 134 C2
  Banbury OX16 .... 16 B3
  Long Compton CV36 .... 27 F3
  Oxford OX1 .... 123 E1
  Uffington SN7 .... 211 E4
Broad Way SN7 .... 211 E3
Broadbrook La OX12 .... 212 C2
Broadfields OX4 .... 142 B1
Broadhead Cl OX2 .... 124 A3
Broadhurst Gdns OX4 .... 142 A1
Broadmarsh Cl OX12 .... 214 B4
Broadwaters Ave OX9 .... 147 F4
Broadway Didcot OX11 .... 218 C4
  Harwell OX11 .... 217 F3
  Kidlington OX5 .... 108 B3
Broadway Cl Harwell OX11 .... 217 F3
  Witney OX8 .... 103 E1
Broadway The OX5 .... 95 D2
Broadwell Cl OX6 .... 65 F2
Broadwell Rd GL7 .... 132 B1
Brocklesby Rd OX4 .... 142 A1
Brocks Way RG9 .... 255 D2
Brode Cl OX14 .... 160 A1
Brogden Cl OX2 .... 140 C4
Brome Pl OX3 .... 124 C2
Bromeswell Cl OX6 .... 62 C3
Bromsgrove SN7 .... 172 C2
Brook Cl HP18 .... 98 B4
Brook Hill OX20 .... 91 D3
Brook La
  Denchworth OX12 .... 196 A2
  Thame OX9 .... 129 F1
  West Hagbourne OX11 .... 218 B3
Brook Rd Bicester OX6 .... 65 E2
  Great Tew OX7 .... 45 E4
Brook St
  Aston Rowant OX9 .... 167 F2
  Benson OX10 .... 204 A2
  Oxford OX1 .... 141 E4
  Sutton Courtenay OX14 .... 200 A4
  Watlington OX9 .... 186 A1
Brook View OX14 .... 143 D1
Brook Way OX8 .... 90 A1
Brooke Rd OX16 .... 16 A2
Brookfield Cl
  Cholsey OX10 .... 221 E3
  Milton-u-W OX7 .... 70 A1
Brookfield Cres OX3 .... 124 A3
Brookhampton Cl OX44 .... 163 E1
Brooklime Wlk [19] OX4 .... 142 C1
Brooklyn Dr RG4 .... 259 D3
Brookmead Dr OX10 .... 221 E3
Brooksby Rd RG31 .... 257 E1
Brookside
  Abingdon OX14 .... 159 F1
  Cholsey OX10 .... 220 C1
  East Hanney OX12 .... 197 D3
  Great Tew OX7 .... 45 E4
  Hook Norton OX15 .... 30 A4
  Oxford OX3, OX44 .... 124 B1
  Thame OX9 .... 129 F1
Brookside Cl OX9 .... 145 F4
Brookside Estate OX14 .... 184 B4
Brookside Way OX15 .... 21 E2
Broome Way OX16 .... 16 C4
Broomfield Rd RG30 .... 258 B1
Broughton Cl RG30 .... 258 B1
Broughton Rd OX15 .... 15 F3
Broughtons Cl OX3 .... 123 F3
Brown's La Charlbury OX7 .... 73 D2
  Woodstock OX20 .... 91 D3
Browning Dr OX6 .... 65 E2
Browning Rd OX16 .... 16 A2
Browns Cl OX2 .... 140 A4
Brookside OX1 .... 217 F4
Bruern Rd OX7 .... 70 A2
Brunel Cres OX12 .... 196 B1
Brunel Dr RG5 .... 260 C1
Brunel Rd OX11 .... 218 B4
Brunstock Beck OX11 .... 200 C2
Bryan Way OX12 .... 214 C3
Bryants Pl RG8 .... 257 D2
Bryony Cl OX4 .... 143 D1
Bryworth La GL7 .... 150 A3
Buchan Rd OX6 .... 65 E2
Buchanan Rd OX6 .... 96 C4
Buckingham Cl OX11 .... 219 D4
Buckingham Cres OX16 .... 65 F2
Buckingham Dr RG4 .... 259 D3

Buckingham Rd
Bicester OX6 .... 65 F2
Brackley NN13 .... 24 A3
Buckingham St OX1 .... 141 E4
Buckland Ct OX5 .... 108 C4
Buckland Rd
Bampton OX18 .... 154 B4
Buckland SN7 .... 174 C4
Charney Bassett OX12 .... 175 F1
Buckler Rd OX2 .... 123 D4
Bucklers Bury Rd OX14 .... 160 A2
Bucknell Ave RG8 .... 256 C3
Bucknell Rd OX6 .... 65 E2
Buckner's Cl OX10 .... 203 F2
Buckthorn La OX10 .... 220 C1
Budd Cl OX20 .... 91 E4
Bulan Rd OX3 .... 142 C4
Bull Baulk
Middleton Cheney OX17 .... 11 D1
Middleton Cheney OX17 .... 17 F4
Bull Cl GL7 .... 132 A3
Bull Hill OX7 .... 72 A4
Bull La OX18 .... 135 F1
Bull Meadow The RG8 .... 248 C3
Bull St OX18 .... 135 F1
Bullingdon Ave OX10 .... 182 B3
Bullingdon Rd OX4 .... 141 F4
Bullmarsh Cl OX6 .... 64 A2
Bullockspits La OX13 .... 176 B4
Bullring The OX15 .... 33 F2
Bulls La Ickford HP18 .... 128 A2
  Kings Sutton OX17 .... 23 F3
Bullsmead OX13 .... 159 F3
Bullstake Cl OX2 .... 122 C1
Bulrush Rd OX4 .... 142 C1
Bulwarks La OX1 .... 123 E1
Bungalow Cl OX3 .... 111 E1
Bunkers Hill OX5 .... 77 D1
Bunyan Rd OX6 .... 65 E2
Burbush Rd OX4 .... 142 C3
Burchester Ave OX3 .... 124 C2
Burchester Pl OX16 .... 16 C4
Burcombe Way RG4 .... 259 D2
Burcot La OX10 .... 182 B2
Burcot Park OX14 .... 181 F3
Burdell Ave OX3 .... 125 D2
Burditch Bank OX20 .... 75 F3
Bure La OX11 .... 201 D1
Bure Pl OX11 .... 65 F1
Burford Rd
  Black Bourton OX18 .... 133 F3
  Brize Norton OX18 .... 115 F4
  Carterton OX18 .... 115 E2
  Chipping Norton OX7 .... 42 C1
  Curbridge OX8 .... 103 D1
  Minster Lovell OX8 .... 102 B1
  Swinbrook OX18 .... 102 B1
  Witney OX8 .... 103 E1
Burford St GL7 .... 150 B2
Burgan Cl OX4 .... 142 B2
Burleigh Mews RG4 .... 259 E3
Burlington Cres OX3 .... 125 D2
Burlington Gdns OX16 .... 16 A2
Burnham Rise RG4 .... 259 E3
Burnhams The HP18 .... 128 B2
Burns Cl HP18 .... 129 E4
Burns Cres OX6 .... 65 E2
Burns Rd OX6 .... 16 A2
Burr Cl OX8 .... 120 A1
Burr St OX11 .... 217 F4
Burra Ct OX4 .... 161 D4
Burrows Cl OX3 .... 124 B2
Burrows Hill OX10 .... 204 C2
Bursill Cl OX3 .... 125 D2
Burswin Rd OX18 .... 115 E3
Burt's La HP18 .... 129 E3
Burton Cl OX14 .... 179 E3
Burton Pl OX4 .... 142 C3
Burwell Cl OX8 .... 117 F4
Burwell Dr OX8 .... 117 F4
Burwell Meadow OX8 .... 117 F3
Bury Mead OX8 .... 138 A4
Bury St OX14 .... 179 F4
Burycroft Rd OX15 .... 30 A3
Burycroft The OX14 .... 180 A2
Buryhook Cnr OX33 .... 126 B1
Buryway La CV36 .... 27 F4
Busby Cl OX8 .... 89 E4
Busby's Cl OX13 .... 152 C4
Buscot Dr OX14 .... 160 A1
Busgrove La RG9 .... 242 A2
Bush Furlong OX11 .... 200 C1
Bush The HP17 .... 130 C3
Bushey Cl OX2 .... 122 A1
Bushey Leys Cl OX3 .... 124 C3
Bushy Row OX18 .... 134 C2
Butcher's Hill OX7 .... 45 E4
Butcher's Row OX16 .... 16 B3
Butler Cl Bloxham OX15 .... 21 F3
  Horspath OX33 .... 143 E3
  Oxford OX2, OX33 .... 123 D2
Butler's Field GL7 .... 150 B3
Butlers CV36 .... 28 A3
Butlers Dr OX18 .... 115 F1
Butlers Orch RG4 .... 252 B2
Butlers Pond RG8 .... 250 B1
Butlers The OX36 .... 28 B3
Buttercup Sq 8 OX44 .... 142 C1
Butterfly Rd HP14 .... 188 C2
Buttermarket OX9 .... 147 F4
Buttermilk La OX8 .... 86 C1
Butterworth Pl OX14 .... 142 C1
Butterwyke Pl OX1 .... 141 E4
Butts Cl OX17 .... 35 E4
Butts Hill Rd RG5 .... 260 C1

Butts La OX3 .... 123 F4
Butts Rd Faringdon SN7 .... 172 C1
  Horspath OX33 .... 143 E3
Butts The Aynho OX17 .... 35 E4
  Long Compton CV36 .... 27 F3
  Merton OX6 .... 95 E4
  Standlake OX8 .... 137 E2
Butts Way OX9 .... 167 E1
Buxton Ave RG4 .... 258 C2
Buzzards Cl OX17 .... 9 E3
Byeway The OX16 .... 16 C4
Byfield Rd OX17 .... 5 F4
Byres The HP17 .... 130 C3
Byron Cl OX14 .... 179 E3
Byron Rd OX6 .... 16 A2
Byron Way OX6 .... 65 E2

Cadogan Cl RG4 .... 259 F2
Cadogan Park OX20 .... 91 D3
Caernarvon Way OX16 .... 15 F3
Caesers Gate NN13 .... 24 A3
Caesars Dene OX18 .... 134 C2
Calais La OX8 .... 136 C3
Calcot Cl OX14 .... 124 C1
Calcroft La
  Clanfield OX18 .... 133 E1
  Kencot OX18 .... 132 C2
Caldecott Cl OX14 .... 179 E3
Caldecott Rd OX14 .... 179 F3
Calder Cl OX16 .... 16 C4
Calder Way OX11 .... 200 C1
Caldicott Cl OX10 .... 203 D3
Caleta Cl RG4 .... 259 E1
Calthorpe Rd OX16 .... 16 B3
Calthorpe St OX16 .... 16 B3
Calves Cl OX5 .... 108 B4
Cam Cl OX11 .... 200 C1
Cambrai Cl OX14 .... 200 C4
Cambridge Terr OX1 .... 141 E4
Camden Cl GL56 .... 26 C3
Camel Cross OX12 .... 214 B3
Camellias The OX16 .... 9 D1
Cameron Ave OX14 .... 160 B1
Camp La Ratley OX15 .... 2 B2
  Warmington OX17 .... 2 B2
Camp Rd OX6 .... 63 E4
Campbell Cl OX6 .... 65 F2
Campbell Rd OX4 .... 142 A3
Campbells Cl OX20 .... 91 E3
Campden Cl OX8 .... 103 F1
Campion Cl
  Carterton OX18 .... 115 F1
  8 Sandford-on-T OX4 .... 142 C1
Campion Hall Dr OX11 .... 219 D4
Campion Rd OX14 .... 180 A4
Canada Cl OX16 .... 16 B4
Canada La SN7 .... 172 C2
Canal Cl OX12 .... 214 B4
Canal La OX15 .... 16 C1
Canal St Banbury OX16 .... 16 B3
  Oxford OX2 .... 123 D1
Canal Way OX14 .... 214 A3
Cane La OX12 .... 214 B4
Canning Cres OX1 .... 141 F3
Cannons Field OX3 .... 123 F3
Canon Hill's Gdns SN6 .... 209 E3
Canterbury Cl OX16 .... 17 D4
Canterbury Rd OX2 .... 123 D2
Capel Cl OX2 .... 123 D4
Caps La OX10 ...... 221 D1
Cardiff Rd RG1 .... 258 C1
Cardigan St
  Oxford OX2 .... 123 D1
  Oxford OX2 .... 123 D2
Cardinal Cl
  Caversham RG4 .... 259 D1
  Oxford OX4 .... 142 A2
Cardwell Cres OX3 .... 124 A1
Carey Cl OX2 .... 108 C1
Cariad Ct RG8 .... 249 D4
Carisbrooke Cl RG4 .... 259 E3
Carleggill Pl RG4 .... 254 C4
Carling Rd RG4 .... 252 C3
Carlisle Rd RG31 .... 257 F2
Carlton Cl OX12 .... 196 B1
Carlton Rd
  Caversham RG4 .... 258 C2
  Cutteslowe OX2 .... 109 D1
Caroline St OX4 .... 123 F1
Carpenter Cl OX4 .... 142 C1
Carr Ave OX18 .... 115 E1
Carse Cl OX14 .... 160 A2
Carswell Cres OX6 .... 63 E4
Carswell La SN7 .... 154 A1
Carter Cl OX3 .... 124 C1
Carter Cres SN7 .... 172 C1
Carters Cl OX18 .... 115 E1
Carters La HP18 .... 129 D4
Carterton Rd OX18 .... 116 A2
Cartwright Gdns OX17 .... 35 E4
Cassington Rd
  Cassington OX8 .... 121 D4
  Eynsham OX8 .... 121 D4
  Yarnton OX5 .... 108 A3
Castle Cl Benson OX10 .... 203 F2
  Bicester OX6 .... 65 F4
Castle Cres SN7 .... 193 F4
Castle Fields OX6 .... 50 A2
Castle La OX10 .... 221 E4
Castle Rd Lewknor OX9 .... 186 B2
  Wootton OX20 .... 75 F3
Castle Sh Ctr OX16 .... 16 B3
Castle Sq OX10 .... 203 F2
Castle St
  Banbury OX15, OX16 .... 16 B3
  Deddington OX15 .... 33 F2
  Marsh Gibbon OX6 .... 67 F2
  Oxford OX1 .... 123 E1

Castle St continued
  Steventon OX13 .... 198 C2
  Wallingford OX10 .... 221 E4
Castle Wlk OX11 .... 200 C1
Caswell La OX8 .... 116 C3
Cat La Ewelme OX10 .... 204 C2
  Stadhampton OX44 .... 163 E1
Cat St OX12 .... 216 B3
Catharine Cl OX14 .... 160 C2
Catherine Cl SN6 .... 209 E3
Catherine St OX4 .... 142 A3
Catmore Cl OX12 .... 214 B4
Catmore Rd RG20 .... 234 C1
Catsham La
  Chadlington OX20 .... 72 B3
  Chilson OX7 .... 72 B3
Catslip RG9 .... 224 C1
Catte St OX1 .... 123 E1
Cattle Mkt OX7 .... 42 C2
Catwell Cl OX4 .... 142 A3
Caudwell Cl Drayton OX14 .... 179 D1
  Grove OX12 .... 196 C1
Causeway Banbury OX16 .... 16 C3
  Bicester OX6 .... 65 F1
  Bletchingdon OX5 .... 93 D4
Causeway The
  East Hanney OX12 .... 197 D3
  Steventon OX13 .... 198 C2
  Woodstock OX20 .... 91 D3
Causmans Way RG31 .... 257 E1
Cavalier Rd OX4 .... 142 B1
Cave St OX4 .... 123 F1
Cavell Rd OX4 .... 142 A3
Cavendish Dr OX3 .... 123 F3
Cavendish Pl OX6 .... 52 B1
Cavendish Rd
  Caversham RG4 .... 259 E3
  Cutteslowe OX2 .... 123 D4
Cavendish Wlk OX9 .... 130 A1
Caversham Park Rd RG4 .... 259 F3
Caversham Rd RG1 .... 259 D1
Cawley Rd OX17 .... 23 D3
Cawsham Gdns RG4 .... 259 E2
Caxton Cl RG30 .... 258 B1
Caxton Ct RG9 .... 244 C1
Cecil Aldin Dr RG31 .... 257 E2
Cecil Sharpe Cl OX3 .... 124 B1
Cedar RG9 .... 244 B1
Cedar Cl OX16 .... 16 B1
Cedar Cres OX9 .... 147 E4
Cedar Ct OX4 .... 142 B3
Cedar Dr Bicester OX6 .... 65 F2
  Pangbourne RG8 .... 256 B2
Cedar Rd Faringdon SN7 .... 172 C2
  N Hinksey Vill OX2 .... 140 B4
Cedar Villa OX16 .... 16 A3
Cedar Wood Cres RG4 .... 259 D2
Cedars The Benson OX10 .... 204 A3
  Reading RG31 .... 257 E1
Celandine Rl 6 OX44 .... 142 C1
Celsea Pl OX10 .... 221 D1

Cemetery Rd
  Abingdon OX14 .... 179 E4
  Bicester OX6 .... 65 F1
Century Pl OX4 .... 143 D1
Centenary Bsns Pk RG9 .... 244 C1
Centre Rise OX33 .... 143 E3
Centre St OX16 .... 16 C4
Centremead OX2 .... 141 D4
Chacombe Rd OX17 .... 10 C1
Chadlington Rd
  Oxford OX2 .... 123 E3
  Spelsbury OX7 .... 72 C4
Chaffinch Wlk OX4 .... 142 C1
Chainhill Rd OX22 .... 214 C1
Chalcraft Cl RG9 .... 254 B4
Chalfont Rd OX2 .... 123 D3
Chalford Cl OX7 .... 42 C2
Chalford Rd OX9 .... 167 D2
Chalgrove Rd OX9 .... 130 A1
Chalgrove Way RG4 .... 259 E3
Chalk Farm Rd HP14 .... 188 B3
Chalk Hill
  Aston Tirrold OX11 .... 237 F4
  Shiplake RG9 .... 254 B3
Chalkhouse Green La
  RG4 .... 253 D1
Chalkhousegreen La RG4 .... 259 D4
Challenor Cl OX14 .... 179 F2
Challow Rd OX12 .... 214 A3
Chalmore Gdns OX10 .... 221 E3
Chalvey Cl OX6 .... 65 E1
Chalvey Rd OX6 .... 65 E1
Chamberlain Pl OX5 .... 92 B1
Champion Rd RG4 .... 259 E1
Champion Way OX4 .... 142 B2
Champs Cl OX14 .... 160 B1
Chancel Way
  Lechlade GL7 .... 150 B2
  Marcham OX13 .... 178 B4
Chandler Cl OX18 .... 134 C2
Chandlers Cl
  Abingdon OX14 .... 160 B1
  Wantage OX12 .... 214 C2
Chapel Cl Lealfield OX8 .... 86 C2
  South Stoke RG8 .... 239 E2
Chapel End NN13 .... 36 B4
Chapel Hill
  Brize Norton OX18 .... 116 A2
  Swerford OX7 .... 30 C2
  Watchfield SN6 .... 191 E1
Chapel La Adderbury OX17 .... 23 D2
  Benson OX10 .... 203 F2
  Berrick Salome OX10 .... 204 A4
  Bledington OX7 .... 54 B1
  Bledlow Ridge HP14 .... 169 F1

Chapel La continued
  Blewbury OX11 .... 237 D4
  Bodicote OX15 .... 22 C4
  Chalgrove OX44 .... 184 B3
  Charney Bassett OX12 .... 175 F1
  Cropredy OX17 .... 4 C1
  Enstone OX7 .... 58 C3
  Fernham SN7 .... 193 D3
  Great Bourton OX17 .... 9 E3
  Great Rollright OX7 .... 29 D2
  Hailey OX8 .... 104 A3
  Kingham OX7 .... 55 D4
  Little Tew OX7 .... 45 D3
  Milton (Banbury) OX15 .... 22 B2
  North Leigh OX8 .... 105 D4
  Northmoor OX8 .... 138 B2
  Oxford OX4, OX44 .... 142 A1
  Ratley OX15 .... 2 A2
  Salford OX7 .... 41 F3
  Shipton-u-W OX7 .... 85 E4
  Standlake OX8 .... 137 E2
  Sutton Courtenay OX14 .... 200 A4
  Turweston NN13 .... 24 A4
  Uffington SN7 .... 211 E4
Chapel Rd Ashbury SN6 .... 228 A4
  South Leigh OX8 .... 119 D3
  Stanford in the V SN7 .... 194 C4
Chapel Sq Deddington OX15 .... 33 F2
  East Hendred OX12 .... 216 C3
Chapel St Bicester OX6 .... 65 F1
  Bloxham OX15 .... 21 F2
  Deddington OX15 .... 34 C2
  Hook Norton OX15 .... 30 A4
  Oxford OX4 .... 141 F4
  Warmington OX17 .... 3 D2
  Watlington OX9 .... 186 A1
Chapel Way Childrey OX12 .... 213 E2
  N Hinksey Vill OX2 .... 122 B1
Chapelwick Cl SN6 .... 209 D3
Chapmans La OX15 .... 34 A2
Chapmans Piece OX18 .... 100 C3
Charbridge La OX6 .... 66 B1
Charbridge Way OX6 .... 66 B1
Charlbury Cl OX5 .... 92 B1
Charlbury Rd Finstock OX7 .... 88 B4
  Oxford OX2 .... 123 E3
  Shrivenham SN6 .... 209 D3
Charles Cl OX16 .... 16 B3
Charles Dr OX9 .... 130 A1
Charles Evans Way RG4 .... 259 E1
Charles Rd OX10 .... 239 D4
Charles St OX4 .... 142 A3
Charlton Park OX12 .... 214 C3
Charlton Rd Aynho OX17 .... 35 E4
  Wantage OX12 .... 214 C3
Charlton Village Rd
  OX12 .... 214 C3
Charney Ave OX14 .... 160 B1
Charter Way OX10 .... 221 E4
Charterville Cl OX8 .... 102 C1
Chartwell Dr OX7 .... 73 E2
Charvil La RG4 .... 260 C2
Chatham Rd OX1 .... 141 E3
Chatsworth Cl RG4 .... 259 E3
Chatsworth Dr OX16 .... 16 C2
Chatterpie La OX8 .... 89 F3
Chaucer Cl Bicester OX6 .... 65 E2
Chaucer St OX4 .... 141 F4
Chaucer's La OX20 .... 91 D3
Chaundy Rd OX5 .... 77 E3
Chaunterell Way OX14 .... 179 E3
Chawley La OX2 .... 140 A3
Chazey Cl RG4 .... 258 B4
Chazey Rd RG4 .... 258 B2
Chearsley Rd HP18 .... 129 F4
Cheatle Cl OX18 .... 100 C2
Checker Wlk OX14 .... 179 F4
Chedworth Dr OX8 .... 117 F4
Chelford Way RG4 .... 258 C2
Chelmscot Row OX10 .... 10 C4
Chelsea Cl RG30 .... 257 F1
Cheney Gdns OX17 .... 10 C1
Cheney La OX3 .... 124 A1
Cheney Rd OX16 .... 16 C2
Cheney Wlk OX14 .... 159 F1
Chepstow Gdns OX16 .... 15 F3
Chepstow Rd RG31 .... 257 E1
Chequers Pl
  Cholsey OX10 .... 220 C1
  Oxford OX3 .... 124 C2
Cherbury Green OX12 .... 214 B4
Cheriton Pl RG4 .... 252 C2
Cherry Cl Caversham RG4 .... 259 E4
  Kidlington OX5 .... 108 C4
  Sandford-on-T OX4 .... 142 C1
  Stratton Audley OX6 .... 52 B1
  Warborough OX10 .... 203 D3
Cherry Orch SN6 .... 190 A3
Cherry Orchard La SN6 .... 190 A3
Cherry Rd OX16 .... 16 A4
Cherry St OX16 .... 52 B1
Cherry Tree Cl Grove OX12 .... 214 C4
  Kingston Bagpuize OX13 .... 176 B4
Cherry Tree Ct OX9 .... 168 B3
Cherrys Cl OX15 .... 21 E2
Cherwell Ave OX5 .... 109 D4
Cherwell Bank RG6 .... 260 C1
Cherwell Business Centre
  OX5 .... 92 B1
Cherwell Cl
  Abingdon OX14 .... 160 A1
  Bicester OX6 .... 65 E1
  Didcot OX11 .... 200 C2
  Wallingford OX10 .... 221 E4

Cherwell Rd
  Berinsfield OX10 .... 182 B3
  Caversham RG4 .... 259 D3
Cherwell St Banbury OX16 .... 16 B4
  Oxford OX4 .... 123 F1
Cheshire Dr OX6 .... 63 E4
Cheshire Rd OX9 .... 148 B4
Chester St Caversham RG4 .... 259 D1
  Oxford OX4 .... 141 F4
Chester Way OX16 .... 15 F3
Chestnut Ave
  Caversham RG4 .... 259 F2
  Faringdon SN7 .... 172 C2
  Oxford OX3 .... 124 B2
  Radley OX14 .... 160 C2
  Thame OX9 .... 147 F4
Chestnut Cl Bix RG9 .... 243 F4
  Chesterton OX6 .... 80 A4
  Launton OX6 .... 66 B1
  Witney OX8 .... 104 A1
Chestnut Dr OX7 .... 71 D1
Chestnut End OX6 .... 65 F3
Chestnut Gr RG8 .... 257 E3
Chestnut Pl OX9 .... 186 A1
Chestnut The
  Abingdon OX14 .... 160 B1
  Benson OX10 .... 203 F2
  N Hinksey Vill OX2 .... 140 B4
Chestnut Tree Cl OX13 .... 159 E1
Chestnuts The
  Abingdon OX14 .... 160 B1
  Berinsfield OX10 .... 116 B2
  Deddington OX15 .... 34 C2
  Kirtlington OX5 .... 78 A2
  Shiplake RG9 .... 255 D2
  Wantage OX12 .... 214 C3
Chetwode OX16, OX17 .... 16 A4
Chetwyn Mead OX18 .... 134 C2
Cheviot Way OX16 .... 8 C1
Cheyne La OX15 .... 34 C2
Chibnall Cl OX44 .... 184 B3
Chichester Cl OX6 .... 65 F1
Chichester Pl OX18 .... 116 B2
Chichester Wlk OX16 .... 9 D1
Chiers Dr OX14 .... 179 E1
Chilbridge Rd OX8 .... 120 B4
Chilbrook OX11 .... 217 F3
Childrey Way
  Abingdon OX14 .... 160 A1
  East Challow OX12 .... 213 F2
Chilgrove Dr OX6 .... 49 F1
Chillingworth Cres OX3 .... 142 C4
Chilswell La
  Sunningwell OX1 .... 141 D1
  Wootton (Oxford) OX1 .... 140 C2
Chilswell Rd OX1 .... 141 E4
Chiltern Bsns Ctr OX4 .... 142 C2
Chiltern Cl Benson OX10 .... 203 F3
  Berinsfield OX10 .... 182 B3
  Chalgrove OX44 .... 184 C3
  Henley-on-T RG9 .... 254 A4
Chiltern Cres OX10 .... 221 D4
Chiltern Gdns OX9 .... 186 B1
Chiltern Gr OX9 .... 148 A4
Chiltern Rd
  Caversham RG4 .... 259 E2
  Rotherfield Peppard RG9 .... 252 C4
Chiltern Ridge HP14 .... 188 B2
Chiltern View
  Little Milton OX44 .... 164 A4
  Purley on T RG8 .... 257 E3
  Tetsworth OX9 .... 166 A4
Chiltern Wlk RG8 .... 256 C3
Chilton Cl OX14 .... 160 A1
Chilton Rd
  Long Crendon HP18 .... 129 E4
  Upton OX11 .... 218 A1
Chilworth Rd OX44 .... 145 E2
Chinalls Cl NN13 .... 24 A3
Chinnock Brook OX11 .... 200 C2
Chinnor Hill OX9 .... 168 C2
Chinnor Rd
  Aston Rowant OX9 .... 167 E1
  Bledlow Ridge HP14 .... 169 E2
  Chinnor OX9 .... 168 A2
  Thame OX9 .... 148 B3
  Towersey OX9 .... 148 C4
Chipmunk Rd OX10 .... 204 B2
Chipperfield Park Rd
  OX15 .... 21 F3
Chipping Norton Rd
  Chadlington OX7 .... 57 D2
  Hook Norton OX15 .... 30 A4
Choicehill Rd OX7 .... 42 C3
Cholsey Cl OX4 .... 142 B2
Cholswell Rd OX13 .... 159 E1
Chorefields OX5 .... 92 B1
Choswell Spring OX4 .... 142 C1
Chowns Cl OX3 .... 123 E2
Christchurch Cl OX16 .... 16 B3
Church Ave
  Henley-on-T RG9 .... 244 C1
  Kings Sutton OX17 .... 23 F3
Church Cl Adderbury OX17 .... 23 D2
  Ascott-u-W OX7 .... 71 D1
  Benson OX10 .... 203 F2
  Black Bourton OX18 .... 133 F3
  Charlbury OX7 .... 73 D2
  Cuddesdon OX44 .... 144 B2
  Cumnor OX2 .... 121 E1
  East Hagbourne OX11 .... 218 C3
  Fringford OX6 .... 52 B4
  Great Bourton OX17 .... 9 E4
  Islip OX5 .... 93 F1
  Longcot SN7 .... 192 B1
  Merton OX6 .... 95 E4
  Wardington OX17 .... 5 F2
  Weston-on-the-G OX6 .... 79 D1

Church Cowley Rd OX4 ..... 142 A3
Church End
Blewbury OX11 .... 219 D1
Croughton NN13 .... 36 B4
Drayton St L OX10 .... 183 D3
South Leigh OX8 .... 119 E3
Standlake OX8 .... 137 E2
Church Fields OX8 .... 89 E4
Church Furlong OX15 .... 20 B4
Church Green
Long Crendon HP18 .... 129 E4
Stanford in the V SN7 .... 194 C4
Witney OX8 .... 118 A4
Church Hill Chilton OX11 ..... 235 E4
Great Haseley OX44 .... 164 C4
Little Milton OX44 .... 163 F3
Stonor RG9 .... 225 E4
Tackley OX5 .... 77 D3
Warmington OX17 .... 3 D2
Church Hill Rd OX4 .... 142 A2
Church La Adderbury OX17 .... 23 D2
Aston Rowant OX9 .... 167 E2
Banbury OX15, OX16, OX17 .... 16 B3
Bicester OX6 .... 65 F1
Bishopstone SN6 .... 227 E2
Bledington OX7 .... 54 B1
Bledlow Ridge HP14 .... 189 F4
Bledlow Ridge HP14 .... 189 E4
Brackley NN13 .... 24 B1
Brightwell-cum-S OX10 .... 202 C2
Burford OX18 .... 100 C3
Cassington OX8 .... 107 E1
Chacombe OX17 .... 10 C2
Chalgrove OX44 .... 184 B3
Charlbury OX7 .... 73 D2
Charlton-on-O OX5 .... 95 D2
Chinnor OX9 .... 168 B3
Chipping Norton OX7 .... 42 C2
Coleshill SN6 .... 191 D4
Croughton NN13 .... 36 B4
Crowmarsh G OX10 .... 221 E1
Drayton OX14 .... 179 E1
Drayton St L OX10 .... 183 D3
Ewelme RG9 .... 206 A1
Fernham SN7 .... 193 D2
Fringford OX6 .... 52 B4
Fulbrook OX18 .... 100 C3
Hailey OX8 .... 104 A3
Hampton Poyle OX5 .... 93 D2
Hanwell OX17 .... 8 C2
Harwell OX11 .... 217 F4
Hornton OX15 .... 7 E3
Horton-cum-S OX33 .... 112 A3
Islip OX5 .... 93 F1
Kirtlington OX5 .... 78 A2
Langford GL7 .... 132 B1
Longworth OX13 .... 156 A2
Lower Heyford OX6 .... 62 B3
Ludgershall HP18 .... 98 B4
Marston OX3 .... 123 F3
Middle Barton OX7 .... 61 D4
Middleton Cheney OX17 .... 10 C1
Milcombe OX15 .... 21 D1
Mixbury OX6 .... 38 C4
Mollington OX17 .... 4 A2
Rotherfield Peppard RG9 ..... 253 D4
Shilton OX18 .... 115 D3
Shiplake RG9 .... 254 C1
South Moreton OX11 .... 219 F3
Steventon OX13 .... 198 C2
Towersey OX9 .... 148 C4
Wallingford OX10 .... 221 E4
Watlington OX9 .... 186 A2
Wendlebury OX6 .... 80 A2
Weston-on-the-G OX6 .... 79 D1
Witney OX8 .... 118 B4
Yarnton OX5 .... 108 A2
Church Meadow OX7 .... 70 A1
Church Mews RG8 .... 257 E3
Church Mill Cl OX8 .... 137 E2
Church Path
Stanford in the V SN7 .... 194 C4
Stokenchurch HP14 .... 188 B3
Church Pl GL56 .... 54 A4
Church Rd Appleton OX13 ... 158 A4
Ardley OX6 .... 50 B2
Benson OX10 .... 203 F2
Brackley NN13 .... 24 A4
Caversham RG4 .... 259 D1
Chadlington OX7 .... 57 E1
Chinnor OX9 .... 168 B3
Cholsey OX10 .... 220 C2
Great Milton OX44 .... 145 D1
Hinton Waldrist SN7 .... 155 F1
Horspath OX33 .... 143 E3
Ickford HP18 .... 127 F2
Lewknor OX9 .... 187 D4
Long Hanborough OX8 .... 106 B4
Lower Odington GL56 .... 54 A4
Milton-u-W OX7 .... 70 A1
North Leigh OX8 .... 105 D4
Pangbourne RG8 .... 256 B3
Radley OX14 .... 160 C2
Sandford-on-T OX4 .... 161 D4
Stokenchurch HP14 .... 188 B3
Thame OX9 .... 129 F1
Weston-on-the-G OX6 .... 79 D1
Wheatley OX33 .... 144 A4
Church Rise OX7 .... 88 B3
Church Row
Bishopstone SN6 .... 227 D2
Childrey OX12 .... 213 E2
Church Sq OX5 .... 93 F1
Church St Ardington OX12 ... 215 F3
Bampton OX18 .... 134 C2
Barford St M OX15 .... 32 C3
Beckley OX3 .... 111 D2
Bicester OX6 .... 65 F1
Church St continued
Bladon OX20 .... 91 D1
Bledington OX7 .... 54 B1
Blewbury OX11 .... 237 D4
Bloxham OX15 .... 21 E2
Bodicote OX15 .... 22 C4
Caversham RG4 .... 259 D1
Charlbury OX7 .... 73 D2
Chipping Norton OX7 .... 42 C2
Deddington OX15 .... 33 F2
Didcot OX11 .... 218 C4
Ducklington OX8 .... 118 A2
East Hendred OX12 .... 216 B3
Eynsham OX8 .... 120 C4
Faringdon SN7 .... 172 C2
Fifield OX7 .... 69 D1
Henley-on-T RG9 .... 244 B1
Idbury OX7 .... 69 D2
Kidlington OX5 .... 92 C1
Kingham OX7 .... 55 D2
Marcham OX13 .... 178 B3
Marsh Gibbon OX6 .... 67 F2
Shellingford SN7 .... 193 F4
Shipton-u-W OX7 .... 85 E4
Stokenchurch HP14 .... 188 B3
Stonesfield OX8 .... 89 E4
Sutton Courtenay OX14 .... 180 A1
Upper Heyford OX6 .... 48 C3
Upton OX11 .... 218 B1
Wantage OX12 .... 214 B2
Wargrave RG10 .... 255 E1
Watlington OX9 .... 186 A1
West Hanney OX12 .... 196 C3
Wootton OX20 .... 75 F2
Wroxton OX15 .... 15 D4
Church View
Ascott-u-W OX7 .... 71 E1
Bampton OX18 .... 134 C2
Banbury OX16 .... 16 A2
Brackley NN13 .... 24 A4
Carterton OX18 .... 115 F1
Charlton-on-O OX5 .... 95 D3
Freeland OX8 .... 106 A3
Stoke Row RG9 .... 241 F3
Church View Rd OX8 .... 117 F4
Church Way
N Hinksey Vill OX2 .... 122 B1
Oxford OX4 .... 141 F2
Sparsholt OX12 .... 212 C2
Church Wlk Banbury OX16 .... 16 B3
Bishopstone SN6 .... 227 E2
Combe OX8 .... 90 A2
Oxford OX2 .... 123 D2
Shipton-u-W OX7 .... 70 B1
Shrivenham SN6 .... 209 E4
Upper Heyford OX6 .... 62 C4
Churchfield RG9 .... 223 E2
Churchfield La OX10 .... 203 F2
Churchill Cl Didcot OX11 ..... 200 B1
Woodstock OX20 .... 91 D3
Churchill Cres OX9 .... 148 A4
Churchill Dr OX3 .... 124 B1
Churchill Gate OX20 .... 91 E3
Churchill Pl OX2 .... 122 C4
Churchill Rd Bicester OX6 ..... 65 F2
Chipping Norton OX7 .... 42 B1
Didcot OX11 .... 200 B1
Kidlington OX5 .... 108 C4
Kingham OX7 .... 55 D4
Churchill Way OX8 .... 106 A4
Churchlea OX17 .... 4 A2
Churchmere Rd OX14 .... 180 A1
Churchward OX11 .... 200 C2
Churchward Cl OX12 .... 196 B1
Churchway RG20 .... 235 D1
Chure The OX5 .... 95 D2
Churnet Cl OX11 .... 201 D1
Cinnaminta Rd OX3 .... 142 C4
Cinnamon Cl OX44 .... 184 B4
Circourt Rd OX12 .... 195 F2
Circular Rd OX6 .... 81 D3
Circus St OX4 .... 141 F4
City Rd HP14 .... 189 E3
Clack's La Benson OX10 .... 222 B4
Crowmarsh G OX10 .... 222 B4
Clanfield Cres RG31 .... 257 E1
Clapcot Way OX10 .... 221 E4
Clare Terr OX18 .... 115 E1
Clarence Pl OX11 .... 218 C4
Clarence Rd RG9 .... 244 B1
Clarendon Cl OX14 .... 180 A4
Clarendon Dr OX9 .... 130 A1
Clarks La CV36 .... 28 A3
Clarkston Rd OX18 .... 115 E1
Clay Bank OX15 .... 30 A4
Clay Cl RG31 .... 257 D1
Clay La OX10 .... 204 B1
Claydon Rd OX17 .... 4 C2
Clayfields SN6 .... 209 D2
Claymond Rd OX3 .... 124 C2
Claypit La SN7 .... 211 D4
Claypits La SN6 .... 209 E4
Clays Cl OX3 .... 124 A3
Cleave The OX11 .... 217 F4
Cleavers OX9 .... 168 A3
Cleavers Sq OX4 .... 142 C1
Cleeve Down RG8 .... 249 E4
Cleeve Rd RG8 .... 249 D4
Cleeves Ave OX7 .... 42 C3
Cleeves Cnr OX7 .... 42 C3
Clematis Pl OX4 .... 142 C1
Clements Cl OX12 .... 214 C3
Clements Green OX11 .... 219 F3
Clements La OX6 .... 67 F1
Clements Mead RG31 .... 257 D1
Clements Rd RG9 .... 244 B2
Clerkenwell Cotts HP17 ...... 130 C3
Cleve Ct RG8 .... 249 D4
Clevedon Rd RG31 .... 257 F2
Cleveland Cl OX5 .... 109 D4
Cleveland Dr OX4 .... 142 B3
Clevelands OX14 .... 160 A1
Cleveley Rd OX7 .... 58 C3
Clevemede RG8 .... 249 E4
Cleycourt Rd SN6 .... 209 D3
Clifden Rd HP18 .... 127 E3
Clifford Pl OX2 .... 122 B4
Clifton Dr OX14 .... 179 F4
Clifton Rd OX15 .... 34 B2
Clifton Rise RG10 .... 255 F1
Clinton Cl OX4 .... 141 F2
Clive Rd OX4 .... 142 B3
Clock Tower SN7 .... 172 C1
Cloisters The
Caversham RG4 .... 259 D2
Wantage OX12 .... 214 B2
Close The Ardington OX12 .... 215 F3
Benson OX10 .... 203 F3
Chipping Warden OX17 .... 5 F3
Epwell OX15 .... 13 D3
Great Bourton OX17 .... 9 E4
Henley-on-T RG9 .... 254 B4
Lechlade GL7 .... 150 B3
Stanton Harcourt OX8 .... 138 A4
Woodcote RG8 .... 250 C4
Closes The OX5 .... 92 C1
Clover Cl OX2 .... 140 A3
Clover Pl Eynsham OX8 .... 120 B4
Oxford OX4 .... 142 C1
Coach La SN7 .... 173 D2
Coach Way OX10 .... 203 F2
Coalport Way RG30 .... 257 F1
Coates La RG9 .... 206 B1
Cobden Cres OX1 .... 141 E4
Cochrane Rd OX10 .... 204 B1
Cockcroft Rd OX11 .... 218 C4
Cockington Green OX16 .... 16 C4
Cockpit Cl OX20 .... 91 D3
Cocks La OX33 .... 125 E4
Cockshoot Cl OX8 .... 89 E4
Cogges Hill Rd OX8 .... 118 B4
Coghill OX5 .... 93 D4
Coker Cl OX6 .... 65 F1
Colborne Rd OX11 .... 218 B4
Coldharbour Cl RG9 .... 254 B4
Coldicutt St RG4 .... 259 E1
Cole Ct OX11 .... 200 C2
Colegrave Rd OX15 .... 21 F3
Colegrove Down OX2 .... 140 A3
Colemans Hill OX3 .... 124 C2
Coleridge Cl Bicester OX6 ..... 65 D2
Oxford OX4 .... 142 B3
Coleridge Dr OX14 .... 179 E3
Colerne Rd OX18 .... 115 F2
Coles La OX44 .... 184 B4
Colesbourne Rd OX15 .... 21 E2
Collcutt Cl OX33 .... 143 E4
College Cl Cholsey OX10 ..... 220 C1
Holton OX33 .... 126 B1
College Farm OX7 .... 57 D1
College Farm Cl OX5 .... 94 C2
College La Oxford OX4 .... 123 E1
Oxford, Littlemore OX4 .... 142 A1
College The OX18 .... 101 F2
College Way OX33 .... 143 D3
Collett OX11 .... 200 C2
Collett Way OX12 .... 196 B1
Colley Wood OX1 .... 141 F1
Collice St OX5 .... 109 F4
Collier's La SN7 .... 173 D2
Collingwood Cl OX14 .... 159 F1
Collingwood Rd OX11 .... 218 B4
Collins St OX4 .... 141 F4
Collinsmith Dr OX12 .... 196 C1
Collinsons Row OX7 .... 73 D2
Collinwood Cl OX3 .... 124 C2
Collinwood Rd OX3 .... 124 C2
Collyer Rd HP14 .... 188 C2
Colmore La RG9 .... 252 C4
Coln Rd OX11 .... 217 D2
Colne Cl Bicester OX6 .... 65 E1
Grove OX12 .... 196 B1
Colne Dr Berinsfield OX10 .... 182 B3
Didcot OX11 .... 201 D2
Colony Rd OX15 .... 19 D4
Colterne Cl OX3 .... 124 A3
Coltman Ave HP18 .... 129 E3
Colton Rd SN6 .... 209 D3
Coltsfoot Sq 5 OX4 .... 142 C1
Columbia Way OX12 .... 214 B4
Columbine Gdns OX4 .... 143 D1
Colvile Cl OX18 .... 134 C2
Colwell Dr Abingdon OX14 ... 179 E4
Oxford OX3 .... 125 D2
Witney OX8 .... 117 F3
Colwell Rd OX10 .... 182 B3
Colyton Way RG8 .... 257 E3
Combe Gate OX8 .... 90 A2
Combe Rd Oxford OX2 .... 123 D1
Stonesfield OX8 .... 89 E4
Combes Cl SN7 .... 173 D2
Combewell OX44 .... 143 E1
Comfrey Rd OX4 .... 142 C2
Common Cl
North Leigh OX8 .... 105 D3
Shrivenham SN6 .... 209 E4
Common La OX7 .... 42 B1
Common Rd Beckley OX3 ..... 110 C2
North Leigh OX8 .... 105 D3
Compass Cl OX4 .... 142 B2
Compton Ave RG31 .... 257 D3
Compton Ct OX14 .... 27 F4
Compton Dr OX14 .... 160 A1
Compton Rd OX16 .... 16 B3
Compton Terr OX10 .... 221 E4
Condor Cl RG31 .... 257 E2
Conduit Hill Rise OX9 .... 147 F4
Conduit Rd OX14 .... 179 F4
Conifer Cl OX2 .... 140 B4
Conifer Dr Bicester OX6 .... 65 F3
Reading RG31 .... 257 D1
Conifer Rise OX16 .... 9 D1
Conigre OX9 .... 168 A3
Conisboro Ave RG4 .... 258 C3
Conisboro Way RG4 .... 258 C3
Coniston Ave OX3 .... 124 A2
Coniston Dr RG30 .... 257 F1
Connolly Dr OX18 .... 115 E2
Constable's Croft OX6 .... 96 C4
Constitution Hill OX10 .... 221 F2
Conway Dr OX16 .... 15 F3
Conway Rd OX13 .... 159 E1
Conyger Cl OX5 .... 93 F1
Cook La OX10 .... 221 F1
Cook's Hill OX15 .... 14 A3
Cooks La OX7 .... 41 F3
Coolidge Cl OX3 .... 124 B1
Coombe Hill Cres OX9 .... 147 F4
Coombe The RG8 .... 248 C3
Coombes Cl OX7 .... 85 E4
Cooper Cl OX7 .... 42 C2
Cooper Pl OX3 .... 124 C2
Cooper Rd RG9 .... 244 B2
Cooper's Court Rd HP14 .... 188 B3
Coopers Gate OX16 .... 16 B4
Coopers Gn OX6 .... 65 F3
Coopers La OX12 .... 214 C3
Coopers Pightle RG4 .... 252 B2
Cope Cl OX2 .... 140 B4
Cope Rd OX16 .... 16 B3
Copenhagen Dr OX13 .... 159 E1
Copperage Rd OX11 .... 234 A1
Coppice Cl OX16 .... 16 C2
Coppock Cl OX3 .... 124 C1
Coppperfield Cl OX12 .... 214 B3
Copse Ave RG4 .... 259 F2
Copse Cl RG31 .... 257 E2
Copse La OX3 .... 124 A3
Copse Mead RG5 .... 260 C1
Copse The Abingdon OX14 ... 160 B1
Wargrave RG10 .... 255 F2
Copson La OX44 .... 163 E1
Copthorne Rd OX5 .... 108 C4
Corbett Rd OX18 .... 115 E1
Cordrey Green OX4 .... 141 F2
Corfe Mews RG4 .... 259 F2
Coriander Way 4 OX4 .... 142 C1
Corn Avill Cl OX14 .... 160 B1
Corn Bar OX8 .... 117 F4
Corn St OX8 .... 118 A4
Corndell Gdns OX8 .... 118 A4
Corneville Rd OX14 .... 179 D1
Cornfield Cl OX8 .... 117 F4
Cornish Rd OX7 .... 42 B1
Cornmarket
Faringdon SN7 .... 172 C2
Thame OX9 .... 147 F4
Cornmarket St OX1 .... 123 E1
Cornwall Cl RG31 .... 257 D2
Cornwallis Cl OX4 .... 142 A3
Cornwallis Rd OX4 .... 142 A3
Coromandel OX14 .... 179 E2
Corunna Cres OX4 .... 142 C3
Cosford Gdns OX6 .... 66 A2
Costar Cl OX4 .... 142 B1
Cot's Gn OX5 .... 92 B1
Cote Rd OX18 .... 135 F2
Cothill Rd OX13 .... 158 C2
Cotman Cl OX14 .... 179 F3
Cotmore Cl OX9 .... 148 A4
Cotmore Gdns OX9 .... 148 A4
Cotshill Gdns OX7 .... 42 C2
Cotswold Cl
Minster Lovell OX8 .... 102 C1
Sibford Ferris OX15 .... 19 D4
Cotswold Cnr OX7 .... 29 D2
Cotswold Cres
Chipping Norton OX7 .... 42 C1
Marston OX3 .... 123 F3
Cotswold Cres Bglws OX7 . 42 C1
Cotswold Meadow OX8 ...... 117 E4
Cotswold Pk OX11 .... 200 B1
Cotswold Rd OX2 .... 140 A3
Cotswold Terr OX7 .... 42 C1
Cotswold View OX7 .... 73 D2
Cotswold Way
Carterton OX18 .... 115 E2
Reading RG31 .... 257 E1
Cottage Rd SN7 .... 194 B4
Cottages The GL7 .... 114 A3
Cottesmore La OX10 .... 204 B3
Cottesmore Rd OX4 .... 142 A2
Cotton Grass Cl OX4 .... 142 C1
Couching St OX9 .... 186 A1
Coulings Cl OX12 .... 216 B4
Council Houses OX7 .... 45 E4
County Rd NN13 .... 24 A3
County Trading Est OX4 ... 142 C2
County View OX15 .... 34 B2
Coupland Rd OX13 .... 159 D3
Court Cl Kidlington OX5 .... 108 B4
Shipton-u-W OX7 .... 85 E4
Warmington OX17 .... 3 D2
Court Close Rd OX9 .... 148 C4
Court Dr OX10 .... 203 D3
Court Farm Rd OX4 .... 141 F2
Court Hill Rd OX12 .... 214 A1
Court Place Gdns OX4 .... 141 F2
Court Rd OX12 .... 214 A1
Court The OX14 .... 159 F1
Courtenay Cl OX14 .... 200 A4
Courtenay Dr RG4 .... 259 D4
Courtenay Rd OX12 .... 214 C3
Courtfield Rd OX33 .... 125 E4
Courthouse HP18 .... 129 E4
Courtiers Green OX14 .... 181 E2
Courtington La OX15 .... 21 E3
Courtland Rd OX4 .... 142 A2
Courtlands Hill RG8 .... 256 B2
Courtlands Rd OX7 .... 85 E4
Courts Gdns OX8 .... 118 B4
Covent Cl OX14 .... 160 A2
Coverley Rd OX3 .... 142 B4
Covert The OX20 .... 91 E3
Cow La Denchworth OX12 .... 195 F2
Didcot OX11 .... 201 D1
Grove OX12 .... 196 C2
Kennington OX1 .... 141 F1
Longworth OX13 .... 156 B2
Moulsford OX10 .... 238 C2
Reading RG1 .... 258 C1
Steeple Aston OX6 .... 62 A4
Cowell Pl OX8 .... 118 A4
Cowleaze OX9 .... 168 A3
Cowleaze Cl SN6 .... 209 D3
Cowley Junc OX4 .... 142 C2
Cowley Pl OX4 .... 141 F4
Cowley Rd Oxford OX4 .... 142 A2
Oxford, Littlemore OX4 .... 142 A4
Cowper Cl OX6 .... 65 D2
Cox La OX7 .... 42 A1
Cox's Alley OX3 .... 124 C2
Cox's La
Crowmarsh G OX10 .... 222 A3
Stoke Row RG9 .... 241 F3
Cox's Rd SN6 .... 209 D3
Coxfield Cl HP14 .... 188 C3
Coxmoor Cl OX7 .... 54 C2
Coxwell Gdns SN7 .... 172 C2
Coxwell Hall Mews SN7 .... 172 C1
Coxwell Rd SN7 .... 172 C1
Coxwell St SN7 .... 172 C2
Cozens La OX7 .... 54 C2
CR Bates Ind Est HP14 ...... 188 C3
Crabhill La OX12 .... 215 D4
Crabtree Cnr OX10 .... 240 B4
Crabtree La OX14 .... 179 D1
Crabtree Pl OX14 .... 180 A4
Crabtree Rd
Haddenham HP17 .... 130 C3
N Hinksey Vill OX2 .... 140 B4
Crafts End OX11 .... 235 F4
Cranbourne Gdns RG30 ..... 258 A1
Cranbrook Ct OX8 .... 118 A3
Cranbrook Dr OX1 .... 160 C4
Crane Furlong SN6 .... 190 A4
Cranesbill Way OX4 .... 142 C1
Cranham St OX2 .... 123 D2
Cranham Terr OX2 .... 123 D2
Cranleigh Cl OX16 .... 16 A2
Cranley Rd OX3 .... 124 C2
Cranmer Cl RG31 .... 257 D2
Cranmer Rd OX4 .... 142 C3
Cranwell Ave OX18 .... 115 F1
Cratlands Cl OX44 .... 163 E1
Craufurd Rd OX4 .... 142 C3
Craven Comm SN7 .... 211 E4
Craven Way OX11 .... 218 C4
Crawborough Rd OX7 .... 73 E2
Crawley Rd OX8 .... 104 A1
Crawshay Dr RG4 .... 259 D4
Cray Ct OX11 .... 200 C2
Creampot Cl OX17 .... 4 C1
Creampot Cres OX17 .... 4 C1
Creampot La OX17 .... 4 C1
Crecy Wlk OX20 .... 91 E3
Cremyll Rd RG1 .... 258 C1
Crescent Cl OX4 .... 142 B3
Crescent Rd Oxford OX4 ..... 142 B3
Reading RG31 .... 257 E1
Crescent The
Adderbury OX17 .... 23 D3
Bicester OX6 .... 65 E2
Carterton OX18 .... 133 E4
Sandford-on-T OX4 .... 161 E4
Shiplake RG9 .... 255 D2
Steeple Aston OX6 .... 62 A4
Witney OX8 .... 104 B1
Crescent Way OX10 .... 220 C1
Cress Hill Pl OX3 .... 124 C2
Crest The
Bledlow Ridge HP14 .... 189 F4
Caversham RG4 .... 259 E3
Crick Rd OX2 .... 123 E2
Cricket Ground HP14 .... 188 B3
Cricket Rd OX4 .... 142 A3
Cricklade Rd SN6 .... 190 A3
Cripley Pl OX2 .... 123 D1
Cripley Rd OX2 .... 123 D1
Crisp Rd RG9 .... 244 B2
Crispin Cl RG4 .... 258 B3
Crispin Pl OX10 .... 221 E4
Croasdell Cl OX14 .... 179 F2
Crockwell Cl OX6 .... 65 F1
Crockwell St CV36 .... 27 F4
Croft Ave OX5 .... 108 C4
Croft Cl Merton OX6 .... 95 E4
Oxford OX3 .... 123 F2
Thame OX9 .... 148 A4
Croft Ctyd HP17 .... 130 C3
Croft End OX12 .... 214 A1
Croft La OX17 .... 23 D2
Croft Rd Goring RG8 .... 249 E3
Oxford OX3 .... 123 F2
Thame OX9 .... 148 A4
Wallingford OX10 .... 221 E4
Croft The
Aston Tirrold OX11 .... 219 F1
Didcot OX11 .... 218 C4

Croft The continued
East Hagbourne OX11 .... 218 C3
Haddenham HP17 .... 130 C3
Harwell OX11 .... 217 F4
Oxford OX3, OX44 .... 124 B2
West Hanney OX12 .... 196 C4
Croft Way RG8 .... 250 C4
Croft's La OX15 .... 30 A3
Crofts The OX8 .... 118 A4
Cromer Cl RG31 .... 257 E1
Cromwell Ave OX9 .... 130 A1
Cromwell Cl
 Chalgrove OX44 .... 184 C3
 Farrington SN7 .... 173 D2
 Henley-on-T RG9 .... 254 C4
 Marston OX3 .... 123 F2
Cromwell Dr OX11 .... 219 D4
Cromwell Park OX7 .... 42 C2
Cromwell Rd
 Banbury OX16 .... 16 A3
 Caversham RG4 .... 259 D1
 Henley-on-T RG9 .... 254 C4
Cromwell St OX4 .... 141 E4
Cromwell Way OX5 .... 109 D4
Cronshaw Cl OX11 .... 200 C1
Crookdale Beck OX11 .... 201 D2
Croom Cotts OX11 .... 217 D4
Cross Ave OX10 .... 204 B1
Cross Cl OX10 .... 204 C1
Cross Hill Rd OX17 .... 22 C2
Cross Keys Rd RG8 .... 239 E2
Cross Leys OX7 .... 42 C1
Cross Rd OX10 .... 220 C1
Cross St OX4 .... 141 F4
Cross Tree La GL7 .... 132 A3
Cross's La OX7 .... 56 C1
Crosslands OX6 .... 52 B3
Crosslands Dr OX14 .... 159 F1
Crossville Cres OX11 .... 200 B1
Crossway OX4 .... 60 C4
Crotch Cres OX3 .... 124 A2
Crouch Hill Rd OX6 .... 16 A2
Crouch St OX16 .... 16 B3
Croughton Rd OX17 .... 35 E4
Crow La OX17 .... 9 E4
Crowberry Rd OX4 .... 142 C1
Crowell Rd OX4 .... 142 B2
Crowmarsh Hill OX10 .... 222 A3
Crowmarsh Rd OX6 .... 64 C3
Crown La Benson OX10 .... 203 F2
 South Moreton OX11 .... 220 A3
Crown Mews OX14 .... 179 F4
Crown Rd Kidlington OX5 .... 108 B4
 Wheatley OX33 .... 144 A4
Crown Sq OX10 .... 204 A2
Crown St OX4 .... 141 F4
Crown Wlk OX6 .... 65 F1
Crowsley Rd RG9 .... 255 D2
Crowsley Way RG4 .... 252 C3
Croxford Gdns OX5 .... 108 C3
Crozier Cl OX2 .... 140 B4
Crumps Butts OX16 .... 65 F1
Crutch Furlong OX10 .... 182 B3
Crutchmore Cres OX5 .... 78 A2
Cuckamus La OX8 .... 105 D3
Cuckoo Cl OX6 .... 65 F3
Cuckoo La Eynsham OX8 .... 106 A2
 Freeland OX8 .... 106 A2
Cuddesdon Cl RG8 .... 250 C4
Cuddesdon Rd OX33 .... 143 F3
Cuddesdon Way OX4 .... 142 C1
Cues La SN6 .... 227 E2
Culham Cl OX14 .... 160 A1
Cullerne Cl OX14 .... 160 A2
Cullerns The SN6 .... 190 A3
Cullum Rd OX33 .... 144 B4
Culworth Rd OX17 .... 5 F3
Cumberford OX15 .... 21 E2
Cumberford Cl OX15 .... 21 E2
Cumberford Hill OX15 .... 21 E2
Cumberland Rd OX4 .... 142 A4
Cumberlege Cl OX3 .... 123 F3
Cummings Cl OX3 .... 124 C1
Cumnor Hill Cumnor OX2 ... 140 A4
 N Hinksey Vill OX2 .... 140 A4
Cumnor Rd Cumnor OX2 .... 139 E4
 Wootton (Oxford) OX13 ..... 159 D4
Cumnor Rise Rd OX2 .... 140 B4
Cunliffe Cl OX2 .... 123 E3
Cup & Saucer OX17 .... 4 C1
Curbridge Rd
 Ducklington OX8 .... 118 A2
 Witney OX8 .... 117 F4
Curie Ave OX11 .... 217 D2
Cursus The GL7 .... 150 B3
Curtis Ave OX14 .... 180 A4
Curtis Rd Kidlington OX5 ..... 92 C1
 Shrivenham SN6 .... 209 D3
Curtiss Cl OX6 .... 66 A2
Curtyn Cl OX14 .... 179 E4
Curzon Gate Ct HP14 .... 188 C3
Cuthwine P1 GL7 .... 150 B3
Cuttesowe Rdbt OX2 .... 109 D1
Cuttlebrook Gdns OX9 .... 129 F1
Cuxham Rd OX9 .... 186 A1
Cwmcarn Rd OX16 .... 258 C3
Cygnet Cl OX6 .... 166 A4
Cypress Gdns OX6 .... 65 F3

Dacey Dr OX6 .... 63 D4
Dacre Ave RG4 .... 259 F2
Daedings The OX15 .... 33 F2
Dagdale Dr OX11 .... 200 C2
Daimler Ave OX16 .... 15 F4

Dairy Meadow OX13 .... 177 E3
Dairyground The OX15 .... 14 A3
Daisy Bank OX14 .... 180 A4
Dale Cl Brackley NN13 .... 24 A4
 Oxford OX1 .... 141 D4
Dale Pl OX5 .... 92 C1
Dale Wlk OX8 .... 118 A3
Dalton Ave OX11 .... 217 D1
Damer Gdns RG9 .... 254 C4
Damson Trees SN6 .... 209 D3
Dancers Hill OX7 .... 73 E3
Danes Rd OX6 .... 65 E1
Danesmoor OX16 .... 16 A4
Danvers Cl OX15 .... 15 E1
Danvers Rd
 Broughton OX15 .... 15 E1
 Oxford OX4 .... 142 A2
Darell Rd RG4 .... 258 C2
Darent Pl OX11 .... 201 D1
Dark La Reading RG31 .... 257 D1
 Sunningwell OX13 .... 159 F3
 Wargrave RG10 .... 255 E1
 Witney OX8 .... 104 A1
 Wroxton OX15 .... 15 D4
Darrell Way OX14 .... 159 F1
Dart Dr OX11 .... 200 C2
Dart Rd OX13 .... 159 E2
Dashwood Ave OX5 .... 108 A3
Dashwood Mews OX5 .... 77 F2
Dashwood Rd
 Banbury OX16 .... 16 B3
 Oxford OX4 .... 142 A2
Dashwood Rise OX6 .... 47 E3
Datchet Gn OX10 .... 202 C1
Daubeny Rd OX4 .... 141 F3
Daubigny Mead OX18 .... 116 B2
Davenant Rd OX2 .... 123 D4
Davenant Rd OX8 .... 103 F1
Daventry Rd OX16 .... 16 C4
David Nicholls Cl OX4 .... 142 A1
David Walter Cl OX2 .... 109 D1
Davis Cl OX18 .... 115 F1
Davis Gdns OX6 .... 65 F1
Davis Cl OX7 .... 71 D1
Dawson Pl OX2 .... 123 D1
Dawson St OX4 .... 141 F4
Day's La OX10 .... 204 C1
Days Ground SN6 .... 209 E4
De Havilland Rd GL54 .... 68 A3
De Montfort Rd RG1 .... 259 D1
De Vitre Pl OX12 .... 214 B4
Deacon Way Banbury OX16 . 16 A3
 Reading RG30 .... 258 A1
Deaconfield RG8 .... 239 E2
Deadman's La RG8 .... 251 E2
Deafort Cl OX5 .... 92 C1
Dean Butler Cl OX12 .... 214 B3
Dean Cl OX16 .... 16 C4
Dean Court Rd OX2 .... 140 A4
Dean Wood Cl RG8 .... 240 C1
Deanes Cl OX13 .... 198 C2
Deanfield Ave RG9 .... 244 B1
Deanfield Rd
 Henley-on-T RG9 .... 244 B1
 N Hinksey Vill OX2 .... 122 A1
Deans Ct OX6 .... 65 F1
Dearlove Cl OX14 .... 159 F1
Deddington Hill OX15 .... 33 F3
Deene Cl OX13 .... 23 D2
Deer Park Rd OX8 .... 117 E4
Deer Wlk OX44 .... 142 C1
Deer's Farm OX15 .... 22 C4
Deer's La RG8 .... 241 E1
Deers Cl OX15 .... 22 C4
Defiant Cl OX6 .... 66 A2
Delafield Cl HP14 .... 188 C2
Delamere Way OX2 .... 140 A4
Delapre Dr OX16 .... 16 C4
Dell Rd RG31 .... 257 E1
Delly Cl OX8 .... 104 A4
Denbigh Cl OX16 .... 16 C4
Denbigh Rd OX9 .... 130 A1
Denby Way RG30 .... 257 F1
Denchfield Rd OX16 .... 16 B1
Denchworth Rd
 Grove OX12 .... 196 B1
 Wantage OX12 .... 214 B3
Dene Hollow OX11 .... 235 F4
Dene Rd OX3 .... 142 B4
Dene Rise OX8 .... 117 F4
Denman's La OX2 .... 139 F3
Denmark St OX4 .... 141 F4
Denton Cl Abingdon OX14 .. 180 A4
 N Hinksey Vill OX2 .... 140 A4
Denton Hill OX44 .... 144 A1
Denton La Cuddesdon OX44 144 A1
 Garsington OX44 .... 143 F1
Dents Cl OX3 .... 124 A3
Derby Rd RG4 .... 259 D2
Derwent Ave Didcot OX11 ... 201 D1
 Oxford OX3 .... 124 A2
 Reading RG30 .... 257 F1
Derwent Cl OX13 .... 159 E1
Derwent Rd OX6 .... 65 E2
Des Roches Sq Ind Est
 OX8 .... 118 A4
Desborough Cres OX4 .... 142 A2
Desmesne Furze OX3 .... 124 B1
Devereux Pl OX4 .... 142 A2
Devil's Hill RG4 .... 253 E3
Devon Cl OX10 .... 204 A2
Devon Dr RG4 .... 259 F2
Devon Pl OX18 .... 115 F1
Devon Way OX16 .... 16 A4
Devonshire Gdns RG31 ...... 257 D2
Dexter Cl OX16 .... 16 B2
Diamond Pl OX2 .... 123 D3
Dickens Cl OX6 .... 65 E2

Dickenson Ct OX7 .... 42 C2
Dickredge The OX6 .... 62 A4
Didcot Rd
 Brightwell-cum-S OX10 ..... 202 B2
 Harwell OX11 .... 218 A4
 Long Wittenham OX14 .... 201 E4
Dido Rd OX11 .... 217 D1
Digberry La RG9 .... 224 B3
Digging La OX13 .... 157 E1
Dirac Pl OX11 .... 219 D4
Diston's La OX7 .... 85 E4
Ditchley Rd OX7 .... 73 F3
Divinity Rd OX4 .... 142 A4
Dobson's La OX9 .... 244 B4
Dobson's La RG9 .... 244 B4
Dodd Dr GL54 .... 68 A2
Dodgson Rd OX4 .... 142 B2
Dodson Ct OX14 .... 179 F4
Doe Lea OX11 .... 200 C2
Dog Cl OX17 .... 22 C2
Dog Kennel La OX7 .... 85 E4
Dog La OX12 .... 213 E2
Doily Cl OX15 .... 30 A4
Dollicot HP17 .... 130 C4
Dolphin La OX18 .... 100 C3
Don Boscoe Cl OX4 .... 142 B3
Don Cl OX11 .... 201 D2
Don Stuart Pl OX4 .... 142 A4
Donegal Cl RG4 .... 259 E2
Donkin Hill RG4 .... 259 E2
Donnington Bridge Rd
 OX4 .... 141 F3
Donnington Cl OX8 .... 117 E4
Donnington Pl OX12 .... 214 B3
Dora Carr Cl OX3 .... 124 A3
Dorchester Cl OX3 .... 124 C1
Dorchester Cres OX14 .... 160 A1
Dorchester Gr OX16 .... 15 F2
Dorchester Pl OX7 .... 147 F4
Dorchester Rd
 Berinsfield OX10 .... 182 C2
 Drayton St L OX10 .... 183 D3
Doris Field Cl OX3 .... 124 A2
Dormer Rd OX9 .... 148 A3
Dormers The SN6 .... 190 A3
Dorn Cl OX7 .... 60 C4
Dorn View OX20 .... 76 A2
Douglas Rd RG4 .... 259 E1
Dove Ct OX18 .... 115 F2
Dove Green OX6 .... 65 D2
Dove House Cl OX2 .... 122 C4
Dove La RG9 .... 252 B4
Dovecote HP17 .... 130 C3
Dovedale Cl RG4 .... 258 C2
Dovehouse Cl OX8 .... 120 C4
Doveleat OX9 .... 168 B4
Dover Ave OX16 .... 15 F3
Dovetrees OX18 .... 115 F2
Down End OX15 .... 30 A4
Downhill La OX8 .... 104 A2
Downlands SN7 .... 192 B1
Downs Cl OX11 .... 217 F3
Downs Rd Aldworth RG20 ... 247 D2
 Curbridge OX8 .... 103 D1
 Didcot OX11 .... 218 B4
 Standlake OX8 .... 137 E3
Downs View SN6 .... 190 A3
Downs Way Chilton OX11 ... 234 C4
 Reading RG31 .... 257 D1
Downside OX11 .... 217 E1
Downside End OX3 .... 125 D2
Downside Rd OX3 .... 125 D2
Downsmead SN8 .... 245 E1
Downsview Rd OX12 .... 214 B4
Doyley Rd Oxford OX2 .... 141 D4
 Wallingford OX10 .... 203 E1
Dragonhill Rd SN7 .... 211 D1
Drake Ave OX11 .... 218 A4
Dray's La RG9 .... 253 D4
Draycott Rd OX13 .... 156 B1
Draymans Croft OX6 .... 65 F1
Drayton Rd
 Abingdon OX14 .... 179 E3
 Dorchester OX10 .... 182 B1
 Milton (Abingdon) OX14 ... 199 F4
Dresden Way RG30 .... 257 F1
Drewitts Cnr OX11 .... 217 F4
Drive The OX7 .... 58 C3
Drivers La GL56 .... 27 D1
Drove Acre Rd OX4 .... 142 A4
Drover's La RG9 .... 226 B4
Droveside OX10 .... 220 C1
Druce Way OX4 .... 142 C2
Druids Wlk Chinnor OX9 ..... 168 B3
 Didcot OX11 .... 200 C1
Dry La Crawley OX8 .... 103 E2
 Curbridge OX8 .... 103 E2
Dryden Ave OX6 .... 65 D2
Drylands Rd OX8 .... 102 C1
Duck End La OX6 .... 120 B1
Duck La HP18 .... 98 B4
Duck Sq OX9 .... 168 B3
Ducklington La OX8 .... 117 F4
Dudgeon Dr OX4 .... 141 F2
Dudley Cl RG31 .... 257 F1
Dudley Gdns OX4 .... 123 F1
Dudley La OX6 .... 226 C4
Dudley Mews RG31 .... 257 F1
Duffield Cl OX14 .... 160 A1
Duffield Pl OX13 .... 178 B4
Duffield Rd RG5 .... 260 C1
Duke of York Ave OX4 .... 199 E2
Duke St Banbury OX16 .... 16 C3
 Henley-on-T RG9 .... 244 C1
 Oxford OX2 .... 141 D4
Dukes Cl HP18 .... 128 B1
Dukes Rd OX6 .... 108 C4

Dulas Cl OX11 .... 200 C1
Dumas Cl OX11 .... 65 E1
Dumbarton Way RG4 .... 259 F3
Dunbar Dr OX9 .... 130 A1
Duncan Cl OX8 .... 120 B4
Duncan Gdns RG8 .... 257 E2
Dundas Cl OX14 .... 180 A4
Dunlin Ct OX6 .... 16 C2
Dunluce Gdns RG8 .... 256 C3
Dunmore Rd OX14 .... 159 F1
Dunnock Way
 Sandford-on-T OX4 .... 142 C1
 Wargrave RG10 .... 255 F2
Dunsden Cl OX11 .... 200 B1
Dunsomer Hill OX11 .... 220 A4
Dunstan Ave OX7 .... 42 C3
Dunstan Rd OX3 .... 124 B2
Dunster Cl RG4 .... 259 E3
Durham Mews OX16 .... 9 D1
Duxford Cl Bicester OX6 ...... 66 A2
 Carterton OX18 .... 115 F2
Dyer Straits OX11 .... 234 C4
Dyer's Hill OX7 .... 73 D2
Dynham Pl OX3 .... 124 B1
Dysonswood La RG4 .... 258 C4

Eady Rd OX6 .... 63 D4
Eagle Ind Est OX8 .... 118 A4
Eagle La SN6 .... 191 E1
Eagle Sq SN7 .... 192 C4
Eagles SN7 .... 172 C2
East Cl OX17 .... 122 C1
Earl's La OX15 .... 23 D2
Earlsfield Cl RG4 .... 259 F2
Earlstoke Cl OX16 .... 16 C4
Early Rd OX8 .... 104 B1
Easington Gdns OX16 .... 16 B2
Easington Rd OX16 .... 16 B2
Eason Dr OX14 .... 160 B1
East Ave OX4 .... 142 A4
East Cl OX16 .... 16 B3
East End OX15 .... 30 A4
East Hawthorn Rd OX6 .... 81 E2
East Lockinge OX12 .... 215 E2
East St Banbury OX15, OX16 16 C4
 Bicester OX6 .... 65 E2
 Bodicote OX15 .... 22 C2
 Didcot OX11 .... 219 D4
 Fritwell OX6 .... 49 F4
 Long Compton CV36 .... 27 F3
 Oxford OX2 .... 123 D1
East St Helen St OX14 .... 179 F3
East View Cl RG10 .... 255 F1
East View Rd RG10 .... 255 F1
East Way OX14 .... 199 D4
Eastbrook Cl OX6 .... 97 F4
Eastbury Ave RG21 .... 257 D3
Eastchurch OX4 .... 141 F2
Eastfield OX12 .... 196 C1
Eastern Ave OX4 .... 142 A2
Eastern By-pass Rd OX4 .... 142 C3
Eastfield OX11 .... 237 D4
Eastfield La
 Whitchurch RG8 .... 256 B4
 Woodcote RG8 .... 250 C3
Eastfield Rd OX8 .... 104 A2
Eastgate OX15 .... 7 F4
Eastmanton La OX12 .... 212 C2
Eastrop SN6 .... 190 A3
Eastwood Rd
 Curbridge OX8 .... 103 E1
 Stokenchurch HP14 .... 188 C2
Eaton Rd OX13 .... 139 D1
Ebbes La OX12 .... 197 D4
Eccles Cl RG4 .... 259 E1
Eden Croft OX14 .... 160 A1
Eden Dr OX3 .... 124 A2
Eden Rd OX3 .... 124 A2
Eden Way OX6 .... 65 D1
Edencroft SN6 .... 190 A4
Edenhall Cl RG31 .... 257 E2
Edgar Milward Cl RG30 ...... 258 A1
Edgecombe Rd OX3 .... 124 C2
Edgehill OX9 .... 129 F1
Edgeway Rd OX3 .... 123 F2
Edgeworth Dr OX18 .... 115 E1
Edinburgh Cl OX16 .... 15 F4
Edinburgh Dr
 Didcot OX11 .... 200 C1
 Kidlington OX5 .... 108 B4
Edinburgh Way OX16 .... 15 F3
Edington Pl OX12 .... 196 B1
Edington Rd OX8 .... 117 E4
Edington Sq OX8 .... 117 E4
Edith Rd OX1 .... 141 E4
Edmonds Cl OX11 .... 218 B4
Edmund Halley Rd OX4 ...... 142 C1
Edmund Rd OX4 .... 142 B3
Edmunds Rd OX16 .... 15 F3
Edward Rd OX1 .... 141 F1
Edward St Abingdon OX14 .. 179 E4
 Banbury OX16 .... 16 C4
Edward Stone Rise OX7 ...... 42 B1
Edwin Rd OX11 .... 218 B4
Eeightein Ct OX14 .... 179 E4
Eighth Ave OX3 .... 142 C4
Eighth St OX11 .... 217 D2
Elbourne OX11 .... 200 C1
Elder Cl RG31 .... 257 E2
Elder Way OX44 .... 143 C1
Elderdene OX9 .... 168 B4
Elderfield Cres OX11 .... 235 E4

Elderfield Rd OX6 .... 65 F4
Eldridge Cl OX14 .... 159 F1
Eleanor Cl OX4 .... 142 A2
Electric Ave OX4 .... 141 D4
Eleventh St OX11 .... 217 D1
Eliot Cl RG4 .... 259 D2
Elizabeth Ave OX14 .... 160 B1
Elizabeth Cl RG9 .... 254 A4
Elizabeth Dr OX12 .... 214 B3
Elizabeth Rd
 Henley-on-T RG9 .... 254 A4
 Stokenchurch HP14 .... 188 C2
Elizabeth Rise OX16 .... 16 A2
Ell's La OX15 .... 21 E4
Ellesmere Cl RG4 .... 259 D2
Ellesmere Rd OX4 .... 142 A2
Elm Bridge Rdbt OX10 ...... 203 F2
Elm Cl Ambrosden OX6 .... 81 E2
 Bicester OX6 .... 65 F2
 Chinnor OX9 .... 168 B3
 Tetsworth OX9 .... 166 A4
 Wheatley OX33 .... 144 B4
 Witney OX8 .... 117 F4
Elm Cres OX7 .... 73 E2
Elm Ct RG4 .... 252 C2
Elm Dr Chinnor OX9 .... 168 B3
 Garsington OX44 .... 143 E1
Elm Gr OX5 .... 108 C3
Elm La OX6 .... 81 E2
Elm Rd Faringdon SN7 .... 172 C2
 Mapledurham RG4 .... 258 B4
 North Moreton OX11 .... 220 A4
 Thame OX9 .... 147 F4
 Wantage OX12 .... 214 C3
Elm Tree Cl OX4 .... 142 A2
Elm Tree Wlk OX13 .... 159 E1
Elm Trees SN6 .... 129 D4
Elmcroft RG8 .... 249 F2
Elmhurst Rd RG8 .... 249 E4
Elmleigh Ct RG4 .... 259 E2
Elms Dr OX3 .... 124 A3
Elms Par OX2 .... 122 B1
Elms Rd Cassington OX8 .... 107 E1
 N Hinksey Vill OX2 .... 122 B1
Elms The Highworth SN6 .... 190 A3
 Langford GL7 .... 132 B1
Elms Way RG9 .... 224 B2
Elmscote Rd OX16 .... 16 B1
Elmstone Dr RG31 .... 257 E1
Elmthorpe Rd OX2 .... 122 C4
Elsfield Rd OX3 .... 123 F3
Elsfield Way OX2 .... 109 D1
Elsley Rd RG31 .... 257 F2
Elstow Ave RG4 .... 259 E3
Elstree Cl RG31 .... 257 E1
Elswith Cl OX12 .... 214 B4
Eltham Ave RG4 .... 258 C3
Elton Cres OX33 .... 144 B4
Elton Rd OX16 .... 16 C1
Elvendon La RG8 .... 250 B4
Elvendon Rd RG8 .... 249 E4
Elwes Cl OX14 .... 180 A4
Elwes Rd OX13 .... 178 B3
Ely Cl Abingdon OX14 .... 179 E3
 Carterton OX18 .... 115 F2
Emma La RG10 .... 255 F1
Emmens Cl RG8 .... 241 E2
Emmer Green Ct RG4 .... 259 E3
Emperor Gdns OX4 .... 142 C1
Eney Cl OX14 .... 160 B1
Enstone Rd
 Charlbury OX7 .... 73 D2
 Little Tew OX7 .... 45 D3
 Middle Barton OX7 .... 60 C4
Epwell Rd OX15 .... 13 F3
Eric Ave RG4 .... 259 D3
Erica Cl Banbury OX16 .... 9 D1
 Oxford OX4 .... 142 C2
Ermont Way OX16 .... 16 A4
Ernest Rd OX11 .... 218 C4
Ernicote Cl OX6 .... 81 F2
Essex Rd OX9 .... 148 A4
Essex St OX4 .... 142 A4
Essex Way RG4 .... 253 D2
Estover Way OX9 .... 168 A3
Ethelhelm Cl OX14 .... 160 B2
Ethelred Ct OX3 .... 124 B2
Eton Cl OX8 .... 118 B4
Euston Way OX12 .... 214 A4
Evans Cl OX8 .... 120 B4
Evans Ct OX5 .... 108 C4
Evans La OX5 .... 108 C4
Evans Rd OX18 .... 115 E1
Evenlode OX16 .... 16 A4
Evelin Rd OX14 .... 159 F1
Evelyn Cl OX2 .... 140 A4
Evenlode OX16 .... 16 A4
Evenlode Cl Bicester OX6 .... 65 F1
 Charlbury OX7 .... 73 D2
 Grove OX12 .... 196 B1
 North Leigh OX8 .... 105 D3
Evenlode Cres OX5 .... 92 A1
Evenlode Dr
 Berinsfield OX10 .... 182 B3
 Didcot OX11 .... 200 C1
 Long Hanborough OX8 ...... 90 A1
Evenlode Park OX14 .... 160 A1
Everard Cl OX3 .... 124 B2
Eversley Cl OX7 .... 57 D1
Evesham Rd RG4 .... 259 D3
Ewart Cl OX6 .... 65 D2
Ewert Pl OX2 .... 123 D3
Ewin Cl OX3 .... 123 F4
Exbourne Rd OX14 .... 179 E4
Exe Cl OX11 .... 201 D1
Exeter Cl OX6 .... 65 F4
Eynham Cl OX3 .... 124 C1
Eyot Pl OX4 .... 141 F3
Eynsford Cl RG4 .... 259 F3
Eynsham Ct OX8 .... 121 D4

Eynsham Rd
Cassington OX8 .... 107 E1
Cumnor OX2 .... 121 F1
N Hinksey Vill OX2 .... 140 A4
Eyot Pl OX4 .... 141 F4
Eyre's La OX10 .... 204 C3
Eyston Way OX14 .... 179 E4

Faber Cl OX4 .... 142 B1
Fair Cl OX6 .... 65 F2
Fair Mile RG9 .... 244 B2
Fair View OX3 .... 142 B4
Fairacres OX14 .... 179 E4
Fairacres Rd Didcot OX11 .. 218 C4
Oxford OX4 .... 141 F3
Fairfax Ave OX3 .... 123 F2
Fairfax Cl Banbury OX16 ... 16 A3
Caversham RG4 .... 259 D2
Oxford OX4 .... 148 A4
Fairfax Gate OX33 .... 144 B4
Fairfax Rd Chalgrove OX44 . 184 B3
Kidlington OX5 .... 108 C3
Oxford OX4, OX44 .... 142 C3
Fairfield OX10 .... 220 C1
Fairfield Cl OX12 .... 214 B4
Fairfield Dr OX8 .... 117 F4
Fairfield Rd OX18 .... 179 F4
Fairfield Rd RG31 .... 249 E4
Fairford Rd RG31 .... 257 E1
Fairford Way OX6 .... 66 A2
Fairhaven Rd OX6 .... 65 F4
Fairlawn End OX2 .... 122 C4
Fairlie Rd OX4 .... 142 A2
Fairmile C1 RG9 .... 244 B2
Fairspear Rd OX8 .... 86 C2
Fairthorne Way SN6 .... 209 D3
Fairview Estate RG9 .... 254 C4
Fairview Rd OX16 .... 16 A1
Fairway The OX16 .... 16 A3
Falcon Cl Banbury OX16 ... 16 A2
Carterton OX18 .... 115 F3
Oxford OX4 .... 142 B1
Falcon Mead OX6 .... 81 D4
Falkland Rd RG4 .... 259 D1
Falkner's Cl OX17 .... 23 D2
Fallow Way OX16 .... 16 C1
Fallowfield Cl RG4 .... 259 D2
Fallowfields OX6 .... 63 F1
Falstaff Cl OX8 .... 120 C4
Fane Cl OX6 .... 65 E2
Fane Dr OX10 .... 182 B3
Fane Rd OX3 .... 123 F3
Fanshawe Pl OX4 .... 142 C3
Fanshawe Rd OX9 .... 148 A4
Faraday Ave OX11 .... 217 D1
Faraday Rd RG12 .... 214 A4
Faringdon Rd
Appleton OX13 .... 139 F1
Kingston Bagpuize OX13 .. 156 C1
Shrivenham SN6 .... 209 E4
Stanford in the V SN7 ...... 194 B4
Watchfield SN6 .... 191 F1
Farleigh Mews RG4 .... 259 F3
Farleigh Rd SN6 .... 209 D3
Farley Cl OX8 .... 89 E4
Farm Cl Aston OX18 .... 135 F1
Chalgrove OX44 .... 184 C3
Kidlington OX5 .... 92 C1
Purley on T RG8 .... 257 E3
Sandford-on-T OX4 .... 142 C1
Farm Close La OX13 .... 143 D3
Farm Close Rd OX33 .... 144 A4
Farm End Grove OX12 ...... 214 B4
Woodstock OX20 .... 91 D4
Farm La OX8 .... 103 E3
Farm Mill La OX8 .... 118 A4
Farm Pl OX9 .... 149 F1
Farm Rd Abingdon OX14 .. 159 F1
Brackley NN13 .... 24 A3
Goring RG8 .... 249 E3
Henley-on-T RG9 .... 254 C4
Farm Way OX16 .... 16 C1
Farman Cres GL54 .... 68 A2
Farmer Pl OX3 .... 123 F2
Farmers Cl OX8 .... 104 A1
Farmfield Rd OX16 .... 16 B2
Farmhouse Cl OX6 .... 138 A4
Farmhouse Meadow OX8 . 117 F4
Farmhouse Mews OX9 .... 186 A1
Farmiloe Cl RG8 .... 257 E2
Farmington Dr OX8 .... 117 F4
Farmstead Cl OX12 .... 196 B1
Farndon Rd OX2 .... 123 D2
Farnham Dr RG4 .... 259 F2
Farrier's Mead OX6 .... 80 A2
Farriers Mews OX14 .... 180 A4
Farriers Rd OX7 .... 60 C4
Farringdon Rd OX14 .... 159 D1
Farthings The OX13 .... 178 B4
Faulder Ave OX18 .... 115 E2
Faulkner St OX1 .... 141 E4
Fawler La OX7 .... 88 B4
Fawler Rd Charlbury OX7 . 73 E1
Kingston Lisle OX12 .... 211 F3
Uffington SN7 .... 211 F3
Fawley Bottom La OX12 .. 226 A1
Fawley Cl OX12 .... 214 B3
Fawley Court RG9 .... 244 C3
Featherbed La
East Hendred OX12 .... 216 C4
Milton (Abingdon) OX14 .. 199 D1
Mixbury OX6 .... 38 B3
Feilden Cl OX8 .... 118 A2
Feilden Gr OX3 .... 124 A2
Felis Cl HP18 .... 129 E3
Feltwell Cl OX18 .... 115 F2
Fencott Rd OX5 .... 95 D2
Fenlock Rd OX8 .... 90 C1

Fennel Way OX14 .... 180 B4
Fenny Compton Rd OX17 .. 1 B1
Fenway OX6 .... 48 A1
Fergusson Pl OX44 .... 180 B4
Fergusson Rd OX6 .... 16 C4
Fermi Ave OX11 .... 217 D1
Fern Glen RG31 .... 257 E1
Fern Hill Rd OX4 .... 142 B3
Fernbrook Rd RG4 .... 258 C3
Ferndale Cl Reading RG31 . 257 E2
Stokenchurch HP14 .... 188 C2
Ferndale Rd OX16 .... 16 B3
Ferndale St SN7 .... 173 D2
Fernham Rd RG8 .... 249 E4
Fernham Rd
Faringdon SN7 .... 172 C1
Fernham SN7 .... 193 E3
Little Coxwell SN7 .... 192 C4
Longcot SN7 .... 192 B1
Shellingford SN7 .... 193 E3
Fernhill Cl Kidlington OX5 . 108 B4
Milcombe OX15 .... 21 D1
Tiddington OX9 .... 146 A3
Fernhill Rd OX5 .... 108 A4
Ferny Cl OX14 .... 160 C2
Ferriston OX6 .... 9 D1
Ferry Hinksey Rd OX2 ..... 123 D1
Ferry La Goring RG8 .... 249 D3
South Stoke RG8 .... 239 D2
Wargrave RG10 .... 255 E1
Ferry Mills OX2 .... 141 D4
Ferry Pool Rd OX2 .... 123 D3
Ferry Rd Oxford OX3 .... 123 F2
South Stoke RG8 .... 239 E2
Ferry Wlk OX14 .... 179 F3
Fetti Pl OX12 .... 214 C3
Fettiplace OX7 .... 70 A1
Fettiplace Cl OX13 .... 158 A4
Fettiplace Rd
Marcham OX13 .... 178 B3
Oxford OX3 .... 124 C3
Witney OX8 .... 117 F4
Fewcott Rd OX6 .... 49 F4
Fidlers Wlk RG10 .... 255 F1
Field Ave OX4 .... 142 C1
Field Cl Ickford HP18 ..... 128 A2
Kidlington OX5 .... 108 C4
Stonesfield OX8 .... 89 E4
Yarnton OX5 .... 108 A3
Field End
Long Crendon HP18 .... 129 F3
Wargrave RG10 .... 255 F1
Field Gdns
East Challow OX12 .... 213 F3
Steventon OX13 .... 199 D3
Field House Dr OX2 .... 123 D4
Field La Cuddesdon OX44 . 144 A2
Murcott OX6 .... 95 F2
Field Rd OX7 .... 54 C2
Field Rd OX7 .... 58 C3
Field The OX13 .... 158 C3
Field View RG4 .... 259 D2
Fielden Cl OX10 .... 204 B1
Fielden Rd OX10 .... 204 B1
Fieldfare Rd OX4 .... 161 F4
Fieldmere Cl OX4 .... 142 C1
Fieldside Abingdon OX14 . 159 E1
East Hagbourne OX11 ..... 219 D3
Long Wittenham OX14 ..... 201 E4
Upton OX11 .... 218 B1
Fiennes Rd Banbury OX16 . 16 A3
Oxford OX4 .... 142 A2
Fifteenth St OX11 .... 217 D1
Fifth Ave NN13 .... 36 C4
Fifth St Croughton NN13 .. 36 C4
Harwell OX11 .... 217 D2
Fifth St E NN13 .... 36 C4
Filkins Rd GL7 .... 132 B1
Finch Cl OX7 .... 124 B1
Finchdale Cl OX18 .... 115 E2
Finches La SN8 .... 245 F1
Finchley La OX6 .... 65 E1
Finham Brook OX11 .... 200 C2
Finmore Cl OX14 .... 179 F4
Finmore Rd OX2 .... 140 B4
Finsbury Pl OX7 .... 42 C2
Fir Cl OX10 .... 240 B4
Fir La OX6 .... 48 A1
Fir Tree Ave OX10 .... 221 D4
Fir Tree Cl OX13 .... 156 C1
Fir Tree Paddock RG20 ... 235 D1
Fir Trees OX14 .... 160 C4
Fircroft OX6 .... 65 F3
Fircroft Cl RG31 .... 257 E1
Firebrass Hill OX10 .... 183 F4
Firs Cl OX7 .... 54 B1
Firs Meadow [1] OX4 ..... 142 C1
Firs The OX15 .... 15 D4
First Ave Didcot OX11 .... 200 B1
Horspath OX33 .... 142 C4
First St Croughton NN13 .. 36 C4
First Turn OX2 .... 122 C4
Fish Ponds La OX9 .... 129 F1
Fisher Cl OX14 .... 179 D1
Fisher Row OX1 .... 123 D1
Fisher's La OX7 .... 73 D2
Fishermans Wharf OX14 . 179 F2
Fishers Cl OX8 .... 104 A3
Fishers Ct RG4 .... 259 E3
Fitzcount Way OX10 ...... 203 E1
Fitzharris Ind Est OX14 .. 179 F4
Fitzharry's Rd OX14 ...... 179 F4
Fitzherbert Cl OX4 .... 141 F2
Five Acre RG31 .... 257 E1
Five Mile Dr OX2 .... 109 D1
Fiveacres OX6 .... 80 A2
Flambards RG4 .... 259 E1

Flatford Pl OX5 .... 92 B1
Flavius Gate NN13 .... 24 A4
Flaxfield Rd OX4 .... 142 C1
Fleet Way OX11 .... 219 D4
Fleetwood Way OX9 .... 129 F1
Fleming Cl OX6 .... 65 E2
Fleming Dr OX7 .... 60 C4
Fleming Rd OX2 .... 91 E3
Flemming Ave OX4 .... 184 B4
Fletcher Cl Faringdon SN7 . 173 D2
Yarnton OX5 .... 108 A3
Fletcher Rd OX4 .... 142 C3
Flexney Pl OX3 .... 124 B1
Flexneys Paddock OX8 ... 138 A4
Flint Hollow OX9 .... 168 A3
Flint St HP17 .... 130 C3
Floral Cl OX12 .... 214 C4
Florence Cl OX5 .... 108 C4
Florence Park Rd OX4 .... 142 A3
Florey's Cl OX8 .... 104 A3
Flowers Hill RG8 .... 256 B2
Floyd's Row OX1 .... 141 E4
Fludger Cl OX10 .... 221 E4
Fococks La OX10 .... 221 F2
Fogwell Rd OX2 .... 122 A1
Foliat Cl OX12 .... 214 B4
Foliat Dr OX12 .... 214 C3
Folland Dr GL54 .... 68 A3
Follets Cl OX5 .... 108 A3
Folly Cl SN6 .... 190 A4
Folly Cres Highworth SN6 . 190 A4
Watchfield SN6 .... 191 F1
Folly Ct OX15 .... 19 E4
Folly Dr SN6 .... 190 A4
Folly Gr RG8 .... 250 C4
Folly Orchard Rd RG8 ... 240 C1
Folly View Cres SN7 ...... 172 C1
Folly View Rd SN7 .... 172 C1
Folly Way SN6 .... 190 A4
Ford La Drayton St L OX10 . 183 D3
East Hendred OX12 .... 216 C3
Garford OX13 .... 178 A4
Ford's Cl HP14 .... 189 F4
Fords Cl OX33 .... 143 E3
Forest Cl Launton OX6 ... 66 B1
Wootton OX1 .... 159 D4
Forest Hill RG30 .... 257 F1
Forest Rd Charlbury OX7 . 73 D2
Oxford OX3 .... 124 C2
Forest Side OX1 .... 141 F1
Foresters
Beacon's Bottom HP14 ... 189 E3
Chinnor OX9 .... 168 A3
Forge Cl Benson OX10 ... 203 F2
Caversham RG4 .... 259 F3
Horton-cum-S OX33 ...... 112 A3
Merton OX6 .... 95 E4
Forge Pl OX6 .... 49 F4
Forgeway OX16 .... 9 D1
Forrest Cl SN6 .... 209 D3
Forster La OX2 .... 139 F2
Forsythia Cl OX16 .... 65 F3
Forsythia Wlk OX16 ...... 9 D1
Fortescue Dr OX6 .... 80 A4
Forties The OX44 .... 145 D1
Fortnam Cl OX3 .... 124 A2
Forty Green OX9 .... 149 F2
Forty The
Bishopstone SN6 .... 227 E3
Chalsey OX10 .... 220 C1
Foscote Rise OX16 .... 16 C2
Fosseway The OX18 ...... 116 B2
Foster Rd OX14 .... 159 F2
Fothergill Pl OX9 .... 147 F4
Foudry Cl OX11 .... 201 D1
Foundry St OX16 .... 16 B3
Fourteenth St OX11 ...... 217 D2
Fourth Ave
Croughton NN13 .... 36 C3
Horspath OX33 .... 143 D4
Fourth St Croughton NN13 . 36 C3
Harwell OX11 .... 217 D2
Fowler Rd OX16 .... 16 C4
Fowler's Rd OX7 .... 55 D2
Fowlers Farm Rd HP14 .. 188 C2
Fox Cl Bampton OX18 .... 134 C2
Chipping Norton OX7 ..... 42 C1
Garsington OX44 .... 143 E1
Hailey OX8 .... 104 A2
Fox Cover OX9 .... 168 B3
Fox Cres OX1 .... 141 F3
Fox Furlong OX4 .... 142 A1
Fox La Bicester OX6 ...... 65 E1
Middle Barton OX7 .... 60 C4
Souldern OX6 .... 35 F2
Wootton (Oxford) OX13 . 159 D4
Foxborough Rd OX14 .... 160 C1
Foxburrow Cl OX8 .... 104 A1
Foxburrow La
Crawley OX8 .... 103 F2
Hailey OX8 .... 103 F2
Foxcombe Ct OX14 .... 179 D1
Foxcombe La OX1 .... 141 D1
Foxcombe Rd OX1 .... 141 D1
Foxcroft Dr OX18 .... 115 E1
Foxdown Cl OX5 .... 92 C1
Foxfield OX7 .... 42 C1
Foxglove La OX11 .... 218 B2
Foxglove Rd OX5 .... 108 B4
Foxhall Rd OX11 .... 200 B1
Foxhill Cl RG4 .... 260 A3
Foxhill La
Caversham RG4 .... 259 F3
Souldern OX6 .... 35 F2
Foxton Cl OX1 .... 108 C1
Foxwell Dr OX3 .... 124 B3
Foxwood OX18 .... 135 F2

Foxwood Cl Aston OX18 . 135 F2
Banbury OX16 .... 16 B1
Framlands Cl OX12 ...... 214 B3
Framlingham Dr RG4 .... 259 F3
Frampton Cl RG5 .... 260 C1
Frances Rd OX7 .... 60 C4
Francis Little Dr OX14 .. 179 E3
Franklin Cl
Chalgrove OX44 .... 184 B3
Abingdon OX5 .... 92 C1
Franklin Rd OX3 .... 124 A2
Franklyn Cl OX14 .... 159 F1
Fraser Ave RG4 .... 259 F3
Fraser Cl OX16 .... 16 C3
Fraser Gdns OX10 .... 221 E3
Frax Cl OX13 .... 156 C1
Frederick Rd OX4 .... 142 B2
Freeborn Cl OX5 .... 92 B1
Freehold St OX6 .... 62 B3
Freelands Rd OX4 .... 141 F3
Freeman Rd OX11 .... 200 B1
Freemans Cl SN7 .... 211 E4
Freemans Rd OX15 ..... 22 C4
French Cl OX8 .... 117 F4
French Laurence Way
OX44 .... 184 B3
Frenchay Rd OX2 .... 123 D3
Frensham Cl OX16 ...... 9 D1
Freshfield St OX18 ...... 100 C2
Friars Cl SN6 .... 209 D3
Friars' Entry OX1 .... 123 E2
Friars Furlong HP18 .... 129 D4
Friars Wharf OX1 .... 141 E4
Friday Ct OX1 .... 123 E1
Friday La OX33 .... 144 A4
Friday St RG9 .... 244 B2
Friends Cl OX8 .... 89 E4
Frilford Rd OX13 .... 178 B3
Frilsham St OX14 .... 200 A4
Fritwell Rd OX6 .... 50 A2
Frog La OX7 .... 70 A1
Frogmore La SN7 .... 194 C4
Frome Rd OX11 .... 217 E1
Fruitlands OX8 .... 120 B4
Frys Hill OX4 .... 142 C1
Fuchsia Wlk OX16 ...... 9 D1
Fullbrook Cres RG31 .. 257 E2
Fullers Field OX44 ..... 145 E1
Fullers Rd OX11 .... 219 F1
Fullwell Cl OX14 .... 159 F1
Fulmar Cl OX6 .... 66 A2
Fulmar Pl OX12 .... 196 B1
Fulton Rd GL54 .... 68 A2
Fulwell Rd NN13 .... 25 D2
Furlong Cl OX4 .... 142 B2
Furlong Row OX18 .... 152 C4
Furlongs The OX9 ..... 147 E3
Fyfield Cl OX12 .... 214 C2
Fyfield Rd OX2 .... 123 E2

Gadge Cl OX9 .... 129 F1
Gainsborough Cres RG9 . 254 B4
Gainsborough Green
OX4 .... 179 F3
Gainsborough Hill RG9 . 254 B4
Gainsborough Rd RG9 . 254 B4
Gaisford Rd OX4 .... 142 B2
Gall Cl OX14 .... 180 A4
Galley Field OX14 ..... 180 A4
Gallowstree Rd RG9 .. 252 C4
Galpin Pl OX9 .... 129 F1
Galsworthy Dr RG4 ... 259 E3
Gangsdown Hill OX10 . 223 F2
Gap The Marcham OX13 . 178 B3
Woodcote RG8 .... 250 C4
Garde Rd RG4 .... 260 C2
Garden Cl Banbury OX16 . 16 B4
Didcot OX11 .... 218 B4
Gardens Cl HP14 ...... 188 C2
Gardens The
Radley OX14 .... 160 C2
South Stoke RG8 ..... 239 E2
Gardiner Cl
Abingdon OX14 .... 180 A4
Wallingford OX33 ... 144 A4
Gardiner St OX3 ...... 124 C1
Garford Cl OX14 ..... 160 A1
Garford Rd OX2 ..... 123 E3
Garne's La OX18 .... 100 C3
Garner Cl OX18 ..... 115 F2
Garrard Way OX11 .. 219 D4
Garsington Rd OX4 .. 142 C2
Garsons La OX10 ... 240 C3
Garston Ct OX12 .... 214 C3
Garston La RG20 .... 235 D2
Garth Rd OX11 ...... 200 C1
Garth The
N Hinksey Vill OX2 . 140 B4
Yarnton OX5 .... 108 A3
Gas La OX7 .... 85 E4
Gascoigne Way OX15 . 21 F1
Gaskells End RG4 .. 258 B3
Gassons Rd GL7 ... 150 B3
Gassons Way GL7 . 150 B2
Gatehampton Rd RG8 . 249 E2
Gathorne Rd OX3 .. 124 B1
Gatteridge St OX16 . 16 B3
Gauntlets Cl OX15 .. 21 F1
Gaveston Gdns OX15 . 33 E2
Gaveston Rd OX15 .. 217 F4
Gavray Dr OX6 ...... 66 A1
Gaydon Cl OX18 .... 115 F2
Gaydon Wlk OX6 ... 65 F1
Gayhurst Cl RG4 ... 259 D3
Gelt Burn OX11 .... 201 D1
Gentian Rd OX4 .... 142 C1
Geoffrey Barbour Rd
OX14 .... 179 F4
Geoffrey Tuttle Dr OX10 . 204 B1
Geoffreyson Rd RG4 . 258 C3

George Moore Cl OX4 . 142 A3
George Rd HP14 ...... 188 C3
George St Banbury OX16 . 16 B3
Bicester OX6 .... 65 E2
Caversham RG4 .... 259 D1
Oxford OX1 .... 123 E1
George Street Mews
OX1 .... 123 D1
Gerard Pl OX4 .... 142 C1
Gerrard Rd GL54 .... 68 A2
Gibbs Cres OX2 ...... 141 D4
Gibbs Rd OX4 .... 16 C4
Gibson Cl OX14 ...... 160 A2
Gibson Dr OX6 .... 63 E4
Gidley Way OX33 ... 143 E4
Giernalls La OX8 ... 104 A3
Giffard Way HP18 .. 129 E4
Gigg La OX13 .... 198 C2
Giles Cl OX4 .... 142 A3
Giles Rd OX4 .... 142 B1
Gill Way OX16 ...... 16 A3
Gillett Cl OX16 ..... 16 A3
Gillett Rd OX16 .... 16 A3
Gillians Way OX4 . 142 A3
Gillotts Cl RG9 .... 254 A4
Gillotts La RG9 .... 254 B4
Gipsy La OX4 ...... 160 A1
Gipsy La Grove OX12 . 214 C4
Oxford OX4 .... 124 A1
Reading RG30 ...... 257 F1
Girdlestone Cl OX3 . 124 B3
Girdlestone Rd OX3 . 124 B1
Glade The RG8 .... 257 E2
Glades The OX6 ... 66 B1
Gladstone Rd OX3 . 124 C2
Glamis Pl OX16 ... 15 F3
Glanville Gdns OX16 . 16 A3
Glanville Rd OX4 . 142 A4
Glebe Cl Ambrosden OX6 . 81 E2
Moulsford OX10 ... 238 C3
Glebe Cotts OX9 .. 166 C2
Glebe Cl OX6 ...... 47 E3
Glebe Rd OX11 ... 24 A4
Glebe Gdns Grove OX12 . 196 C1
Sonning RG4 ...... 260 C2
Glebe House Dr MK18 . 25 F3
Glebe La OX6 ..... 66 A2
Glebe Rd Cumnor OX2 . 139 F3
Didcot OX11 ...... 218 C4
Purley on T RG8 . 257 D3
Stanford in the V SN7 . 194 B4
Glebe Ride RG8 . 250 C4
Glebe St OX4 .... 123 F1
Glebe The Aldworth RG8 . 247 F2
Aynho OX17 ...... 35 E4
Culham OX14 .... 180 A2
Cumnor OX2 ..... 139 F3
Didcot OX11 ..... 213 E3
Hook Norton OX15 . 30 A4
Lewknor OX9 .... 187 D4
Rotherfield Peppard RG9 . 254 A4
Standlake OX8 .. 137 E2
Shrivenham SN6 . 144 A4
Glebelands Bampton OX18 . 134 C2
Oxford OX3 ..... 142 B4
Glen Cl OX6 ... 52 B1
Glenham Rd OX9 . 148 A1
Glenmore Rd OX18 . 115 E2
Glenrhondda RG4 . 258 C3
Glimbers Gr OX9 . 168 B3
Gloucester Court Mews
OX8 .... 104 A1
Gloucester La OX1 . 123 D1
Gloucester Mews SN7 . 172 C2
Gloucester Pl Oxford OX8 . 123 E1
Witney OX8 ..... 104 A1
Gloucester St
Faringdon SN7 . 172 C2
Oxford OX1 ...... 123 E1
Glover's Cl OX7 . 42 C1
Glovers Cl OX20 . 91 E3
Glovers La OX17 . 10 C1
Glyme Cl Abingdon OX14 . 160 A1
Woodstock OX20 . 91 D4
Glyme Dr OX10 ... 182 B3
Glyme Way OX8 . 106 A4
Glympton Rd OX20 . 75 F3
Glyn Ave OX11 . 218 B4
Glyn Rd OX3 .... 124 C2
Glyncastle RG4 . 258 C3
Glyndebourne Gdns OX16 . 9 D1
Glynswood OX9 . 168 B3
Gobles Ct OX6 . 65 F1
Goddard's La OX7 . 42 C2
Godfrey Cl OX14 . 179 F3
Godfreys Cl Brill HP18 . 98 A1
Godstow Cl RG5 . 260 C1
Godstow Rd OX2 . 122 C4
Godwyn Cl OX14 . 179 F4
Goffe Cl OX9 .... 148 C4
Goggs The OX9 . 186 A1
Golafre Rd OX14 . 179 E2
Gold Cl OX4 .... 161 F4
Goldcrest Way OX4 . 81 D4
Golden Cross OX1 . 123 E1
Golden Hills OX9 . 168 B3
Golden Rd OX4 . 142 A4
Golden Villa Cl OX16 . 16 A3
Golder's Cl HP18 . 127 F2
Goldfinch La OX10 . 221 D1
Goldfinch Cl OX6 . 65 D2
Goldsmith's La OX10 . 221 E4
Goldsworth Cl OX4 . 201 C2
Goodall Cl OX9 . 200 C2
Goodlake Ave SN7 . 173 D2

Goodlife Gdns RG31 ...... 257 E2
Goodrich Cl OX4 .... 259 F3
Goodrington Cl OX16 ...... 16 A3
Goodson Wlk OX12 .... 123 F2
Goodsons Ind Mews
.... 147 F4
Goor La SN8 .... 245 D2
Goose Green OX15 .... 33 F2
Goose Green Cl OX2 ...... 122 C4
Goose La OX15 .... 22 B4
Goose La OX14 .... 21 E2
Goosacre OX14 .... 160 C1
Goosey La OX12 .... 195 D2
Gordon Cl OX3 .... 123 F3
Gordon Dr OX14 .... 160 B1
Gordon Pl RG30 .... 258 B1
Gordon St OX1 .... 141 E3
Goring Rd RG8 .... 250 C4
Gorse Leas OX3 .... 124 A3
Gorselands RG4 .... 259 D3
Gorton Playne OX7 .... 70 B1
Gorwell OX9 .... 186 A1
Gosbrook Rd RG4 .... 259 D1
Gosford Cl OX5 .... 108 C3
Goslyn Cl OX1 .... 124 B1
Gould Cl OX6 .... 66 A3
Gouldland Gdns OX3 ...... 124 A3
Goulds Villas OX16 .... 16 A3
Gower Rd OX12 .... 214 A4
Grafton Rd OX4 .... 168 B4
Grafton Orch OX9 .... 168 B4
Graham Cl OX11 .... 237 D4
Graham Rd OX6 .... 65 E2
Grahame Ave RG8 .... 256 B3
Grammar School Hill
OX7 .... 73 D2
Gramps Hill OX12 .... 231 F3
Grange Ave RG9 .... 253 D4
Grange Beck OX11 .... 201 D2
Grange Cl Goring RG8 ... 249 D3
  Highworth SN6 .... 190 A3
Grange Cl OX2 .... 140 A4
Grange Farm Rd HP14 ... 189 D4
Grange La OX15 .... 19 E4
Grange Park OX6 .... 48 A1
Grange Rd Banbury OX16 16 B2
  Henley-on-T RG9 .... 244 C1
  Oxford OX4 .... 142 A1
Grange The RG4 .... 258 B3
Grants Mews OX14 .... 141 F4
Granville Way OX6 .... 66 A1
Grasmere Ave RG30 .... 257 F1
Grass Hill RG4 .... 258 C2
Grates The OX14 .... 142 B2
Gravel Hill
  Caversham RG4 .... 259 D3
  Henley-on-T RG9 .... 244 B1
  Sonning Common RG4 . 252 C3
Gravel Hill Cres RG4 ..... 252 C3
Gravel La Drayton OX14 . 179 D1
  Warborough OX10 .... 203 D4
Gravel Pits La OX5 .... 108 A3
Gravel Rd RG9 .... 253 F1
Gravel Wlk
  Drayton St L OX10 .... 183 D3
  Faringdon SN7 .... 172 C2
Graveney Dr RG4 .... 258 C2
Gravenhill Rd N OX6 ..... 81 D4
Gravett Cl RG9 .... 254 B3
Grays Cl OX44 .... 184 B4
Grayshott Rd OX4 .... 124 A1
Graysleaze RG4 .... 252 B2
Great Clarendon St OX2 123 D1
Great Close Rd OX5 .... 108 B3
Great Western Dr OX11 . 200 C1
Grebe Cl Abingdon OX14 179 F3
  Sandford-on-T OX4 ...... 142 C1
Grebe Rd OX6 .... 16 C2
Grebe Sq GL54 .... 68 A2
Green Cl Benson OX10 ... 204 A3
  Bicester OX6 .... 65 F1
  Didcot OX11 .... 218 C3
  Steventon OX13 .... 198 C3
  Wallingford OX10 .... 221 E4
Green Dean Hill RG4 ..... 252 B1
Green End Rd HP14 .... 189 F3
Green Farm OX17 .... 23 D2
Green Furlong OX10 ...... 182 B3
Green Heart Way OX13 .. 156 C1
Green Hill OX4 .... 143 D1
Green Hitchings OX44 ... 145 E1
Green La Abingdon OX13 159 D3
  Banbury OX5, OX16, OX17 16 B2
  Bledlow Ridge HP14 ..... 189 E3
  Caversham RG4 .... 258 C2
  Chesterton OX6 .... 79 F4
  Ewelme OX10 .... 204 B2
  Henley-on-T RG9 .... 254 B4
  Little Tew OX7 .... 44 B3
  Longworth OX13 .... 156 B1
  Milton-u-W OX7 .... 70 A1
  N Hinksey Vill OX2 ...... 140 A4
  North Leigh OX8 .... 105 D4
  Pangbourne RG8 .... 256 B2
  Sonning Common RG4 . 252 C3
  South Newington OX15 31 F4
  Stokenchurch HP14 ..... 188 B3
  Sunningwell OX13 .... 160 A3
  Swalcliffe OX15 .... 14 A1
  Upper Arncott OX6 ...... 96 C4
  Warborough OX10 .... 203 D4
  Woodcote RG8 .... 250 C4
  Woodstock OX20 .... 91 D4
Green N The OX1 .... 203 E4
Green Pl OX1 .... 141 E3

Green Rd Didcot OX11 .... 218 C4
  Kidlington OX5 .... 108 C4
  Oxford OX3 .... 124 C2
Green Ridges OX3 .... 125 D2
Green S The OX10 .... 203 E4
Green St OX4 .... 142 A4
Green The Adderbury OX17 23 D2
  Alvescot OX18 .... 133 E3
  Ascott-w-W OX7 .... 71 E1
  Aston Rowant OX9 .... 167 E2
  Barford St M OX15 .... 32 C2
  Bladon OX20 .... 91 D1
  Cassington OX8 .... 107 E1
  Chalgrove OX44 .... 184 B3
  Charlbury OX7 .... 73 E2
  Charney Bassett OX12 . 176 A1
  Chesterton OX6 .... 79 F4
  Chilton OX11 .... 235 F4
  Chipping Norton OX7 ... 42 C1
  East Hanney OX12 .... 179 D1
  East Hanney OX12 .... 197 D4
  Fernham SN7 .... 193 D2
  Fifield OX7 .... 69 E1
  Fringford OX6 .... 52 B3
  Garsington OX44 .... 143 F1
  Great Bourton OX17 ..... 9 F4
  Great Milton OX44 .... 145 D1
  Great Rollright OX7 ...... 29 D2
  Highworth SN6 .... 190 A3
  Hook Norton OX15 .... 30 A4
  Hornton OX15 .... 7 A3
  Horspath OX33 .... 143 E3
  Horton-cum-S OX33 ..... 112 A3
  Launton OX6 .... 66 C1
  Milcombe OX15 .... 20 C1
  North Leigh OX8 .... 89 E1
  Shrivenham SN6 .... 209 D3
  Standlake OX8 .... 137 E2
  Stanton Harcourt OX8 . 138 A4
  Steventon OX13 .... 199 D3
  Swalcliffe OX15 .... 19 A4
  Tackley OX5 .... 77 D3
  Uffington SN7 .... 211 E4
  West Hanney OX12 ...... 176 B1
  West Hanney OX12 ...... 196 C3
Green's Rd OX6 .... 120 C4
Greenacres OX14 .... 179 D1
Greenacres Dr OX12 ..... 214 B2
Greenacres La OX18 ..... 135 E2
Greenfield Cres
  Stonesfield OX8 .... 89 E4
  Wallingford OX10 .... 221 D4
Greenfield Rd OX8 .... 89 E4
Greenfields OX6 .... 96 B4
Greenfinch Cl OX4 .... 142 C1
Greenhill Ct OX16 .... 16 B2
Greenhills Park OX15 .... 21 E2
Greenleas Ave RG4 .... 259 D4
Greenmere OX10 .... 202 C2
Greenmoor RG8 .... 250 C4
Greens Garth OX15 .... 21 F3
Greens Keep HP17 .... 130 C3
Greenswrd The OX17 .... 5 F1
Greenway
  Haddenham HP17 .... 130 C3
  Lower Heyford OX5 ...... 63 D2
Greenway The OX12 ...... 216 A3
Greenwich La OX8 .... 87 D2
Greenwood Ave OX9 ..... 168 B3
Greenwood Dr OX6 .... 65 D2
Greenwood Meadow OX8 168 B3
Gregory Estate OX9 ...... 185 E2
Grenoble Rd
  Garsington OX4 .... 143 D1
  Sandford-on-T OX4 ...... 142 B1
Grenville Way OX9 .... 130 A1
Gresham Way RG30 .... 258 A1
Greygoose La GL56 .... 41 D3
Greyhound La OX9 .... 129 F1
Greys Cl OX16 .... 15 F3
Greys Hill RG9 .... 244 B1
Greys Rd RG9 .... 254 B4
Greystoke Rd RG4 .... 259 F2
Griffin Rd OX9 .... 148 B4
Griffiths Cl OX8 .... 138 B2
Griffiths Gdns OX6 .... 66 A4
Grimmer Way RG8 .... 250 C4
Grimsbury Dr OX16 ...... 16 C4
Grimsbury Green OX16 . 16 C4
Grimsbury Sq OX16 ...... 16 C4
Grosvenor Rd
  Banbury OX16 .... 16 B3
  Caversham RG4 .... 259 E2
  N Hinksey Vill OX2 ...... 140 C3
Grove Cotts
  Caversham RG4 .... 259 D3
  Little Coxwell SN7 .... 192 C4
Grove Hill
  Caversham RG4 .... 259 D2
  Highworth SN6 .... 190 A4
Grove La OX10 .... 205 D3
Grove Park Dr
  Ardington OX12 .... 215 E4
  Wantage OX12 .... 214 C3
Grove Rd Bladon OX20 .. 91 E2
  Caversham RG4 .... 259 D3
  Grove OX12 .... 214 C4
  Harwell OX11 .... 217 E4
  Henley-on-T RG9 .... 244 C1
  Sonning Common RG4 . 252 C3
Grove St Banbury OX16 . 16 B3
  Cutteslowe OX2 .... 123 D4
  Wantage OX12 .... 214 C3
Grove The Abingdon OX14 144 A1
  Bourton SN6 .... 209 D2
  Deddington OX15 .... 33 F2
Grovelands OX5 .... 108 B4
Grovelands Centre OX12 196 B1

Grovelands Rd OX3 .... 125 D1
Grundy Cl OX14 .... 180 A4
Grundy Cres OX14 .... 141 F1
Grunsell Cl OX3 .... 124 B3
Guelder Rd OX4 .... 142 B1
Guildenford OX18 .... 100 C3
Gullicote La OX17 .... 8 C2
Gulliver's Cl OX15 .... 8 A2
Gurden Pl OX3 .... 124 C2
Gurl Cl OX3 .... 124 C2
Gurney Cl RG4 .... 258 B3
Gurney Dr RG4 .... 258 B3
Gwyneth Rd OX4 .... 142 A1
Gwynne Cl RG31 .... 257 E2

Hackers La OX7 .... 55 F2
Hadden Hill OX11 .... 201 E1
Haddenham Aerodrome
  Ind Est
  HP17 .... 130 C4
Haddenham & Thame
  Parkway Sta HP17 .... 130 C3
Hadland Rd OX4 .... 180 B4
Hadleigh Rise RG4 .... 259 F3
Hadow Rd OX3 .... 124 A2
Hadrians Gate NN13 ..... 24 A4
Hafod RG4 .... 258 C3
Hagbourne Cl RG8 .... 250 C4
Hagbourne Rd
  Aston Tirrold OX11 ...... 219 E1
  Didcot OX11 .... 219 D4
  East Hagbourne OX11 . 219 D1
Hailey Ave OX7 .... 42 C1
Hailey Cft OX7 .... 168 A3
Hailey Cres OX7 .... 42 C1
Hailey Rd
  Chipping Norton OX7 ... 42 B1
  Witney OX8 .... 104 A2
Haines Ct OX14 .... 178 B4
Haldane Rd
  Caversham RG4 .... 258 C3
  Oxford OX4 .... 142 C1
Hale Rd OX10 .... 203 F3
Halfpenny La OX10 .... 238 C3
Halifax Rd OX4 .... 66 A2
Hall Cl OX7 .... 186 A2
Hall Cl The OX6 .... 66 A3
Halliday Hill OX3 .... 124 A3
Halls Cl Drayton OX14 ... 179 E1
  N Hinksey Vill OX2 ...... 140 A4
Halse La OX12 .... 197 D4
Halse Water OX11 .... 201 D1
Halton Rd OX18 .... 115 F1
Ham La OX18 .... 135 F1
Ham Rd OX12 .... 214 B2
Hamble Dr OX4 .... 160 A1
Hamble Rd OX11 .... 201 D1
Hambleden Dr OX10 ..... 221 D4
Hambleside OX6 .... 65 D1
Hambridge La GL7 .... 150 B3
Hamel The OX1 .... 123 D1
Hamfield OX12 .... 214 A2
Hamilton Ave OX3 .... 124 C1
Hamilton Rd
  Cutteslowe OX2 .... 123 D4
  Thame OX9 .... 130 A1
  Wargrave RG10 .... 255 F1
Hamlet The RG4 .... 252 A3
Hamlyn Cl OX12 .... 214 A1
Hammer La OX10 .... 183 D1
Hammett Pl OX18 .... 115 E1
Hampden Ave OX9 .... 147 F4
Hampden Cl Banbury OX16 15 F3
  Bicester OX6 .... 66 A2
  Chalgrove OX44 .... 184 B3
  Faringdon SN7 .... 173 D2
Hampden Dr OX5 .... 108 C3
Hampden Rd
  Caversham RG4 .... 259 D1
  Oxford OX4 .... 142 B2
  Wantage OX12 .... 214 C3
Hampden Way OX10 ..... 204 C2
Hampstead Hill RG4 ..... 260 B4
Hampton Dr OX17 .... 23 F3
Hanborough Cl OX8 ...... 120 C4
Hanborough Rd OX8 ..... 120 C4
Handlo Pl OX3 .... 124 C2
Hanney Rd
  Kingston Bagpuize OX13 176 B4
  Steventon OX13 .... 198 B3
Hannis Rd OX7 .... 42 B1
Hanover Cl OX7 .... 73 E2
Hanover Gdns OX6 .... 65 F1
Hans Ave OX12 .... 214 C3
Hanson Rd OX14 .... 159 F2
Hanwell Ct OX17 .... 8 C2
Hanwood Cl RG5 .... 260 B1
Harberton Mead OX3 .... 123 F2
Harbord Rd OX2 .... 109 D1
Harborne Rd OX5 .... 77 E3
Harcourt Cl RG9 .... 244 B1
Harcourt Green OX12 ... 214 C3
Harcourt Hill OX2 .... 140 C3
Harcourt Rd
  Stokenchurch HP14 ..... 188 C2
  Wantage OX12 .... 214 C3
Harcourt Terr OX3 .... 124 A1
Harcourt Way
  Abingdon OX14 .... 159 F1
  Wantage OX12 .... 214 C3
Harding Rd OX14 .... 179 E4
Hardings OX44 .... 184 B3
Hardings Cl OX14 .... 142 A2
Hardings Strings OX18 . 128 C4
Hardwell Cl OX12 .... 196 B1
Hardwick Ave OX16 ...... 16 C4
Hardwick Park OX16 ..... 8 C1

Hardwick Rd Hethe OX6 . 52 A4
  Whitchurch RG8 .... 256 B4
Hardy Cl RG4 .... 259 E1
Harebell Rd OX4 .... 142 C1
Harecourt OX12 .... 214 C2
Harefields OX2 .... 109 D4
Harewood Rd OX16 .... 16 C1
Harlech Ave RG4 .... 259 E3
Harlech Cl OX16 .... 15 F3
Harlequin Way OX16 ..... 9 D1
Harley Rd
  Caversham RG4 .... 259 D1
  Oxford OX2 .... 122 C1
Harlington Ave OX12 .... 196 C1
Harlow Way OX3 .... 123 F4
Harmon Cl OX6 .... 66 A3
Harold White Cl OX3 .... 124 C1
Harolde Cl OX3 .... 124 B2
Harolds Cl OX3 .... 87 D2
Harper Cl OX6 .... 96 B4
Harpes Rd OX2 .... 123 D4
Harpsden Rd RG9 .... 254 C4
Harpsichord Pl OX4 ...... 123 F1
Harrier Park OX11 .... 200 B2
Harrier Way OX6 .... 66 A2
Harriers View OX16 ...... 16 B2
Harris Rd OX6 .... 63 E4
Harris's La OX13 .... 156 B1
Harrison Pl OX3 .... 129 F1
Harrison's La OX20 ...... 91 D3
Harrisville OX6 .... 62 A4
Harrold HP18 .... 129 E3
Harrogate Rd RG4 .... 258 C2
Harrow Rd OX14 .... 142 C2
Harrowby Rd OX16 .... 16 B1
Harsden Way RG9 .... 254 C4
Hart Ave SN7 .... 172 C2
Hart Cl OX14 .... 180 B4
Hart Pl OX6 .... 66 A3
Hart St Henley-on-T RG9 244 C1
  Oxford OX2 .... 123 D1
  Wallingford OX10 .... 221 E4
Harthmoor Cl HP14 ...... 188 C2
Harts Cl OX5 .... 108 B4
Hartslock Ct RG8 .... 256 A3
Hartslock View RG8 ..... 249 F1
Hartslock Way RG1 .... 257 E1
Harwell OX12 .... 200 A4
Harwell Ind Bsns Ctr OX11 217 D1
Harwell Rd OX14 .... 199 F3
Harwood Rd OX11 .... 218 C3
Haselmere Gdns OX2 ... 109 D1
Haslemere Way OX16 ... 16 C3
Hastings Cl OX16 .... 15 F3
Hastings Dr OX18 .... 115 F1
Hastings Hill OX3 .... 55 F3
Hastings Rd OX16 .... 15 F4
Hatch Cl OX5 .... 77 F2
Hatch End OX5 .... 77 F2
Hatch Gate La RG10 ..... 255 F4
Hatch Way OX5 .... 77 F2
Hatchet Hill SN6 .... 227 D1
Hatching La OX18 .... 87 D2
Hatfield Pits La OX8 ..... 104 A4
Hathaways OX3 .... 144 A4
Havelock Rd OX4 .... 142 B3
Haven Cl OX10 .... 202 B4
Havers Ave OX14 .... 199 E1
Haw La Aldworth RG8 ... 247 F1
  Bledlow Ridge HP14 .... 189 F4
Hawke La OX5 .... 24 E1
Hawke's La OX15 .... 19 E4
Hawker Sq GL54 .... 68 A2
Hawkins St OX4 .... 141 F4
Hawkins Way OX13 ...... 159 D3
Hawksmead Rd OX6 ..... 81 D4
Hawksmoor Rd OX2 ..... 109 D1
Hawkswell Gdns OX2 ... 123 E4
Hawkswell Ho OX2 .... 123 E4
Hawksworth Cl OX12 ... 200 B2
Hawthorn Ave Oxford OX3 124 B2
  Thame OX9 .... 147 E4
Hawthorn Cl
  N Hinksey Vill OX2 ...... 140 B4
  Wallingford OX10 .... 221 E4
Hawthorn Cres OX12 ... 214 C4
Hawthorn Gr OX18 .... 115 E1
Hawthorn Rd
  Eynsham OX8 .... 120 C1
  Kidlington OX5 .... 108 C4
Hawthorn Way
  Kidlington OX5 .... 108 C4
  Sonning RG4 .... 260 C1
Hawthorne Ave OX13 ... 159 E1
Hawthorne Rd RG4 ...... 259 F2
Hawthornes RG31 .... 257 D2
Hawthorns The OX16 ... 16 B2
Hayden La RG9 .... 224 A2
Haydon Rd OX11 .... 200 C1
Hayes Ave OX13 .... 156 A4
Hayes Cl OX3 .... 123 F2
Hayfield Rd OX2 .... 123 D3
Haynes Rd OX3 .... 123 F3
Hayward Dr OX18 .... 115 E1
Hayward Rd OX2 .... 109 D1
Haywards Cl
  Henley-on-T RG9 .... 244 B1
  Wantage OX12 .... 214 C3
Haywards Rd OX14 .... 199 D4
Hazel Ave OX12 .... 147 F4
Hazel Cres OX5 .... 108 C3
Hazel End OX14 .... 143 E1
Hazel Gdns RG4 .... 252 C3
Hazel Gr Bicester OX6 .. 65 F2
  Wallingford OX10 .... 221 E4
Hazel Rd N Hinksey Vill OX2 122 B1
  Purley on T RG8 .... 257 E2
Hazel Wlk OX5 .... 108 C3

Hazeldene Gdns OX16 ... 16 B2
Hazell's La SN6 .... 209 E3
Hazells La GL7 .... 132 A3
Hazelmoor La RG4 .... 252 B2
Hazelnut Path OX14 ..... 160 C4
Hazelrig Cl OX9 .... 148 A4
Hazelton Cl OX9 .... 147 F4
Hazelwood Cl RG31 ...... 257 E1
Headington Rd OX3 ...... 124 A1
Headington Rdbt OX3 ... 124 C2
Headley Way OX3 .... 124 A2
Healey Cl OX14 .... 179 F3
Hean Cl OX14 .... 160 A1
Hearns La RG4 .... 252 B3
Hearthway OX16 .... 16 C3
Heath Cl Milcombe OX15 20 C1
Heath End Rd OX6 .... 68 B4
Heath Dr RG9 .... 254 A1
Heath La OX20 .... 91 D1
Heathcote Ave OX16 ..... 16 C1
Heathcote Pl OX14 .... 160 B1
Heather Cl
  Carterton OX18 .... 115 E3
  Sonning Common RG4 . 253 D3
Heather Pl OX3 .... 123 F2
Heather Rd Bicester OX6 65 F3
  Milton (Abingdon) OX14 199 E3
Heathfield Ave RG9 ...... 254 A1
Heathfield Cl RG9 .... 254 A1
Hedge End OX20 .... 91 E3
Hedge Hill Rd OX12 ...... 213 F3
Hedgemead Ave OX14 .. 160 B1
Hedgerley OX9 .... 168 A3
Helen Rd OX2 .... 122 C1
Hellebourine Cl OX4 .... 142 C1
Helwys Pl OX5 .... 92 B1
Hemdean Hill RG4 .... 259 D2
Hemdean Rd RG4 .... 259 D2
Hemdean Rise RG4 ...... 259 D2
Hemingway Dr OX6 ...... 65 E1
Hempton Rd OX15 .... 33 F2
Hendon Pl OX6 .... 66 A2
Hendred St OX4 .... 142 A3
Hendred Way OX14 ...... 160 A1
Henfield View OX10 ..... 203 D4
Hengest Gate OX11 ...... 217 F4
Hengrove Cl OX3 .... 124 B2
Henley Ave OX4 .... 142 A3
Henley Dr SN6 .... 190 A4
Henley Gdns OX6 .... 65 F1
Henley Rd
  Caversham RG4 .... 260 B4
  Dorchester OX10 .... 202 C4
  Henley-on-T RG9 .... 244 B3
  Shiplake RG4 .... 260 B4
Henley St OX4 .... 141 F4
Henleys La OX14 .... 179 D1
Hennef Way OX16 .... 16 C4
Henor Mill Cl OX14 ...... 160 A1
Henrietta Rd OX4 .... 130 A1
Henry Rd OX2 .... 122 C1
Henry Taunt Cl OX3 ..... 124 C3
Hensington Cl OX20 ..... 91 D3
Hensington Rd OX20 .... 91 D3
Henwood Dr OX1 .... 140 A1
Herald Way OX6 .... 66 A2
Herbert Cl OX4 .... 142 A4
Hereford Way OX16 ..... 9 D1
Heritage La OX7 .... 71 D1
Herman Cl OX14 .... 180 A4
Hermitage Rd OX14 ...... 179 F3
Hernes Cl OX2 .... 123 D4
Hernes Cres OX2 .... 123 D4
Hernes Rd OX2 .... 123 D4
Heron Cl OX18 .... 115 E2
Heron Ct OX6 .... 66 A2
Heron Island RG4 .... 259 E1
Heron Rd OX10 .... 204 B2
Heron Shaw RG8 .... 249 E4
Heron's Wlk OX14 .... 159 F1
Herons Pl OX2 .... 123 D4
Herringcote OX10 .... 182 B1
Herschel Cres OX4 .... 142 B2
Hertford Cl Bicester OX6 65 F2
  Caversham RG4 .... 259 E3
Hertford St OX4 .... 142 A4
Hethe Rd Cottisford NN13 38 A2
  Hardwick NN13 .... 51 E4
Hewett Ave RG4 .... 258 B2
Hewett Cl RG4 .... 258 B2
Hewetts Cl OX8 .... 87 D2
Hewgate Ct RG4 .... 244 C1
Heycroft OX18 .... 120 C4
Heydons Terr OX17 ...... 3 F4
Heyford Cl OX4 .... 142 C1
Heyford Hill La OX4 ..... 141 F1
Heyford Hill Rdbt OX4 . 141 F1
Heyford Mead OX5 .... 92 B1
Heyford Rd
  Kirtlington OX5 .... 77 F2
  Middleton Stoney OX6 . 64 A2
  Steeple Aston OX6 ...... 62 A4
Hicks Cl OX8 .... 104 A3
Hid's Copse Rd OX2 ..... 140 A4
Higgs Cl OX11 .... 219 D3
High Acres OX16 .... 16 C2
High Cross Way OX3 .... 124 C3
High Furlong OX16 .... 16 A4
High House Cl OX3 .... 152 C4
High Land Cl HP18 .... 98 A1
High Meadow
  Caversham RG4 .... 258 B2
  Sibford Gower OX15 ... 13 D1
High Rd Beckley OX3 .... 111 D2
Brightwell-cum-S OX10 202 C2
Brightwell-cum-S, Slade End
OX10 .... 203 D1

High St
Abingdon OX13, OX14 ...... 179 F4
Adderbury OX17 ...... 23 D2
Ascott-u-W OX7 ...... 71 E1
Ashbury SN6 ...... 228 A4
Aston OX18 ...... 135 E2
Aston Rowant OX9 ...... 167 F2
Bampton OX18 ...... 134 C2
Banbury OX15, OX16, OX17 ... 16 B3
Barford St M OX15 ...... 32 C3
Benson OX10 ...... 203 F2
Bishopstone SN6 ...... 227 E2
Bloxham OX15 ...... 21 F3
Bodicote OX15 ...... 22 B4
Bodicote OX18 ...... 100 C3
Chalgrove OX44 ...... 184 B4
Charlton-on-O OX5 ...... 95 D2
Charney Bassett OX12 ...... 175 F1
Childrey OX12 ...... 213 E2
Chinnor OX9 ...... 168 B4
Chipping Norton OX7 ...... 42 C2
Clifton Hampden OX14 ...... 181 E2
Cropredy OX17 ...... 4 C1
Croughton NN13 ...... 36 B4
Cuddesdon OX44 ...... 144 A1
Cullom OX14 ...... 180 A2
Cumnor OX2 ...... 139 E3
Deddington OX15 ...... 33 F2
Didcot OX11 ...... 218 C4
Dorchester OX10 ...... 182 B1
Drayton OX14 ...... 179 D1
Drayton St L OX10 ...... 183 D3
East Hendred OX12 ...... 216 C3
Ewelme OX10 ...... 204 C2
Eynsham OX8 ...... 120 C4
Fernham SN7 ...... 193 D2
Fifield OX7 ...... 69 D1
Finstock OX7 ...... 88 A3
Goring RG8 ...... 249 E3
Great Rollright OX7 ...... 29 D2
Haddenham HP17 ...... 130 C3
Harwell OX11 ...... 217 F4
Highworth SN6 ...... 190 A3
Hinton Waldrist SN7 ...... 155 F1
Hook Norton OX15 ...... 30 A4
Islip OX5 ...... 93 F1
Lechlade GL7 ...... 150 B2
Lewknor OX9 ...... 187 D4
Long Crendon HP18 ...... 129 E3
Long Wittenham OX14 ...... 201 E4
Ludgershall HP18 ...... 98 A4
Middleton Cheney OX17 ...... 17 F4
Milton (Abingdon) OX14 ...... 199 E3
Milton-u-W OX7 ...... 70 A1
Nettlebed RG9 ...... 224 B1
North Moreton OX11 ...... 220 A4
Oxford OX1 ...... 123 E1
Pangbourne RG8 ...... 256 C3
Ramsden OX7 ...... 88 A2
Ratley OX15 ...... 2 A2
Shipton-u-W OX7 ...... 85 E4
Shrivenham SN6 ...... 209 E3
Shutford OX15 ...... 14 A3
Sonning RG4 ...... 260 B2
Souldern OX6 ...... 35 F2
South Newington OX15 ...... 31 F4
Standlake OX8 ...... 137 E2
Stanford in the V SN7 ...... 194 C4
Steventon OX13 ...... 199 D2
Stonesfield OX8 ...... 89 E4
Streatley RG8 ...... 249 D3
Sutton Courtenay OX14 ...... 200 A4
Swerford OX7 ...... 166 A4
Thame OX9 ...... 129 F1
Uffington SN7 ...... 211 E4
Upper Heyford OX6 ...... 48 C1
Upton OX11 ...... 218 B1
Wallingford OX10 ...... 221 E4
Wargrave RG10 ...... 255 E1
Watchfield SN6 ...... 191 E1
Watlington OX9 ...... 186 A1
Wheatley OX33 ...... 144 A4
Whitchurch RG8 ...... 256 B4
Witney OX8 ...... 118 A4
Woodstock OX20 ...... 91 D3
Wootton OX20 ...... 75 F2
High View OX12 ...... 214 A2
Highbridge Cl RG4 ...... 259 F2
Highclere Gdns
Banbury OX16 ...... 15 F3
Wantage OX12 ...... 214 B3
Highdown Ave RG4 ...... 259 F4
Highdown Hill Rd
Caversham RG4 ...... 259 D4
Mapledurham RG4 ...... 259 D4
Highfield HP18 ...... 129 E4
Highfield Ave OX4 ...... 124 B1
Highfield Cl OX9 ...... 147 F4
Highfield Park RG10 ...... 255 F1
Highfield Rd RG31 ...... 257 E2
Highlands 9 D1
Highlands La RG9 ...... 254 A4
Highmoor Rd RG4 ...... 258 C2
Hightown Gdns OX16 ...... 16 B2
Hightown Leys OX16 ...... 16 B2
Hightown Rd OX16 ...... 16 B2
Highworth Pl OX18 ...... 118 A4
Highworth Rd
Faringdon SN7 ...... 172 C1
Shrivenham SN6 ...... 209 D4
Highworth Way RG31 ...... 257 D1
Hill Bottom Cl RG8 ...... 250 C2
Hill Cl Charlbury OX7 ...... 73 E2
Chipping Norton OX7 ...... 42 C1
East Challow OX12 ...... 214 A2
Hill Cres OX7 ...... 88 B3
Hill Farm Cl OX9 ...... 168 B3
Hill Farm La OX6 ...... 47 E3

Hill Gdns RG8 ...... 249 D3
Hill La OX18 ...... 152 B4
Hill Lands RG10 ...... 255 E1
Hill Piece OX11 ...... 235 F4
Hill Rd Chinnor OX39 ...... 168 B3
Lewknor OX9 ...... 187 D4
Lewknor OX9 ...... 187 E3
Watchfield SN6 ...... 191 E1
Watlington OX9 ...... 206 C4
Hill Rise
Great Rollright OX7 ...... 29 D2
Horspath OX33 ...... 143 E3
Woodstock OX20 ...... 91 D4
Hill The Aynho OX17 ...... 35 E4
Bourton SN6 ...... 209 D2
Burford OX18 ...... 100 C2
Garsington OX44 ...... 143 F1
Hill Top La OX9 ...... 168 C2
Hill Top Rd OX4 ...... 142 A4
Hill View Carterton OX18 ...... 115 E2
Kingston Lisle OX12 ...... 212 A2
Oxford OX3 ...... 125 D2
Uffington SN7 ...... 211 E4
Hill View Cres OX16 ...... 16 A4
Hill View La OX13 ...... 159 D4
Hillary Way OX33 ...... 144 B4
Hillcraft Rd OX33 ...... 125 E4
Hilliat Fields OX14 ...... 179 D1
Hilliers Cl OX14 ...... 200 A4
Hillsborough Cl OX4 ...... 142 A2
Hillsborough Rd OX4 ...... 142 A2
Hillside Harwell OX11 ...... 217 F2
Whitchurch RG8 ...... 256 B4
Hillside Cl Banbury OX16 ...... 16 C2
Upper Arncott OX6 ...... 96 C4
Hillside Rd OX4 ...... 46 C1
Hilltop Rd OX3 ...... 129 E3
Hilltop Gdns OX5 ...... 93 F1
Hilltop Rd RG4 ...... 258 B3
Hillview Cl RG31 ...... 257 D1
Hillview Rd Abingdon OX14 ...... 159 F1
Oxford OX4 ...... 123 D1
Hillwerke OX9 ...... 168 B3
Hilly Lawn Ct OX7 ...... 42 C2
Hingthaysel Barns OX4 ...... 200 A4
Hilton Rd OX16 ...... 16 A3
Hinksey Hill OX1 ...... 141 D2
Hinksey Hill Intc OX1 ...... 141 E2
Hinton Hill SN6 ...... 227 D2
Hinton Rd
Hinton Waldrist OX13 ...... 156 A2
Longworth OX13 ...... 156 A2
Hinton Springs SN6 ...... 227 D2
Hirstwood RG30 ...... 257 F1
Hiskins OX12 ...... 214 A3
Hitchman Dr OX7 ...... 42 C2
Hithercroft Cholsey OX10 ...... 220 B3
South Moreton OX10 ...... 220 B3
Hithercroft Ct OX10 ...... 221 D3
Hithercroft Rd OX10 ...... 221 D4
Hive Mews OX14 ...... 179 F3
Hixet Wood OX7 ...... 73 D2
HM Prison (Bullingdon)
OX6 ...... 97 D3
Hobbs Cl OX14 ...... 180 A4
Hobby Ct OX4 ...... 142 C1
Hobson Rd OX2 ...... 123 D4
Hocker Bench SN6 ...... 227 E2
Hocketts Cl RG8 ...... 250 C2
Hockmore St OX4 ...... 142 B2
Hodge Ct OX1 ...... 141 E4
Hodgson Cl OX6 ...... 49 F4
Hogarth Pl OX14 ...... 179 F3
Hogg End Bloxham OX15 ...... 21 F2
Chipping Norton OX7 ...... 5 F3
Holborn Hill OX12 ...... 231 E4
Holcombe La OX10 ...... 183 E3
Holford Rd OX18 ...... 117 F4
Holis Cl OX18 ...... 118 B4
Holkham Cl RG30 ...... 257 F1
Holland Cl OX9 ...... 148 A4
Holland Pl OX3 ...... 124 C4
Holland Rd OX14 ...... 160 A1
Hollandbridge La RG4 ...... 207 E2
Hollands Rise OX17 ...... 23 F2
Holley Cres OX3 ...... 124 C2
Holliers Cl Sydenham OX9 ...... 167 E4
Thame OX9 ...... 147 F4
Holliers Cres OX7 ...... 60 C4
Hollington HP18 ...... 129 D4
Hollow Furlong OX8 ...... 107 F4
Hollow Way Aynho OX17 ...... 35 E4
Childrey OX12 ...... 213 E2
Oxford OX3, OX4 ...... 142 B3
Holloway Hill OX15 ...... 12 A1
Holloway
Compton Wynyates OX15 ...... 12 A1
Ibstone RG9 ...... 207 F3
Holloway Rd OX33 ...... 144 A4
Holloway Rd The SN7 ...... 192 A4
Holloway The
Harwell OX11 ...... 217 F3
Mollington OX17 ...... 4 A2
Holly Cl Bicester OX6 ...... 65 F3
Kidlington OX5 ...... 108 C4
Rotherfield Peppard RG9 ...... 242 C3
Hollybush Rd
Carterton OX18 ...... 115 E1
Hook Norton OX15 ...... 30 A4
Hollybush Row OX1 ...... 123 D1
Holm Sq OX6 ...... 65 F3
Holm Way OX6 ...... 65 F3
Holme Park Farm La RG4 ...... 260 B1
Holmemoor Dr RG4 ...... 260 C1
Holmlea Rd RG8 ...... 249 E3
Holoway Rd OX18 ...... 118 A4
Holt The Abingdon OX14 ...... 179 F4

Mollington OX17 ...... 3 F2
Purley on T RG8 ...... 257 E2
Holt Weer Cl OX10 ...... 221 D1
Holyoake Rd OX3 ...... 124 B2
Holyrood Cl RG4 ...... 259 E3
Holywell Cl OX14 ...... 160 B1
Holywell St OX1 ...... 123 E1
Home Cl Carterton OX18 ...... 115 F1
Cuttleslowe OX2 ...... 122 B4
Kidlington OX5 ...... 92 C1
Wootton (Boars Hill) OX13 ...... 159 D3
Home Croft RG31 ...... 257 D1
Home Farm OX10 ...... 204 B3
Home Farm Cl
Ambrosden OX6 ...... 81 E2
East Hendred OX12 ...... 216 B4
Shipton-u-W OX7 ...... 85 E4
Home Farm Ct OX17 ...... 23 D2
Homefield Cl HP14 ...... 188 C2
Homeleaze Rd SN6 ...... 209 F4
Homestall OX12 ...... 122 A1
Homestead Cres OX6 ...... 63 D4
Homestead Rd OX16 ...... 16 C1
Homestead The
Bladon OX20 ...... 91 E2
Kidlington OX5 ...... 108 B4
Thame OX9 ...... 129 F1
Hone Ct OX7 ...... 73 D2
Honey La OX10 ...... 220 C1
Honeybottom La OX13 ...... 159 D3
Honeyham OX18 ...... 116 B2
Honeysuckle Cl OX6 ...... 65 F3
Honeysuckle Gr OX4 ...... 143 D1
Honor Cl OX5 ...... 108 C4
Hook End La RG8 ...... 249 D1
Hook Norton Rd OX15 ...... 19 D4
Hookend La RG8 ...... 251 E4
Hooks Cl GL7 ...... 132 C1
Hop Gdns RG9 ...... 244 B1
Hopcraft Cl OX6 ...... 96 C4
Hopcraft La OX15 ...... 33 F2
Hopkins Ct OX4 ...... 142 B3
Hopton Rd OX9 ...... 130 A1
Horley Path Rd OX15 ...... 8 A1
Horn Hill OX15 ...... 32 C3
Horn Hill Rd OX17 ...... 22 C2
Horn La Adlestrop OX12 ...... 40 A3
East Hendred OX12 ...... 216 B3
Hornbeam Cl Banbury OX16 ...... 16 A3
Purley on T RG8 ...... 257 E3
Hornbeam Dr OX4 ...... 143 D1
Horne OX6 ...... 66 A4
Hornsea Cl RG30 ...... 257 F1
Horrton Hollow OX15 ...... 22 C2
Horse Cl The RG4 ...... 259 E2
Horse Close Cotts OX44 ...... 164 B4
Horse Fair
Banbury OX15, OX16 ...... 16 B3
Chipping Norton OX7 ...... 42 C2
Horse Shoe La OX15 ...... 33 F2
Horse Shoe Rd OX12 ...... 72 A4
Horsecroft SN7 ...... 194 C4
Horseman Cl OX3 ...... 124 A3
Horsemere La OX8 ...... 105 D4
Horsepond Rd OX4 ...... 252 A3
Horseshoe La OX10 ...... 75 F2
Horseshoe Park RG8 ...... 256 B3
Horseshoe Rd
Bledlow Ridge HP14 ...... 189 E4
Pangbourne RG8 ...... 256 B3
Horseshoes La OX10 ...... 203 F2
Horsham Cl OX16 ...... 8 C1
Horspath Driftway OX3 ...... 142 C4
Horspath Rd OX4 ...... 142 C3
Horton Ave OX9 ...... 148 A4
Horton Cl OX9 ...... 148 A4
Horton La OX15 ...... 21 D1
Horton View OX16 ...... 16 B2
Horwood OX3 ...... 124 B2
Hosker Cl OX3 ...... 125 D2
Hound Cl OX14 ...... 160 B1
Howard Ave OX12 ...... 196 C1
Howard Cornish Rd OX13 ...... 178 B4
Howard Rd OX16 ...... 16 C3
Howard St OX4 ...... 142 A4
Howbery Farm OX10 ...... 221 F4
Howe Cl OX33 ...... 144 A4
Howe Rd OX9 ...... 206 B4
Howes La OX6 ...... 65 D3
Howgate Dr RG8 ...... 249 E4
Howland Rd OX9 ...... 148 A3
Hoyle Cl OX8 ...... 104 A2
Huckleberry Cl RG8 ...... 257 E2
Hudson Ave OX10 ...... 204 B1
Hudson St Bicester OX6 ...... 65 E2
Deddington OX15 ...... 33 F2
Hugh Allen Cres OX3 ...... 123 F2
Hughes Cl OX7 ...... 73 E1
Hughes Cres SN7 ...... 192 B2
Humber Cl Didcot OX11 ...... 201 D1
Wantage OX12 ...... 214 C3
Humber St OX15 ...... 21 F2
Humber Wlk OX16 ...... 15 F4
Humfrey Rd OX3 ...... 124 C3
Humphries Cl OX18 ...... 115 F2
Hundred Acre Cl OX4 ...... 142 A2
Hunsdon Rd OX4 ...... 142 A2
Hunt Cl OX6 ...... 65 F1
Hunt Rd OX9 ...... 148 A4
Hunt's Cl OX8 ...... 89 E4
Hunter Cl Abingdon OX14 ...... 160 A2
Oxford OX4 ...... 142 C3
Huntercombe End La
RG9 ...... 224 A2
Hunters Chase RG4 ...... 258 C3
Hunters Cl OX12 ...... 196 B1
Hunters Field SN7 ...... 194 C4

Hunters Piece SN6 ...... 209 D1
Hunters Point OX9 ...... 168 B3
Hunts Cl OX18 ...... 100 C2
Hurdeswell OX8 ...... 90 A1
Hurdlers Green OX9 ...... 186 A1
Hurst Cl OX10 ...... 221 E3
Hurst La Cumnor OX2 ...... 140 B4
Freeland OX8 ...... 106 A4
Hurst Rise Rd OX2 ...... 140 B4
Hurst St OX4 ...... 141 F4
Huscarle Way RG31 ...... 257 E2
Hutchcomb Rd OX2 ...... 140 B4
Hutchcombe Farm Cl
OX2 ...... 140 B4
Huxley Cl Bicester OX6 ...... 65 E2
Wootton (Oxford) OX13 ...... 159 D3
Hyacinth Wlk OX4 ...... 143 D1
Hyde Copse OX13 ...... 178 B4
Hyde Gr OX15 ...... 21 E2
Hyde Pl OX14 ...... 179 E3
Hyde Rd OX12 ...... 196 A3
Hyde The OX14 ...... 179 E3
Hydrangea Wlk OX16 ...... 9 D1
Hythe Bridge St OX1 ...... 123 D1
Ian Mikardo Way RG4 ...... 259 E1
Ibstone Ave RG4 ...... 259 F3
Ibstone Rd HP14 ...... 188 B2
Ickford Rd
Shabbington HP18 ...... 128 B1
Tiddington OX9 ...... 145 F4
Worminghall HP18 ...... 127 F3
Ickleton Rd
East Challow OX12 ...... 214 A2
Wantage OX12 ...... 214 A2
Icknield Cl
Aston Rowant OX9 ...... 168 A2
Didcot OX11 ...... 200 B1
Icknield La OX12 ...... 214 C2
Icknield Pl RG8 ...... 249 E4
Icknield Rd RG8 ...... 249 E4
Icknield Way SN6 ...... 227 E2
Idbury Cl OX8 ...... 117 F4
Iden Ho SN6 ...... 209 D1
Iffley Rd OX4 ...... 141 F4
Iffley Turn OX4 ...... 142 A3
Ilchester Mews RG4 ...... 259 E2
Ilex Cl RG4 ...... 252 C2
Ilges La OX10 ...... 221 D1
Ilkley Rd RG4 ...... 258 C2
Illingworth Ave RG4 ...... 259 F3
Ilsley Cl RG4 ...... 252 C3
Ilsley Rd OX3 ...... 124 C1
Independent Bsns Pk
HP14 ...... 188 B3
Ingham La OX9 ...... 186 A1
Ingle Cl OX3 ...... 124 A2
Inglewood Cl RG4 ...... 252 C3
Ingrebourne Way OX11 ...... 200 C2
Inkerman Cl OX14 ...... 159 E1
Innsworth Rd OX18 ...... 115 F2
Inott Furze OX3 ...... 142 B4
Insall Rd OX7 ...... 42 C2
Ireton Cl OX44 ...... 184 B3
Ireton Ct OX9 ...... 129 F1
Iron Down Hill
Barford St M OX15 ...... 32 B2
South Newington OX15 ...... 30 B4
Ironstone Hollow OX15 ...... 30 B4
Ironstones OX16 ...... 16 A4
Isis Ave OX6 ...... 65 D1
Isis Bsns Ctr OX4 ...... 142 C3
Isis Cl Abingdon OX14 ...... 160 B2
Oxford OX4 ...... 106 A4
Islip Rd Bletchingdon OX5 ...... 93 D4
Cuttleslowe OX2 ...... 123 D4
Islsley Rd OX3 ...... 124 C2
Itchen Cl OX11 ...... 201 D2
Ivatt Wlk OX16 ...... 16 C4
Ivy La Mollington OX17 ...... 4 A2
Oxford OX3 ...... 124 B2
Ivybank RG31 ...... 257 E1
Ivybridge SN6 ...... 258 B1
Jack Argent Cl ⊠ OX4 ...... 142 C1
Jack Straw's La OX3 ...... 124 A2
Jackdaw La OX4 ...... 141 F4
Jackies La OX33 ...... 144 B4
Jackman Cl OX14 ...... 180 A3
Jackson Cl OX18 ...... 115 E1
Jackson Dr OX1 ...... 141 F1
Jackson Rd Bledington OX7 ...... 54 B1
Cuttleslowe OX2 ...... 109 D1
Jacobs Cl OX8 ...... 104 A4
Jago Ho OX7 ...... 60 C4
James Cl OX18 ...... 152 C4
James St OX4 ...... 141 F4
James Wolfe Rd OX4 ...... 142 C4
Jane Seaman Ct OX4 ...... 143 D1
Japonica Cl OX6 ...... 65 D1
Japonica Wlk OX16 ...... 9 D1
Jarn Way OX1 ...... 140 B1
Jarvis La OX6 ...... 66 A1
Jasmine Cl OX4 ...... 142 C2
Jasmine Pl OX6 ...... 65 D1
Javelin Way OX10 ...... 204 B2
Jay Cl OX6 ...... 81 D4
Jaynes Cl OX16 ...... 16 B1
Jefferson Cl RG4 ...... 259 E4
Jefferson Way OX9 ...... 148 A4
Jeffersons Piece OX7 ...... 73 E3
Jemmetts Cl OX10 ...... 182 B1
Jennings La OX11 ...... 217 F4
Jericho St OX2 ...... 123 D2
Jerome Way OX5 ...... 92 B3
Jersey Dr OX16 ...... 9 D1

Jersey Rd OX4 ...... 142 A2
Jervis Cl OX7 ...... 60 C4
Jespers Hill SN7 ...... 173 D2
Jesse's La OX18 ...... 129 E3
Jessops Cl OX3 ...... 123 F3
Jethro Tull Gdns OX10 ...... 221 F4
Jeune St OX4 ...... 141 F4
Joan Lawrence Pl OX3 ...... 124 C1
John Buchan Rd OX3 ...... 124 A3
John Garne Way OX3 ...... 124 A1
John Lopes Rd OX8 ...... 120 C4
John Mason Rd OX14 ...... 180 A4
John Morris Rd OX14 ...... 179 F3
John Piers La OX1 ...... 141 E3
John Snow Pl OX3 ...... 124 C2
John Towle Cl OX1 ...... 141 E3
Johnson Cl OX44 ...... 143 E1
Johnston's Way OX7 ...... 42 C1
Johnstone Pl OX10 ...... 221 E4
Jordan Cl Caversham RG4 ...... 259 F3
Didcot OX11 ...... 201 D1
Jordan Hill OX2 ...... 109 D1
Josey Cl RG4 ...... 252 C3
Jourdain Rd OX4 ...... 142 C1
Jowett Wlk OX1 ...... 123 E1
Joyce's Rd SN7 ...... 194 B4
Jubilee Cl OX6 ...... 62 A4
Jubilee Cotts OX12 ...... 215 F3
Jubilee La OX6 ...... 16 B3
Jubilee Rd OX18 ...... 188 C2
Jubilee Way OX11 ...... 219 D4
Jubillee La OX7 ...... 85 D4
Judd's Cl OX8 ...... 118 B4
Judges Cl OX5 ...... 108 C4
Junction Rd Banbury OX16 ...... 16 C3
Churchill OX7 ...... 55 F2
Oxford OX4 ...... 142 B3
Juniper Cl OX16 ...... 9 D1
Juniper Dr OX4 ...... 142 C1
Juniper Gdns OX6 ...... 65 F3
Juniper Way RG31 ...... 257 E1
Juxon St OX2 ...... 123 D2
Kames Cl OX4 ...... 142 A3
Katchside OX14 ...... 199 F3
Katherine's Wlk GL7 ...... 150 B2
Keats Cl OX6 ...... 65 D2
Keats Rd OX16 ...... 16 A2
Keble Cl GL7 ...... 150 B3
Keble Rd Bicester OX6 ...... 65 F2
Oxford OX1 ...... 123 E2
Kedleston Rise OX16 ...... 16 C1
Keene Cl OX44 ...... 161 D4
Keens La OX9 ...... 168 B3
Keeys Cl OX6 ...... 50 B2
Kelburne Rd OX4 ...... 142 A2
Kelham Hall Dr OX33 ...... 144 A4
Kelly's Rd OX13 ...... 143 F4
Kelmscott Cl RG4 ...... 258 C2
Kelso Mews RG4 ...... 259 F3
Kelvedon Way RG4 ...... 258 C3
Kemps Rd OX17 ...... 23 D2
Kempson Cres OX4 ...... 142 A1
Kempster Cl OX14 ...... 180 A4
Kendal Ave RG4 ...... 259 F3
Kendal Cres OX2 ...... 109 D1
Kendal Piece OX7 ...... 73 E2
Kenhill Rd OX15 ...... 6 B1
Kenilworth Ave OX4 ...... 142 A4
Kenilworth Rd OX2 ...... 139 F2
Kenilworth Way OX16 ...... 15 F3
Kenley Ave OX18 ...... 115 E2
Kennedy Cl OX4 ...... 142 C4
Kennedy Cres OX10 ...... 220 C1
Kennedy Dr RG8 ...... 256 C3
Kennedy Rd OX6 ...... 65 E1
Kennel La
Chipping Norton OX7 ...... 42 A1
Steventon OX13 ...... 199 D3
Kennet Cl Berinsfield OX10 ...... 182 B2
Bicester OX6 ...... 65 E1
Grove OX12 ...... 196 B1
Kennet Rd Abingdon OX14 ...... 160 A1
Harwell OX11 ...... 217 E1
Kennett Rd OX3 ...... 124 B1
Kennington Rd
Kennington OX1 ...... 141 F1
Radley OX14 ...... 160 C3
Kennington Rdbt OX1 ...... 141 F2
Kennylands Rd RG4 ...... 253 D2
Kensington Cl
Abingdon OX14 ...... 179 F2
Kings Sutton OX17 ...... 23 F3
Kent Cl Abingdon OX14 ...... 180 A4
Oxford OX4 ...... 142 C2
Kentons La RG10 ...... 255 E4
Kentwood Cl
Oxford OX10 ...... 220 C1
Reading RG30 ...... 257 F1
Kentwood Hill RG31 ...... 257 F1
Kenville Rd OX1 ...... 141 F1
Kernham Dr RG31 ...... 257 D2
Kerosene Cl OX6 ...... 9 D1
Kersington Cres OX4 ...... 142 B2
Kerwood Cl OX20 ...... 91 D4
Keston Cl RG4 ...... 259 E1
Kestrel Cl OX18 ...... 115 E2
Kestrel Cres OX4 ...... 142 C1
Kestrel Pl OX4 ...... 142 B1
Kestrel Way OX6 ...... 81 D4
Kestrels The OX12 ...... 196 B1
Ketchmere Cl HP18 ...... 129 E3
Kew Win OX11 ...... 201 D1
Keydale Rd OX33 ...... 143 F4

Keyser Rd OX15 .... 22 C4
Keyte's Cl OX17 .... 23 D2
Kibble Cl OX11 .... 219 D4
Kiddington Rd OX7 .... 60 C4
Kidlington Business Park
OX5 .... 92 B1
Kiddington Ctr OX5 ...... 92 C1
Kiddington Rd OX5 .... 93 F1
Kidmore End Rd
  Caversham RG4 .... 259 D4
  Mapledurham RG4 .... 259 D4
Kidmore La RG4 .... 252 C2
Kidmore Rd RG4 .... 258 C3
Kilbale Cres OX16 .... 16 B2
Kildare Gdns RG4 .... 259 E2
Kilkenny La OX18 .... 115 F3
Kiln Cl OX4 .... 161 E4
Kiln La Garsington OX44 . 143 E1
  Oxford OX3, OX33, OX44 . 124 C1
  Shiplake RG9 .... 254 B1
  Wheatley OX33 .... 144 A4
Kiln Rd RG4 .... 259 E4
Kimbells Cl HP18 .... 128 B1
Kimber Cl OX33 .... 144 A4
Kimber Rd OX14 .... 179 E4
Kimbers Cl OX12 .... 196 A2
Kinecroft OX10 .... 221 E4
Kineton Rd OX1 .... 141 E4
King Alfred Dr OX11 ..... 200 C1
King Edward St OX1 ..... 123 E1
King James Way RG9 .... 254 B4
King St OX2 .... 123 D2
King Wlk OX11 .... 200 C1
King's Ave OX6 .... 65 E1
King's Cl OX7 .... 147 F4
King's Cross Rd OX2 ..... 123 D4
King's End OX6 .... 65 E1
King's head La OX5 ...... 93 F1
King's Head Mews OX7 .. 42 C2
King's La SN7 .... 192 A2
King's Mill La OX3 .... 123 F1
King's Rd Banbury OX16 . 16 A3
  Henley-on-T RG9 .... 244 B2
  Thame OX9 .... 148 A4
Kingfisher Cl OX14 ...... 179 F2
Kingfisher Dr OX16 ...... 16 C2
Kingfisher Grn OX4 ...... 142 C1
Kingfisher Way OX6 ..... 81 E4
Kingfishers OX12 .... 214 C4
Kingham Dr OX18 .... 115 E1
Kingham Rd OX7 .... 55 F3
Kings Ave
  Highworth SN6 .... 190 A3
  Sandford-on-T OX4 .... 178 B4
Kings Cl Ashbury SN6 ... 228 A4
  Brightwell-cum-S OX10 . 202 C2
  Henley-on-T RG9 .... 244 B1
  Worminghall HP18 ..... 127 E3
Kings Farm La RG9 ...... 253 F3
Kings La Harwell OX11 .. 217 F4
  Kencot OX18 .... 132 B2
Kingsclere Rd RG4 .... 259 E1
Kings Stile OX17 .... 10 C1
Kings Way Dr OX5 .... 109 D4
Kingsclere Rd OX6 ...... 65 E1
Kingsey Rd OX6 .... 130 B1
Kingsholme Cl OX11 .... 128 C3
Kingsley Rd OX6 .... 65 D2
Kingsmead GL7 .... 150 B3
Kingston Cl OX14 .... 179 F4
Kingston Hts OX35 ...... 105 D4
Kingston Hill OX9 .... 188 A4
Kingston Rd OX2 .... 123 D2
Kingsway Banbury OX16 . 16 A3
  Caversham RG4 .... 259 F3
Kingswood La HP18 ..... 98 C3
Kinson Rd RG30 .... 258 A1
Kipling Cl OX6 .... 65 E2
Kirby Cl
  Middle Barton OX7 ..... 60 C4
  South Moreton OX11 .. 219 F3
Kirby Dr OX14 .... 142 B3
Kirby Rd GL54 .... 68 A2
Kirk Cl Cutteslowe OX2 . 109 D1
  Kennington OX1 .... 160 C4
Kirkfell Cl RG31 .... 257 E1
Kirkham Cl OX4 .... 259 F3
Kirtlington Rd OX6 ...... 63 D4
Kit La RG9 .... 241 E3
Knapp Cl OX14 .... 179 E4
Knappe Cl RG9 .... 254 B4
Knapton's Croft OX6 .... 62 B3
Knighton Cl RG4 .... 259 D4
Knighton Hill SN7 .... 210 C1
Knights Rd OX4 .... 142 B1
Knights Way RG4 .... 259 D3
Knightsbridge La OX9 .. 186 A3
Knoll Cl OX12 .... 231 F4
Knoll The RG31 .... 257 D2
Knolles Rd OX4 .... 142 B2
Knollys Cl OX14 .... 160 A2
Knowlands SN6 .... 190 A4
Knowle Cl RG4 .... 258 B2
Knowle La OX6 .... 96 C4
Knowsley Rd RG31 ...... 257 E2
Kybald St OX1 .... 123 E1
Kyetts Cnr OX17 .... 4 C1
Kynaston Rd OX4 .... 218 C4
Kysbie Cl OX14 .... 159 F2

Laburnum Ave OX13 .... 159 E1
Laburnum Cl OX5 .... 81 E2
Laburnum Cres OX5 .... 108 C3

Laburnum Gr
  Banbury OX16 .... 16 B1
  Didcot OX11 .... 218 C4
Laburnum Rd OX2 .... 140 B4
Lacemakers Chinnor OX9 168 B3
  Long Crendon HP18 ... 129 E4
Lacey Cl OX9 .... 148 A4
Lackmore Gdns RG8 .... 250 C4
Ladburn La OX18 .... 115 D3
Ladder Hill OX33 .... 144 A4
Ladman Rd OX4 .... 142 C2
Lady Gr OX14 .... 201 D2
Lady Jane Ct RG4 .... 259 E2
Lady Wlk SN7 .... 211 E4
Ladygrove Paddock
OX14 .... 179 E3
Ladywell Cl OX18 .... 105 E3
Laggots Cl SN7 .... 155 F1
Lake Rd
  East Hagbourne OX11 . 218 C3
  Shrivenham SN6 .... 209 E4
Lake St OX1 .... 141 E3
Lake View NN13 .... 38 A2
Lakefield Rd OX14 ...... 160 A2
Lakeside OX2 .... 108 C1
Lakeside Ind Est OX8 .. 137 F4
Lamarsh Rd OX2 .... 122 C1
Lamb La OX20 .... 91 D1
Lamb's Cres OX16 ...... 16 C3
Lamb's La OX20 .... 75 F2
Lambe Ave OX14 .... 199 E2
Lambert Wlk OX12 ..... 129 F1
Lamborough Hill OX13 . 159 D3
Lambourn Rd OX4 ...... 142 A2
Lambourne Cres OX6 .. 65 F1
Lambourne Rd RG4 .... 252 C3
Lambrick Way OX14 ... 179 F2
Lambridge La RG9 ..... 244 B2
Lambridge Wood Rd
RG9 .... 244 A2
Lammas Cl OX5 .... 92 C1
Lambton Cl OX14 ...... 142 C3
Lambwath Stream OX11 . 200 C2
Lammas Cl OX14 .... 159 F1
Lamorna Cres RG31 .... 257 E1
Lampitts Green OX15 .. 15 D4
Lancaster Ave OX14 ... 204 B2
Lancaster Cl OX26 ..... 66 A2
Lancaster Pl OX18 ..... 115 F1
Lanchester Dr OX16 ... 15 F4
Lancott La OX8F 137 D2
Lancut Rd OX8 .... 103 F1
Landells OX18 .... 134 C2
Landseer Wlk OX14 ... 179 F3
Lane Cl Horley OX15 ... 8 A2
  Kidlington OX5 .... 108 B4
Lane End OX10 .... 222 A4
Lane The Bloxham SN6 . 227 D2
  Chastleton GL56 ...... 40 B4
  Chilton OX11 .... 235 F4
  Cuddesdon OX44 ...... 144 B1
  Denchworth OX15 ..... 33 D2
  Fritwell OX6 .... 49 F4
  Great Tew OX7 .... 45 E4
  Lower Heyford OX6 ... 62 B3
Lanes The OX18 .... 134 C2
Langdale Gate OX18 .. 118 A4
Langdale Rd OX9 ...... 148 A4
Langford Cl OX4 .... 259 E3
Langford Gdns OX6 ... 65 E1
Langford La Kidlington OX5 92 A1
  Wendlebury OX5 ...... 80 A1
Langhams Way RG10 . 255 F1
Langley Cl OX3 .... 124 B1
Langley La OX18 ...... 152 B3
Langley Rd Abingdon OX14 159 F1
  Chalgrove OX44 ...... 184 B2
Langley's La OX4 ...... 137 E1
Langston Cl OX7 ...... 55 F3
Langton Ave OX4 ..... 81 E2
Lanham Way OX4 ..... 142 A1
Lansdown Cl OX16 ... 16 A4
Lansdowne Rd SN7 .. 173 D2
Lansdowne Rd OX13 . 159 D3
Lapwing Cl OX6 ...... 81 D4
Lapwing La OX10 .... 221 D1
Larch Cl Bicester OX6 . 65 F3
  Kingston Bagpuize OX13 . 156 C1
Larch End OX44 ..... 143 E1
Larches The
  Carterton OX18 ..... 115 E1
  Oxford OX3 .... 125 D2
Larissa Cl RG31 .... 257 E1
Lark Hill OX12 ...... 215 D1
Larkdown OX12 .... 214 C2
Larkfield OX10 ..... 221 D1
Larkfields OX3 ..... 124 C1
Larkhill Pl OX14 ... 179 E4
Larkhill Rd OX14 .. 179 E4
Larkins La OX3 .... 124 B2
Larksfield Cl OX18 . 133 E4
Larksfield Rd OX16 . 16 B1
Larkswood Cl RG31 . 257 D2
Larsen Rd OX6 .... 63 E4
Lashbrook Mead RG9 255 D2
Lashbrook Rd RG9 . 255 D2
Lashford La OX13 . 158 C4
Lashford Rd OX13 . 158 C4
Lashlake Rd OX9 .. 129 F1
Latchford La OX44 . 164 C4
Lathbury Rd OX2 .. 123 D3
Latimer Rd
  Carterton OX18 .... 115 F1
  Oxford OX3 .... 124 B1
Latton Ct Chilton OX11 . 235 F4
  Kingston Bagpuize OX13 . 156 B1
Laud's Cl RG9 ..... 244 B1
Laughton Hill OX8 . 89 E4

Launceston Ave RG4 ... 259 F3
Laundry La OX18 .... 135 E2
Launton Rd Bicester OX6 66 A1
  Stratton Audley OX6 .. 52 B1
Laurel Cl Banbury OX16 . 16 B1
  Carterton OX18 .... 115 E2
  Chalgrove OX44 ...... 184 B4
Laurel Cres OX12 ...... 214 C4
Laurel Dr
  Kingston Bagpuize OX13 . 156 C1
  Reading RG31 .... 257 D3
Laurel Farm Cl OX3 ... 124 B2
Laurels The Fringford OX6 52 B3
  Great Coxwell SN7 ... 192 B4
  Stadhampton OX44 .. 163 E1
  Tetsworth OX9 .... 166 A4
Lavender Cl OX16 .... 9 D1
Lavender Pl OX18 .... 115 E1
Lavender Sq OX18 ... 134 C2
Lawns The HP18 ..... 98 A1
Lawrence Cl OX12 ... 213 E2
Lawrence La OX18 ... 100 C3
Lawrence Leys OX15 . 21 F3
Lawrence Rd OX4 ... 142 B3
Lawrence Way OX6 . 65 E1
Lawson Dr RG4 ..... 258 C3
Lawson La OX11 .... 235 E4
Lawton Ave OX10 .. 115 E1
Lay Ave OX10 ...... 182 B3
Laym Rise RG31 ... 257 E2
Lea Gr OX11 .... 200 C1
Lea Rd RG4 .... 252 C2
Leabrook Cl OX16 . 16 B1
Leach Rd
  Berinsfield OX10 .. 182 B3
  Bicester OX6 ...... 65 E1
Leafield Rd Crawley OX8 . 103 F3
  Oxford OX4 .... 142 B3
  Shipton-u-W OX7 . 86 A3
Leamington Dr SN7 . 172 C1
Leander Way OX4 .. 65 E1
Lechlade Rd Buscot SN7 171 E4
  Faringdon SN7 .... 172 B3
  Highworth SN6 .... 190 A4
  Langford GL7 ..... 132 B1
Leckford Pl OX2 ... 123 D2
Leckford Rd OX2 .. 123 D2
Ledbury Cl RG30 .. 258 A1
Ledgers Cl OX4 ... 142 B1
Lee Ave OX14 .... 180 A4
Lee Cl Charlbury OX7 . 73 E2
  Kidlington OX5 ... 92 B1
Lee Ct OX9 .... 147 F4
Lee Rd HP27 ..... 169 F3
Lees Hts OX7 .... 73 E2
Lees The SN7 ... 172 C2
Leicester St RG9 . 244 B2
Leiden Rd OX3 .. 142 C4
Leigh Cl OX8 ... 105 D3
Leigh Gr OX16 .. 16 B3
Lely Ct OX4 .... 179 F3
Lennox Gdns OX16 . 16 A2
Lenthall OX5 ... 93 D4
Lenthall Rd
  Abingdon OX14 . 179 F4
  Oxford OX4 .... 141 F2
Lenton Rd OX16 . 16 B1
Leon Cl OX4 ... 141 F4
Leopold St OX4 . 142 A4
Lerwick Croft OX6 . 65 F2
Lester Cl OX17 . 23 D3
Lester Way OX10 . 221 D4
Letcombe Ave OX14 . 179 F4
Letcombe Hill OX12 . 214 A2
Letcombe Wlk OX12 . 196 B1
Letts Alley OX7 . 186 A1
Levence Cl OX16 . 16 C3
Leverkus Ho OX9 . 168 B3
Levery Cl OX14 . 180 B4
Lewell Ave OX4 . 123 F2
Lewin Cl OX4 .. 142 B2
Lewington Cl OX44 . 164 B4
Lewis Cl OX15 . 22 B1
Lewis Rd OX7 . 42 B1
Lewknor Cl OX9 . 187 D4
Ley The OX20 . 91 E3
Leybourne Gdns OX9 . 168 B4
Leyes The OX5 . 33 F2
Leysland Ct OX16 . 16 A2
Leys App OX7 . 42 C1
Leys Cl OX15 . 15 D4
Leys Pl OX4 . 142 A4
Leys Rd OX2 . 139 E3
Leys The Adderbury OX17 22 C2
  Chipping Norton OX7 . 42 B1
  Salford OX7 . 41 F3
Leys Villas OX8 . 118 A4
Leyshon Rd OX33 . 144 B4
Library Ave OX11 . 217 D1
Liddell Rd OX4 . 142 B2
Lidderdale Rd GL54 . 68 A2
Liddiard Cl
  Kennington OX1 . 160 C4
  Wantage OX12 . 214 B3
Liddon Rd OX44 . 184 B3
Lido Rd OX11 . 234 C4
Lidsey Rd OX16 . 16 A3
Lilac Cl RG8 . 257 E3
Limborough Rd OX12 . 214 B3
Lime Ave OX16 . 16 C2
Lime Cres OX6 . 65 F3
Lime Gr Chinnor OX9 . 168 B3
  Kingston Bagpuize OX13 . 156 B1
Lime Kiln Rd OX5 . 77 F2
Lime Rd OX2 . 140 B4
Lime Tree Cl OX18 . 115 E2
Lime Tree Rd RG8 . 249 D3
Lime Wlk OX3 . 124 B1

Limes The
  Dorchester OX10 ... 182 B1
  Stratton Audley OX6 . 52 B1
Limes Way HP18 ... 128 B1
Limetree Cl OX12 . 196 B1
Limetrees OX11 ... 217 F1
Linacre Cl OX11 ... 219 D4
Lince La OX5 ..... 77 F1
Lincoln Cl Banbury OX16 16 B1
  Bicester OX6 .... 66 A2
  Standlake OX8 .. 137 E2
Lincoln Gdns OX11 . 219 D4
Lincoln Pl OX9 .. 147 F4
Lincoln Rd OX1 .. 141 E3
Lincombe La OX1 . 159 F4
Lincraft Cl OX5 .. 108 C4
Linden Cres OX12 . 196 C1
Linden Gate OX11 . 217 F4
Linden Rd OX6 .. 65 F3
Lindsay Dr OX14 . 160 A1
Link The Banbury OX16 . 16 A3
  Marston OX3 .... 123 F2
  Oxford OX3 ..... 124 C2
Links Rd OX1 ... 160 C4
Links Rd OX3 ... 221 F4
Linkside Ave OX2 . 108 C1
Linkwood Rd OX8 . 103 E1
Linnet Cl
  Clifton Hampden OX14 . 182 A2
  Oxford OX4 .... 142 B1
Linton Rd OX2 .. 123 E3
Lion Meadow RG9 . 224 B1
Lipscombe Pl OX18 . 115 E2
Lipstick Pl OX11 . 200 C1
Lister Cl RG8 ... 257 F2
Litchfield Cl OX7 . 58 C3
Lithgow Rd GL54 . 68 A2
Little Acreage OX3 . 123 F3
Little Blenheim OX5 . 108 A3
Little Bowden La RG8 . 256 C2
Little Brewery St OX4 . 123 F1
Little Bridge Rd OX15 . 21 E2
Little Croft Rd RG8 . 249 E3
Little Glebe RG4 . 260 C2
Little Green OX15 . 21 E2
Little Howe Cl OX14 . 160 C2
Little La Aynho OX17 . 35 E4
  Milton (Abingdon) OX14 . 199 E3
Little Lees OX7 . 73 E2
Little Paddock OX6 . 52 B4
Littlebrook Meadow
OX7 .... 70 B1
Littlegate St OX1 . 141 E4
Littlehay Rd OX4 . 142 B2
Littlejohns La RG30 . 258 B1
Littlemore Rd OX4 . 142 B2
Littlemore Rdbt OX4 . 142 A2
Littlestead Cl RG4 . 259 F3
Littlewood HP14 . 188 C3
Littlemore Bsns Ctr
OX33 .... 143 F4
Littleworth Hill OX12 . 214 B3
Littleworth Rd
  Benson OX10 .. 203 F2
  Wheatley OX33 . 144 A4
Lobelia Rd OX4 . 142 C1
Lock Cres OX5 . 108 C3
Lockheart Cres OX4 . 142 B2
Lockheed Cl OX16 . 16 B4
Lockinge Cl OX11 . 218 C2
Locks La OX12 . 214 B2
Lockstile Mead RG8 . 249 E3
Lockstile Way RG8 . 249 E3
Lockway OX14 . 199 D4
Locombe Hill GL7 . 131 D4
Loddon Ave OX10 . 182 B3
Loddon Cl
  Abingdon OX14 . 160 A1
  Bicester OX6 .. 65 E1
Loddon Dr Didcot OX11 201 D1
  Wargrave RG10 . 255 D1
Loder Rd OX11 . 217 F4
Loder's Field GL7 . 150 B2
Loders The GL7 . 150 B2
Lodge Cl Banbury OX16 16 B2
  Bicester OX6 .. 65 F3
  Marston OX3 .. 123 F4
Lodge Rd OX5 . 90 C1
Logic La OX1 . 123 E1
Lombard St
  Abingdon OX14 . 179 F4
  Eynsham OX8 .. 120 C4
Lombard Way OX16 . 17 D3
Lomond Ave RG4 . 259 F3
London La OX7 . 71 E1
London Pl OX4 . 123 F1
London Rd Bicester OX6 80 C4
  Blewbury OX11 . 236 C4
  Chipping Norton OX7 . 43 D2
  Great Haseley OX9 . 146 A2
  Headington OX3 . 124 B1
  Oxford OX3, OX33 . 126 A1
  Tiddington OX9 . 145 F3
  Upton OX11 .. 236 C4
  Wheatley OX33 . 144 B4
  Woodstock RG5 . 144 B4
London St SN7 . 173 D2
Long Cl N Hinksey Vill OX2 122 A1
  Oxford OX2, OX3 . 142 C4
Long Crendon Ind Est
HP18 .... 129 E4
Long Crendon Rd HP18 128 B2
Long Ford Cl OX1 . 141 E4
Long Furlong HP17 . 130 C3
Long Furlong Rd OX13 . 158 C4
Long Ground OX14 . 142 C1

Long La Oxford OX4 .... 142 B2
  Purley on T RG31 ..... 257 D2
  Reading RG31 .... 257 D2
Long Toll RG8 .... 251 D3
Long Tow OX13 .... 159 E1
Long Wall HP17 ...... 130 C3
Long Wittenham Rd
OX11 .... 220 A4
Longcot Rd Longcot SN7 192 A1
  Shrivenham SN6 .... 209 E3
Longelandes Cl OX16 . 16 A4
Longelandes Way OX16 16 A4
Longfellow Cl OX6 ... 65 E2
Longfellow Dr OX14 . 179 E3
Longfellow Rd OX16 . 16 A4
Longfields Bicester OX6 65 F1
  Marcham OX13 ..... 178 B4
Longford Way OX11 . 200 C1
Longhurst Cl OX4 ... 258 B3
Longlands Rd OX4 .. 142 C2
Longleat Cl OX16 ... 16 C1
Longleat Dr RG31 .. 257 D2
Longmead OX14 ... 159 F1
Longmore Ave GL54 . 68 A2
Longore OX8 .... 89 E4
Longore Cl OX8 .... 89 E4
Longwall OX4 ...... 142 A2
Longwall St OX1 ... 123 E1
Longworth Cl OX16 . 16 C4
Longworth Rd
  Charney Bassett OX12 . 176 A2
  Oxford OX2 ...... 123 D2
Lonsdale Rd OX2 .. 123 D4
Lord Cl OX18 ..... 72 B1
Lords Piece Rd OX7 . 42 B2
Lovatt Cl OX18 ... 115 E3
Love La OX9 ..... 186 A1
Lovegrove's La RG8 . 241 E2
Lovelace Cl OX14 . 160 A2
Lovelace Dr OX5 . 109 D4
Lovelace Rd OX2 . 109 D1
Lovell Cl Ducklington OX8 118 A2
  Henley-on-T RG9 . 254 B4
  Swinbrook OX18 . 102 A2
Lower Armour Rd RG31 257 E1
Lower Bungalows RG8 249 E4
Lower Cherwell St OX16 16 B3
Lower Church St HP14 188 C3
Lower Cl OX15 .. 22 C4
Lower Common SN7 . 211 E4
Lower Cres OX9 . 102 C2
Lower Elmstone Dr RG31 257 E1
Lower End
  Great Milton OX44 . 145 D2
  Piddington OX6 .. 97 F4
  Salford OX7 .... 41 F2
  Shutford OX15 .. 14 A3
Lower Farm Cl HP18 . 128 B2
Lower Farm La OX17 . 3 F2
Lower Hades Rd OX5 77 D3
Lower Henley Rd RG4 259 E2
Lower Heyford Rd OX6 63 D3
Lower Icknield Way OX9 168 B4
Lower Rd
  Aston Rowant OX9 . 166 C2
  Blackthorn OX6 .. 82 A2
  Chilton OX11 .... 235 E4
  Chinnor OX9 .... 168 B4
  Long Hanborough RG8 90 C1
Lower St
  Barford St M OX15 . 32 C3
  Islip OX5 .... 93 F1
Lower Wharf OX10 . 221 E4
Lower Whitley Rd OX2 139 E4
Lowes Cl Shiplake RG9 255 D2
  Stokenchurch HP14 . 188 B3
Lowfield Green RG4 . 259 F2
Lowfield Rd RG4 .. 259 E3
Loyd Cl OX14 .... 160 A2
Loyd Rd OX11 ... 218 B3
Lucca Dr OX14 .. 179 F3
Lucerne Ave OX4 . 163 E1
Lucerne Rd OX2 . 123 C4
Lucey Cl RG31 .. 257 D2
Lucky La OX4 ... 16 B3
Ludford Gdns OX15 . 22 B1
Luggershall Rd OX6 . 97 F4
Ludlow Dr OX9 .. 148 A4
Lugsden Gr OX9 . 148 A4
Luker Ave RG9 .. 244 B2
Lumberd Rd OX14 . 160 A1
Lune Cl OX11 ... 201 D1
Lupton Rd Thame OX9 148 A4
  Wallingford OX10 . 221 D4
Luscombe Cl RG4 . 259 E2
Luther Ct OX1 .. 141 E4
Lych Gate La OX44 . 145 D3
Lycroft Cl RG8 .. 249 E4
Lydalls Cl OX11 . 200 C1
Lydalls Rd OX11 . 200 C1
Lydia Cl OX3 ... 124 C2
Lydsee Gate OX12 . 214 A3
Lye Valley OX3 . 142 B4
Lyefield Cl RG4 . 259 D3
Lyford Cl OX11 . 179 D1
Lyford Way OX14 . 160 A1
Lymbrook Cl OX8 . 119 E3
Lyme Gr RG31 . 257 D2
Lymington Gate RG4 258 C2
Lynch The OX12 . 216 B3
Lyndene Rd OX11 . 200 B2
Lyndhurst Rd
  Goring RG8 ... 249 E1
  Reading RG30 . 258 A1
Lyndworth Cl OX3 . 124 C2
Lyndworth Mews OX3 124 C2
Lyneham Cl OX18 . 115 E1

Lyneham Rd Bicester OX6 ...... 66 A2
Milton-u-W OX7 .... 70 A2
Lynges Cl OX14 .... 160 A1
Lynmouth Rd Didcot OX11 .. 218 C4
Reading RG1 .... 259 D1
Lynn Cl OX3 .... 123 F2
Lynt Rd SN6 .... 170 A3
Lynton La OX18 .... 107 E1
Lyon Cl OX14 .... 160 A1
Lysander Cl OX6 .... 66 A2
Lytham End RG31 .... 257 D2
Lytton Rd OX4 .... 142 A3

Maberley Cl OX14 .... 179 E3
Mably Way OX12 .... 214 B4
Macaulay Cl OX6 .... 65 E2
Macdonald Cl OX11 .... 200 B1
Mackenzie Cl OX6 .... 65 E2
Mackley Cl OX15 .... 33 F2
Macray Rd OX8 .... 118 A2
Mafeking Row OX9 .... 186 C2
Magdalen Cl OX6 .... 65 F2
Magdalen Ct OX11 .... 219 D4
Magdalen Pl OX18 .... 115 E1
Magdalen Rd OX4 .... 142 A4
Magdalen St OX1 .... 123 E1
Magnolia Cl OX5 .... 108 C4
Magnolias The
   Banbury OX16 .... 9 D1
   Bicester OX6 .... 65 F3
Magpie La OX1 .... 123 E1
Maidcroft Rd OX4 .... 142 B3
Maiden's Cl SN6 .... 191 E1
Maidley Cl OX4 .... 104 B1
Main Ave OX4 .... 161 E4
Main Rd Broughton OX15 ...... 15 E1
   Curbridge OX8 .... 117 E3
   East Hagbourne OX11 .... 218 C3
   Fyfield OX13 .... 157 E1
   Long Hanborough OX8 .... 90 B1
   Middleton Cheney OX17 ...... 17 F4
   Sutton Courtenay OX14 ..... 200 C4
   West Hanney OX12 .... 196 C3
Main St Adlestrop OX12 .... 40 B2
   Bledington OX7 .... 54 B1
   Chilton OX11 .... 235 E4
   Duns Tew OX6 .... 47 E3
   East Hanney OX12 .... 197 D3
   Finstock OX7 .... 88 C4
   Fringford OX6 .... 52 B3
   Grove OX12 .... 196 C1
   Hanwell OX17 .... 8 C2
   Hethe OX6 .... 52 A4
   Letcombe Bassett OX12 ..... 214 A1
   Mollington OX17 .... 4 A2
   North Newington OX15 ...... 15 D2
   Over Norton OX7 .... 42 C3
   Shalstone MK18 .... 25 F3
   Sibford Gower OX15 .... 19 D4
   Sibford Gower OX15 .... 19 D4
   Tadmarton OX15 .... 20 B4
   Turweston NN13 .... 24 B4
   West Hagbourne OX11 .... 218 B2
   Westbury NN13 .... 25 D2
   Wroxton OX15 .... 15 D4
Majors Rd SN6 .... 191 F1
Makins Rd RG8 .... 254 B4
Malet Cl HP14 .... 188 C3
Malford Rd OX3 .... 124 C2
Mall The SN6 .... 209 F4
Mallard Cl OX4 .... 142 B1
Mallard Way OX12 .... 196 B1
Mallins La SN7 .... 192 B2
Mallory Ave RG4 .... 259 E3
Maltfield Rd OX3 .... 124 A3
Malthouse
   Bodicote OX15 .... 22 B4
   Dorchester OX10 .... 182 B1
   Long Compton CV36 .... 27 F3
   Shutford OX15 .... 174 C4
Malthouse Paddock SN7 .. 174 C4
Maltings Ct OX15 .... 21 E2
Maltings The RG20 .... 235 D1
Maltsters
   Kidlington OX5 .... 108 C4
Malvarsh Ave OX11 .... 200 B1
Malvern Cl Banbury OX16 .... 16 B1
   Didcot OX11 .... 200 B1
Malyns Cl OX9 .... 168 B4
Mandarin Pl OX12 .... 196 B1
Mandeville Cl OX14 .... 160 A1
Mandhill Cl OX12 .... 214 C4
Manning Cl OX15 .... 21 F1
Mannings Cl OX15 .... 19 D4
Manor Cl Aston OX18 .... 135 F1
   Cassington OX8 .... 107 E1
   Drayton OX14 .... 179 D1
   Great Bourton OX17 .... 9 E4
   Shrivenham SN6 .... 209 D4
   Sutton Courtenay OX14 ..... 200 C4
   West Hagbourne OX11 .... 218 B2
Manor Cres Didcot OX11 .... 200 B1
   Standlake OX8 .... 137 E3
   Stanford in the V SN7 .... 194 C4
Manor Ct Abingdon OX14 .... 179 F3
   Banbury OX16 .... 16 C4
   Chadlington OX7 .... 57 E1
Manor Dr OX33 .... 143 E3
Manor Farm Cl
   Kingham OX7 .... 54 C3
   Merton OX6 .... 95 E4
Manor Farm Ct OX20 .... 75 F2
Manor Farm La RG8 .... 256 B1
Manor Farm Rd
   Dorchester OX10 .... 182 B1
   Horspath OX33 .... 143 E3
Manor Field OX12 .... 214 A1
Manor Gn OX11 .... 217 F4

Manor Gr OX1 .... 160 C4
Manor La Clanfield OX18 .... 152 C4
   East Hendred OX12 .... 216 A3
   Shrivenham SN6 .... 209 D3
Manor Orch OX15 .... 8 A2
Manor Park OX17 .... 1 B1
Manor Pl OX1 .... 123 D2
Manor Rd Adderbury OX17 .... 22 C2
   Banbury OX16, OX17 .... 16 C4
   Bladon OX20 .... 91 D1
   Brize Norton OX18 .... 116 A2
   Carterton OX18 .... 115 E3
   Chinnor OX9 .... 149 D3
   Didcot OX11 .... 200 B1
   Ducklington OX8 .... 118 A2
   Fringford OX6 .... 52 B4
   Goring RG8 .... 249 D3
   Great Bourton OX17 .... 9 E4
   Henley-on-T RG9 .... 254 B4
   Middle Barton OX7 .... 46 B1
   Oxford OX1 .... 123 F1
   South Hinksey OX1 .... 141 D3
   Wantage OX12 .... 232 B3
   Whitchurch RG8 .... 256 B4
   Witney OX8 .... 118 B4
   Woodstock OX20 .... 91 D4
Manor Way OX5 .... 92 C1
Manor Wood Gate RG9 ...... 255 D2
Manor Wood Rd OX6 .... 65 F1
Mansell Cl OX8 .... 106 B3
Mansfield Gdns OX11 .... 219 D4
Mansfield Rd OX1 .... 123 E1
Mansion Hill OX17 .... 17 F4
Mansmoor Rd OX5 .... 94 C3
Manston Cl OX6 .... 66 A2
Manzel Rd OX6 .... 66 A3
Maple Ave OX5 .... 108 C4
Maple Cl Banbury OX16 .... 16 C1
   N Hinksey Vill OX2 .... 140 B4
   Sonning Common RG4 .... 253 D2
Maple Ct Goring RG8 .... 249 D3
   Kidlington OX5 .... 108 C4
Maple Rd Bicester OX6 .... 65 F1
   Faringdon SN7 .... 173 D2
   Thame OX9 .... 147 E4
Maple Way OX7 .... 71 D1
Maple Well OX8 .... 89 E4
Maplederm Rd RG8 .... 258 C2
Maplederm Rd RG8 .... 257 E3
Maplederham View RG31 ... 257 E1
Maples The
   Carterton OX18 .... 115 E1
   Grove OX12 .... 196 B1
March Rd OX17 .... 3 E2
Marcham Rd
   Abingdon OX13, OX14 .... 179 D4
   Drayton OX14 .... 179 D1
   Marcham OX13 .... 179 D4
Marchwood Ave RG4 .... 259 E4
Margaret Ct Banbury OX16 ... 16 A3
   Bicester OX6 .... 65 E2
Margaret Rd
   Adderbury OX17 .... 23 D3
   Oxford OX3 .... 124 C1
Maria Cres OX12 .... 16 C4
Marie Cl OX6 .... 67 F4
Marigold Cl OX4 .... 142 C1
Marines Dr SN7 .... 172 C1
Marjoram Cl OX4 .... 143 D1
Mark Rd OX3 .... 124 C2
Market End Way OX6 .... 65 E2
Market Pl Abingdon OX14 ... 179 F4
   Banbury OX15, OX16 .... 16 B3
   Deddington OX15 .... 33 F2
   Faringdon SN7 .... 172 C2
   Henley-on-T RG9 .... 244 B1
   Lechlade GL7 .... 150 B2
   Wallingford OX10 .... 221 E4
Market Sq Bicester OX6 ...... 65 F1
   Witney OX8 .... 118 A4
Market St Charlbury OX7 ..... 73 D2
   Chipping Norton OX7 .... 42 C2
   Oxford OX1 .... 123 E1
   Woodstock OX20 .... 91 D3
Marlborough Ave OX5 .... 92 B1
Marlborough Cl
   Carterton OX18 .... 115 F1
   Eynsham OX8 .... 120 C4
   Faringdon SN7 .... 172 D2
   Kidlington OX5 .... 92 B1
   Kings Sutton OX17 .... 23 F3
   Oxford OX4 .... 142 A1
Marlborough Cr
   Long Hanborough OX8 ...... 106 A4
   Woodstock OX20 .... 91 D4
Marlborough Ct OX2 .... 122 C1
Marlborough Dr OX18 .... 107 E1
Marlborough Gdns SN7 .... 172 C1

Marlborough Pl
   Banbury OX16 .... 16 B3
   Charlbury OX7 .... 73 D2
   Eynsham OX8 .... 120 C4
   Faringdon SN7 .... 172 C1
Marlborough Rd
   Banbury OX16 .... 16 B3
   Chipping Norton OX7 .... 42 C2
   Oxford OX1 .... 141 E4
Marlborough St SN7 .... 172 C2
Marley Ind Est OX16 .... 16 B4
Marley La OX44 .... 184 B4
Marley Way OX16 .... 16 B4
Marling Cl RG31 .... 257 E1
Marlow Cl OX10 .... 221 D4

Marlow Rd
   Beacon's Bottom HP14 ...... 189 D1
   Henley-on-T RG9 .... 244 C2
Marlowe Cl OX16 .... 15 F3
Marmion Rd RG9 .... 254 C4
Marriott Cl OX2 .... 109 D1
Marriotts Cl HP17 .... 130 C3
Marriotts La HP17 .... 130 C3
Marriotts Way HP17 .... 130 C3
Marsack St RG4 .... 259 E1
Marsh Cl OX5 .... 108 B3
Marsh Cl OX14 .... 179 F4
Marsh End OX9 .... 147 D1
Marsh La Clanfield OX18 .... 152 C4
   Fyfield OX13 .... 157 D2
   Marston OX3 .... 124 A3
Marsh Rd Oxford OX4 .... 142 B3
   Shippon HP18 .... 128 B2
Marsh Way SN7 .... 211 D3
Marshall Cl
   Chipping Norton OX7 .... 42 C1
   Reading RG4 .... 258 C3
Marshall Cres OX7 .... 46 C1
Marshall Rd OX4 .... 142 B3
Marshalls Cl OX15 .... 6 B1
Marshland Sq RG4 .... 259 D3
Marston Ferry Rd
   Cutteslowe OX2 .... 123 E3
   Marston OX2 .... 123 E3
Marston Rd
   Oxford OX3, OX4 .... 123 F2
   Thame OX9 .... 130 A1
Marston St OX4 .... 141 F4
Marten Gate OX16 .... 16 B2
Marten Pl RG31 .... 257 D2
Martens Cl SN6 .... 209 D3
Martens Rd SN6 .... 209 D3
Martin Cl OX6 .... 80 D4
Martin's La OX10 .... 182 B1
Martyn's Way OX10 .... 204 C2
Mayfield Cl OX12 .... 214 C2
Marygreen OX12 .... 214 B4
Marylands Green OX44 ...... 162 B1
Marymead OX10 .... 220 C1
Mascall Ave OX3 .... 142 C4
Mascord Cl OX16 .... 16 A3
Mascord Rd OX16 .... 16 A3
Masefield Cl OX6 .... 65 E2
Masefield Cres OX14 .... 179 E3
Masefield Rd OX16 .... 16 A2
Mason's Rd OX3 .... 124 C1
Massey Cl OX14 .... 124 B1
Mather Rd OX3 .... 124 C2
Mathews Way OX13 .... 178 C2
Mattock Rd RG4 .... 258 C2
Matson Dr RG9 .... 244 C1
Mattock Way OX14 .... 160 A2
Mattock's Cl OX3 .... 124 B1
Maud Cl OX6 .... 65 E2
Maunder Cl OX16 .... 15 F4
Maunds The OX15 .... 33 F2
Mavor Cl OX20 .... 91 D4
Mawles La SN7 .... 85 E4
Maxwell Ave OX13 .... 159 D1
Maxwell Cl OX4 .... 49 F4
Mayfair Rd OX4 .... 142 A2
Mayfield Ave OX12 .... 196 C1
Mayfield Cl
   Carterton OX18 .... 115 E1
   Chinnor OX9 .... 184 B3
Mayfield Dr RG4 .... 259 E2
Mayfield Rd Banbury OX16 ... 16 B1
   Cumnor OX2 .... 121 D1
   Cutteslowe OX2 .... 123 D4
Mayott's Rd OX14 .... 179 F4
McCraes Wlk RG10 .... 255 E1
McKee Sq OX10 .... 204 B1
McMullan Cl OX10 .... 221 E4
Mead La RG8 .... 249 F1
Mead Platt HP14 .... 188 B3
Mead Rd OX15 .... 21 E2
Mead The OX17 .... 3 F2
Mead Way OX5 .... 92 C1
Mead Wlk OX11 .... 200 C1
Meaden Hill OX3 .... 124 A3
Meadow Bank SN7 .... 172 C2
Meadow Cl Cumnor OX2 .... 121 D2
   Goring RG8 .... 249 E3
   Grove OX12 .... 196 C1
   Moulsford OX10 .... 238 C2
   Shipton-u-W OX7 .... 70 B1
Meadow La
   Cromarsh & OX10 .... 222 A3
   Fulbrook OX18 .... 100 C3
   Oxford OX4 .... 141 F3
   Thame OX9 .... 130 A2
Meadow Prospect OX2 ...... 122 B4
Meadow Rd Didcot OX11 .... 200 C1
   Henley-on-T RG9 .... 244 C1
   Reading RG1 .... 258 C1
   Watchfield SN6 .... 191 F1
Meadow View
   Adderbury OX17 .... 23 D2
   Banbury OX16, OX17 .... 16 C2
   Kidlington OX5 .... 92 C1
   Long Crendon HP18 .... 129 F2
   Witney OX8 .... 118 A3
Meadow View Rd OX1 ...... 160 C4
Meadow Way Didcot OX11 .. 218 B4
   Faringdon SN7 .... 172 C2
   Kingham OX7 .... 54 C2
   Thame OX9 .... 129 F1
   Yarnton OX5 .... 108 B3
Meadowbank Cl
   Ascott-u-W OX7 .... 71 D1
   Long Crendon HP18 .... 129 E4

Meadows The OX9 .... 186 A1
Meadowside
   Abingdon OX14 .... 179 F3
   Reading RG8 .... 257 D1
Meadowside Ct OX14 .... 179 F4
Meadowside Rd RG8 .... 256 B3
Meads Cl OX14 .... 179 D1
Meads The OX12 .... 196 C4
Meadside OX10 .... 202 C4
Meashill Way OX11 .... 234 C4
Medcroft Rd OX5 .... 77 D3
Medhill Cl RG8 .... 250 C4
Medina Cl OX14 .... 201 D1
Medina Gdns OX6 .... 65 D1
Medlar Rd SN6 .... 209 E4
Medlicott Dr OX14 .... 179 E3
Medlock Gr OX11 .... 200 C2
Medway Cl OX13 .... 197 D3
Medway Rd OX13 .... 159 E2
Medway Rd OX13 .... 159 E2
Melbourne Cl OX16 .... 16 C2
Melford Green RG4 .... 259 E2
Melton Dr OX11 .... 200 C1
Melville Cl OX6 .... 65 D1
Membury Way OX12 .... 214 B4
Memorial Ave RG9 .... 254 C1
Mendip Hts OX11 .... 200 B1
Menmarsh Rd HP18 .... 127 F3
Menpes Rd RG12 .... 257 E2
Mercury Cl OX14 .... 134 C2
Mercury Rd OX4 .... 143 D1
Mere Dyke Rd OX13 .... 155 D3
Mere Rd Cutteslowe OX2 .... 122 C4
   Finmere MK18 .... 39 E3
Meredith Cl OX6 .... 65 E2
Mereland Rd OX11 .... 218 C4
Merewood Ave OX3 .... 124 C4
Merganser Dr OX6 .... 81 D4
Meriden Cl OX10 .... 221 E4
Merlin Cl OX18 .... 115 E2
Merlin Rd Abingdon OX14 . 159 D1
   Oxford OX4 .... 142 C1
Merlin Way OX6 .... 81 D4
Merritt Rd OX11 .... 200 B1
Merrivale's La OX15 .... 21 F2
Merrymouth Rd OX7 .... 69 D1
Mersey Way OX13 .... 201 D2
Merton Cl Didcot OX11 .... 219 D4
   Eynsham OX8 .... 120 B4
Merton Rd OX6 .... 81 E2
Merton St Banbury OX16 .... 16 C3
   Oxford OX1 .... 123 E1
Merton Way OX5 .... 108 A3
Merton Wlk OX6 .... 65 F2
Metcalf Cl OX15 .... 179 F2
Metcalfe Cl OX15 .... 15 E4
Meteor Cl OX6 .... 66 A2
Mewburn Rd OX16 .... 16 B1
Mews The Highworth SN6 .. 190 A4
   Watchfield SN6 .... 191 E1
Micklands Rd RG4 .... 259 F2
Mickle Way OX33 .... 125 F2
Middle Aston La
   North Aston OX6 .... 48 A3
   Steeple Aston OX6 .... 48 A3
Middle Furlong OX11 .... 201 D1
Middle Hill OX15 .... 30 A4
Middle La Shottswell OX17 ... 8 B4
   Wendlebury OX6 .... 14 B4
Middle Rd OX18 .... 135 D1
Middle Row OX7 .... 42 C2
Middle St OX5 .... 93 F1
Middle Way Chinnor OX9 .. 168 A3
   Cutteslowe OX2 .... 123 D4
   Islip OX5 .... 93 F1
Middleton Rd
   Banbury OX16, OX17 .... 16 C4
   Bucknell OX6 .... 64 C4
   Chacombe OX17 .... 10 C2
Middleton Stoney Rd
   OX6 .... 66 A3
Middleway Bottom OX12 .. 213 E1
Middleway Rd OX12 .... 213 E1
Midget Cl OX14 .... 179 E3
Midsummer Meadow
   RG4 .... 258 C3
Midway OX17 .... 11 D1
Miles Dr OX12 .... 214 C4
Milestone Ave RG4 .... 260 C3
Milestone Rd OX18 .... 115 E1
Milestone Way RG4 .... 259 E3
Mileway Gdns OX3 .... 124 B1
Milford Rd Reading RG1 .... 258 C1
   Wootton OX20 .... 76 A2
Milking La OX6 .... 104 A2
Mill Cl Bix RG9 .... 243 F4
   Chadlington OX7 .... 57 D1
   Charlton-on-O OX5 .... 95 D3
   Deddington OX15 .... 33 F2
   Souldern OX6 .... 49 E1
Mill End OX5 .... 93 D1
Mill Green Bampton OX18 . 134 C1
   Caversham RG4 .... 259 D1
Mill Green OX18 .... 134 C1
Mill La Adderbury OX17 .... 23 D2
   Alvescot OX18 .... 133 E3
   Banbury OX15, OX16, OX17 .. 16 A3
   Benson OX10 .... 203 F2
   Black Bourton OX18 .... 133 F3
   Brackley NN13 .... 24 A3
   Chalgrove OX44 .... 184 B3
   Chinnor OX9 .... 168 A4
   Chipping Warden OX17 .... 5 F3
   Clanfield OX18 .... 152 C4
   Croughton NN13 .... 36 B4
   Drayton (Banbury) OX15 ... 15 F4
   East Hendred OX12 .... 216 A3
   Great Haseley OX44 .... 164 B4

Mill continued
Grove OX12 .... 214 C4
Haddenham HP17 .... 130 A2
Henley-on-T RG9 .... 254 C4
Horton-cum-S OX33 .... 112 A3
Kidmore End RG4 .... 252 B1
Kings Sutton OX17 .... 23 F2
Kirtlington OX5 .... 77 F2
Lechlade GL7 .... 150 C2
Lower Heyford OX6 .... 62 B3
Marston OX3 .... 123 F4
Middle Barton OX7 .... 60 C4
Milton (Abingdon) OX14 .... 199 E3
Oxford
   OX3, OX33, OX4, OX44 .... 141 F2
Shiplake RG9 .... 255 D1
South Moreton OX11 .... 220 A3
Stokenchurch HP14 .... 188 B3
Sutton Courtenay OX14 .... 200 C4
Upper Arncott OX6 .... 96 C4
Upper Heyford OX6 .... 48 C1
Wallingford OX10 .... 221 E4
Westbury NN13 .... 25 D2
Weston-on-the-G OX6 .... 79 D1
Wootton OX20 .... 76 C2
Mill Orch OX12 .... 197 D3
Mill Paddock
   Abingdon OX14 .... 179 F3
   Letcombe Bassett OX12 ... 214 A1
Mill Rd
   Abingdon OX13, OX14 ...... 179 E3
   Caversham RG4 .... 259 E1
   Cutteslowe OX2 .... 122 B4
   Goring RG8 .... 249 E4
   Marston OX3 .... 178 B3
   Nettlebed RG9 .... 224 C2
   Shiplake RG9 .... 255 D2
   Stokenchurch HP14 .... 188 B3
   Stratton Auley OX6 .... 52 A4
Mill St OX2 Eynsham OX8 ... 120 C4
   Islip OX5 .... 109 F4
   Kidlington OX5 .... 92 C1
   Oxford OX2, OX33 .... 123 D1
   Stanton St John OX33 ..... 125 F4
   Steventon OX13 .... 198 C2
   Wantage OX12 .... 214 B3
   Witney OX8 .... 104 A1
Mill St Mews OX18 .... 120 C4
Millaway La OX12 .... 195 E3
Millbank OX2 .... 141 D4
Millbrook Cl
   Blewbury OX11 .... 219 D1
   Wallingford OX10 .... 221 E4
Milldown Ave RG8 .... 249 E4
Milldown Rd RG8 .... 249 E4
Miller Rd Banbury OX16 .... 16 A3
   Wheatley OX33 .... 144 B4
Miller's Acre OX2 .... 109 D1
Millers Cl Chalgrove OX44 . 184 B4
   Goring RG8 .... 249 D4
Millers La OX15 .... 7 E4
Millers Turn OX9 .... 168 A3
Millfield Ave OX6 .... 67 F2
Millfield Cl OX6 .... 67 F2
Millham The OX12 .... 216 A3
Millmoor Cres OX18 ...... 120 C4
Mills La OX15 .... 12 C4
Millstream Ct OX2 .... 122 B4
Millview OX7 .... 42 C1
Millway Cl OX12 .... 122 C4
Millway La OX13 .... 157 F3
Millwood End OX8 .... 90 A1
Millwood Vale OX8 .... 90 A1
Millwright Cl OX16 .... 16 A3
Milne Pl OX3 .... 124 A3
Milton Cl Bicester OX6 ...... 65 E2
   Banbury OX16 .... 16 A3
Milton Cres OX33 .... 125 F2
Milton La OX13 .... 199 D3
Milton Manor Dr OX44 .... 163 F3
Milton Park OX14 .... 199 F2
Milton Rd Bloxham OX15 .. 21 B1
   Milton (Banbury) OX15 ...... 22 B1
   Oxford OX4, OX44 .... 142 A3
   Shipton-u-W OX7 .... 70 B1
   Sutton Courtenay OX14 .... 199 F3
   Sutton Courtenay OX14 .... 200 A2
Milton St OX16 .... 16 B3
Milvery Way OX44 .... 142 A2
Minchery Farm Cotts
   OX4 .... 142 B1
Minchery Rd OX4 .... 142 B1
Minchins Ct OX14 .... 180 B4
Minnow La OX18 .... 99 E3
Minns Ind Est OX2 .... 122 B4
Minns Rd OX12 .... 196 C1
Minster Rd
   Brize Norton OX18 .... 116 A3
   Oxford OX4 .... 142 A4
Minster Riding OX6 .... 102 C2
Minton Cl RG30 .... 257 F1
Minty Cl OX18 .... 115 E1
Mirfield Rd OX8 .... 117 F4
Mistletoe Gn OX4 .... 142 C1
Mitchell Cl Thame OX9 .... 147 F4
   Wootton OX20 .... 159 D4
Moat Cl OX18 .... 116 A2
Moat La OX6 .... 67 F1
Moat The OX7 .... 54 C3
Moat's Cres OX9 .... 148 A4
Mobbs La OX15 .... 30 A4
Moberly Cl OX4 .... 141 F4
Moir Ct OX12 .... 214 B3
Mold Cres OX16 .... 16 A4
Mole Pl **IB** OX4 .... 142 C1

Mollington La OX17 .... 3 D2
Molyneux Ave OX4 .... 22 C4
Monarchs Ct OX10 .... 203 F2
Monique Ct OX16 .... 9 D1

Monks Cl
Dorchester OX10 .... 182 C1
Oxford OX4 .... 142 B1
West Hanney OX12 .... 196 C3
Monks Lode OX11 .... 200 C2
Monks Mead OX10 .... 202 C1
Monmouth Rd OX1 .... 141 E3
Mons Way OX14 .... 159 E1
Montabaur Rd NN13 .... 24 A4
Montagu Rd OX2 .... 140 B4
Montague St RG4 .... 259 E1
Montgomery Rd OX6 .... 66 A4
Montpelier Dr RG4 .... 259 E3
Montrose Way OX9 .... 148 A4
Monument Ind Park
OX44 .... 184 C4
Monument Rd OX44 .... 184 C3
Monument St OX16 .... 16 B3
Moody Rd OX3 .... 123 F2
Moor Ave OX8 .... 104 A1
Moor La OX15 .... 31 F4
Moor Pond Cl OX6 .... 65 F1
Moorbank OX4 .... 142 C2
Moorbrook OX11 .... 200 B2
Moorend La Thame OX9 .... 129 F1
Thame OX9 .... 130 A1
Moorfield Ct OX16 .... 16 C3
Moorgate GL7 .... 150 A2
Moorhen Wlk OX44 .... 142 C1
Moorland Rd OX8 .... 117 F4
Moorlands Cl OX8 .... 103 F1
Moorlands The
Benson OX10 .... 204 A2
Kidlington OX5 .... 92 C1
Moors Cl OX8 .... 118 A3
Moors Drive The OX17 .... 17 F4
Moors The Kidlington OX5 .... 92 B1
Pangbourne RG8 .... 256 B3
Morecambe Ave RG4 .... 258 C3
Moreton Ave OX10 .... 221 D4
Moreton La Northmoor OX8 .... 156 C4
Thame OX9 .... 147 F4
Moreton Rd
Aston Tirrold OX11 .... 219 F1
Cutteslowe OX2 .... 123 D3
Morgan Cl OX16 .... 15 F4
Morlais RG4 .... 259 D3
Morland Cl OX33 .... 144 A4
Morland Rd OX13 .... 178 B3
Morlands OX12 .... 197 D4
Morrell Ave OX4 .... 142 A4
Morrell Cl OX5 .... 108 B4
Morrell Cres OX4 .... 142 A1
Morrells Cl OX11 .... 200 B1
Morris Cres OX4 .... 142 A3
Morris Dr OX16 .... 15 F4
Morse Rd OX11 .... 218 B3
Mortimer Dr OX3 .... 123 F2
Mortimer Rd OX4 .... 141 F2
Morton Ave OX5 .... 108 C4
Morton Cl Abingdon OX14 .... 180 B4
Kidlington OX5 .... 108 C4
Morton King Cl HP18 .... 128 B2
Mosquito La OX10 .... 204 B1
Moss Cl RG4 .... 259 E2
Motte The OX14 .... 179 F4
Mount Owen Rd OX18 .... 135 D2
Mount Pl OX2 .... 123 D1
Mount Pleasant
Bishopstone SN6 .... 227 E2
Lechlade GL7 .... 150 B2
Mount St OX2 .... 123 D1
Mount The
Caversham RG4 .... 258 C2
Tetsworth OX9 .... 166 A4
Mount View RG9 .... 244 B1
Mount View Ct RG9 .... 244 B1
Mountfield RG8 .... 249 E4
Mountfield Rd OX8 .... 117 F4
Mousey La OX10 .... 221 E4
Mowbray Dr
RG1 & RG30 & RG31 .... 258 A1
Mowbray Rd OX11 .... 218 C3
Mowforth Cl RG8 .... 240 C1
Mulberries The OX12 .... 197 D3
Mulberry Dr Bicester OX6 .... 65 F3
Wheatley OX33 .... 144 A4
Mulcaster Ave OX5 .... 108 C4
Mullard Way OX14 .... 179 F4
Mumbery Hill RG10 .... 255 F1
Murcott Rd OX6 .... 96 B3
Murdock Cl OX15 .... 33 F2
Murdock Rd OX6 .... 66 A1
Murren The OX10 .... 221 E3
Museum Rd OX1 .... 123 D1
Musgrave Rd OX9 .... 168 B4
Musgrave Wlk HP14 .... 188 C3
Mustard La RG4 .... 260 C1
Myrtle Cl
Long Hanborough OX8 .... 90 A1
Reading RG31 .... 257 E2

Naldertown OX12 .... 214 B3
Napier Ct OX14 .... 180 A4
Napier Rd OX4 .... 142 B3
Nappins Cl HP18 .... 129 E3
Naseby Cl OX9 .... 130 A1
Nash Dr OX14 .... 179 E3
Nash La OX8 .... 106 A4
Neal's La OX15 .... 242 A1
Needlemakers HP18 .... 129 E4

Neithrop Ave OX16 .... 16 A4
Neithrop Cl OX16 .... 16 A4
Nell Hill SN6 .... 227 E2
Nelson Cl OX10 .... 221 E4
Nelson Rd RG4 .... 259 E1
Nelson St Oxford OX2 .... 123 D1
Thame OX9 .... 147 F4
Nene Gr OX11 .... 201 D1
Nene Rd OX13 .... 159 E1
Nether Cl NN13 .... 24 A4
Netheravon Cl OX18 .... 115 F1
Nethercote La OX10 .... 167 D1
Nethercote Rd OX5 .... 77 E3
Netherton La OX13 .... 157 E2
Netherton Rd OX13 .... 157 F3
Netherwoods Rd OX3 .... 124 C2
Netherworton Rd OX15 .... 32 C3
Netley Cl RG4 .... 259 F3
Netting St OX15 .... 30 A4
Nettlebed Mead OX4 .... 142 C1
Nettleton Dr OX6 .... 63 E4
Neunkirchen Way OX6 .... 81 D4
Neville Way SN7 .... 194 C4
Nevis Rd RG31 .... 257 E2
New Cotts HP18 .... 129 E3
New Cross Rd OX3 .... 124 C2
New High St OX3 .... 124 B1
New Inn Rd OX8 .... 257 E3
New Inn Hall St OX1 .... 123 E1
New Inn Rd OX3 .... 111 D1
New Pond La OX5 .... 95 D3
New Rd Adderbury OX17 .... 22 C2
Bampton OX18 .... 134 C2
Banbury OX15, OX16, OX17 .... 16 B3
Bledington OX7 .... 54 B1
Bletchingdon OX5 .... 93 D4
Charney Bassett OX12 .... 175 F1
Childrey OX12 .... 213 D3
East Hagbourne OX11 .... 219 D3
Great Tew OX7 .... 45 E3
Hailey OX8 .... 104 A3
Kingham OX7 .... 54 C2
Long Hanborough OX8 .... 90 A1
Marcham OX13 .... 178 B3
Oxford OX1, OX3 .... 123 D1
Radley OX14 .... 160 C1
Ratley OX15 .... 2 A2
Shiplake RG9 .... 255 D2
Shotteswell OX17 .... 8 B4
Stokenchurch HP14 .... 188 C2
Wallingford OX10 .... 221 E4
Warborough OX10 .... 203 D3
Watlington OX9 .... 186 A1
Woodstock OX7 .... 91 D3
Wootton OX20 .... 75 E4
New Row OX6 .... 64 C4
New St Abingdon OX14 .... 179 F4
Bicester OX6 .... 65 F2
Chipping Norton OX7 .... 42 C2
Deddington OX15 .... 33 F2
Henley-on-T RG9 .... 244 C1
New Town La SN6 .... 227 E2
New Yatt La OX8 .... 104 C4
New Yatt Rd Hailey OX8 .... 104 B2
Witney OX8 .... 104 B2
Newalls Rise RG10 .... 255 F1
Newbery Cl RG31 .... 257 E1
Newbold Cl OX16 .... 16 C2
Newbury Rd OX12 .... 216 C3
Newbury St OX12 .... 214 B2
Newcombe Cl OX3 .... 124 B1
Newells Cl OX4 .... 163 E1
Newfield Rd RG4 .... 252 C3
Newgate Rd OX6 .... 95 F3
Newington Rd OX44 .... 163 E1
Newland Cl OX8 .... 104 B1
Newland Ct OX8 .... 120 C4
Newland Pl OX16 .... 16 B3
Newland Rd OX16 .... 16 B3
Newland St OX8 .... 120 C4
Newlands Ave
Caversham RG4 .... 259 D2
Didcot OX11 .... 218 C4
Newlands Dr OX12 .... 196 B1
Newlands La RG9 .... 242 A3
Newlands Mill OX8 .... 104 B1
Newlin Cl OX4 .... 141 F2
Newman Ct Curbridge OX8 .... 103 E1
Oxford OX4 .... 123 F1
Newman La OX11 .... 179 D1
Newman Rd OX4 .... 142 A2
Newmans Cl OX11 .... 218 B2
Newmill La OX8 .... 103 F1
Newnham Green OX12 .... 221 F4
Newnhamhill Bottom
RG9 .... 242 A3
Newport Cl OX5 .... 108 B4
Newport Rd RG1 .... 259 D1
Newton Ave RG4 .... 259 E3
Newton Rd OX1 .... 141 E4
Newton Way OX10 .... 204 A3
Newton Gdns RG4 .... 254 C4
Newtown Rd RG9 .... 254 C4
Niagara Rd RG9 .... 254 C4
Nicholas Ave OX3 .... 123 F2
Nicholas Rd RG9 .... 254 A4
Nicholson Rd OX3 .... 123 F2
Nightingale Ave OX4 .... 142 C1
Nightingale La SN6 .... 208 A3
Nightingale Pl OX16 .... 81 D4
Nine Acres Cl OX7 .... 73 D2
Nine Acres La OX7 .... 73 D2
Nineteenth St OX11 .... 217 D1
Ninety Cut Hill OX18 .... 102 A2
Ninth Ave OX11 .... 142 C4
Ninth St OX11 .... 217 D1
Nixon Rd OX4 .... 141 F3
Nizewell Head OX6 .... 62 A4

Nobles Cl Grove OX12 .... 196 B1
N Hinksey Vill OX2 .... 140 A4
Nobles La OX12 .... 140 A4
Nor Brook Cl OX14 .... 180 B3
Norcot Rd RG30 .... 258 A1
Norfolk Cl OX14 .... 160 C1
Norfolk St OX1 .... 141 E4
Norham Gdns OX2 .... 123 E2
Norham Rd OX2 .... 123 E2
Norman Ave
Abingdon OX14 .... 160 A1
Henley-on-T RG9 .... 244 C1
Norman Rd RG4 .... 259 E2
Norman Smith Rd
OX4 .... 142 C1
Norman Way OX10 .... 221 E4
Normandy Cres OX4 .... 142 C3
Norreys Ave OX1 .... 141 E3
Norreys Cl OX11 .... 218 B4
Norreys Rd Cumnor OX2 .... 139 F3
Didcot OX11 .... 218 B4
Norries Dr OX10 .... 203 E1
Norris Cl Abingdon OX14 .... 160 B1
Adderbury OX17 .... 22 C1
Norris Rd OX6 .... 96 C4
North Aston Rd OX6 .... 47 E3
North Ave OX14 .... 160 A1
North Bar Pl OX16 .... 16 B3
North Bar St OX16 .... 16 B3
North Cl OX9 .... 145 F4
North Croft OX11 .... 218 C3
North Dr Grove OX12 .... 196 C1
Harwell OX11 .... 217 E2
North Green OX12 .... 196 C4
North Hill HP18 .... 98 A1
North Hinksey La OX2 .... 140 C4
North Hinksey Village
OX2 .... 140 C4
North La OX6 .... 79 D1
North Leigh Bsns Pk OX8 .... 105 E4
North Manor Estate The
OX44 .... 143 F1
North Mill Rd OX9 .... 149 F3
North Parade Ave OX2 .... 123 E2
North Pl OX3 .... 124 B2
North Quay OX14 .... 179 F4
North Rd Didcot OX11 .... 200 B1
Moulsford OX10 .... 238 C2
North Side OX6 .... 48 A1
North St Aston OX18 .... 135 F2
Banbury OX16 .... 16 B3
Bicester OX6 .... 65 F1
Caversham RG4 .... 259 D1
Fritwell OX6 .... 49 F4
Islip OX5 .... 93 F1
Marcham OX13 .... 178 B3
Middle Barton OX7 .... 60 C4
Oxford OX2 .... 123 D1
Thame OX9 .... 129 F1
Watchfield SN6 .... 191 E1
North Way Cutteslowe OX2 .... 109 D1
Oxford OX3 .... 124 C3
Steventon OX13 .... 198 C2
Northampton Rd OX1 .... 141 E3
Northbrook Rd RG4 .... 259 E3
Northcourt La OX14 .... 160 A1
Northcourt Rd OX14 .... 159 F1
Northcourt Wlk OX14 .... 180 A4
Northern By-pass Rd
Cutteslowe OX2 .... 108 C1
Marston OX2 .... 124 B3
Oxford OX2 .... 124 B3
Northfield Ave RG9 .... 255 D2
Northfield Cl OX14 .... 142 B1
Northfield Cl RG9 .... 244 B2
Northfield End RG9 .... 244 B2
Northfield Rd
Abingdon OX14 .... 160 A2
Oxford OX3 .... 124 C2
Reading RG1 .... 259 D1
Shiplake RG9 .... 255 D2
Northford Cl SN6 .... 209 E4
Northford Hill SN6 .... 209 E4
Northmead La OX12 .... 196 A4
Northmoor Rd OX2 .... 123 E3
Northolt Rd OX18 .... 115 F2
Northwood Cres OX16 .... 115 F2
Norton Cl Oxford OX3 .... 124 B1
Norton Ct OX3 .... 124 B1
Norton Pk OX7 .... 42 C2
Norton Rd OX12 .... 115 F2
Norwood Ave OX13 .... 156 C1
Nottwood La RG9 .... 242 A3
Nowell Rd OX4 .... 141 F2
Nuffield Cl Bicester OX6 .... 65 F2
Didcot OX11 .... 219 D4
Nuffield Dr OX16 .... 16 A4
Nuffield Hill RG9 .... 223 D2
Nuffield La OX10 .... 222 C3
Nuffield Rd OX3 .... 124 C1
Nuffield Way OX14 .... 179 E4
Nuneham Sq OX14 .... 179 F4
Nunhide La RG8 .... 256 C1
Nunnery Cl OX4 .... 142 B1
Nuns Acre RG8 .... 249 D4
Nurseries Rd OX5 .... 108 B4
Nursery Cl OX3 .... 124 B1
Nursery Gdns OX11 .... 16 B4
Nursery Gdns RG8 .... 257 D3
Nursery La OX16 .... 16 B4
Nursery Rd OX8 .... 105 E4
Nursery The OX4 .... 200 A4
Nuthatch Cl OX4 .... 142 C1
Nyatt Rd OX14 .... 180 B4

Oak Dr OX5 .... 92 C1
Oak End Way OX9 .... 168 B3
Oak Farm Cl OX9 .... 166 A4
Oak La Ambrosden OX6 .... 81 E2
Stanford in the V SN7 .... 194 C3
Oak Rd SN6 .... 191 E1
Oak St GL7 .... 150 B2
Oak Tree Copse RG31 .... 257 F2
Oak Tree Rd RG31 .... 257 E3
Oak Tree Wlk RG8 .... 257 E3
Oakdene RG8 .... 250 C4
Oakdown Cl RG8 .... 250 C2
Oakey Cl OX18 .... 133 E3
Oakfield Rd OX18 .... 115 E1
Oaklands Ind Est OX8 .... 120 B3
Oakham Cl RG31 .... 257 E1
Oakham Rd GL56 .... 27 D1
Oakland Cl OX18 .... 105 F4
Oakland Rd OX16 .... 16 B1
Oakley La OX9 .... 168 A3
Oakley Rd
Caversham RG4 .... 258 C2
Chinnor OX9 .... 168 B3
Oaks Rd RG9 .... 255 D2
Oaksmere OX13 .... 158 A3
Oakthorpe Pl OX2 .... 123 D3
Oakthorpe Rd OX2 .... 123 D3
Oasis Park OX8 .... 120 B3
Oatland Rd OX11 .... 218 C4
Oatlands Rd OX2 .... 122 C1
Observatory Cl OX10 .... 204 A2
Observatory St OX2 .... 123 D2
Ock Dr OX10 .... 182 B3
Ock Mill Cl OX14 .... 179 E3
Ock St OX14 .... 179 F3
Ockley Brook OX11 .... 201 D1
Octavian Way NN13 .... 24 A4
Oddley La HP27 .... 169 E4
Odiham Ave RG4 .... 259 F3
Odiham Cl OX18 .... 115 F2
Offas Cl OX10 .... 203 F2
Ogbourne Cl OX12 .... 214 A3
Old Arncott Rd OX6 .... 81 E2
Old Barn Cl Benson OX10 .... 204 A2
Caversham RG4 .... 259 D3
Old Bath Rd RG4 .... 260 B3
Old Bridge Rd OX15 .... 21 F2
Old Buildings OX10 .... 221 E4
Old Burford Rd OX7 .... 54 B1
Old Chapel Ct OX5 .... 92 C1
Old Coachyard The OX8 .... 104 A1
Old Copse Gdns RG4 .... 252 C3
Old Croft Cl OX9 .... 167 F2
Old Dashwood Hill OX14 .... 189 F1
Old Farm Cl
Abingdon OX14 .... 180 B4
Worminghall HP18 .... 127 E3
Old Farm Cres RG31 .... 257 E1
Old Field OX44 .... 164 A4
Old Forge Cl OX7 .... 54 B1
Old Forge Rd OX7 .... 29 D2
Old George Yd OX18 .... 100 C3
Old Glebe OX15 .... 20 B4
Old Greyfriars St OX1 .... 141 E4
Old Grimsbury Rd OX16 .... 16 C4
Old High St OX3 .... 124 B2
Old Kiln The RG9 .... 224 C1
Old London Rd
Benson OX10 .... 204 A2
Tiddington OX9 .... 145 F2
Wheatley OX33 .... 144 B4
Old Maltings The OX9 .... 129 F1
Old Manor Ct OX12 .... 214 A1
Old Marston Rd OX3 .... 123 F2
Old Mill Cl OX12 .... 196 C1
Old Moor OX11 .... 199 E3
Old Moor Cl OX10 .... 221 E4
Old Nursery View OX1 .... 141 E1
Old Orchard OX9 .... 149 F1
Old Parr Cl OX16 .... 16 B3
Old Parr Rd OX16 .... 16 B3
Old Place Yd OX6 .... 65 F1
Old Plough Wlk OX15 .... 33 D2
Old Pound The OX13 .... 159 D3
Old Rd East Hendred OX12 .... 216 C2
Great Tew OX7 .... 45 E4
Oxford OX3, OX33 .... 124 C1
Ratley OX15 .... 2 A2
Wheatley OX33 .... 143 F4
Old Reading Rd OX10 .... 221 F3
Old Rectory Ct OX6 .... 80 A2
Old Sawmills Rd SN7 .... 172 C1
Old School Cl Bicester OX6 .... 65 F4
Stokenchurch HP14 .... 188 C3
Old School Ct OX12 .... 213 F3
Old Stables The OX3 .... 124 B2
Old Stables Yard OX12 .... 214 A1
Old Station Yd OX14 .... 179 F4
Old Town NN13 .... 24 A4
Old Wharf Rd SN7 .... 210 B4
Old Windmill Way HP18 .... 129 E4
Old Witney Rd OX8 .... 120 B4
Oliver Rd OX4 .... 142 C3
One End La OX10 .... 203 F2
Onslow Dr OX9 .... 130 A1
Onslow Gdns RG4 .... 259 E2
Oracle Parkway RG4 .... 260 A1
Orange Cl SN6 .... 209 E4
Orchard Ave RG4 .... 252 C3
Orchard Cl Abingdon OX14 .... 160 A1
Banbury OX15, OX16 .... 16 A3
Bucknell SN7 .... 174 C4
Cassington OX8 .... 107 E1
Chalgrove OX44 .... 184 B4
Charney Bassett OX12 .... 175 F1
Cholsey OX10 .... 221 E3
Combe OX8 .... 90 A2

Orchard Cl continued
Didcot OX11 .... 200 C1
East Hanney OX12 .... 197 D3
East Hendred OX12 .... 216 C4
Eynsham OX8 .... 120 C4
Henley-on-T RG9 .... 244 C1
Lechlade GL7 .... 150 B2
Purley on T RG31 .... 257 E2
Salford OX7 .... 41 F2
Thame OX9 .... 254 C1
Upton OX11 .... 218 B1
Warborough OX10 .... 203 D4
Wheatley OX33 .... 144 A4
Orchard Combe RG8 .... 250 B2
Orchard Field RG4 .... 252 C3
Orchard Field La OX20 .... 91 E2
Orchard Gdns OX12 .... 213 E3
Orchard Gr Bloxham OX15 .... 21 E2
Caversham RG4 .... 259 F2
Orchard Ground OX7 .... 69 E1
Orchard Haven OX10 .... 202 B4
Orchard Hill SN7 .... 172 C2
Orchard La Cropredy OX17 .... 4 C1
East Hendred OX12 .... 216 B3
Upper Heyford OX6 .... 62 C4
Wootton OX4 .... 140 B1
Orchard Piece OX17 .... 4 A2
Orchard Pl NN13 .... 25 D2
Orchard Rd Ardley OX6 .... 50 A2
Buckland SN7 .... 174 C4
Hook Norton OX15 .... 30 A4
N Hinksey Vill OX2 .... 140 A4
Orchard Rise OX4 .... 79 F4
Orchard Row OX18 .... 100 C3
Orchard The
Appleton OX13 .... 158 A4
East Challow OX12 .... 214 A3
Merton OX6 .... 95 E4
Orchard View OX17 .... 4 C1
Orchard Way
Banbury OX16, OX17 .... 16 A3
Bicester OX6 .... 65 E2
Chinnor OX9 .... 168 B3
Harwell OX11 .... 217 E4
Kidlington OX5 .... 108 C4
Kingham OX7 .... 54 C2
Marcham OX13 .... 178 B3
Middle Barton OX7 .... 46 C1
Oxford OX4 .... 142 B2
Wantage OX12 .... 214 C2
Witney OX8 .... 118 A4
Orchard Wlk OX9 .... 186 B1
Orchids The OX11 .... 235 E4
Ordnance Rd OX11 .... 200 B1
Oregon Ave RG31 .... 257 E2
Oriel Cl OX11 .... 219 D4
Oriel Sq OX1 .... 123 E1
Oriel St OX1 .... 123 E1
Oriel Way OX6 .... 65 F2
Orkney Pl OX18 .... 117 F4
Ormond Rd Thame OX9 .... 130 A1
Wantage OX12 .... 214 C2
Orpwood Way OX14 .... 179 E3
Orwell Cl RG4 .... 258 C2
Orwell Dr OX11 .... 201 D1
Osberton Rd OX2 .... 123 D4
Osborne Cl Bicester OX6 .... 65 E1
Cutteslowe OX2 .... 122 C4
Kidlington OX5 .... 108 B4
Osiers The OX10 .... 183 D3
Osler Rd OX3 .... 124 B2
Osney Cl OX15 .... 30 A4
Osney La OX1 .... 123 D1
Osney Mead OX2 .... 141 D4
Osprey Cl OX4 .... 81 D4
Osterley Dr RG4 .... 259 F3
Osterley Gr OX16 .... 16 A2
Oswestry Rd OX1 .... 141 E3
Otmoor La Beckley OX3 .... 111 D2
Charlton-on-O OX5 .... 95 D2
Otters Reach OX1 .... 141 F1
Ottery Way OX11 .... 201 D1
Otwell Cl OX14 .... 160 A1
Ouseley Cl OX3 .... 123 F2
Outram Rd OX4 .... 142 A3
Oval The Bicester OX6 .... 65 E2
Didcot OX11 .... 200 B1
Oxford OX4 .... 142 A2
Over Norton Rd OX7 .... 42 C3
Overbrooke Gdns OX4 .... 143 D1
Overdale Cl OX13 .... 124 C2
Overdown Rd RG31 .... 257 E1
Overlanders End RG31 .... 257 F2
Overmead OX14 .... 180 A4
Overmead Green OX4 .... 142 C1
Overstrand Cl OX6 .... 66 A2
Overthorpe Rd OX16 .... 16 C3
Overton Dr OX9 .... 130 A1
Owlington Cl OX2 .... 122 B1
Ox Cl OX14 .... 180 A4
Oxen Piece OX44 .... 145 E1
Oxeye Ct OX4 .... 161 F4
Oxford Bsns Pk N OX4 .... 142 B3
Oxford Bsns Pk S OX4 .... 142 B2
Oxford Cl OX5 .... 77 F2
Oxford Cres OX11 .... 218 B4
Oxford Hill OX8 .... 118 A4
Oxford La OX12 .... 196 C1
Oxford Rd
Abingdon OX13, OX14 .... 160 A3
Adderbury OX17 .... 23 D2
Banbury OX15, OX16, OX17 .... 16 B2
Benson OX10 .... 203 F2
Bicester OX6 .... 80 B4
Bletchingdon OX5 .... 93 D4
Burford OX18 .... 100 C2
Clifton Hampden OX14 .... 181 F3

Oxford Rd *continued*
Cumnor OX2 .... 139 F3
Cumnor, Farmoor OX2 .... 139 F3
Cutteslowe OX2 .... 109 D2
Deddington OX15 .... 33 F1
Dorchester OX10 .... 182 B1
Enstone OX7 .... 58 C3
Eynsham OX8 .... 120 C4
Garsington OX44 .... 143 E1
Hampton Poyle OX5 .... 93 D2
Horspath OX33 .... 143 D3
Kennington OX1 .... 160 A3
Kidlington OX5 .... 108 C4
Kirtlington OX5 .... 77 F2
Marston OX3 .... 123 F3
Middleton Stoney OX6 .... 64 A2
North Aston OX6 .... 47 F3
Oxford, Blackbird Leys OX4 .... 142 C2
Oxford, Littlemore OX4 .... 142 A2
Oxford, Temple Cowley OX4 .... 142 B3
Reading RG30 .... 258 A1
Steeple Aston OX6 .... 47 F3
Stokenchurch HP14 .... 188 B3
Thame OX9 .... 147 F4
Tiddington OX9 .... 145 F3
Woodcote RG8 .... 240 C1
Woodstock OX20 .... 91 E3
Oxford Sq SN6 .... 191 E1
Oxford St
Cumnor RG4 .... 259 D1
Woodstock OX20 .... 91 D3
Oxhey Hill OX17 .... 4 B2
Oxhey Rise OX15 .... 31 D4
Oxlease OX8 .... 118 B4
Oxon Pl SN6 .... 227 E2
Oxpens Rd OX1 .... 141 D4

Pack & Prime La RG9 .... 244 B1
Packhorse La OX3 .... 178 B3
Paddick Cl RG4 .... 260 C2
Paddock Cl Benson OX10 .... 204 A2
Chalgrove OX44 .... 184 B4
Wantage OX12 .... 214 C3
Paddock Farm La OX15 .... 22 B4
Paddock Rd Ardley OX6 .... 50 A2
Caversham RG4 .... 259 E1
Wallingford OX10 .... 221 E4
Paddock The
Highworth SN6 .... 190 A3
Longworth OX13 .... 156 B1
Upper Heyford OX6 .... 48 C3
Paddocks The
Bampton OX18 .... 134 C1
Deddington OX15 .... 33 F2
East Hanney OX12 .... 197 D3
Mollington OX17 .... 3 F2
Souldern OX6 .... 35 F2
Yarnton OX5 .... 108 A3
Paddox Cl OX2 .... 123 D4
Paddox The OX2 .... 123 D4
Page Furlong OX10 .... 182 B1
Pages La OX15 .... 7 D3
Pages Orch RG4 .... 252 C3
Paget Rd OX4 .... 142 C3
Pagisters Rd OX14 .... 160 B1
Paines Hill OX6 .... 62 A4
Painswick Cl OX8 .... 103 F1
Painters Cl OX15 .... 21 E2
Palmer Ave OX6 .... 96 C4
Palmer Pl OX14 .... 179 F3
Palmer Rd OX3 .... 124 C1
Palmers OX12 .... 214 C3
Pampas Cl OX18 .... 115 F1
Panbourne Hill RG8 .... 256 B3
Pangbourne St RG20 .... 258 A1
Panters Rd OX4 .... 221 D1
Paper Mill La OX11 .... 220 A3
Papist Way OX10 .... 238 C4
Parade The OX5 .... 108 C3
Paradise La OX15 .... 21 D1
Paradise Mews RG9 .... 244 B1
Paradise Rd RG9 .... 244 B1
Paradise Sq OX1 .... 123 D1
Paradise St OX1 .... 123 D1
Paradise Terr OX7 .... 42 B1
Park Ave Highworth SN6 .... 190 A3
Kidlington OX5 .... 92 B1
Shrivenham SN6 .... 209 E4
Park Cl
Avon Dassett OX17 .... 2 C4
Banbury OX16, OX17 .... 16 B3
Bladon OX20 .... 91 D2
Cutteslowe OX2 .... 109 D1
Didcot OX11 .... 218 B4
Hanwell OX17 .... 8 C2
Hook Norton OX15 .... 30 A3
Kirtlington OX5 .... 77 F3
Middleton Stoney OX6 .... 64 A2
North Leigh OX8 .... 105 E3
Sonning Common RG4 .... 253 D3
Yarnton OX5 .... 108 A2
Park Cres OX14 .... 179 F4
Park End Bodicote OX15 .... 16 C1
Croughton NN13 .... 36 B4
Park End Cl OX15 .... 16 C1
Park End Ct OX15 .... 16 C1
Park End Pl OX1 .... 123 D1
Park End St OX1 .... 123 D1
Park Hill Hailton OX33 .... 126 A4
Hook Norton OX15 .... 30 A4
Park La Appleton OX13 .... 158 A4
Aston Rowant OX9 .... 167 F2
Bladon OX20 .... 91 D1
Checkendon RG8 .... 251 F3
Long Hanborough OX8 .... 90 B1
North Newington OX15 .... 15 E2
Stanford in the V SN7 .... 195 D3
Stokenchurch HP14 .... 188 C3

Park La *continued*
Stonor RG9 .... 225 E3
Swalcliffe OX15 .... 19 F4
Woodstock OX20 .... 91 D3
Park Rd Abingdon OX14 .... 179 F4
Banbury OX15, OX16 .... 16 A3
Chipping Norton OX7 .... 42 C2
Combe OX8 .... 90 A3
Didcot OX11 .... 218 B4
Ducklington OX8 .... 118 A2
Faringdon SN7 .... 172 C2
Henley-on-T RG9 .... 244 C1
Hook Norton OX15 .... 30 A4
North Leigh OX8 .... 105 D3
Witney OX8 .... 103 F1
Park Rise OX6 .... 81 E2
Park Side Marcham OX13 .... 178 B3
Woodstock OX20 .... 91 E3
Park St Bladon OX20 .... 91 D1
Charlbury OX7 .... 73 D2
Thame OX9 .... 148 A4
Woodstock OX20 .... 91 D3
Park Terr OX9 .... 148 A4
Park The Cumnor OX2 .... 139 F2
Harwell OX11 .... 217 F3
Park Town OX2 .... 123 E2
Park View
Crowmarsh OX10 .... 222 A3
Sydenham OX9 .... 148 C1
Wantage OX12 .... 214 C3
Park Wall La RG8 .... 249 E1
Park Way OX3 .... 123 F4
Park Wlk RG8 .... 257 E3
Parker St OX4 .... 141 F3
Parkers Cl SN7 .... 173 D2
Parkers Hill OX9 .... 166 A4
Parkhill Dr RG31 .... 257 E1
Parklands Banbury OX16 .... 16 A4
Freeland OX8 .... 105 F4
Parks Rd OX1 .... 123 E1
Parkside Cuddesdon OX44 .... 144 A2
Henley-on-T RG9 .... 244 B1
North Leigh OX8 .... 105 E3
Parkway Dr RG4 .... 260 C2
Parliament Rd OX9 .... 129 F1
Parrs Rd HP14 .... 188 C2
Parry Cl OX3 .... 123 F2
Parson's La OX10 .... 204 C2
Parson's St OX16 .... 16 B3
Parsonage Cl OX12 .... 215 D3
Parsons Mead OX14 .... 159 F1
Parsons Pl OX4 .... 142 A4
Parsons St OX17 .... 23 D2
Partridge Chase OX6 .... 81 D4
Partridge Cl OX12 .... 214 C2
Partridge Pl OX1 .... 92 B1
Partridge Wlk OX4 .... 143 D1
Pascall Pl OX16 .... 9 D1
Passey Cres OX14 .... 204 A2
Patemore La OX9 .... 206 C1
Paternoster La OX10 .... 220 C1
Patrick Haugh Rd OX6 .... 74 A4
Patrick Rd RG4 .... 259 D1
Patricks Orch SN7 .... 211 E4
Pattison Pl OX14 .... 142 A2
Pauling Rd OX3 .... 124 C1
Pauls Way OX9 .... 186 A1
Paxmans Pl OX16 .... 16 B2
Paynes End OX6 .... 63 F3
Peachcroft Centre OX14 .... 160 A1
Peachcroft Rd OX14 .... 160 A1
Peacock Rd OX3 .... 123 F2
Peaks La OX8 .... 89 E4
Pear Tree Cl OX7 .... 70 A1
Pearce Cl OX9 .... 147 F4
Pearce Dr OX7 .... 42 C1
Pearce Way OX9 .... 148 A4
Pearces Meadow RG9 .... 224 B2
Pearces Orch RG9 .... 244 B2
Pearson Rd RG4 .... 260 B2
Peartree Cl ▮ OX4 .... 142 C1
Peartree Interchange
OX2 .... 108 C1
Peacroft HP18 .... 129 E3
Peat Moors OX3 .... 142 B4
Pebble Cl OX18 .... 101 E3
Pebble Dr OX11 .... 219 D4
Pebble La NN13 .... 24 A4
Peel Cl Caversham RG4 .... 259 C1
Ducklington OX8 .... 118 A2
Peel Pl Carterton OX18 .... 115 F1
Oxford OX1 .... 141 E3
Peep-o-day La OX14 .... 179 F2
Pegasus Ct OX4 .... 142 A2
Pegasus Rd OX4 .... 142 C1
Pegswell La OX44 .... 145 D1
Pelham Rd OX9 .... 130 A1
Pelican Pl OX8 .... 120 C4
Pembroke Ct OX4 .... 141 F4
Pembroke La OX14 .... 199 E3
Pembroke Pl
Bampton OX18 .... 134 C2
Caversham RG4 .... 259 E2
Pembroke Sq OX1 .... 141 E4
Pembroke St OX1 .... 123 E1
Pembroke Way OX6 .... 65 F2
Pemscott Cl OX18 .... 133 E3
Pen Way OX16 .... 9 E1
Pendennis Ave RG4 .... 259 F3
Penley Cl OX9 .... 168 A3
Penn Cl Abingdon OX14 .... 160 B1
Caversham RG4 .... 259 D3
Pennington Pl OX9 .... 130 A1
Pennycress Rd OX4 .... 143 D1
Pennyfarthing Pl OX1 .... 123 E1
Pennygreen La OX10 .... 202 C1
Pennypiece RG8 .... 249 E4
Pennywell Dr OX2 .... 109 D1

Penpont Water OX11 .... 201 D1
Penrhyn Cl OX16 .... 15 F4
Penrose Cl OX14 .... 16 A3
Penrose Dr OX16 .... 16 A3
Pensclose OX8 .... 104 B1
Pensfield OX10 .... 203 F2
Penson's Gdns OX4 .... 123 F1
Pentagon The OX14 .... 180 A4
Peppard Hill RG9 .... 252 C4
Peppard La RG9 .... 254 C4
Peppard Rd
Caversham RG4 .... 253 D2
Sonning Common RG4 .... 253 D2
Pepper Alley OX15 .... 34 C2
Peppercorn Ave OX3 .... 142 C4
Percy St OX4 .... 141 F3
Peregrine Rd OX4 .... 142 B1
Peregrine Way
Bicester OX6 .... 81 D4
Grove OX12 .... 196 B1
Perian Cl RG9 .... 254 B4
Perimeter Rd OX11 .... 217 E1
Periwinkle Pl OX4 .... 143 D1
Perkins OX1 .... 141 E1
Perkins Cl OX15 .... 7 C2
Perrin St OX3 .... 124 B1
Perrinsfield GL7 .... 150 B3
Perrott Cl OX8 .... 105 D4
Perry's Rd SN7 .... 194 B4
Perserverance Hill RG9 .... 254 A3
Peter's Way OX4 .... 142 B3
Peterley Rd OX4 .... 142 C3
Pether Rd OX1 .... 124 C1
Pethers Piece OX18 .... 100 B3
Petre Pl OX5 .... 92 C1
Pettiwell OX44 .... 162 B4
Pevensey Ave RG4 .... 259 F3
Pheasant Wlk OX4 .... 142 A1
Phelps The OX5 .... 108 B4
Philcote St OX15 .... 33 F2
Phillimore Rd OX4 .... 142 C3
Phipps Rd OX4 .... 142 B2
Phoebe Ct OX2 .... 123 D3
Phyllis Ct Dr RG9 .... 244 C2
Pickett Ave OX3 .... 142 C4
Picklers Hill OX14 .... 160 A1
Picton Way RG4 .... 259 D2
Piddington Rd OX18 .... 98 A4
Pieces The OX18 .... 134 C2
Pierces Hill RG31 .... 257 E1
Pigeon Farm Rd HP14 .... 188 C3
Pigeon House La OX8 .... 106 B3
Pigeonhouse La OX6 .... 95 F2
Piggotts Rd RG4 .... 259 E2
Piggy La OX6 .... 65 F1
Pike Terr OX1 .... 141 E4
Pikeshaw Way RG31 .... 257 E1
Pill La GL56 .... 26 C2
Pimpernel Cl OX4 .... 143 D1
Pine Cl Bicester OX6 .... 65 F3
Garsington OX44 .... 143 E1
Oxford OX4, OX44 .... 142 C2
Pine Woods Rd OX13 .... 156 A1
Pinecroft OX18 .... 115 E1
Pines The SN7 .... 172 C2
Pinetree Ct RG4 .... 259 D3
Pinewood Dr RG4 .... 258 C3
Pingle Dr OX6 .... 80 C4
Pinhill Rd OX16 .... 16 A4
Pinkhill La OX8 .... 120 C3
Pinnocks Way OX2 .... 140 A4
Pinsley Rd OX8 .... 106 A4
Pioneer Rd Ambrosden OX6 .... 81 D3
Faringdon SN7 .... 172 C1
Piper St OX3 .... 124 B1
Pipers Croft OX16 .... 16 A2
Pipit Cl OX4 .... 142 C1
Pipits Croft OX6 .... 81 D4
Pipkin Way OX4 .... 142 A3
Pitch The HP14 .... 189 E2
Pitreavie Ave OX18 .... 115 F2
Pitters Piece HP18 .... 129 D4
Pitts Rd OX3 .... 124 C2
Pixey Pl OX2 .... 122 C4
Pixton Cl OX11 .... 218 B4
Plain Rd The OX15 .... 14 A3
Plain The OX4 .... 141 F4
Plane Tree Way OX20 .... 91 E3
Plantation Rd
Chilton OX11 .... 234 C4
Oxford OX2 .... 123 D2
Plantation The OX17 .... 4 C1
Playfield Rd OX1 .... 160 C4
Playford Ct OX9 .... 147 F4
Playhatch Rd RG4 .... 260 A3
Playing Field Rd NN13 .... 25 D2
Pleck La OX9 .... 167 F2
Plot Rd OX15 .... 14 A3
Plough Cl Cutteslowe OX2 .... 122 C4
Warborough OX10 .... 203 D3
Plough Cnr OX9 .... 148 C1
Plough La RG9 .... 254 C1
Ploughley Cl Ardley OX6 .... 50 B2
Kidlington OX5 .... 108 B4
Ploughley Rd OX6 .... 81 E2
Plover Dr OX4 .... 142 C1
Plowden Park OX44 .... 167 F2
Plowden Way RG9 .... 254 C1
Plum La OX7 .... 85 E4
Plumbe Ct OX12 .... 214 B3
Pluto Rd OX11 .... 234 C4
Plym Dr OX11 .... 201 D1
Pochard Pl OX4 .... 142 C1
Pococks Cl OX18 .... 134 C2
Poffley End La OX8 .... 104 A3
Polecat End La OX33 .... 125 F2
Polstead Rd OX2 .... 123 D2
Polsted Rd RG31 .... 257 E1

Pond End Rd RG4 .... 253 D3
Pond Hill OX8 .... 89 E4
Pond La RG4 .... 257 F4
Ponds La OX3 .... 123 F3
Pony Rd OX4 .... 142 C3
Pool Close Cotts GL56 .... 26 C1
Pooles La OX7 .... 73 D2
Poolside Cl OX16 .... 16 A3
Popes Acre HP17 .... 130 C3
Popes Piece OX8 .... 103 F1
Poplar Cl Banbury OX16 .... 16 B2
Garsington OX44 .... 143 E1
Kidlington OX5 .... 108 C4
Poplar Farm Cl OX7 .... 70 A1
Poplar Farm Rd OX44 .... 184 B4
Poplar Gr OX1 .... 160 C4
Poplar Rd OX2 .... 122 B1
Poplars The OX6 .... 66 B1
Port Hill RG9 .... 224 A1
Port Hill Rd OX10 .... 203 F3
Port Way
Crowmarsh OX10 .... 221 F2
East Challow OX12 .... 214 A4
Kirtlington OX5 .... 78 A4
Lower Heyford OX6 .... 62 C3
Wantage OX12 .... 215 D3
Portal Dr OX6 .... 63 E4
Portal Dr N OX6 .... 63 E4
Portal Dr S OX6 .... 63 E4
Portland Pl OX7 .... 42 C2
Portland Rd
Cutteslowe OX2 .... 123 D4
Milcombe OX15 .... 21 D1
Portman Rd RG30 .... 258 B1
Portway Aynho OX17 .... 35 E4
Banbury OX16, OX17 .... 16 A4
Croughton NN13 .... 36 C4
Didcot OX11 .... 218 B4
Faringdon SN7 .... 172 C2
Wantage OX12 .... 214 B2
Portway Cres NN13 .... 36 C4
Portway Dr NN13 .... 36 B4
Portway Gdns OX17 .... 35 E4
Post Office La
Letcombe Bassett OX12 .... 214 A1
Stanton St John OX33 .... 125 E4
Potenger Way OX14 .... 179 E3
Potkiln La RG8 .... 250 C4
Pott's Cl OX44 .... 145 D2
Pottery Piece OX4 .... 142 C1
Pottery Rd RG30 .... 257 F1
Pottle Cl OX2 .... 122 A1
Poultney Pl OX18 .... 115 F2
Poulton Pl OX4 .... 142 C2
Pound Cl
Ducklington OX8 .... 118 A2
Kirtlington OX5 .... 77 F2
Yarnton OX5 .... 108 A3
Pound Croft OX12 .... 214 B4
Pound Field Cl OX13 .... 124 C3
Pound Hill OX7 .... 73 D2
Pound La Cassington OX8 .... 107 E1
Cholsey OX10 .... 220 C1
Clanfield OX18 .... 133 F1
Sibford Gower OX15 .... 13 D1
Sonning RG4 .... 260 C1
Stanton St John OX33 .... 125 E4
Upton OX11 .... 218 B1
Pound Piece SN6 .... 228 A4
Pound The Bloxham OX15 .... 21 F3
North Newington OX15 .... 15 D2
Wantage OX12 .... 215 D3
Pound Way OX4 .... 142 B3
Powell Cl OX13 .... 125 F2
Powys Gr OX16 .... 15 F4
Preachers La OX1 .... 141 E4
Prescott Ave OX16 .... 16 B3
Prescott Cl OX16 .... 16 A3
Preston Rd OX14 .... 179 F2
Prestwick Burn OX11 .... 200 C2
Price's Forge OX2 .... 109 D1
Prior's La SN7 .... 155 F2
Priory Ave RG4 .... 259 D1
Priory Cl Bicester OX6 .... 65 F1
Horton-cum-S OX33 .... 112 A3
Priory Copse RG4 .... 252 C3
Priory Ct OX6 .... 65 F1
Priory Green SN6 .... 190 A3
Priory La Bicester OX6 .... 65 F1
Burford OX18 .... 100 C3
Lyneham OX7 .... 70 B3
Marcham OX13 .... 178 B3
Priory Mead SN7 .... 192 B1
Priory Mews OX10 .... 221 E4
Priory Orch OX12 .... 214 B3
Priory Rd Bicester OX6 .... 65 F1
Lyneham OX7 .... 70 B3
Oxford OX4 .... 142 B1
Wantage OX12 .... 214 B2
Priory Vale Rd OX16 .... 16 C4
Pritchard Cl OX10 .... 182 B3
Promenade Rd RG4 .... 259 D1
Prospect Cl OX8 .... 89 E4

Prospect Pl OX9 .... 186 A1
Prospect Rd Banbury OX16 .... 16 B3
Upton OX11 .... 218 B1
Prospect St RG4 .... 259 D1
Prunus Cl OX4 .... 142 C2
Puck La OX8 .... 104 A1
Puddleduck La SN7 .... 192 A4
Pudlicote La OX7 .... 71 F3
Pudsey Cl OX14 .... 179 F2
Pugsden La OX13 .... 199 D2
Pulker Cl OX4 .... 142 B2
Pullens Cl OX13 .... 124 A1
Pullens La OX3 .... 124 A1
Pulling Cl SN7 .... 172 C2
Pumbro OX8 .... 89 E4
Purcell Rd OX4 .... 123 F2
Purfield Dr RG10 .... 255 F1
Purland Cl OX4 .... 142 B3
Purley La RG8 .... 257 E3
Purley Rise RG8 .... 256 C3
Purley Village RG8 .... 257 E3
Purley Way RG8 .... 256 C3
Pursiane OX14 .... 160 A4
Pusey La OX1 .... 123 E1
Pusey Ls OX1 .... 123 E1
Pusey St OX1 .... 123 E1
Putman Cl OX3 .... 148 A4
Putman Pl RG9 .... 244 C1
Pye St SN7 .... 173 D2
Pykes Cl OX14 .... 160 A1
Pym Wlk OX9 .... 129 F1
Pyrton La OX9 .... 186 A1
Pytenry Cl OX14 .... 160 A2
Pytt's La OX18 .... 100 C3

Quadrangle The
Bicester OX6 .... 65 F1
Woodstock OX20 .... 91 E4
Quadrant The OX14 .... 180 A4
Quaker La OX10 .... 203 D4
Quantock Ave RG4 .... 259 E3
Quantock View OX11 .... 200 B1
Quarhill Cl OX7 .... 42 C3
Quarry Cl Bloxham OX15 .... 21 E2
Enstone OX7 .... 59 D3
Long Crendon HP18 .... 129 E4
Quarry End OX5 .... 108 A4
Quarry High St OX3 .... 124 C2
Quarry Hollow OX3 .... 124 C1
Quarry La OX7 .... 73 E2
Quarry Rd Chadlington OX7 .... 57 D2
Oxford OX3 .... 124 C1
Sunningwell OX13 .... 159 F4
Witney OX8 .... 104 A2
Quarry School Pl OX3 .... 124 C1
Quartermain Cl OX4 .... 142 A3
Quartermain Rd OX44 .... 184 B3
Quebec Rd RG9 .... 254 C4
Queen Annes Gate OX14 .... 259 E2
Queen Cl RG9 .... 244 C1
Queen Elizabeth Cl OX11 .... 219 D4
Queen Emmas Dyke OX8 .... 117 F4
Queen St Abingdon OX14 .... 179 F4
Bampton OX18 .... 134 C2
Caversham RG4 .... 259 D2
Dorchester OX10 .... 182 B1
Eynsham OX8 .... 120 C4
Henley-on-T RG9 .... 244 C1
Hook Norton OX15 .... 30 A4
Middleton Cheney OX17 .... 17 F4
Oxford OX1 .... 123 E1
Queens Cl
Dorchester OX10 .... 182 B1
N Hinksey Vill OX2 .... 140 A4
Thame OX9 .... 129 F1
Queens Ct OX6 .... 65 F1
Queens La OX1 .... 120 C4
Queens Rd
Caversham RG4 .... 259 E1
Cholsey OX10 .... 220 C1
Queens St OX15 .... 13 D1
Queens Way OX11 .... 219 F4
Queensborough Dr RG4 .... 258 C3
Queensway Banbury OX16 .... 16 A2
Caversham RG4 .... 259 E3
Didcot OX11 .... 218 C3
Quickset Cl OX7 .... 72 C4
Quintan Ave OX6 .... 81 E2

Rack End OX8 .... 137 E2
Radbone Hill OX7 .... 42 C3
Radcliffe Rd OX4 .... 141 F3
Radcliffe Sq OX1 .... 123 E1
Radcot Cl RG5 .... 260 C1
Radcot Rd SN7 .... 172 C3
Radford Cl OX4 .... 141 F2
Radley Rd OX14 .... 160 B1
Radnage Common Rd
HP14 .... 189 E3
Radnage La HP14 .... 169 E1
Radnor Cl RG9 .... 244 C1
Radnor Rd OX10 .... 221 D4
Raghouse La OX6 .... 49 F3
Raglan Gdns RG4 .... 259 E2

Ragley Mews RG4 .... 259 E3
Ragnall's La Beckley OX3 ... 111 F4
Horton-cum-S OX33 .... 112 A3
Rahere Rd OX4 .... 142 B2
Railway La OX4 .... 142 A1
Railways Cotts RG8 ...... 249 E3
Rainbow Way OX14 .... 160 A2
Raincliffe Cl OX17 ...... 35 E4
Raleigh Cres OX8 .... 117 E4
Raleigh Park Rd OX2 ..... 140 C4
Rampion Cl OX4 .... 143 D1
Ramsay Rd OX3 .... 124 C2
Ramsons Way OX14 ...... 180 B4
Randall Rd GL54 .... 68 A2
Randolph Rd RG1 .... 259 D1
Randolph St OX4 .... 141 F4
Range Rd OX8 .... 103 E1
Rannal Dr OX9 .... 168 B3
Rattlecombe Rd OX15 ..... 6 B1
Rau Cl OX6 .... 66 A4
Raven Rd HP14 .... 188 C2
Ravencroft OX4 .... 81 D4
Ravensbourne Dr RG5 .... 260 C1
Ravenscroft Rd RG2 ..... 244 B1
Ravensmead Banbury OX16 . 16 A2
Chinnor OX9 .... 168 B3
Rawlings Gr OX14 .... 179 E4
Rawlins' Ct OX7 .... 23 D1
Rawlinson Cl OX7 .... 57 D1
Rawlinson Rd OX2 .... 123 D3
Rawson Cl OX2 .... 108 C1
Rawthey Ave OX11 ...... 200 C2
Ray Ct OX11 .... 201 D1
Raymond Rd OX6 .... 65 E2
Raymund Rd OX3 .... 123 F3
Raynham Cl OX18 .... 115 F2
Reade Ave OX14 .... 180 A4
Reade Cl OX7 .... 70 A1
Reade's La RG4 .... 252 B2
Reading Rd Aldworth RG8 . 248 A1
East Hendred OX12 ..... 216 A4
Goring RG8 .... 249 F3
Harwell OX11 .... 217 E3
Henley-on-T RG9 ...... 244 C1
Kidmore End RG4 ...... 252 A2
Moulsford OX10 .... 239 D4
Pangbourne RG8 .... 256 B3
Streatley RG8 .... 249 D3
Wallingford OX10 ..... 221 E2
Woodcote RG8 .... 240 C1
Recreation Rd
Wargrave RG10 .... 255 F1
Woodstock OX20 ...... 91 E3
Rectory Cl
Marsh Gibbon OX6 .... 67 F2
Warmington OX17 ..... 3 D2
Wendlebury OX6 ...... 80 A2
Rectory Cres OX7 ..... 60 C4
Rectory Ct OX9 ...... 187 D4
Rectory Farm Cl OX12 . 196 C4
Rectory Gdns OX15 ... 15 E4
Rectory Hill RG9 .... 206 A1
Rectory La Blewbury OX11 . 237 F4
Fringford OX6 .... 52 B3
Kingston Bagpuize OX13 . 176 C4
Letcombe Bassett OX12 . 231 F4
Lewknor OX9 .... 166 C1
Longworth OX13 ..... 156 A2
Middleton Cheney OX17 . 10 C1
Woodstock OX20 ..... 91 D3
Rectory Meadow OX9 .. 168 B4
Rectory Rd
Caversham RG4 ...... 259 D1
Great Haseley OX44 .. 164 C4
Hook Norton OX15 ... 30 A4
Oxford OX4, OX44 ... 141 F4
Streatley RG8 ...... 248 B4
Red Bridge Hollow OX1 . 141 E2
Red Copse Rd OX1 .... 140 C1
Red Cross Rd RG8 .... 249 E3
Red Hill RG9 .... 253 F3
Red House Dr RG4 .... 253 D3
Red House Rd OX15 ... 22 C4
Red La Ewelme RG9 ... 206 B1
Watlington OX9 ..... 206 B1
Woodcote RG8 ...... 240 B2
Red Lion Sq OX7 .... 42 B3
Red Lion Sq OX7 .... 123 E1
Red Lion St Cropredy OX17 . 4 C1
Kings Sutton OX17 .. 23 F3
Red Poll Cl OX16 ... 16 A4
Redberry Cl RG4 .... 259 E3
Redc Cl OX3 .... 124 C1
Redland Rd OX3 .... 124 A3
Redmoor Cl OX44 ... 142 B1
Redmoor Ct OX6 .... 65 E2
Redwing Cl OX6 .... 66 A1
Redwood Cl
Garsington OX4 .... 143 D1
Kingston Bagpuize OX13 . 156 C1
Redwood Way RG31 .. 257 E2
Reedmace Cl OX4 ... 143 D1
Regal Way SN7 ..... 172 C2
Regency Hts RG4 ... 258 C2
Regent Gdns OX14 .. 219 D4
Regent Mall OX12 .. 214 B2
Regent Mews SN7 ... 172 C2
Regent St OX4 ..... 141 F4
Regis Pl OX12 ..... 214 A1
Reid Cl OX16 ...... 16 A3
Reid Pl OX6 .... 63 D4
Remenham La RG9 .. 244 C2
Remus Gate NN13 .. 24 A3
Rest Harrow OX4 .. 142 C1
Retford Cl RG5 .... 260 C1

Retreat Gdns OX10 .. 221 F4
Retreat La HP14 .... 169 E1
Rewley Rd OX1 ..... 123 D1
Reynolds Cl OX7 ... 70 B1
Reynolds Way
Abingdon OX14 ..... 179 F3
East Challow OX12 .. 213 F3
Rhigos RG4 .... 258 C3
Richards La OX2 ... 123 D4
Richards Way OX3 .. 124 C1
Richens Dr OX18 ... 115 E1
Richfield Ave RG1 .. 258 C1
Richman Gdns OX16 . 15 F4
Richmere Rd OX4 ... 218 C4
Richmond Rd
Caversham RG4 ..... 258 C2
Oxford OX1 .... 123 D1
Richmond St OX17 .. 23 F3
Rickyard The
Ardington OX12 ... 215 E3
Chilton OX11 ..... 100 C3
Riddell Pl OX2 ... 109 D1
Ride The OX3 ..... 158 A3
Riders Way OX3 ... 168 B3
Ridge Cl OX16 .... 16 B2
Ridge Hall Cl RG4 . 258 C2
Ridge The RG8 .... 249 F1
Ridge Way OX12 ... 214 A4
Ridgefield Rd OX4 . 142 A4
Ridgemont Cl OX2 . 123 D4
Ridgemount Cl RG31 . 257 D1
Ridgeway Wargrave RG10 . 255 F1
Wootton (Oxford) OX1 . 140 B1
Ridgeway Cl RG30 .. 223 E2
Ridgeway Rd Didcot OX11 . 218 C4
Oxford OX3 ...... 124 C2
Ridgeway The
Bloxham OX15 .... 21 F2
Caversham RG4 ... 259 D2
Nettlebed RG9 ... 224 B1
Riding La OX8 ... 103 E4
Riding The OX8 .. 86 C1
Ridings The
Caversham RG4 ... 259 E4
Kidlington OX5 .. 92 B1
Oxford OX3 ...... 142 C4
Ridley Rd OX4 ... 142 C3
Riely Cl OX8 .... 90 B1
Riley Cl OX14 ... 179 E3
Riley Dr OX16 ... 15 F4
Rimes Cl OX13 ... 156 C1
Ringwood Rd Oxford OX3 . 125 D2
Reading RG30 ... 258 A1
Ripley Rd RG30 . 258 A1
Rippington Ct OX14 . 179 D1
Rippington Dr OX3 . 123 F2
Rise The Adderbury OX17 . 23 D3
Aston Rowant OX9 . 167 F3
Caversham RG4 ... 259 D2
Islip OX5 .... 93 F1
Rissington Cl RG31 . 257 F2
Rissington Dr OX8 . 117 F4
Rivacres RG8 .... 250 C2
River Cl OX14 ... 179 F3
River Gdns RG8 .. 257 E3
River Rd RG4 .... 258 B2
River View Kennington OX1 . 141 F1
Sandford-on-T OX4 . 161 D4
Rivermead Rd OX4 . 141 F2
Riverside OX16 .. 16 C3
Riverside Gdns OX8 . 104 A1
Riverside Rd OX2 . 122 C1
Riverview Rd RG8 . 256 B3
Rivy Cl OX14 .... 180 B4
Road Eight OX11 . 217 D1
Road Eighteen OX11 . 217 D1
Road Eleven OX11 . 217 D1
Road Fifteen OX11 . 217 D1
Road Five OX11 .. 217 D1
Road Four OX11 .. 217 D1
Road Fourteen OX11 . 217 D1
Road Nine OX11 .. 217 D1
Road One OX11 ... 217 D1
Road Six OX11 ... 217 D1
Road Thirteen OX11 . 217 D1
Road Twelve OX11 . 217 D1
Road Two OX11 ... 217 D1
Robert Robinson Ave
OX4 .... 142 B1
Robert Sparrow Gdns
OX10 .... 222 A3
Roberts Cl OX3 .. 125 D2
Robin Hill OX8 .. 90 A2
Robin Pl OX4 ... 142 C1
Robins Cl
Barford St M OX15 . 32 C3
Great Kulbright OX7 . 29 D2
Robins Platt OX9 . 168 A3
Robins Way OX6 . 81 D4
Robinson Cl OX18 . 115 E2
Robinswood OX16 . 16 A2
Robsart Pl OX2 . 139 F2
Rochester Ave RG5 . 260 C1
Rochester Pl OX7 . 73 E2
Rochester Way OX17 . 23 D3
Rochford Gdns OX6 . 66 A2
Rock Cl OX18 ... 115 E2
Rock Edge OX3 . 124 B1
Rock Farm La OX4 . 161 D4
Rock Hill OX7 .. 42 B2
Rock Rd OX18 .. 115 E2
Rock The OX15 . 33 D2
Rockbourne Gdns RG30 . 258 A1
Rocky La RG9 .. 243 D2
Roding Way OX11 . 201 D1
Rodway Rd RG30 . 257 F1
Roebuck Ct OX11 . 219 D4
Roentgen Ave OX11 . 217 D1

Rofford La OX44 . 164 A2
Rogers St OX2 .. 123 D4
Rokeby Dr RG4 . 258 B4
Rolfe Pl OX3 ... 124 C4
Rolls Ct OX12 .. 214 B3
Roman Pl OX11 . 200 B1
Roman Rd OX3 . 144 B4
Roman Way Beckley OX3 . 111 D2
Bicester OX6 .. 65 F1
Brackley NN13 . 24 A4
Lechlade GL7 .. 150 B3
Oxford OX3, OX44 . 142 C3
Wantage OX12 . 214 B3
Romany Cl RG30 . 258 A1
Romany La RG30 . 258 A1
Romney Rd OX16 . 16 B3
Romsey Rd RG30 . 258 A1
Romulus Way NN13 . 24 A3
Rookery Cl
Abingdon OX13 . 159 D1
Bodicote OX15 . 22 C4
Rookery The OX5 . 92 B1
Rookery Way OX6 . 65 E2
Rooks La OX9 . 147 F4
Roosevelt Dr OX3 . 124 B1
Roosevelt Rd OX8 . 106 A4
Rope Way OX15 . 30 A3
Rope Wlk OX16 . 16 B3
Roper Rd OX4 . 63 E4
Rosamund Dr OX2 . 91 D4
Rosamund Rd OX2 . 122 C4
Rose Ave OX14 . 159 F2
Rose Cl OX18 . 115 E1
Rose Cnr HP14 . 188 C3
Rose Ct OX4 . 142 A2
Rose Gdns OX2 . 140 B4
Rose Hill OX4 . 142 B2
Rose La OX1 . 123 E1
Rose Pl OX1 . 141 E4
Rosebay Cres OX12 . 214 B4
Rosebery Rd RG4 . 258 B4
Rosedale Ave OX16 . 9 D1
Rosehill Park OX4 . 259 E4
Rosemary La OX18 . 134 C2
Rosemead Ave RG31 . 257 D2
Roses La OX7 . 41 F3
Rosina Wlk OX6 . 9 D1
Ross Rd RG1 . 259 D1
Rossendale Rd RG4 . 259 E2
Rotha Field Rd OX2 . 109 D1
Rother Garth OX11 . 201 D2
Rotherfield Rd RG4 . 259 E2
Rotherfield Way RG4 . 259 D2
Rothwell Gdns RG5 . 260 C1
Rothwell Wlk RG4 . 259 E1
Rothwells Cl OX10 . 221 D1
Rotten Row OX10 . 182 B1
Round Close Rd
Adderbury OX17 . 22 C2
Hook Norton OX15 . 30 A4
Roundham Cl OX5 . 92 B1
Roundhead Dr OX9 . 129 F1
Roundhill Rd OX17 . 4 A2
Roundhills Mead SN6 . 190 A4
Roundtown OX17 . 35 E4
Roundway The OX3 . 124 C2
Rouses La GL7 . 132 A3
Rousham Rd OX5 . 77 E4
Routh Rd OX3 . 124 C2
Roves La SN6 . 208 A4
Row La RG4 . 259 F4
Row The SN7 . 155 F1
Rowallan Cl RG4 . 259 E3
Rowan Cl
Carterton OX18 . 115 E2
Kidlington OX5 . 108 C4
Sonning Common RG4 . 252 C2
Rowan Gr OX4 . 143 D1
Rowan Rd OX2 . 122 C4
Rowel Dr OX5 . 92 A1
Rowell Way OX7 . 42 C2
Rowland Cl
Cutteslowe OX2 . 122 C4
Wallingford OX10 . 203 E1
Rowland Rd OX10 . 221 D1
Rowles Cl OX1 . 141 F1
Rowney Pl OX4 . 142 A2
Rowstock OX11 . 217 D4
Royal Borough OX11 . 200 B2
Royal Berkshire Ct OX11 . 218 C4
Royal Mansions RG9 . 244 C1
Ruck Keene Cl OX4 . 65 E1
Rufus Isaacs Rd RG4 . 259 D1
Rumbolds Cl OX10 . 203 F3
Rumseys La OX11 . 237 D4
Rupert Cl RG9 . 244 C2
Rupert House Sch RG9 . 244 C1
Rupert Rd Chalgrove OX44 . 184 B3
Oxford OX4 . 142 C3
Rupert Way OX9 . 130 A3
Rupert's La RG9 . 244 C2
Ruscote Ave OX16 . 16 A4
Ruscote Sq OX16 . 16 A4
Rushall Rd OX9 . 130 A1
Rushmead Copse OX14 . 160 B1
Ruskin Ave OX14 . 179 F3
Ruskin Cl OX11 . 219 D4
Ruskin Rd OX16 . 16 B2
Ruskin Wlk OX6 . 65 E2
Russell Jackson Cl OX10 . 182 B3
Russell Rd RG4 . 258 B4
Russell St OX2 . 123 D1
Russet Cl OX12 . 252 C3
Russet Glade RG4 . 259 E4
Russet Rd OX6 . 50 B2
Rutherford Cl OX14 . 160 A1
Rutherford Ave OX11 . 217 D2
Rutherway OX2 . 123 D2

Rutten La OX5 . 108 A3
Rutters Cl OX5 . 108 B4
Rycote La OX9 . 146 B3
Rydal Ave RG30 . 257 F1
Rydes Cl OX15 . 22 C4
Rydes The OX15 . 22 C4
Rye Cl OX16 . 8 C1
Rye Grass OX20 . 91 E3
Ryecroft Cl
Wargrave RG10 . 255 F1
Woodstock RG5 . 260 C1
Rymans Cres OX11 . 219 D3
Rymers La OX4 . 142 A3

Sackville Cl OX17 . 8 C2
Sadler Wlk OX1 . 141 D4
Sadlers Croft OX44 . 143 F1
Sadlers Ct OX14 . 160 A2
Saffron Ct OX14 . 180 A4
Sage Cl OX16 . 9 D1
Sage Wlk 🖪 OX4 . 142 C1
St Alban's Cl OX10 . 221 E4
St Aldates OX1 . 141 E4
St Amand Dr OX14 . 179 F3
St Andrew Ct OX9 . 147 F4
St Andrew's La OX3 . 124 B2
St Andrew's Rd
Chinnor OX9 . 168 B3
Didcot OX11 . 218 C4
Oxford OX3 . 124 B2
St Andrews Cl OX14 . 160 B1
St Andrews Ho OX9 . 168 B3
St Andrews Rd
Caversham RG4 . 258 C2
Henley-on-T RG9 . 254 B4
St Anne's Cl RG9 . 244 B1
St Anne's Rd Banbury OX16 . 16 B2
Oxford OX3 . 124 B1
St Annes Cl OX15 . 65 F2
St Annes Ct OX11 . 219 D4
St Annes Rd RG4 . 259 D1
St Barnabas Rd RG4 . 259 D2
St Barnabas St OX2 . 123 D1
St Bernard's Rd OX2 . 123 D2
St Birinus Ct GL7 . 150 B3
St Christopher's Pl OX4 . 142 B3
St Clement's St OX4 . 123 E1
St Cross Rd OX1 . 123 E1
St Davids Cl RG4 . 258 C3
St Denys Cl SN7 . 194 C4
St Ebbes St OX1 . 141 E4
St Edburg's Cl OX6 . 65 E1
St Edith's Way OX6 . 65 E1
St Edmund's La OX4 . 179 F3
St Edward's Ave OX2 . 123 D4
St Francis Rd HP14 . 189 E2
St George's Cres OX16 . 16 B2
St George's Pl OX1 . 123 D1
St George's Rd SN7 . 154 B1
St Georges Green OX10 . 203 E1
St Georges Rd OX10 . 221 E4
St Giles OX5 . 93 D4
St Giles' OX1 . 123 E1
St Giles Cl OX6 . 80 A2
St Helen's Ave OX10 . 203 F2
St Helen's Cres OX10 . 204 A2
St Helen's Ct OX14 . 179 F3
St Helen's Mews OX14 . 179 F3
St Helen's Pas OX1 . 123 E1
St Helen's Way OX10 . 203 F2
St Helen's Wharf OX14 . 179 F3
St Hilda's Cl OX6 . 65 E1
St Hildas Cl OX11 . 219 D4
St Hugh's Cl Bicester OX6 . 65 F2
Stokenchurch HP14 . 188 C2
St Hugh's Pl HP14 . 188 C2
St Hughs Cl OX16 . 16 B2
St Hughs Rise OX11 . 219 D4
St Ives La OX12 . 214 C4
St Ives Rd OX12 . 214 B3
St James
St James Cl RG8 . 256 B3
St James Ct OX8 . 89 E4
St James Cl OX4 . 160 C2
St James Terr OX14 . 160 C1
St James View OX17 . 197 D4
St John St OX1 . 123 E1
St John's Cl Didcot OX11 . 219 D4
Fyfield OX13 . 157 D1
St John's Green OX10 . 221 E3
St John's Rd
Abingdon OX14 . 180 A4
Banbury OX16 . 16 B3
Caversham RG4 . 259 D1
Wallingford OX10 . 221 E4
St John's Row OX14 . 201 E4
St John's St Bicester OX6 . 65 F1
Lechlade GL7 . 150 B2
St John's Way OX15 . 33 D2
St Johns Dr
Carterton OX18 . 115 F2
Kidlington OX5 . 92 C1
St Johns Rd
Caversham RG4 . 259 E1
Tackley OX5 . 77 D3
St Katherines Rd RG9 . 254 B4
St Kenelm's Cl OX8 . 102 C1
St Lawrence Cl OX10 . 203 D4
St Lawrence Rd
South Hinksey OX1 . 141 D3
St Leonard's Cl OX16 . 16 B3
St Leonard's La OX10 . 221 E4
St Leonard's Rd OX3 . 124 C1
St Leonard's Sq OX10 . 221 E4
St Leonards Cl OX9 . 186 A1
St Lucian's La OX10 . 221 E3
St Luke's Rd OX4 . 142 B3

St Lukes Way RG4 . 259 D2
St Margaret's Rd OX2 . 123 D2
St Marks Rd RG9 . 254 B4
St Martin's Rd OX4 . 142 A2
St Martin's St OX10 . 221 E4
St Mary Cl OX44 . 184 B3
St Mary's Cl Bicester OX6 . 65 E1
Kidlington OX5 . 92 C1
Oxford OX4 . 142 A1
St Mary's Ct OX8 . 118 A4
St Mary's Green OX14 . 159 F1
St Mary's La OX7 . 30 C2
St Mary's Mead OX8 . 118 A4
St Mary's Rd
Adderbury OX17 . 22 C1
East Hendred OX12 . 216 C3
Oxford OX4 . 141 F4
St Mary's St OX10 . 221 E4
St Mary's Way OX12 . 214 B3
St Marys Ave RG8 . 257 E3
St Marys Cl
Henley-on-T RG9 . 254 B4
Wheatley OX33 . 144 A4
St Michael's Ave
Abingdon OX14 . 179 F4
Highworth SN6 . 190 A3
St Michael's Cl OX6 . 52 B3
St Michael's La OX5 . 107 F4
St Michael's St OX1 . 123 E1
St Michael's Way OX13 . 198 C2
St Michaels Cl OX7 . 85 E4
St Nicholas' Green OX14 . 159 F1
St Nicholas Rd Oxford OX4 . 142 B1
Tackley OX5 . 77 E3
Wallingford OX10 . 221 E4
St Omer Rd OX4 . 142 B3
St Paul's Cres OX2 . 140 B4
St Peter's Cl
Cassington OX8 . 107 E1
Stoke Lyne OX6 . 51 D3
Wootton (Oxford) OX13 . 159 D3
St Peter's Cres OX6 . 65 F1
St Peter's Pl OX10 . 221 E4
St Peter's Rd
Abingdon OX14 . 160 B1
Brackley NN13 . 24 A4
Cutteslowe OX2 . 122 C4
Didcot OX11 . 218 C4
St Peter's St OX18 . 221 E4
St Peters Ave RG4 . 258 C2
St Peters Gate NN13 . 24 A4
St Peters Hill RG4 . 258 C2
St Peters Rd RG4 . 24 A4
St Ruald's Cl OX10 . 221 E4
St Rumbold's Rd OX10 . 221 E4
St Stephens Cl RG4 . 259 D1
St Swithun's Rd OX1 . 160 C4
St Thomas St OX15 . 33 D2
St Thomas' St OX1 . 123 D1
St Thomas's Cl SN7 . 155 F1
Salegate La OX4 . 142 B3
Salesian Gdns OX4 . 142 B3
Salford Rd OX3 . 123 F2
Salisbury Cres OX2 . 123 D4
Sallow Cl OX6 . 65 F3
Salmon Cl OX15 . 21 F3
Salop Cl SN6 . 209 D3
Salt La OX9 . 166 C1
Salter Cl OX1 . 141 E4
Salters La HP18 . 98 B4
Salvia Cl OX16 . 9 D1
Samian Way OX10 . 202 B4
Samor Way OX11 . 218 B4
Samphire Rd OX4 . 142 C1
Sanctuary Rd OX4 .
Sand Hill SN6 . 209 D4
Sand View SN7 . 172 C1
Sandcroft Rd RG4 . 258 C3
Sandell Cl OX14 . 160 A2
Sanderling Wlk OX16 . 16 C2
Sandfield Rd OX3 . 124 A2
Sandfine Rd OX15 . 15 D1
Sandford Cl
Abingdon OX14 . 160 A1
Woodcote RG8 . 250 C4
Sandford Dr RG5 . 260 C1
Sandford Green OX16 . 15 F4
Sandford La OX1 . 160 C4
Sandford Park OX7 . 73 E2
Sandford Rd OX4 . 142 A1
Sandford Rise OX7 . 73 E2
Sandgate Ave RG30 . 257 F2
Sandhill Rd OX5 . 108 A4
Sandleigh Rd OX13 . 159 D4
Sandpiper Cl OX6 . 81 D4
Sandpit Hill HP18 . 39 E3
Sandringham Dr OX11 . 219 D4
Sandringham Rd OX17 . 23 F3
Sands Cl Bletchingdon OX5 . 93 D4
Cumnor OX2 . 139 D4
Sands La OX5 . 31 F4
Sands Rd OX11 . 219 F2
Sands The Benson OX10 . 204 B1
Ewelme OX10 . 204 B3
Milton-u-W OX7 . 70 A1
Sandy Cl OX16 . 9 D1
Sandy Way OX10 . 203 D2
Sandy La Beckley OX3 . 111 D2
Cholsey OX10 . 220 C2
Church Westcote GL54 . 68 A3
Kingston Bagpuize OX13 . 156 C3
Long Crendon HP18 . 129 D1
Oxford OX1, OX33, OX44 . 142 C2
Shrivenham SN6 . 209 D3
Stanford in the V SN7 . 174 B3
Tiddington OX9 . 145 F2
Wootton (Oxford) OX1 . 140 B1
Yarnton OX5 . 108 B3
Sandy La W OX4 . 142 B3
Sandy Lane Ct GL54 . 68 A3

Sarajac Ave OX12 ... 213 F2
Sarsden Cl OX7 ... 57 D1
Sarum Cl OX18 ... 115 F2
Satin La OX15 ... 33 F2
Satwell Cl RG9 ... 243 D2
Saunders Cl OX9 ... 186 A1
Saunders Ct RG8 ... 257 D3
Saunders Rd OX4 ... 142 A3
Saunders Wood Copse HP14 ... 188 C2
Savile Rd OX1 ... 123 E1
Savile Way OX12 ... 196 B1
Saw Cl OX44 ... 184 B4
Sawpit Rd OX4 ... 142 C2
Sawpits La GL56 ... 40 A1
Saxel Cl OX18 ... 135 F2
Saxifrage Sq OX4 ... 142 C1
Saxon Ct OX12 ... 221 E4
Saxon Pl OX12 ... 214 A3
Saxon Way Oxford OX3 ... 124 A2
  Witney OX8 ... 118 A4
Saxons Heath OX14 ... 201 E4
Saxons Way OX11 ... 219 D4
Saxton Rd OX14 ... 179 F3
Sayers Orch OX11 ... 200 B1
Scafell Cl RG31 ... 257 E1
Scampton Cl OX6 ... 66 A2
Schilling St OX6 ... 63 D4
Schofield Ave OX8 ... 104 A2
Schofield Gdns OX8 ... 104 A2
Schofields Way OX15 ... 21 F3
Scholar Pl OX2 ... 140 B4
Scholars Acre OX18 ... 115 E2
Scholars Cl RG4 ... 258 C2
Schongau Cl OX14 ... 179 E2
School Cl Ickford HP18 ... 128 A2
  Long Compton CV36 ... 27 F3
  Longworth OX13 ... 156 B2
  Steventon OX13 ... 198 C2
School End OX17 ... 35 E4
School Hill
  Minster Lovell OX8 ... 102 C2
  Mollington OX17 ... 3 F2
  Wargrave RG10 ... 255 E1
School La
  Aston Rowant OX9 ... 167 F2
  Banbury OX15, OX16, OX17 ... 16 B3
  Black Bourton OX18 ... 133 F3
  Caversham RG4 ... 259 D1
  Caversham, The Common RG4 ... 259 D3
  Chilson OX7 ... 71 F3
  Coleshill SN6 ... 191 D4
  Great Bourton OX17 ... 9 E4
  Harwell OX11 ... 217 F4
  Kingston Bagpuize OX13 ... 156 C1
  Middleton Stoney OX6 ... 64 A2
  Milton (Abingdon) OX14 ... 199 E2
  Milton (Abingdon) OX14 ... 199 E3
  Minster Lovell OX8 ... 102 C2
  North Newington OX15 ... 15 E2
  Shabbington HP18 ... 128 B3
  Stadhampton OX44 ... 163 E1
  Stoke Row RG9 ... 241 F2
  Sutton Courtenay OX14 ... 200 C4
  Upper Heyford OX6 ... 62 C4
  Wargrave RG10 ... 255 E1
  Warmington OX17 ... 3 D2
School Paddock OX6 ... 64 C4
School Pl OX1 ... 141 E3
School Rd
  Ardington OX12 ... 215 E3
  Finstock OX7 ... 88 B3
  Kidlington OX5 ... 92 C1
  West Hanney OX12 ... 196 C3
School View OX16 ... 16 C3
School Yd OX44 ... 163 E1
Schooler's La OX12 ... 40 B2
Scotland End OX15 ... 30 A4
Scotsgrove Cotts HP17 ... 130 A2
Scott Cl Bicester OX6 ... 65 E2
  Caversham RG4 ... 259 D3
  Kidlington OX5 ... 108 B4
Scott Rd OX4 ... 123 D4
Scotts Cnr NN13 ... 25 D2
Scotts La OX4 ... 67 F1
Scours La RG30 ... 258 A1
Scruton Cl OX3 ... 124 C2
Seacourt Rd OX2 ... 122 B1
Sealham Rd OX8 ... 118 A2
Second Ave OX11 ... 200 B1
Second St Croughton NN13 ... 36 C3
  Harwell OX11 ... 217 E2
Sedgefield Cl RG4 ... 252 C3
Sedgemoor Dr OX9 ... 130 A1
Sedgewell Rd RG4 ... 252 C3
Seelscheid Way OX6 ... 81 D4
Seeson Way OX12 ... 214 C2
Sefton Pl OX15 ... 22 C2
Sefton Rd OX3 ... 124 C2
Segsbury Rd OX12 ... 214 A3
Selborne Gdns RG30 ... 258 A1
Sellwood Dr OX8 ... 115 F2
Sellwood Rd OX14 ... 159 F1
Selwyn Cres OX14 ... 160 C1
Send Rd RG4 ... 259 E1
Sermon Cl OX3 ... 124 C1
Seven Acres
  Long Crendon HP18 ... 129 D4
  Thame OX9 ... 148 A4
Sevenfields SN6 ... 190 A4
Seventeenth St OX11 ... 217 D1
Seventh Ave OX33 ... 142 C4
Seventh St OX11 ... 217 D2
Severalls Cl OX10 ... 203 E4
Severn Cl OX6 ... 65 D2
Severn Rd Abingdon OX13 ... 159 E1
  Harwell OX11 ... 217 D1

Sewell Cl OX14 ... 160 B1
Sewell's La OX9 ... 167 F4
Shackleton Cl OX6 ... 66 A2
Shades The OX16 ... 16 B3
Shadwell Rd OX10 ... 182 B3
Shaftesbury Rd OX3 ... 124 C3
Shakespeare Cl RG4 ... 259 E3
Shakespeare Dr OX6 ... 65 E2
Shakespeare Rd OX8 ... 120 B4
Shannon Cl OX12 ... 196 C1
Shannon Rd OX6 ... 65 D1
Sharland Cl OX12 ... 214 C4
Sharman Beer Ct OX9 ... 147 F4
Shaw Cl OX6 ... 65 E2
Shaw's Copse OX14 ... 160 C1
Sheards La SN7 ... 194 C4
Shearings The OX15 ... 30 A4
Shearwater Dr OX6 ... 81 D4
Sheen Cl OX6 ... 65 F3
Sheep St Bicester OX6 ... 65 F1
  Burford OX18 ... 100 C3
  Charlbury OX7 ... 73 D2
  Highworth SN6 ... 190 A3
Sheep Wlk RG4 ... 259 D2
Sheepwash La OX13 ... 199 D3
Sheepway Ct OX4 ... 142 A2
Sheepways La RG4 ... 258 A4
Sheerstock HP17 ... 130 C3
Sheldon Rd HP18 ... 128 A2
Sheldon Way OX4 ... 142 B2
Shelford Pl OX3 ... 124 B1
Shelley Cl Abingdon OX14 ... 160 A1
  Banbury OX16 ... 16 A2
  Bicester OX6 ... 65 E2
  Oxford OX3 ... 124 C1
Shelley Rd OX4 ... 142 A3
Shepard Way OX7 ... 42 C2
Shepherd Gdns OX14 ... 179 E3
Shepherds Cl Grove OX12 ... 196 B1
  Weston-on-the-G OX6 ... 79 D1
Shepherds Hill
  Sandford-on-T OX4 ... 142 C1
  Woodstock RG5 ... 260 B1
Shepherds La RG4 ... 258 B3
Sheraton Dr RG31 ... 257 E1
Sherborne St GL7 ... 150 B2
Sherborne Rd OX8 ... 117 E4
Sheridan Ave RG4 ... 259 D2
Sheriff's Dr OX2 ... 122 C4
Sherwood Ave OX14 ... 180 A4
Sherwood Cl OX6 ... 66 A3
Sherwood Gdns RG9 ... 254 B4
Sherwood Pl RG8 ... 257 D2
Sherwood Rd OX11 ... 218 B4
Sherwood Rise RG8 ... 257 D3
Shifford La OX8 ... 137 E1
Shilbrook Manor OX18 ... 133 E2
Shilbrook Ave OX18 ... 115 E3
Shildeane Dr OX18 ... 115 E2
Shilton Rd Burford OX18 ... 100 C2
  Carterton OX18 ... 115 E2
Shiplake Bottom RG4 ... 252 C3
Shipston Rd CV36 ... 27 F4
Shipton Cl RG31 ... 257 E1
Shipton Rd Ascott-u-W OX7 ... 71 D1
  Shipton-u-W OX7 ... 70 A1
  Woodstock OX20 ... 91 F3
Shirburn Rd OX9 ... 186 B1
Shirburn St OX9 ... 186 B1
Shirelake Cl OX1 ... 141 E4
Shires Rd NN13 ... 24 A3
Shirvell's Hill RG8 ... 250 C4
Shoe La
  East Hagbourne OX11 ... 218 C3
  Oxford OX1 ... 123 E1
Shooters Hill RG8 ... 256 A3
Short Furlong OX11 ... 201 D1
Short St Caversham RG4 ... 259 D1
  Pangbourne RG8 ... 256 B3
  Watchfield SN6 ... 191 E1
Short The RG8 ... 257 E3
Shortlands Hill OX10 ... 238 B2
Shotover SN7 ... 211 E3
Shrieves Cl OX14 ... 160 A1
Shrivenham Hundred SN6 ... 191 E1
Shrivenham Rd
  Highworth SN6 ... 190 A2
  Longcot SN7 ... 192 B1
Shute Ave SN6 ... 209 E4
Shutford Rd
  North Newington OX15 ... 15 D2
  Tadmarton OX15 ... 20 C4
Sibford Rd
  Hook Norton OX15 ... 30 A4
  Shutford OX15 ... 13 F2
Sideleigh Rd OX15 ... 22 C4
Sidings Rd OX7 ... 55 F3
Sidney St OX4 ... 141 F4
Signet End OX18 ... 100 C2
Silkdale Cl OX4 ... 142 B3
Silver Birches OX33 ... 125 F4
Silver La OX12 ... 197 D2
Silver Rd OX4 ... 142 A4
Silver St Bourton SN6 ... 209 D1
  Chacombe OX17 ... 10 C2
  Fernham SN7 ... 193 D2
  Tetsworth OX9 ... 166 A1
  Wroxton OX15 ... 15 D4
Silverdale Rd RG10 ... 255 F1
Silvermead HP18 ... 127 E3
Silverthorne Dr RG4 ... 258 C3
Simmonds Wlk OX12 ... 214 B3
Simmons Rd RG9 ... 244 B3
Simons Way OX9 ... 129 F1
Simon's Cl OX33 ... 144 A4
Simons Cl RG31 ... 257 E2

Simons Way OX9 ... 85 E4
Simpsons Way OX14 ... 160 C4
Sinclair Ave OX16 ... 16 A4
Sinclair Dr OX16 ... 16 A4
Singer La RG9 ... 244 C1
Singers Cl RG9 ... 254 C4
Sinnels Field OX7 ... 85 F4
Sinodun Cl OX14 ... 201 E4
Sinodun Rd Didcot OX11 ... 218 C4
  Wallingford OX10 ... 203 E1
Sinodun Way OX10 ... 203 D4
Sint Niklaas Cl OX14 ... 179 E2
Sir Georges La OX17 ... 23 D2
Siskin Rd GL54 ... 68 A3
Sixpenny La OX44 ... 184 C3
Sixteenth St OX11 ... 217 D2
Sixth St Croughton NN13 ... 36 C4
  Harwell OX11 ... 217 D2
Skarries View RG4 ... 258 B4
Skene Cl OX3 ... 124 B1
Skerrit Way RG8 ... 257 E2
Skilton Rd RG31 ... 257 E2
Skimmingdish La OX6 ... 65 F3
Skimmingdish Rd OX6 ... 66 A2
Skinner Rd OX6 ... 66 A3
Skippett La OX7 ... 88 A2
Skippon Way OX9 ... 129 F1
Skittle Alley OX17 ... 35 E4
Slade Cl OX3 ... 124 B1
Slade End OX10 ... 203 D1
Slade End Rdbt OX10 ... 203 D1
Slade Rd Cholsey OX10 ... 221 D1
  Didcot OX11 ... 200 B1
  Stokenchurch HP14 ... 188 C2
Slade The Charlbury OX7 ... 73 E2
  Oxford OX3 ... 142 C4
Slave Hill HP17 ... 130 C3
Slaymaker Cl OX3 ... 124 C1
Sloan Ct RG8 ... 249 E3
Slopes The RG4 ... 259 E1
Small Ho OX15 ... 19 E4
Smith Barry Cres GL54 ... 68 A2
Smith Barry Rd GL54 ... 68 A2
Smith Cl RG4 ... 252 C3
Smith's Cl OX18 ... 135 F1
Smiths Farm La OX11 ... 200 B1
Smiths Hill OX12 ... 231 F3
Smiths Rickyard OX12 ... 216 B4
Snakehill La OX15 ... 33 D2
Snipe Rd GL54 ... 68 A2
Snowdon Mede OX3 ... 124 A2
Snows La OX33 ... 125 E4
Snowshill Dr OX8 ... 103 E1
Snowsill Dr OX18 ... 117 E4
Snowswick La SN7 ... 170 C3
Snuff La OX17 ... 8 B4
Snuggs La OX12 ... 197 D4
Soden Rd OX6 ... 63 E4
Solters Cl HP18 ... 98 B4
Somerton Rd Ardley OX6 ... 50 A2
  North Aston OX6 ... 48 A4
Somerville OX11 ... 219 D4
Somerville Cl OX17 ... 23 E2
Somerville Dr OX6 ... 65 F2
Songers Cl OX4 ... 140 A4
Sonning La OX4 ... 260 B2
Sonning Meadows RG4 ... 260 B1
Soot La OX17 ... 3 D2
Sopwith Rd GL54 ... 68 A3
Sorrel Rd OX4 ... 143 D1
Sotwell St OX10 ... 202 C1
South Ave Abingdon OX14 ... 159 F1
  Henley-on-T RG9 ... 254 C4
  Kidlington OX5 ... 108 C3
South Bar St OX16 ... 16 B3
South Cl OX5 ... 108 C3
South Dr Harwell OX11 ... 217 E2
  Sonning RG4 ... 260 B1
South End
  Great Rollright OX7 ... 29 D2
  Haddenham HP17 ... 130 C3
South Gate Ct GL54 ... 68 A2
South Hills HP17 ... 98 A1
South Leigh Rd OX8 ... 119 D4
South Mere OX18 ... 116 B2
South Newington Rd
  Barford St M OX15 ... 32 B3
  Bloxham OX15 ... 21 D1
South Par OX2 ... 123 D4
South Park Ave OX11 ... 218 B4
South Parks Rd OX1 ... 123 E1
South Row OX11 ... 235 E4
South Side OX6 ... 62 A4
South St Banbury OX16 ... 16 C4
  Blewbury OX11 ... 237 D4
  Caversham RG4 ... 259 D1
  Lechlade Bassett OX12 ... 214 A1
  Lower Heyford OX6 ... 62 C3
  Middle Barton OX7 ... 60 C4
  Oxford OX2 ... 141 D4
  Watchfield SN6 ... 191 E1
South Stoke Rd RG8 ... 240 A1
South View OX17 ... 4 A3
South View Ave RG4 ... 259 E1
South View Park RG4 ... 259 E1
Southam Rd
  Banbury OX16, OX15 ... 9 E2
  Cropredy OX17 ... 4 B2
  Great Bourton OX17 ... 9 E2
  Mollington OX17 ... 4 A3
Southampton St SN7 ... 172 C2
Southbank OX10 ... 221 D4
Southchurch Dr ... 123 F3
Southdale Rd OX2 ... 123 D4
Southdown Ct SN7 ... 194 C4
Southdown Rd RG4 ... 259 D3

Southend OX44 ... 162 C4
Southern By-pass Rd
  Kennington OX1 ... 141 E2
  N Hinksey Vill OX2 ... 140 C4
  Oxford OX1 ... 141 F2
  South Hinksey OX1 ... 141 D2
Southern Rd OX9 ... 147 F4
Southerndene Cl RG31 ... 257 E1
Southfield Dr OX14 ... 199 F4
Southfield La OX6 ... 49 F4
Southfield Park OX4 ... 142 A4
Southfield Rd OX4 ... 142 A4
Southlands OX18 ... 135 F1
Southlawn OX8 ... 117 F4
Southmoor Pl OX2 ... 123 D2
Southmoor Rd OX2 ... 123 D2
Southmoor Way OX14 ... 179 F4
Southrop RG15 ... 30 A3
Southwold OX6 ... 65 F3
Southwood Rd OX4 ... 142 B2
Sovereign Cl OX11 ... 219 D4
Sovereign Ct OX4 ... 142 B2
Spa Cl SN6 ... 190 A4
Span Hall RG4 ... 260 B4
Spareacre La OX8 ... 120 C4
Sparrow Way OX4 ... 142 C1
Sparsey Pl OX2 ... 109 D1
Sparsholt St OX12 ... 212 C2
Spears The OX5 ... 108 A3
Speedwell St OX1 ... 141 E4
Spencer Ave OX5 ... 108 A3
Spencer Cress OX4 ... 142 A2
Spencers Cl SN7 ... 194 B4
Spenlove Cl OX14 ... 159 F1
Spenser Cl OX6 ... 65 E2
Spey Rd OX13 ... 159 E1
Speyside Cl OX18 ... 115 E3
Spier's La OX6 ... 67 F1
Spindleberry Cl OX4 ... 142 C1
Spindlers OX5 ... 92 C1
Spinfieldside OX6 ... 65 F3
Spinney Cl RG4 ... 259 D4
Spinney Dr OX16 ... 16 C2
Spinney Field OX4 ... 142 C1
Spinney The
  Abingdon OX14 ... 159 E1
  Launton OX6 ... 66 B1
  Lechlade GL7 ... 150 B2
Spinneys Cl OX14 ... 160 C2
Spinneys The OX7 ... 58 C3
Spitfire Cl OX6 ... 66 A2
Spooner Cl OX3 ... 124 C2
Spriggs Holly La HP14 ... 189 D4
Spring Cl OX18 ... 118 A4
Spring Copse OX4 ... 141 E2
Spring Farm OX9 ... 47 E3
Spring Gdns OX14 ... 179 E4
Spring Hill OX13 ... 176 B4
Spring Hill Rd OX5 ... 107 F4
Spring La
  Aston Tirrold OX11 ... 237 F4
  Caversham RG4 ... 260 A3
  Great Bourton OX17 ... 9 E4
  Horspath OX33 ... 143 E4
  Idbury OX7 ... 69 D2
  Oxford OX3, OX33, OX4 ... 142 C3
  Oxford,Headington Quarry OX3 ... 124 C1
  Wallingford OX9 ... 186 B1
Spring Path OX9 ... 147 F4
Spring Pl OX7 ... 42 C1
Spring Rd OX14 ... 179 E4
Spring Terr OX14 ... 122 B1
Spring Wlk RG10 ... 255 E1
Springdale OX10 ... 221 E4
Springfield OX17 ... 8 C2
Springfield Ave OX16 ... 16 B2
Springfield Cl
  Shrivenham SN6 ... 209 D3
  Watlington OX9 ... 186 B1
Springfield End RG8 ... 249 E4
Springfield Gdns OX9 ... 168 B4
Springfield Oval OX8 ... 103 F1
Springfield Park OX8 ... 103 F1
Springfield Rd
  Bicester OX6 ... 65 E4
  Kidlington OX5 ... 108 C4
  N Hinksey Vill OX2 ... 140 B4
  Stokenchurch HP14 ... 188 C2
  Wantage OX12 ... 214 C2
Springhill Rd RG8 ... 249 E4
Springs The OX8 ... 118 A4
Springwell Hill OX5 ... 78 A1
Springwood La RG9 ... 252 C4
Spruce Dr OX6 ... 65 F3
Spruce Gdns OX4 ... 161 F4
Spruce Rd OX5 ... 108 C4
Spur The RG10 ... 255 F2
Square Firs OX3 ... 90 A3
Square The
  Abingdon OX3, OX14 ... 179 F4
  Aston OX18 ... 135 F2
  Aynho OX17 ... 35 E3
  Ducklington OX8 ... 118 A2
  Eynsham OX8 ... 120 C4
  Kings Sutton OX17 ... 23 F3
  Long Crendon HP18 ... 129 E3
  Longworth OX13 ... 156 A2
  N Hinksey Vill OX2 ... 122 B1
  Pangbourne RG8 ... 256 B3
  Swalcliffe OX15 ... 19 F4
Squire's Wlk OX4 ... 221 E3
Squires Cl OX18 ... 116 B2
Squires Leys OX6 ... 81 D4
Squitchey La OX2 ... 123 D4
Stable Cl MK18 ... 39 E4
Stable Rd OX6 ... 65 F2
Staddlestone Cl RG31 ... 257 E1

Stadhampton Rd
  Drayton St L OX10 ... 183 D3
  Little Milton OX44 ... 163 F3
Stadium Way RG30 ... 258 A1
Staffordshire Cl RG30 ... 257 F1
Stainer Pl OX3 ... 123 F2
Stainfield Rd OX3 ... 124 A3
Stainswick La SN6 ... 209 E2
Stallpits Rd SN6 ... 209 D4
Stanbridge Cl OX16 ... 16 A3
Standlake Rd
  Ducklington OX8 ... 118 B2
  Northmoor OX8 ... 138 A1
Stanford Dr OX14 ... 179 F4
Stanford Rd SN7 ... 173 D2
Stanier Pl OX16 ... 16 C2
Stanley Cl OX2 ... 140 B4
Stanley Rd OX4 ... 141 F4
Stanmore Cres OX18 ... 115 F2
Stansfeld Pl OX3 ... 124 C1
Stansfield Cl OX3 ... 124 C1
Stanton Cl OX8 ... 117 F4
Stanton Harcourt Rd
  South Leigh OX8 ... 119 E3
  Witney OX8 ... 118 B4
Stanton Rd
  Forest Hill OX33 ... 125 F2
  N Hinksey Vill OX2 ... 140 C3
Stanville Rd OX2 ... 140 A4
Stanway Cl OX8 ... 103 E1
Stanway Rd OX3 ... 125 D2
Stanwell Cl OX17 ... 11 D1
Stanwell Dr OX17 ... 11 D1
Stanwell Lea OX17 ... 11 D1
Stanwell Rd OX17 ... 9 E4
Stapleton Rd OX3 ... 124 B1
Star La SN6 ... 191 E1
Star Rd RG4 ... 259 E1
Starina Croft OX16 ... 9 D1
Starnham Rd OX8 ... 118 A2
Starwort Path OX4 ... 142 C1
Station App Bicester OX6 ... 65 F1
  Kidlington OX5 ... 92 B1
Station Field Ind Est OX5 ... 92 B1
Station La OX8 ... 118 A3
Station Rd Ardley OX6 ... 50 B2
  Ashbury SN6 ... 228 A4
  Aynho OX17 ... 35 D3
  Bampton OX18 ... 134 C3
  Black Bourton OX18 ... 133 F3
  Blackthorn OX6 ... 82 A2
  Bletchingdon OX5 ... 93 D4
  Brize Norton OX18 ... 116 B2
  Chinnor OX9 ... 168 B3
  Chipping Norton OX7 ... 42 B1
  Cholsey OX10 ... 220 C1
  Churchill OX7 ... 54 C2
  Cropredy OX17 ... 4 C2
  Culham OX14 ... 180 C2
  Didcot OX11 ... 200 C1
  Eynsham SN7 ... 120 C4
  Faringdon SN7 ... 172 C2
  Goring RG8 ... 249 E3
  Grove OX12 ... 214 C2
  Haddenham HP17 ... 130 C3
  Henley-on-T RG9 ... 244 C1
  Highworth SN6 ... 190 A3
  Hook Norton OX15 ... 30 B4
  Kingham OX7 ... 54 C2
  Launton OX6 ... 66 C2
  Lechlade GL7 ... 150 B3
  Lower Heyford OX6 ... 62 B3
  Marsh Gibbon OX6 ... 67 F2
  Pangbourne RG8 ... 256 B3
  Shiplake RG9 ... 255 D2
  Shipton-u-W OX7 ... 70 C1
  Shrivenham SN6 ... 209 D3
  South Leigh OX8 ... 119 E3
  Uffington SN7 ... 211 E4
  Upton OX11 ... 218 C1
  Wallingford OX10 ... 221 E4
  Wargrave RG10 ... 255 E1
  Wheatley OX33 ... 144 A4
Station Yard Ind Est OX17 ... 23 D1
Station Yd Steventon OX13 ... 199 D2
  Thame OX9 ... 148 A4
Staunton Rd OX3 ... 124 A2
Staverton Rd OX2 ... 123 D3
Steady's La OX8 ... 138 A4
Steep Rise OX3 ... 124 A3
Steeple Cl OX15 ... 21 F2
Steepness Hill OX15 ... 32 C2
Stenton Cl OX14 ... 179 F3
Stephen Rd OX3 ... 124 B2
Stephenson Rd OX12 ... 214 B4
Steptoe Cl OX12 ... 196 B1
Sterling Cl Bicester OX6 ... 66 A2
  Kidlington OX5 ... 108 C4
Sterling Rd OX5 ... 108 C4
Sterling Road App OX5 ... 108 C4
Sterling Way RG30 ... 258 A1
Stert Rd OX9 ... 167 F2
Stert St OX14 ... 179 F4
Stevens La RG9 ... 252 B4
Stevenson Cl OX6 ... 65 E2
Stevenson Dr OX14 ... 179 E4
Steventon Rd
  Drayton OX14 ... 199 D3
  East Hanney OX12 ... 197 F4
Stewart St OX1 ... 141 E3
Stile Rd OX3 ... 124 B2
Stimpsons Cl OX2 ... 122 A1
Stirling Cl Carterton OX18 ... 115 E2
  Caversham RG4 ... 259 E3
  Wantage OX12 ... 214 C3

Stirling Ct OX16 ...... 15 F3
Stirlings Rd OX12 ...... 214 B2
Stockey End OX14 ...... 160 B1
Stockham Park OX12 ...... 214 B3
Stockham Way OX12 ...... 214 B3
Stocking La OX15 ...... 6 B1
Stockleys Rd OX3 ...... 124 A3
Stockmore St OX4 ...... 141 C4
Stocks La OX13 ...... 198 C2
Stocks Tree Cl OX5 ...... 108 A3
Stoke Lyne Rd OX6 ...... 52 B1
Stoke Pl OX3 ...... 124 B2
Stoke Row Rd RG9 ...... 252 C4
Stokes View RG8 ...... 256 B3
Stone Cl OX2 ...... 122 A1
Stone Ct OX7 ...... 29 D2
Stone Hill OX15 ...... 21 E2
Stone House Cl OX13 ...... 156 C1
Stone Quarry La OX4 ...... 142 A2
Stone St Oxford OX4 ...... 142 A4
   Reading RG30 ...... 258 A1
Stonebridge Rd OX13 ...... 198 C3
Stoneburge Cres OX6 ...... 65 F2
Stonehay Cl OX12 ...... 214 C3
Stonefield Dr SN6 ...... 190 A2
Stonefield Way SN6 ...... 209 E3
Stonefields Riding OX8 ...... 89 E4
Stonehill OX14 ...... 179 E2
Stonehill Cl OX13 ...... 176 B4
Stonehill Wlk OX14 ...... 179 F2
Stoneleigh Cl OX7 ...... 57 D1
Stoneleigh Dr OX18 ...... 115 E3
Stonesfield OX11 ...... 219 D4
Stonesfield La OX7 ...... 73 E1
Stonesfield Rd OX8 ...... 90 A3
Stonesfield Riding OX7 ...... 74 B1
Stoney La OX9 ...... 185 F4
Stonhouse Cres OX14 ...... 160 C1
Stonor Cl OX11 ...... 200 C1
Stonor Gn OX9 ...... 186 A1
Stonor Ho RG9 ...... 226 A4
Stonor Pl OX4 ...... 124 A1
Stort Cl OX11 ...... 200 C2
Stour Cl OX11 ...... 201 D1
Stoutsfield Cl OX5 ...... 108 A3
Stow Ave OX8 ...... 117 E4
Stow Rd Bledington OX7 ...... 54 B1
   Fifield OX7 ...... 69 D1
Stowford Rd OX3 ...... 124 C2
Stowhill OX12 ...... 213 E2
Stowood Cl OX3 ...... 124 C2
Strachey Cl RG8 ...... 256 B1
Strafford Way OX9 ...... 148 A4
Strainges Cl OX14 ...... 118 A2
Stratfield Rd
   Cutteslowe OX2 ...... 123 D3
   Kidlington OX5 ...... 108 C3
Stratford Dr OX8 ...... 120 B4
Stratford La OX20 ...... 76 A1
Stratford Rd
   Drayton (Banbury) OX15 ...... 15 F4
Stratford Rd continued
   Shenington OX15 ...... 6 C3
   Wroxton OX15 ...... 14 C4
Stratford St OX4 ...... 141 F4
Stratton Au OX18 ...... 115 F3
Stratton Audley Rd
   Fringford OX6 ...... 52 B3
   Stoke Lyne OX6 ...... 51 D3
Stratton Way OX14 ...... 179 F4
Strawberry Hill OX15 ...... 21 F3
Strawberry Path OX4 ...... 142 C1
Strawberry Terr OX15 ...... 21 F3
Stream Rd OX11 ...... 218 B1
Streatley & Goring Bridge
   RG8 ...... 249 D3
Streatley Hill RG8 ...... 248 C3
Street The
   Crowmarsh G OX10 ...... 221 F4
   Crowmarsh, Ipsden OX10 ...... 240 B4
   Crowmarsh G, N Stoke OX10 ...... 221 E1
   Moulsford OX10 ...... 239 D2
   South Stoke RG8 ...... 239 D2
   Stoke Lyne OX6 ...... 51 D3
   Tidmarsh RG8 ...... 256 B1
Stuart Cl RG4 ...... 259 D3
Stuart Way OX9 ...... 130 A1
Stubble Cl OX2 ...... 140 A4
Stubbs Ave OX3 ...... 142 C4
Studdridge Ct HP14 ...... 188 B2
Sturges Cl OX3 ...... 124 C2
Sturt Cl OX7 ...... 73 E1
Sturt Rd OX7 ...... 73 E2
Styles Cl OX6 ...... 67 F1
Styles The OX11 ...... 217 E4
Sudbury Ct SN7 ...... 173 D2
Sudbury La OX13 ...... 156 B2
Suffolk Cl OX6 ...... 67 F2
Suffolk Way OX14 ...... 179 E3
Sugarswell La OX15 ...... 6 A3
Sugworth Cres OX14 ...... 160 C3
Sugworth La OX14 ...... 160 B3
Sulham La
   Pangbourne RG8 ...... 256 C2
   Purley on T RG8 ...... 256 C2
   Reading RG8 ...... 256 C2
Summer Fields OX14 ...... 160 A2
Summer Ley OX15 ...... 32 C2
Summerfield OX1 ...... 141 E3
Summerfield Rd OX2 ...... 123 D4
Summerfield Rise RG8 ...... 249 E4
Summerhill Rd OX2 ...... 123 D4
Summers Cl OX17 ...... 23 D3
Summerside Rd SN7 ...... 174 C4
Summerton Pl OX7 ...... 42 C2

Summertown OX12 ...... 197 D3
Summertown Ct OX2 ...... 123 D4
Sunderland Ave OX2 ...... 109 D1
Sunderland Dr OX6 ...... 66 A2
Sundew Cl OX4 ...... 143 D1
Sunningwell Rd
   Oxford OX1 ...... 141 E3
   Sunningwell OX13 ...... 159 F2
Sunny Rise OX33 ...... 143 E3
Sunnyside
   Benson OX10 ...... 203 F3
   Oxford OX33, OX4 ...... 142 B3
   Wheatley OX33 ...... 144 B4
Surley Row RG4 ...... 259 D3
Sussex Dr OX9 ...... 9 D1
Sutton Cl OX14 ...... 179 F4
Sutton Courtenay Rd
   OX14 ...... 180 A1
Sutton La OX8 ...... 120 A1
Sutton Rd
   Milton (Abingdon) OX14 ...... 199 F3
   Oxford OX3 ...... 124 A3
Sutton Wick La OX14 ...... 179 E1
Suzan Cres OX12 ...... 214 C3
Swalcliffe Rd
   Swalcliffe OX15 ...... 20 A4
Swale Dr OX1 ...... 201 D1
Swallow Cl Bicester OX6 ...... 81 D4
   Sandford-on-T OX4 ...... 142 C1
Swan Cl Grove OX12 ...... 196 B1
   Lechlade GL7 ...... 150 B2
   Middleton Cheney OX17 ...... 17 F4
Swan Close Rd OX16 ...... 16 B3
Swan Ct OX8 ...... 118 A4
Swan Gdns OX9 ...... 166 A4
Swan Ind Est OX16 ...... 16 B3
Swan La Burford OX18 ...... 100 C3
   Farington SN7 ...... 172 C2
   Great Bourton OX17 ...... 9 E4
   Long Hanborough OX8 ...... 90 A1
Swan Lane OX18 ...... 100 C3
Swan St Eynsham OX8 ...... 120 C4
   Oxford OX2 ...... 123 E1
Swan Wlk OX9 ...... 147 F4
Swanhall La OX8 ...... 104 A3
Swansea Rd RG1 ...... 259 D1
Swansea Terr RG31 ...... 257 E1
Swansfield Bicester OX6 ...... 81 D4
   Lechlade GL7 ...... 150 B3
Swanston La RG8 ...... 256 B4
Swarbourne Cl OX11 ...... 200 C2
Sweeps La OX18 ...... 100 C3
Sweet Briar OX13 ...... 178 B3
Sweetmans Rd OX2 ...... 140 B4
Swerford Rd OX15 ...... 30 B1
Swift Cl Bicester OX6 ...... 65 E2
   Sandford-on-T OX4 ...... 142 C1
Swift Way OX10 ...... 204 B2
Swin La OX18 ...... 101 F3
Swinbourne Rd OX4 ...... 142 A1
Swinbrook Cl RG31 ...... 257 E2
Swinbrook Rd
   Carterton OX18 ...... 115 E3
   Shipton-u-W OX7 ...... 85 F3
Swinburne Rd
   Abingdon OX14 ...... 180 A4
   Oxford OX4 ...... 141 F3
Swindon Rd SN6 ...... 190 A3
Swindon St SN6 ...... 190 A3
Swingburn Pl OX8 ...... 118 A4
Swinstead Ct OX44 ...... 184 B3
Sworford La OX44 ...... 144 C3
Sycamore Cl
   Abingdon OX13 ...... 159 E1
   Long Crendon HP18 ...... 129 E3
   Sibford Gower OX15 ...... 19 D4
   Watlington OX9 ...... 186 A1
   Witney OX8 ...... 104 B1
Sycamore Cres OX14 ...... 160 C4
Sycamore Dr
   Banbury OX16 ...... 16 B1
   Carterton OX18 ...... 115 E2
   Thame OX9 ...... 147 F4
Sycamore Gdns OX6 ...... 65 F2
Sycamore Rd
   Ambrosden OX6 ...... 81 E2
   Launton OX6 ...... 66 C1
   N Hinksey Vill OX2 ...... 140 B4
Sycamore Wlk OX2 ...... 196 B1
Sydenham Gr OX9 ...... 167 F4
Sylvester Cl OX18 ...... 134 B4
Sympson Cl OX14 ...... 179 F3
Synderford Cl OX11 ...... 201 D1
Syringa Wlk OX16 ...... 9 D1

Tackley Pl OX2 ...... 123 D2
Tadmarton Rd
   Bloxham OX15 ...... 21 D3
   Tadmarton OX15 ...... 21 D3
Taggs Gate OX3 ...... 124 C3
Tait Dr OX6 ...... 65 E2
Talbot Cl Banbury OX16 ...... 15 F4
   Caversham RG4 ...... 259 E1
Talbot Fields OX18 ...... 135 D2
Talbot Rd OX2 ...... 109 D1
Talbot Way RG31 ...... 257 E2
Talisman Rd OX6 ...... 80 C4
Tamar Cres OX6 ...... 65 D2
Tamar Way OX11 ...... 201 D1
Tamarisk Gdns OX6 ...... 65 F3
Tangmere Ave OX18 ...... 115 F2
Tangmere Cl OX6 ...... 66 A2
Tanner's La OX18 ...... 100 B3
Tanners Ct OX7 ...... 73 D2
Tanners La
   Adderbury OX17 ...... 22 C2
   Eynsham OX8 ...... 120 C4
   Mapledurham RG4 ...... 258 C4

Tannery Cl OX18 ...... 100 C3
Taphouse Ave OX8 ...... 104 A1
Tarragon Dr OX4 ...... 142 C1
Tarrant Ave OX8 ...... 104 B1
Taston Rd OX7 ...... 73 D4
Tatham Rd OX14 ...... 159 F1
Tatlings Rd OX13 ...... 198 C3
Taverner Pl OX3 ...... 123 F2
Tavistock Ave OX11 ...... 218 B4
Tavy Cl OX11 ...... 200 C2
Tawney St OX4 ...... 142 A4
Taylor Cl OX6 ...... 65 E3
Tchure The OX15 ...... 33 F2
Teal Cl Banbury OX16 ...... 16 C2
   Grove OX12 ...... 196 B1
   Sandford-on-T OX4 ...... 142 C1
Teale Cl OX6 ...... 96 C4
Teescroft OX11 ...... 201 D2
Telford Cres RG5 ...... 260 C1
Telford Rd OX6 ...... 66 A2
Templar Rd OX2 ...... 109 D1
Templars OX33 ...... 144 A4
Templars Sq OX4 ...... 142 B2
Temple Cloisters OX4 ...... 142 B3
Temple Rd OX4 ...... 142 B3
Temple St Brill HP18 ...... 98 A1
Tenby Ave RG4 ...... 259 E3
Tenlands OX17 ...... 17 F4
Tennis The OX8 ...... 107 E1
Tennyson Cl OX16 ...... 16 A2
Tennyson Dr OX14 ...... 179 E3
Tenpenny OX10 ...... 202 B4
Tenth St OX11 ...... 217 D2
Tern Wlk OX4 ...... 142 C1
Terrace The OX7 ...... 70 A1
Terrington Cl OX14 ...... 160 A1
Tessa Rd RG1 ...... 259 D1
Tetbury Cl OX18 ...... 103 E1
Tew La OX20 ...... 75 F3
Tewer The OX8 ...... 89 E4
Thackley End OX2 ...... 123 D3

Thrift Pl OX4 ...... 142 C1
Thrupp La OX14 ...... 160 B1
Thurne View OX11 ...... 201 D1
Thurston Cl OX14 ...... 179 F3
Tichborne OX9 ...... 148 A4
Ticknell Piece Rd OX7 ...... 73 E2
Tidmarsh La Oxford OX1 ...... 123 D1
   Pangbourne RG8 ...... 256 A1
   Tidmarsh RG8 ...... 256 B2
Tidmarsh Rd
   Pangbourne RG8 ...... 256 B2
   Tidmarsh RG8 ...... 256 B2
Tidmarsh St RG30 ...... 258 B2
Tidmore La OX8 ...... 240 C1
Tilbury Cl RG4 ...... 259 E2
Tilbury La OX2 ...... 122 B1
Tilehouse Cl RG9 ...... 244 B1
Tilehouse Ct OX3 ...... 124 C2
Tilgarsley Rd OX8 ...... 120 B4
Tilling Cl RG31 ...... 257 D1
Tilsley Rd OX7 ...... 42 B1
Timber Way OX9 ...... 168 B3
Timbers La RG9 ...... 223 E1
Timms Rd OX16 ...... 16 B1
Timothy Way OX14 ...... 142 C1
Tinker's La OX6 ...... 65 F1
Tinkerbush La OX12 ...... 214 B3
Tinkers La OX17 ...... 2 B2
Tippings OX11 ...... 188 C3
Tippings La RG5 ...... 260 C1
Tirrold Way OX12 ...... 214 C3
Titchener Cl OX6 ...... 65 E2
Tite La OX15 ...... 30 A4
Tithe Ct OX16 ...... 16 A3
Tithe La OX15 ...... 34 B3
Tithings The OX15 ...... 19 F4
Titup Hall La OX3 ...... 124 C1
Tiverton Cl RG5 ...... 260 C1
Tokers Green Rd RG4 ...... 258 C4
Tokersgreen La
   Caversham RG4 ...... 258 B3
   Mapledurham RG4 ...... 258 B3
Tollgate Rd OX14 ...... 180 A2
Tollington Ct SN7 ...... 172 C1
Tompkins La OX6 ...... 67 F1
Toot Hill Butts OX3 ...... 124 C2
Top Station Rd NN13 ...... 24 A4
Torridge Dr OX11 ...... 201 D1
Tothill OX7 ...... 70 B1
Tower Cl
   Abingdon OX13, OX14 ...... 179 E3
   Caversham RG4 ...... 259 E4
   Marcham OX13 ...... 178 B3
Tower Cres OX1 ...... 123 E1
Tower Gdns OX10 ...... 203 F3
Tower Hill OX8 ...... 117 F4
Tower Rd OX10 ...... 182 B3
Tower View SN7 ...... 172 C1
Towersey Dr OX9 ...... 148 A4
Towersey Rd OX9 ...... 148 B4
Town Cl Fremere MK18 ...... 39 E3
   Sutton Courtenay OX14 ...... 200 A4
Town End Rd
   Bledlow Ridge HP14 ...... 189 E4
   Faringdon SN7 ...... 172 C1
Town Furlong
   Appleton OX13 ...... 158 A4
   Bodicote OX15 ...... 22 B4
Town Furze OX3 ...... 142 B4
Town Green The OX5 ...... 92 C1
Town Pond La OX13 ...... 176 B4
Townhill OX15 ...... 2 A2
Townsend
   Abingdon OX14 ...... 179 F3
   Banbury OX15, OX16 ...... 16 A3
   Barford St M OX15 ...... 32 C3
   Harwell OX11 ...... 217 F4
   Harwell, Chilton OX11 ...... 217 E1
   Marsh Gibbon OX6 ...... 67 F1
Townsend La
   Marsh Gibbon OX6 ...... 67 F1
   Middleton Cheney OX17 ...... 11 F3
Townsend Rd
   Aldworth RG8 ...... 247 F2
   Shrivenham SN6 ...... 209 D3
   Streatley RG8 ...... 249 D4
Townsend Sq OX4 ...... 141 F3
Townside HP17 ...... 130 C3
Toy La OX7 ...... 42 B1
Toynbee Cl OX4 ...... 140 B4
Trafford Rd Oxford OX3 ...... 124 C2
   Reading RG1 ...... 258 C1
Traitor's Ford La OX15 ...... 18 B2
Tramhill HP18 ...... 98 A1
Tramway Rd OX16 ...... 16 C3
Treadwells SN7 ...... 194 C4
Tredegar Rd RG4 ...... 259 D3
Tree La OX4 ...... 142 A2
Treeground Pl OX5 ...... 108 C4
Trefoil Pl OX4 ...... 143 D1
Treforgan Rd RG4 ...... 258 C3
Trelawney Dr RG31 ...... 257 E1
Trenchard Ave OX14 ...... 199 E2
Trenchard Cl OX10 ...... 221 E4
Trenchard Cres OX16 ...... 49 E1
Trendell Pl OX14 ...... 159 F1
Trent Cres OX6 ...... 65 D2
Trent Rd OX11 ...... 201 D1
Trenthams Cl RG8 ...... 257 D3
Trevor Pl OX4 ...... 142 A3
Trill Mill Ct OX1 ...... 141 E4
Trinder Rd OX12 ...... 214 C2
Tring Rd RG31 ...... 257 E2
Trinity Cl Abingdon OX14 ...... 160 A1
   Banbury OX16 ...... 15 F4
   Bicester OX6 ...... 66 B2
Trinity Pl OX4 ...... 141 F3
Trinity Rd OX3 ...... 124 C1

Trinity St OX1 ...... 141 E4
Trinity Way OX17 ...... 23 E2
Tristram Rd OX8 ...... 118 A2
Troika Ct OX16 ...... 9 D1
Trot's La OX7 ...... 85 E4
Troy La OX5 ...... 77 F2
Truelocks Way OX12 ...... 214 C3
Truemper Gr OX6 ...... 65 F4
Trust Cnr RG9 ...... 254 C4
Tubb Cl OX6 ...... 65 E1
Tubbs Cl OX12 ...... 214 B4
Tubbs La OX6 ...... 80 A4
Tuck's La OX13 ...... 156 A2
Tucker Rd OX4 ...... 142 C2
Tuckers La SN6 ...... 227 D2
Tuckers Rd SN7 ...... 173 D2
Tudor Cl Banbury OX16 ...... 16 B1
   Oxford OX4 ...... 142 C2
Tudor Ct OX2 ...... 140 A4
Tuer Dr OX8 ...... 120 C4
Tullis Cl OX14 ...... 199 F4
Tulwick La OX12 ...... 197 D1
Tumbledown Hill OX2 ...... 139 E3
Tuns La RG9 ...... 244 C1
Turberville Cl OX14 ...... 179 E3
Turl St OX1 ...... 123 E1
Turley La OX8 ...... 104 A4
Turnagain La OX14 ...... 179 F3
Turnberry Cl OX6 ...... 66 A2
Turner Cl OX4 ...... 142 B3
Turner Rd OX14 ...... 179 E3
Turners Cl OX14 ...... 160 C1
Turnfields HP18 ...... 128 A2
Turnpike Rd
   Bicester OX6 ...... 66 A3
   Cumnor OX2 ...... 140 A3
   Highworth SN6 ...... 190 A3
Turnstone Green OX6 ...... 81 D4
Tuscan Cl RG30 ...... 257 F1
Tweed Cres OX6 ...... 65 D2
Tweed Dr OX11 ...... 200 C2
Twelfth St OX11 ...... 217 D2
Twelve Acre Dr OX14 ...... 160 B2
Twentieth St OX11 ...... 216 C1
Twin Oaks RG4 ...... 259 D3
Two Rivers Ind Est OX8 ...... 118 A3
Two Tree Hill RG9 ...... 254 A4
Twyford Ave OX17 ...... 23 D3
Twyford Gdns OX17 ...... 23 D3
Twyford Gr OX17 ...... 23 D3
Twyford Rd OX17 ...... 23 E4
Twynhams Rd OX5 ...... 77 E3
Tyburn Glen OX11 ...... 200 C1
Tyler Cl RG4 ...... 258 C3
Tylorstown RG4 ...... 258 C3
Tyndale Pl OX33 ...... 144 B4
Tyndale Rd OX4 ...... 141 F4
Tyne Ave OX11 ...... 200 C1
Tyne Rd OX13 ...... 159 C1
Tyrell Cl SN7 ...... 194 B4
Tyrrell's Way OX14 ...... 199 F3
Tyrrells Cl OX11 ...... 217 E3

Ulfgar Rd OX2 ...... 122 C4
Ullswater Dr RG31 ...... 257 E2
Ulster Cl RG4 ...... 259 E3
Underhill OX10 ...... 239 D2
Underhill Circus OX3 ...... 124 C2
Unicorn St OX15 ...... 21 E2
Union St Banbury OX16 ...... 16 A3
   Oxford OX4 ...... 141 F4
   Woodstock OX20 ...... 91 D4
Union Way OX8 ...... 117 F4
Unity Cl RG4 ...... 259 D3
Untons Pl SN7 ...... 173 D2
Upavon Way OX18 ...... 115 F2
Upland Park Rd OX2 ...... 123 D4
Upland Rise OX17 ...... 9 E3
Uplands Rd RG4 ...... 258 C3
Upper Barr OX4 ...... 142 B2
Upper Brook Hill OX20 ...... 91 D3
Upper Campsfield Rd
   OX20 ...... 91 F3
Upper Comm La SN7 ...... 211 E4
Upper Crale SN7 ...... 194 B4
Upper Cres OX8 ...... 120 A1
Upper Cross La OX11 ...... 218 C3
Upper End OX18 ...... 100 C4
Upper Fisher Row OX1 ...... 123 D1
Upper Gn SN7 ...... 194 C4
Upper High St SN7 ...... 147 F4
Upper Rd OX1 ...... 141 F1
Upper Red Cross Rd RG8 ...... 249 D3
Upper Warren Ave RG4 ...... 258 B2
Upper Windsor St OX16 ...... 16 B2
Upperway RG8 ...... 258 B3
Upperway Furlong OX11 ...... 201 D1
Uppingham Dr RG5 ...... 260 C1
Uppingham Gdns RG4 ...... 259 E3
Upthorpe Dr OX12 ...... 214 C3
Upton Cl Abingdon OX14 ...... 160 A1
   Oxford OX4 ...... 142 C1
Upway Rd OX3 ...... 124 A3
Upwood Dr OX18 ...... 115 F2
Urquhart La OX14 ...... 241 D4
Usk Way OX11 ...... 201 D2
Uxmore Rd RG8 ...... 241 F2

Vale Ave OX11 ...... 196 C1
Vale Cres RG30 ...... 257 F1
Vale Rd OX12 ...... 214 C2
Vale Rd Harwell OX11 ...... 217 D2
   Witney OX8 ...... 117 F4
Valence Cres OX18 ...... 103 F1
Valentia Cl OX5 ...... 92 C4
Valentia Rd OX3 ...... 124 B1
Valentine Cres RG4 ...... 259 E3

Valetta Way OX10 .... 204 B2
Valley Cl Brackley NN13 .... 24 A4
 Caversham RG4 .... 259 D2
 Goring RG8 .... 249 E3
Valley Cres NN13 .... 24 A4
Valley Rd Banbury OX16 .... 16 B2
 Brackley NN13 .... 24 A4
 Finmere MK18 .... 39 E3
 Henley-on-T RG9 .... 254 A4
 Horspath OX33 .... 143 F3
Valley Rise NN13 .... 24 A4
Valley View
 Great Bourton OX17 .... 9 E4
 Lower Heyford OX6 .... 62 C3
Van Dieman's OX7 .... 194 B4
Van Dieman's Rd OX9 ...... 147 F4
Van Diemens Cl OX9 .... 168 B4
Van-Dieman's La OX4 ...... 142 B2
Vanalloys Business Park
 RG9 .... 242 A2
Vanbrugh Cl OX20 .... 91 D4
Vane Rd OX9 .... 130 A1
Vanner Rd OX8 .... 104 B2
Vastern Rd RG1 .... 259 D1
Vauxhall Way OX11 .... 200 B1
Venables Cl OX2 .... 123 D2
Venetia Cl OX14 .... 259 E4
Venners Water OX11 .... 201 D2
Ventfield Cl OX33 .... 112 A3
Ventnor Rd RG31 .... 257 E1
Venwell Cl OX7 .... 42 C1
Verbena Way OX4 .... 142 C1
Verlam Gr OX11 .... 201 D1
Vermont Dr OX20 .... 91 D4
Vernon Ave OX2 .... 140 C3
Vestry Cl OX12 .... 196 B3
Vetch Pl OX4 .... 142 C1
Vicarage Cl Aston OX18 ... 135 E2
 Chalgrove OX44 .... 184 B4
 Grove OX12 .... 196 C1
 Oxford OX4, OX44 .... 142 A1
Vicarage Gdns OX17 .... 4 C1
Vicarage Hill OX12 .... 214 C1
Vicarage La
 Highworth SN6 .... 190 A3
 Long Compton CV36 .... 27 F3
 Oxford OX1 .... 141 E3
 Piddington OX6 .... 97 F3
 Shrivenham SN6 .... 209 E3
Vicarage Rd Didcot OX11 .. 218 C4
 Henley-on-T RG9 .... 254 C4
 Kidlington OX5 .... 92 C1
 Oxford OX1 .... 141 E3
 Steventon OX13 .... 198 C2
Vicarage Wood Way
 RG31 .... 257 D1
Vickers Rd GL54 .... 68 A3
Victor St OX2 .... 123 D1
Victoria Ct Bicester OX6 .. 65 F1
 Henley-on-T RG9 .... 244 C1
 Oxford OX1 .... 123 E1
Victoria Mead OX9 .... 148 A4
Victoria Pl Banbury OX16 .. 16 C1
 Chipping Norton OX7 ..... 42 C2
Victoria Rd Abingdon OX14 . 179 E4
 Bicester OX6 .... 65 F1
 Caversham RG4 .... 259 D2
 Cuttleslowe OX2 .... 123 D4
 Reading RG31 .... 257 E1
 Wargrave RG10 .... 255 F1
Viking Dr OX11 .... 219 D4
Viking Terr OX10 .... 204 B2
Village Farm Ct OX6 ...... 79 D1
Villeboys Cl OX14 .... 180 B4
Villiers La OX4 .... 142 A2
Villiers Rd OX6 .... 65 E1
Vine The HP18 .... 128 B2
Viner Cl OX18 .... 104 B2
Vinery The RG10 .... 255 E1
Vineyard OX14 .... 179 F4
Vineyard Cl OX16 .... 16 B4
Violet Way OX4 .... 161 F4
Virginia Gdns HP14 .... 189 F4
Virginia Way OX14 .... 179 E2
Vorda Rd SN6 .... 190 A4

Wadard's Meadow OX8 ...... 118 B4
Wadham Cl OX6 .... 65 F2
Wainwrights HP18 .... 129 E1
Waites Cl OX18 .... 135 F1
Wales St OX17 .... 23 F3
Walk The OX5 .... 93 F1
Walker Dr OX9 .... 148 A4
Walker's Cl OX18 .... 101 F2
Walker's Ht OX7 .... 88 B3
Walkers Cl OX8 .... 106 A3
Wallace Cl OX17 .... 179 F3
Walled Gdn The RG10 ...... 255 E1
Walled Gdns The OX6 ...... 65 F1
Waller Ct RG4 .... 259 D1
Waller Dr OX16 .... 16 A2
Wallingford Rd
 Cholsey OX10 .... 221 D2
 Crowmarsh G OX10 .... 222 C3
 Reading RG8 & OX10 ...... 239 E3
 South Stoke RG8 & OX10 .. 239 E3
 Streatley RG8 .... 249 D4
 Warborough OX10 .... 203 D3
Wallingford St OX12 ...... 214 C2
Walls The SN7 .... 194 C1
Walmer Rd RG5 .... 260 C1
Walnut Cl Bicester OX6 ... 65 F3
 Deddington OX15 .... 34 C2
 Long Crendon HP18 .... 129 E4
 Sonning Common RG4 ...... 252 C3
 Wootton OX20 .... 75 F2
Walnut Rise OX6 .... 48 C3

Walnut Tree Ct RG8 .... 249 E3
Walnut Trees Hill SN6 .... 228 A4
Walpole Cl OX6 .... 65 D2
Walterbush Rd OX7 .... 42 C1
Waltham Gdns OX16 .... 17 D3
Walton Ave
 Adderbury OX17 .... 23 D3
 Henley-on-T RG9 .... 254 C4
Walton Cl OX15 .... 22 C4
Walton Cres OX1 .... 123 D1
Walton La OX1 .... 123 D1
Walton St OX1, OX2 .... 123 D1
Walton Well Rd OX2 .... 123 D2
Wanbourne La RG9 .... 224 B1
Wandhope Way RG31 .... 257 E1
Wandle Beck OX11 .... 200 C2
Wansbeck Dr OX6 .... 65 D1
Wansbeck Wood OX11 .... 201 D2
Wantage Rd Didcot OX11 ... 218 B4
 Harwell OX11 .... 217 E3
 Streatley RG8 .... 248 C4
 Wallingford OX10 .... 203 D1
Wapping HP18 .... 129 E3
War Memorial Pl RG9 ...... 254 C4
Warbler Wlk OX4 .... 142 C1
Warborough Rd
 Letcombe Bassett OX12 ... 232 A4
 Warborough OX10 .... 203 D3
Warbreck Dr RG31 .... 257 D2
Warburg Cres OX4 .... 142 C2
Ward Rd NN13 .... 24 A3
Warddington Rd OX17 ...... 10 B3
Wardle Ave RG31 .... 257 E1
Wards Cres OX15 .... 22 C4
Wards Rd OX4 .... 42 C2
Ware Leys Cl OX6 .... 67 F2
Ware Rd SN7 .... 194 B4
Wargrave Hill RG10 .... 255 E2
Wargrave Rd
 Cockpole Green RG9 ...... 255 D4
 Henley-on-T RG9 .... 244 C2
Warkworth Cl OX16 .... 15 F4
Warkworth Rd OX17 .... 17 F4
Warley Rise RG31 .... 257 E2
Warmans Cl OX12 .... 214 A3
Warnborough Rd OX2 .... 123 D2
Warneford La OX3 .... 124 A1
Warneford Rd OX4 .... 142 A4
Warner Cres OX11 .... 218 B4
Warren Cres OX3 .... 142 B4
Warren Hill OX44 .... 163 E1
Warren Rd RG5 .... 260 B1
Warren Row Rd RG10 .... 255 F4
Warren The Abingdon OX14 . 180 A4
 Caversham RG4 .... 258 C2
Warwick Cl Abingdon OX14 . 180 A4
 Carterton OX18 .... 115 F2
 Stanford in the V SN7 ... 194 C4
Warwick Ct OX6 .... 66 A2
Warwick Rd
 Banbury OX16, OX17 ...... 8 C2
 Hanwell OX17 .... 8 C2
Warwick St OX4 .... 141 F3
Wasborough Ave OX12 ...... 214 B3
Washford Glen OX11 .... 201 D1
Washington Rd RG4 .... 259 D1
Wastie's Orch OX8 .... 90 A1
Watcombe Rd OX9 .... 146 A4
Water Eaton La OX5 .... 109 D4
Water Eaton Rd OX2 .... 123 E4
Water End Rd HP14 .... 189 E2
Water La Adderbury OX17 .. 23 D2
 Ardley OX6 .... 50 A2
 Bloxham OX15 .... 21 F3
 Brackley NN13 .... 24 A4
 Drayton St L OX10 .... 183 D3
 Little Tew OX7 .... 45 D3
 Steeple Aston OX6 .... 62 A4
Water St OX6 .... 48 C3
Waterloo Dr OX16 .... 16 C3
Waterman Pl RG1 .... 259 D1
Watermans Rd RG9 .... 254 C4
Watermans Way RG10 .... 255 F1
Watermead OX5 .... 109 D4
Watermill Way OX12 .... 125 D2
Waterperry Ct OX16 .... 16 C3
Waterperry Rd HP18 .... 127 E3
Waters La OX17 .... 11 D1
Waterside Rd RG8 .... 257 E3
Waterslade Pens HP17 ..... 130 C3
Watery La Brackley NN13 .. 24 A4
 Clifton Hampden OX14 .... 181 E2
 Hook Norton OX15 .... 30 A4
 Sparsholt OX12 .... 212 C2
Wates Way OX16 .... 16 C4
Watling La OX10 .... 182 B1
Watlington Ind Est OX9 ... 186 A1
Watlington Rd
 Benson OX10 .... 203 F2
 Garsington OX44 .... 162 B4
 Lewknor OX9 .... 186 C3
 Oxford OX4, OX44 .... 142 C2
Watlington St RG9 .... 224 C1
Watson Cres OX13 .... 159 D4
Watsons Cl OX18 .... 115 F1
Watts La OX11 .... 237 D4
Watts Way OX5 .... 92 C1
Waveney Cl Bicester OX6 .. 65 D1
 Didcot OX11 .... 201 D1
Wavers Ground OX18 .... 115 F2
Waxes Cl OX14 .... 160 B1
Wayfaring Cl OX4 .... 161 F4
Wayfarings OX4 .... 65 F3
Wayland Ave OX12 .... 214 A4
Wayland Cres OX11 .... 217 E1
Wayland Rd OX12 .... 196 B1
Waynflete Rd OX3 .... 125 D2

Wayside Green RG8 .... 240 C1
Weald Rise RG30 .... 257 F1
Weald St OX18 .... 134 C1
Wealden Way RG30 .... 257 F1
Wear Rd OX6 .... 65 D1
Weaver Croft OX11 .... 201 D2
Weavers Cl OX18 .... 118 A4
Weavers Row OX15 .... 14 A3
Webb Cl OX16 .... 16 C1
Webb Cres OX7 .... 42 B1
Webb's Cl OX2 .... 122 B4
Webb's Way OX5 .... 92 C1
Webbs Cl OX7 .... 57 D1
Webster Cl OX9 .... 129 F1
Webster's Cl OX14 .... 106 A3
Wedgewood Way RG30 .... 257 F1
Wedgwood Rd OX6 .... 66 A2
Weedon Ct OX10 .... 221 E4
Weeping Cross OX15 .... 22 C4
Weighbridge Row RG1 ...... 258 C1
Weir La OX6 .... 82 A2
Weirs La OX1 .... 141 E3
Welch Way OX8 .... 118 A4
Weldon Rd OX3 .... 123 F2
Weldon Way OX8 .... 118 A4
Welford Gdns OX14 .... 160 A1
Well Bank OX15 .... 30 A4
Well Hill OX7 .... 88 B3
Well La Curbridge OX8 .... 117 E3
 Stonesfield OX8 .... 89 E4
Well Vew RG9 .... 241 F2
Welland Ave OX11 .... 201 D1
Welland Cl Abingdon OX13 . 159 E1
 Reading RG1 .... 257 E1
Welland Croft OX6 .... 65 D2
Weller Cl OX10 .... 204 A4
Wellesbourne Cl OX14 ..... 180 A4
Wellington Cl OX6 .... 66 A2
Wellington Pl OX1 .... 123 E1
Wellington Sq Oxford OX1 . 123 E1
 Watchfield SN6 .... 191 E1
Wellington St Oxford OX2 . 123 D1
 Thame OX9 .... 148 A4
Wellshead La OX11 .... 217 F3
Wellsprings OX10 .... 202 C1
Welham Rd OX8 .... 117 F4
Wenlock Cl OX11 .... 200 B1
Wenman Rd OX9 .... 148 A3
Wenric Dr OX8 .... 102 C1
Wensum Cres OX6 .... 65 D2
Wensum Dr OX11 .... 201 D1
Wentworth Rd
 Cuttleslowe OX2 .... 123 D4
 Thame OX9 .... 148 A4
Wesley Cl Bicester OX6 ... 65 E2
 Oxford OX4 .... 142 C2
Wesley Dr OX16 .... 16 A4
Wesley La OX6 .... 65 F1
Wesley Pl OX17 .... 10 C2
Wessex Cl SN7 .... 173 D2
Wessex Rd OX11 .... 218 C4
Wessex Way Grove OX12 .... 214 B4
 Highworth SN6 .... 190 A4
West Ave OX14 .... 160 A1
West Bar St OX16 .... 16 B3
West Chiltern RG8 .... 250 C4
West Cotts OX6 .... 52 B1
West Cross OX8 .... 102 C1
West Dr Harwell OX11 ..... 217 D2
 Sonning RG4 .... 260 C1
West End
 Brightwell-cum-S OX10 ... 202 B1
 Chipping Norton OX7 ..... 42 C1
 Cholsey OX10 .... 220 C1
 Combe OX8 .... 90 A2
 Hornton OX15 .... 7 A2
 Kingham OX7 .... 54 C2
 Launton OX6 .... 66 B1
 Witney OX8 .... 104 A1
 Wootton OX20 .... 75 F2
West End Cl OX6 .... 66 B1
West End Ind Est OX8 ..... 104 A1
West La
 Bishopstone SN6 .... 227 E2
 Merton OX6 .... 95 E4
West Hawthorn Rd OX4 ..... 81 E2
West Hill OX12 .... 214 B2
West Lockinge OX12 .... 215 E2
West Oxon Ind Park OX18 .. 115 F2
West Rd RG9 .... 242 A1
West St Banbury OX15, OX16 16 C4
 Bicester OX6 .... 65 E2
 Childrey OX12 .... 213 D2
 Chipping Norton OX7 ..... 42 C1
 Henley-on-T RG9 .... 244 B1
 Kingham OX7 .... 54 C2
 Oxford OX2 .... 123 D1
 Shutford OX15 .... 14 A3
 Sparsholt OX12 .... 212 C2
West St Helen St OX14 .... 179 F3
West View Oxford OX4 ..... 142 A2
 Upper Heyford OX6 ...... 49 D3
West Way Lechlade GL7 .... 150 B3
 N Hinksey Vil OX2 ...... 122 B1
Westacott Rd OX6 .... 81 D3
Westbeech Ct OX16 .... 16 B3
Westbourne Ct OX15 .... 21 F2
Westbrook Faringdon SN7 .. 172 C2
 Oxford OX2 .... 196 C1
Westbrook Green OX11 ..... 236 C4
Westbrook Rd RG30 .... 258 B1
Westbrook St OX11 .... 236 C4
Westbury Cres OX4 .... 142 A1
Westbury La RG8 .... 257 D3
Westcot La OX12 .... 212 C3
Westcote Cl OX16 .... 117 E4
Westdene Cres RG4 .... 258 C2

Western Ave
 Henley-on-T RG9 .... 254 C4
 Woodstock RG5 .... 260 C1
Western By-pass Rd
 Cutteslowe OX2 .... 108 C1
 Wytham OX2 .... 122 B3
Western Cres OX16 .... 16 C2
Western Oaks RG31 .... 257 F1
Western Rd
 Henley-on-T RG9 .... 254 C4
 Oxford OX1 .... 141 E4
Westfield OX11 .... 217 E4
Westfield Cl Benson OX10 . 204 A2
 Grove OX12 .... 214 B4
 Oxford OX4 .... 142 A3
Westfield Cres RG9 .... 255 D2
Westfield Rd Benson OX10 . 204 A2
 Caversham RG4 .... 259 D1
 Cholsey OX10 .... 238 B4
 Long Wittenham OX14 ..... 201 E4
 Wheatley OX33 .... 144 A4
 Witney OX8 .... 104 A1
Westfield Way OX12 .... 215 D3
Westfields OX14 .... 179 E4
Westholm Ct OX6 .... 65 F1
Westland Rd SN7 .... 172 C1
Westland Way OX20 .... 91 D4
Westlands Ave OX6 .... 79 D1
Westlands Dr OX3 .... 124 A3
Westleigh Dr RG4 .... 252 C2
Westminster Cl NN13 ...... 24 A4
Westminster Cres NN13 .... 24 A4
Westminster Way
 Banbury OX16 .... 16 C3
 N Hinksey Vil OX2 ...... 140 A4
Weston Cl CV36 .... 28 A3
Weston La OX9 .... 146 C4
Weston Rd OX9 .... 187 D4
Westonbirt Dr RG4 .... 258 C2
Westridge Ave RG8 .... 257 F3
Westrop SN6 .... 190 A3
Westrop Cl OX3 .... 123 F2
Westwater Way OX11 .... 201 D1
Westway RG8 .... 249 E4
Westwood Glen RG31 .... 257 E1
Westwood Rd
 Curbridge OX8 .... 103 E1
 Reading RG31 .... 257 E1
Westwood Row RG31 .... 257 E1
Wetherby Cl RG4 .... 259 E3
Wey Rd OX10 .... 182 B3
Weycroft OX11 .... 201 D2
Weyland Rd OX3 .... 124 C1
Whales La OX6 .... 67 F1
Wharf Cl OX14 .... 179 F3
Wharf La Henley-on-T RG9 . 244 C1
 Lechlade GL7 .... 150 B2
 Souldern OX6 .... 35 D2
Wharf Rd OX10 .... 203 D3
Wharton Rd OX3 .... 124 B2
Whatleys Orch SN6 .... 227 E2
Wheatcroft Cl OX14 ...... 160 A1
Wheatfields OX11 .... 218 B4
Wheatley Campus
 (Brookes Univ) OX33 .... 126 B1
Wheatley Cl OX16 .... 16 C1
Wheatley Rd
 Garsington OX44 .... 143 F2
 Islip OX5 .... 109 F4
 Stanton St John OX33 ... 125 F2
Wheeler Ct RG31 .... 257 F1
Wheeler Rd OX9 .... 168 B3
 Brackley NN13 .... 36 A4
Whimbrel Way OX16 .... 16 C2
Whimorel Cl OX6 .... 66 A1
Whirlwind Way OX10 ...... 204 B2
Whitamore Row RG9 .... 254 C4
Whitby Green RG4 .... 259 E3
Whitchurch Rd RG8 .... 256 B3
White Cross OX13 .... 159 E2
White Hart HP18 .... 98 A4
White Hart Cl OX10 ...... 203 F2
White Hart Wlk SN7 ...... 172 C2
White Hill
 Bishopstone SN6 .... 227 D1
 Burford OX18 .... 101 D2
 Henley-on-T RG9 .... 244 C1
 Shiplake RG9 .... 254 A3
White Hill La OX1 .... 140 A1
White Horse Cres OX12 ... 214 B4
White House Rd OX10 ..... 239 F4
White La RG9 .... 243 F4
White Leys Cl OX11 ...... 200 C1
White Lion Wlk OX16 ..... 16 B3
White Lodge Cl RG31 ..... 257 D2
White Mews OX18 .... 100 C2
White Post Rd OX15 ...... 16 C1
White Rd Chilton OX11 ... 235 E4
 East Hendred OX12 ...... 216 C4
 Oxford OX4 .... 142 C3
White Shoot OX11 .... 237 D3
White Way OX5 .... 108 C4
White's La OX14 .... 160 B2
Whitecross Rd HP17 ...... 130 C3
Whitehall Cl OX8 .... 102 B1
Whitehall La RG8 .... 241 E2
Whitehills Green RG8 .... 249 E3
Whitehorn Way OX4 .... 142 C1
Whitehorns Way OX14 ..... 179 D2
Whitehouse Cl OX13 ...... 159 E1
Whitehouse La OX7 .... 42 C2
Whitehouse Rd
 Oxford RG8 .... 141 E4
 Woodcote RG8 .... 250 C4
Whitelock Rd OX14 .... 159 F1
Whitemoor La RG8 .... 249 E1
Whites Forge OX13 .... 158 A4
Whiteway OX17 .... 3 F2

Whitings La OX4 .... 104 A4
Whitley Cres OX6 .... 66 A2
Whitley Dr OX6 .... 63 E4
Whitley Rd OX10 .... 221 D3
Whitson Pl OX4 .... 142 A4
Whittall St OX17 .... 23 F3
Whittington Pl OX18 ..... 115 E1
Whittle Rd OX9 .... 148 A4
Whitton Cl OX15 .... 30 A4
Wick Cl Abingdon OX14 ... 160 B1
Wick Green OX12 .... 196 B1
Wicks Cl OX18 .... 152 C4
Widmere La RG4 .... 253 D3
Widnell La OX6 .... 97 E4
Wigan's La HP14 .... 169 E3
Wigginton Rd OX15 .... 31 E4
Wigmore La RG30 .... 258 B1
Wigod Way OX10 .... 203 E1
Wilberforce St OX3 ...... 124 B1
Wilcote La OX8 .... 88 A2
Wilcote Rd OX3 .... 124 C2
Wilcote Riding OX7 ...... 88 B3
Wilcote View OX8 .... 105 E3
Wilcox Rd OX7 .... 42 C2
Wilder Rd RG8 .... 256 C3
Wilding Rd OX10 .... 203 E1
Wildmere Cl OX16 .... 16 C4
Wildmere Rd OX16 .... 9 F1
Wildmoor Gate OX14 ...... 159 F1
Wilkins Rd OX4 .... 142 B3
Willes Cl SN7 .... 172 C2
William Bliss Ave OX7 ... 42 C1
William Cl OX10 .... 15 F4
William Kimber Cres OX3 . 124 C2
William Orchard Cl OX3 .. 124 B2
William St OX3 .... 123 F2
Williamscot Hill OX17 ... 10 A3
Williamson Way OX4 ...... 142 A2
Willis Ct OX7 .... 70 B1
Willoughby Rd OX16 ...... 16 B1
Willow Cl Garsington OX44 143 E1
 Wallington OX9 .... 186 A1
 Yarnton OX5 .... 108 A3
Willow Court La OX10 .... 238 C3
Willow End GL56 .... 27 D1
Willow Gdns OX5 .... 257 D1
Willow La
 Milton (Abingdon) OX14 . 199 E3
 Wantage OX12 .... 214 B2
 Reading RG2 .... 255 E2
Willow Mead OX44 .... 184 B3
Willow Rd Ambrosden OX6 . 81 E2
 Banbury OX16 .... 16 B1
 Brackley NN13 .... 24 A3
 Chinnor OX9 .... 168 B3
 Thame OX9 .... 129 F1
Willow Tree Cl OX13 ..... 159 E1
Willow Way Begbroke OX5 . 92 A1
 Kennington OX1 .... 160 C4
 Oxford OX4 .... 142 C1
Willowbrook OX13 .... 137 F4
Willows Edge OX8 .... 120 B4
Willows The
 Caversham RG4 .... 259 D1
 Grove OX12 .... 214 B4
 Highworth SN6 .... 190 A3
 Witney OX8 .... 104 B1
 Wootton (Oxford) OX13 .. 159 D4
Willowside RG5 .... 260 C1
Wills Rd OX11 .... 200 B1
Wilmot Cl OX8 .... 117 F3
Wilmot Way OX12 .... 214 C3
Wilmots OX44 .... 162 A3
Wilsdon Way OX5 .... 92 B1
Wilsham Rd OX14 .... 179 F2
Wilson Ave RG9 .... 254 C4
Wilson Way OX6 .... 65 F4
Wilsons Cl OX14 .... 201 E4
Wilwyne Cl RG4 .... 259 E2
Wimble Straw Rd OX10 .... 182 B2
Wimblestraw Rd OX10 ..... 182 B3
Wimborne Ave OX16 .... 16 A3
Wimbourne Gdns RG30 ..... 258 A1
Winaway OX11 .... 217 E3
Winchelsea Cl OX16 ...... 8 C1
Winchester Cl OX16 ...... 16 C4
Winchester Rd OX2 .... 123 D2
Winchester Way OX12 ..... 214 B3
Wincroft Rd RG4 .... 258 C3
Windale Ave OX4 .... 142 C1
Windmill Mews OX11 ...... 201 D2
Windle Gdns OX6 .... 65 E1
Windmill Ave OX6 .... 65 F2
Windmill Cl
 Banbury OX16, OX16 ..... 16 B2
 Deddington OX15 .... 33 F2
 North Leigh OX8 .... 105 D3
 Towersey OX9 .... 148 C4
Windmill Heights OX8 .... 105 D3
Windmill La OX33 .... 144 A4
Windmill Pl OX12 .... 213 F2
Windmill Rd
 Haddenham HP17 .... 130 C3
 North Leigh OX8 .... 105 D3
 Oxford OX3 .... 124 B1
 Thame OX9 .... 130 C1
 Towersey OX9 .... 148 C4
Windmill St Brill HP18 .. 98 A1
 Deddington OX15 .... 33 F2
Windrush OX16 .... 16 A4

Windrush Cl Bicester OX6 .... 65 E1
Windrush Ct
Burford OX18 .... 100 C2
Grove OX12 .... 196 B1
Witney OX8 .... 103 F1
Windrush Ct
Abingdon OX14 .... 179 E4
Burford OX18 .... 100 C2
Windrush Park Rd OX8 .... 103 E1
Windrush Rd OX10 .... 182 B2
Windrush Valley Rd OX8 .. 103 F1
Windrush Way
Abingdon OX14 .... 160 A1
Standlake OX8 .... 137 E3
Windsor Cl Carterton OX18 .. 115 E1
Didcot OX11 .... 219 D4
Kings Sutton OX17 .... 23 F3
Windsor Cres
East Hagbourne OX11 ...... 218 C3
Marston OX3 .... 123 F3
Windsor St Banbury OX16 .... 16 B3
Oxford OX3 .... 124 B1
Windsor Terr OX16 .... 16 B3
Windy Ridge SN7 .... 173 D2
Wingate Cl OX4 .... 142 C2
Wingfield Cl OX10 .... 204 C2
Winnyards The OX2 .... 139 F2
Winsmore La OX14 .... 179 F3
Winston Cl OX5 .... 108 C4
Winston Way RG8 .... 257 D3
Winter La OX12 .... 196 C4
Winter's Field OX10 .... 221 F4
Winterberry Way RG4 ..... 258 C3
Winterborne Rd OX14 ..... 179 E4
Winterbourne Cl OX6 .... 65 E1
Winterbrook OX10 .... 221 E3
Winterbrook La OX10 ...... 221 E3
Wintergreen La OX10 ...... 221 E3
Winters Way OX15 .... 21 E2
Wintringham Way RG8 ..... 257 E3
Wise Ave OX5 .... 92 B1
Wise Cl OX15 .... 22 C4
Wise Cres OX8 .... 52 B3
Wisteria The OX16 .... 9 D1
Witan Way Wantage OX12 .. 214 B3
Witney OX8 .... 118 A4
Wither's Ct OX7 .... 42 C2
Withers Way OX7 .... 42 C1
Withington Ct OX14 .... 179 F4
Withington Rd OX6 .... 65 F1
Withycombe Dr OX16 .... 15 F3

Witney La OX8 .... 86 C2
Witney Rd
Brize Norton OX18 .... 116 B3
Crawley OX8 .... 103 F2
Ducklington OX8 .... 118 A3
Eynsham OX8 .... 120 B4
Finstock OX7 .... 88 A3
Leafield OX8 .... 87 D1
Long Hanborough OX8 ...... 90 A1
Standlake OX8 .... 137 D2
Witney St OX18 .... 100 C3
Wittenham Ave RG31 ...... 257 D3
Wittenham Cl
Wallingford OX10 .... 203 E1
Woodcote RG8 .... 250 C4
Wittenham La OX10 .... 202 B4
Woburn Cl Banbury OX16 .... 16 C4
Caversham RG4 .... 258 C2
Wolseley Cl OX16 .... 16 A4
Wolsey Ct OX20 .... 91 F2
Wolsey Rd
Caversham RG4 .... 259 D1
Cutteslowe OX2 .... 109 D1
Wolvercote Green OX2 .... 122 C4
Wolvercote Rdbt OX2 ...... 108 C1
Wood End OX16 .... 16 C2
Wood Farm Rd OX3 .... 124 C1
Wood Gr RG8 .... 250 C4
Wood La Hailey OX8 .... 104 A4
Kidmore End RG4 .... 252 B2
Leafield OX8 .... 87 F1
Sonning Common RG4 ..... 252 C3
Woodcote RG8 .... 250 B4
Wood Lane Cl RG4 .... 252 C3
Wood St OX10 .... 221 E4
Wood's Farm Rd OX12 .... 216 B4
Woodberry Cl RG4 .... 259 D2
Woodbine Pl OX1 .... 123 D1
Woodbridge Cl OX18 ...... 135 F1
Woodcote Rd Bicester OX6 .. 66 A4
Caversham RG4 .... 258 C2
South Stoke RG8 .... 239 F2
Woodcote Way
Abingdon OX14 .... 179 F2
Caversham RG4 .... 258 B3
Woodcroft OX1 .... 141 F1
Woodfield OX16 .... 16 A4
Woodfield Dr OX7 .... 73 E2
Woodfield Rd OX6 .... 65 F2
Woodford Cl
Caversham RG4 .... 258 C2
Enstone OX7 .... 58 C3
Woodgate Cl OX12 .... 196 B1

Woodgreen Ave OX16 ...... 16 A3
Woodgreen Hill OX8 .... 104 B1
Woodhall Dr OX16 .... 16 C2
Woodhill Dr OX12 .... 214 B4
Woodhill La OX12 .... 214 A4
Woodhouse Way OX4 ..... 142 A2
Woodland Rise OX8 .... 89 E4
Woodlands Freeland OX8 .. 106 A4
Kidlington OX5 .... 109 D4
Standlake OX8 .... 137 E2
Woodlands Cl
Milton-u-W OX7 .... 70 A1
Oxford OX3 .... 124 A2
Woodlands Gr RG4 .... 259 F2
Woodlands Rd Oxford OX3 .. 124 A2
Shiplake RG9 .... 254 C2
Sonning Common RG4 .... 252 C3
Witney OX8 .... 104 B1
Woodlands The OX6 .... 79 F4
Woodley Cl OX14 .... 159 F2
Woodpecker Gn 🟦 OX4 .. 142 C1
Woodperry Rd OX3 .... 111 D1
Woodpiece Rd OX6 .... 96 C4
Woodruff Cl OX4 .... 142 C1
Woods Rd RG4 .... 259 F2
Woodside OX8 .... 105 E3
Woodside La RG4 .... 252 B3
Woodstock Cl OX2 .... 123 D4
Woodstock Rd
Begbroke OX5 .... 108 B2
Charlbury OX7 .... 73 E1
Cutteslowe OX2 .... 108 B2
Kidlington OX5 .... 91 F2
Oxford OX2 .... 123 D3
Stonesfield OX8 .... 89 E4
Witney OX8 .... 104 B1
Yarnton OX5 .... 108 B2
Woodview SN7 .... 172 C2
Woodview Rd RG8 .... 256 B3
Woodville OX9 .... 168 B3
Woodway Rd
Blewbury OX11 .... 237 D4
Middle Barton OX7 .... 60 C4
Sibford Ferris OX15 .... 19 D4
Woolgate OX8 .... 118 A4
Woolstone Rd
Uffington SN7 .... 211 D3
Woolstone SN7 .... 211 D3
Wootten Dr OX4 .... 142 A2
Wootten End OX8 .... 89 E4
Wootton Rd
Abingdon OX13, OX14 ...... 159 F1
Henley-on-T RG9 .... 254 B4

Worcester Dr OX11 .... 219 D4
Worcester Pl OX1 .... 123 D1
Worcester Rd OX7 .... 42 B1
Worcester St OX1 .... 123 D1
Wordsworth Cl Bicester OX6 .. 65 D2
Stanford in the V SN7 ...... 194 B4
Wordsworth Ct RG4 .... 259 E4
Wordsworth Rd OX14 ...... 179 E3
Workhouse La OX15 .... 21 E3
Wormald Rd OX10 .... 221 E3
Worminghall Rd HP18 .... 127 F2
Wormsley Cres HP14 ...... 188 B2
Wortham Rd OX11 .... 200 B1
Worthington Way OX12 .. 214 B3
Worton Rd OX7 .... 46 C1
Wotton End HP18 .... 98 B4
Wren Rd OX2 .... 109 E1
Wrenfield Dr RG4 .... 258 C3
Wright Cl GL54 .... 68 A3
Wright Rd GL54 .... 68 A3
Wrightson Cl OX33 .... 143 E3
Wroslyn Rd OX8 .... 106 A4
Wroxton Ct OX15 .... 15 D4
Wyatt Rd OX2 .... 109 D1
Wychcotes RG4 .... 258 C2
Wychwood Cl Benson OX10 204 A2
Carterton OX18 .... 115 E3
Charlbury OX7 .... 73 E2
Milton-u-W OX7 .... 85 D4
Sonning Common RG4 ..... 252 C3
Witney OX8 .... 117 F4
Wychwood Dr OX7 .... 70 A1
Wychwood Gdns OX16 ...... 16 A2
Wychwood La OX3 .... 125 D1
Wychwood Paddocks OX7 .. 73 D2
Wychwood View OX8 ...... 102 C1
Wycombe Rd
Beacon's Bottom HP14 ..... 189 E2
Stokenchurch HP14 .... 189 E2
Wycombe Way OX18 .... 115 F1
Wye Cl OX6 .... 65 D2
Wyfold La RG9 .... 252 B4
Wyfold Rd RG4 .... 252 A3
Wykeham Cres OX4 .... 142 A2
Wykeham Gate HP17 ...... 130 C3
Wykeham Park OX9 .... 148 A4
Wykeham Rise OX9 .... 168 B3
Wykeham Way HP17 .... 130 C3
Wykham Gdns OX16 .... 16 A2
Wykham La
Banbury OX15, OX16 .... 16 A1
Broughton OX15 .... 15 F1
Wykham Pl OX16 .... 16 A2

Wylie Cl OX3 .... 124 B1
Wynbush Rd OX4 .... 142 A2
Wyncies The SN6 .... 227 E2
Wyndale Cl RG9 .... 244 C1
Wyndham Cres RG5 .... 260 B1
Wyndham Gdns OX10 ...... 221 E3
Wyndham Way OX2 .... 123 D4
Wyndyke Furlong OX14 ... 179 E4
Wyre Ct RG31 .... 257 E2
Wysdom Way OX18 .... 100 C2
Wytham Cl OX8 .... 120 C4
Wytham St OX1 .... 141 E3
Wytham View OX8 .... 120 C4

Yare Cl OX11 .... 201 D1
Yarnell's Hill OX2 .... 140 B4
Yarnell's Rd OX2 .... 140 B4
Yarnton Cl RG4 .... 259 E3
Yarnton Ct OX5 .... 108 C4
Yarnton La OX5 .... 108 B3
Yarnton Rd Cassington OX8 . 107 E2
Kidlington OX5 .... 108 C4
Yarrow Cl OX4 .... 142 C1
Yatesbury Rd OX18 .... 115 F2
Yealm Cl OX11 .... 200 C2
Yeates Cl OX9 .... 129 F1
Yeats Cl OX4 .... 142 C3
Yeftly Dr OX4 .... 142 A1
Yeld Hall Rd OX14 .... 160 A1
Yeomans Cl NN13 .... 24 A4
Yew Cl Bicester OX6 .... 65 F3
Garsington OX4 .... 143 D1
Yew Tree Cl OX9 .... 166 A4
Yew Tree Ct RG8 .... 249 E3
Yew Tree Mews OX14 ...... 179 F4
Yew Tree Rise NN13 .... 36 B4
Yolsum Cl HP17 .... 130 C3
York Ave OX3 .... 124 C1
York Cl OX6 .... 66 A2
York Pl OX4 .... 123 F1
York Rd Carterton OX18 ... 115 F2
Henley-on-T RG9 .... 244 B1
Oxford OX3 .... 124 C1
Reading RG1 .... 259 D1
West Hagbourne OX11 ..... 218 B2
Youghal Cl SN6 .... 209 D3
Ypres Way OX14 .... 159 E1

Ordnance Survey

MOTORING ATLAS

Britain

The best-selling *OS Motoring Atlas Britain* uses unrivalled and up-to-date mapping from the Ordnance Survey digital database. The exceptionally clear mapping is at a large scale of 3 miles to 1 inch (Orkney/Shetland Islands at 5 miles to 1 inch).

A special feature of the atlas is its wealth of tourist and leisure information. It contains comprehensive directories, including descriptions and location details, of the properties of the National Trust in England and Wales, the National Trust for Scotland, English Heritage and Historic Scotland. There is also a useful diary of British Tourist Authority Events listing more than 300 days out around Britain during the year.

Available from all good bookshops or direct from the publisher:
Tel: 01933 443863

The atlas includes:

◆ **112 pages of fully updated mapping**
◆ **45 city and town plans**
◆ **8 extra-detailed city approach maps**
◆ **route-planning maps**
◆ **restricted motorway junctions**
◆ **local radio information**
◆ **distances chart**
◆ **county boundaries map**
◆ **multi-language legend**

STREET ATLASES

ORDER FORM

The Street Atlases are available from all good bookshops or by mail order direct from the publisher. Orders can be made in the following ways. **By phone** Ring our special Credit Card Hotline on **01933 443863** during office hours (9am to 5pm) or leave a message on the answering machine, quoting your full credit card number plus expiry date and your full name and address. **By post or fax** Fill out the order form below (you may photocopy it) and post it to: **Philip's Direct, 27 Sanders Road, Wellingborough, Northants NN8 4NL** or fax it to: **01933 443849**. Before placing an order by post, by fax or on the answering machine, please telephone to check availability and prices.

COLOUR LOCAL ATLASES		
	PAPERBACK	
	Quantity @ £3.50 each	£ Total
CANNOCK, LICHFIELD, RUGELEY	☐ 0 540 07625 2	➤
DERBY AND BELPER	☐ 0 540 07608 2	➤
NORTHWICH, WINSFORD, MIDDLEWICH	☐ 0 540 07589 2	➤
PEAK DISTRICT TOWNS	☐ 0 540 07609 0	➤
STAFFORD, STONE, UTTOXETER	☐ 0 540 07626 0	➤
WARRINGTON, WIDNES, RUNCORN	☐ 0 540 07588 4	➤

COLOUR REGIONAL ATLASES				
	HARDBACK	SPIRAL	POCKET	
	Quantity @ £10.99 each	Quantity @ £8.99 each	Quantity @ £4.99 each	£ Total
MERSEYSIDE	☐ 0 540 06480 7	☐ 0 540 06481 5	☐ 0 540 06482 3	➤
	Quantity @ £12.99 each	Quantity @ £8.99 each	Quantity @ £5.99 each	£ Total
BERKSHIRE	☐ 0 540 06170 0	☐ 0 540 06172 7	☐ 0 540 06173 5	➤
	Quantity @ £12.99 each	Quantity @ £9.99 each	Quantity @ £4.99 each	£ Total
DURHAM	☐ 0 540 06365 7	☐ 0 540 06366 5	☐ 0 540 06367 3	➤
EAST KENT	☐ 0 540 07483 7	☐ 0 540 07276 1	☐ 0 540 07277 X	➤
	Quantity @ £12.99 each	Quantity @ £9.99 each	Quantity @ £5.50 each	£ Total
GREATER MANCHESTER	☐ 0 540 06485 8	☐ 0 540 06486 6	☐ 0 540 06487 4	➤
TYNE AND WEAR	☐ 0 540 06370 3	☐ 0 540 06371 1	☐ 0 540 06372 X	➤
	Quantity @ £12.99 each	Quantity @ £9.99 each	Quantity @ £5.99 each	£ Total
BIRMINGHAM & WEST MIDLANDS	☐ 0 540 07603 1	☐ 0 540 07604 X	☐ 0 540 07605 8	➤
BUCKINGHAMSHIRE	☐ 0 540 07466 7	☐ 0 540 07467 5	☐ 0 540 07468 3	➤
CHESHIRE	☐ 0 540 07507 8	☐ 0 540 07508 6	☐ 0 540 07509 4	➤
DERBYSHIRE	☐ 0 540 07531 0	☐ 0 540 07532 9	☐ 0 540 07533 7	➤
EDINBURGH & East Central Scotland	☐ 0 540 07653 8	☐ 0 540 07654 6	☐ 0 540 07656 2	➤
NORTH ESSEX	☐ 0 540 07289 3	☐ 0 540 07290 7	☐ 0 540 07292 3	➤
SOUTH ESSEX	☐ 0 540 07294 X	☐ 0 540 07295 8	☐ 0 540 07297 4	➤

PHILIP'S

COLOUR REGIONAL ATLASES

	HARDBACK	SPIRAL	POCKET	
	Quantity @ £12.99 each	Quantity @ £9.99 each	Quantity @ £5.99 each	£ Total
GLASGOW & West Central Scotland	☐ 0 540 07648 1	☐ 0 540 07649 X	☐ 0 540 07651 1	➤ ☐
NORTH HAMPSHIRE	☐ 0 540 07471 3	☐ 0 540 07472 1	☐ 0 540 07473 X	➤ ☐
SOUTH HAMPSHIRE	☐ 0 540 07476 4	☐ 0 540 07477 2	☐ 0 540 07478 0	➤ ☐
HERTFORDSHIRE	☐ 0 540 06174 3	☐ 0 540 06175 1	☐ 0 540 06176 X	➤ ☐
WEST KENT	☐ 0 540 07366 0	☐ 0 540 07367 9	☐ 0 540 07369 5	➤ ☐
OXFORDSHIRE	☐ 0 540 07512 4	☐ 0 540 07513 2	☐ 0 540 07514 0	➤ ☐
SURREY	☐ 0 540 06435 1	☐ 0 540 06436 X	☐ 0 540 06438 6	➤ ☐
EAST SUSSEX	☐ 0 540 07306 7	☐ 0 540 07307 5	☐ 0 540 07312 1	➤ ☐
WEST SUSSEX	☐ 0 540 07319 9	☐ 0 540 07323 7	☐ 0 540 07327 X	➤ ☐
WARWICKSHIRE	☐ 0 540 07560 4	☐ 0 540 07561 2	☐ 0 540 07562 0	➤ ☐
SOUTH YORKSHIRE	—	☐ 0 540 07667 8	☐ 0 540 07669 4	➤ ☐
WEST YORKSHIRE	☐ 0 540 07671 6	☐ 0 540 07672 4	☐ 0 540 07674 0	➤ ☐
	Quantity @ £14.99 each	Quantity @ £9.99 each	Quantity @ £5.99 each	£ Total
LANCASHIRE	☐ 0 540 06440 8	☐ 0 540 06441 6	☐ 0 540 06443 2	➤ ☐
NOTTINGHAMSHIRE	☐ 0 540 07541 8	☐ 0 540 07542 6	☐ 0 540 07543 4	➤ ☐
STAFFORDSHIRE	☐ 0 540 07549 3	☐ 0 540 07550 7	☐ 0 540 07551 5	➤ ☐

BLACK AND WHITE REGIONAL ATLASES

	HARDBACK	SOFTBACK	POCKET	
	Quantity @ £11.99 each	Quantity @ £8.99 each	Quantity @ £3.99 each	£ Total
BRISTOL AND AVON	☐ 0 540 06140 9	☐ 0 540 06141 7	☐ 0 540 06142 5	➤ ☐
	Quantity @ £12.99 each	Quantity @ £9.99 each	Quantity @ £4.99 each	£ Total
CARDIFF, SWANSEA & GLAMORGAN	☐ 0 540 06186 7	☐ 0 540 06187 5	☐ 0 540 06207 3	➤ ☐

Name..

Address..

....

....

..........................Postcode.......................

◆ Add £2 postage and packing per order

◆ All available titles will normally be dispatched within 5 working days of receipt of order but please allow up to 28 days for delivery

☐ Please tick this box if you do not wish your name to be used by other carefully selected organisations that may wish to send you information about their products and services

Registered Office: 2-4 Heron Quays, London E14 4JP
Registered in England number: 3597451

Total price of order £☐

(including postage and packing at £2 per order)

I enclose a cheque/postal order, for £☐

made payable to Octopus Publishing Group Ltd,

or please debit my ☐ Mastercard ☐ American Express

☐ Visa account by £☐

Account no
☐☐☐☐ ☐☐☐☐ ☐☐☐☐ ☐☐☐☐
Expiry date ☐☐ ☐☐

Signature..

Post to: Philip's Direct, 27 Sanders Road, Wellingborough, Northants NN8 4NL

OS Ordnance Survey

STREET ATLASES ORDER FORM

OS Ordnance Survey
STREET ATLAS
South Essex
BEST BUY AUTO EXPRESS
Unique comprehensive coverage
SOUTHEND-ON-SEA
Plus Chingford, Dagenham, Ilford, Romford
PHILIP'S

OS Ordnance Survey
STREET ATLAS
West Yorkshire
NEW EDITION
COMPLETE COUNTY-WIDE COVERAGE
PHILIP'S

OS Ordnance Survey
STREET ATLAS
Glasgow
and West Central Scotland
Comprehensive coverage from Stirling to Ayr and Greenock to Lanark
PAISLEY
PHILIP'S

PHILIP'S